The Essentials of American History

since 1865

RICHARD N. CURRENT

University of North Carolina at Greensboro

T. HARRY WILLIAMS

Louisiana State University

FRANK FREIDEL

Harvard University

W. ELLIOT BROWNLEE

University of California, Santa Barbara

The Essentials of American History

since 1865

Second Edition

ALFRED A. KNOPF   NEW YORK

THIS IS A BORZOI BOOK PUBLISHED BY ALFRED A. KNOPF, INC.

Second Edition
987654321
Copyright © 1977 by Alfred A. Knopf, Inc.

Library of Congress Cataloging in Publication Data
Main entry under title:

The Essentials of American history since 1865.

  Text consists of the 2d pt. of the 1-vol. 2d ed. published in 1976 under title: The Essentials of American history.
  Bibliography: p.
  Includes index.
  1.   United States — History — 1865-   I.   Current, Richard Nelson.
E661.E87   1977   973   76-40922
ISBN 0-394-31284-8

Design: Meryl Sussman Levavi
Manufactured in the United States of America

To the Memory of William Best Hesseltine (1902–1963)

PREFACE

The four years since the first edition of this book appeared have witnessed a swift torrent of historical scholarship and an even more rapid flow of national events. In revising *The Essentials of American History* we have sought to bring the book up to date in terms of both recent scholarship and current history. As part of that effort we have expanded our treatment of the role of minorities and women in American history. Also, we have revised the historiographical essays, "Where Historians Disagree," expanded the treatment of economic and social history, and reorganized the coverage of politics since 1865.

Despite substantial revision, *The Essentials of American History* remains a brief textbook that provides the main themes of American history while omitting much of the factual and illustrative material commonly found in longer texts. The organization—with chapters grouped in chronological units and with an introduction for each period—is intended to make the overall structure quite clear and at the same time to allow a good deal of flexibility in assignments. The list of readings at the end of each unit is highly selective, presenting examples of the best available writings as judged by both readability and scholarly importance. Books published in comparatively low-priced softcover editions are so indicated on each list. Since the variety of paperbacks on the market continually grows and changes, current issues of the quarterly publication *Paperbound Books in Print* should also be consulted. The brief historiographical essays included in the text introduce the student to several of the most serious conflicts of historical interpretation and thus, it is hoped, help him to understand that the study of history involves far more than merely collecting and memorizing "facts."

In preparing this revision, we have profited from the expertise of the editors at Alfred A. Knopf, Inc. Of particularly great assistance was Suzanne Thibodeau, the project editor of this edition. We also want to thank Edward D. Bridges, Douglas L. Crane, Jr., Virginia M. Noelke, and Germaine M. Reed for their helpful critiques of the first edition. We shall be grateful for suggestions regarding improvements to be made in future reprintings and revisions of this text.

R.N.C.

T.H.W.

F.F.

W.E.B.

CONTENTS

1917–1941 • PART SIX
From Total War Through Depression   246

Appendices

Index

Maps

Where Historians Disagree

The
Essentials
of
American
History
since 1865

When Americans of a later generation looked back on the 1860s and 1870s, it seemed to many of them that there had been a sharp break between the Civil War and the ensuing period of Reconstruction. The war itself, for all its suffering and sacrifice, was remembered on the whole as an ennobling experience, one of high purpose and gallantry on both sides. The postwar years, by contrast, appeared to have been a time of low, unscrupulous politics, a time when vengeful men among the victors disgraced the country while unnecessarily delaying a real, heartfelt reunion of the North and the South.

That view contains elements of historical reality, but it misses an essential truth about the troubled postwar period. The struggle over Reconstruction was, in part, a continuation of the Civil War. It was a struggle, as the war had been, that involved (among other things) the question of both state rights and human rights. The victory for Union and emancipation had not been completely won on the battlefield. In the postwar years an effort was made to confirm the supremacy of the national government over the Southern states and to assure the benefits of freedom to the millions of emancipated slaves. This effort, provoking resistance as it did, had the effect of keeping the country psychologically divided.

The struggle over Reconstruction ended in the Compromise of 1877. This arrangement, a combination of "reunion and reaction," brought the sections together at the expense of the black people. The federal government gave up the attempt to enforce the Negro's rights and left the Southern states in the hands of conservative whites. Yet two great charters of human liberty still stood as documents of the Reconstruction era—the Fourteenth and Fifteenth amendments to the federal Constitution—which had been intended to assure citizenship and the suffrage to the former slaves. For the time being, these documents were disregarded, but a day was to come, several decades later, when they would provide the legal basis for a renewed drive to bring true freedom and equality to all Americans.

Chapter 16.   RADICAL RECONSTRUCTION

Congress Takes Over

When Congress met in December 1865, it denied admission to the senators and representatives from the states that President Johnson had "restored." The Radical leaders explained that the Southerners should be excluded until Congress knew more about conditions in the South. Congress must first be assured that the former Confederates had accepted the results of the war and that Southern Negroes and loyal whites were safe. Accordingly, Congress set up the Joint Committee on Reconstruction to investigate opinions in the South and to advise Congress in laying down a Reconstruction policy.

During the next few months the Radicals, though disagreeing among themselves, advanced toward a more severe program than their first plan, the Wade-Davis Bill of 1864. The Radicals gained the support of moderate Republicans because of Johnson's intransigent attitude. Johnson insisted that Congress had no right even to consider a policy for the South until his own plan had been accepted and the Southern congressmen and senators had been admitted.

Northern opinion was aroused by the so-called Black Codes, which the Southern legislatures adopted during the sessions of 1865–1866. These measures were the South's solution to the problem of the free Negro laborer, and they were also the South's substitute for slavery as a white-supremacy device. They all authorized local officials to apprehend unemployed Negroes, fine them for vagrancy, and hire them out to private employers to satisfy the fine. Some of the codes tried to force Negroes to work on the plantations by forbidding them to own or lease farms or to take other jobs except as domestic servants.

An appropriate agency for offsetting the Black Codes was the Freedmen's Bureau, but its scheduled year of existence was about to end. It had been losing some of its original functions. With the passing of the immediate postwar emergency, there was decreasing need for the bureau's relief activities. And President Johnson had been pardoning so many former rebels — thus restoring to them their confiscated plantations — that there was less and less land available for resettling former slaves.

In February 1866 Congress passed a bill to prolong the life of the bureau and to widen its powers by authorizing special courts for settling labor disputes. Thus the bureau could set aside work agreements that might be forced upon Negroes under the Black Codes. Johnson vetoed the bill, denouncing it as unconstitutional.

In April Congress again struck at the Black Codes by passing the Civil Rights Bill, which made United States citizens of Negroes and empowered the federal government to intervene in state affairs when necessary for protecting the rights of citizens. Johnson vetoed this bill, too. With moderates and Radicals acting together, Congress had the necessary two-thirds majority, and it promptly overrode the veto. Then, Congress repassed the Freedmen's Bureau Bill and overcame another veto.

The Joint Committee on Reconstruction submitted to Congress in April a proposed amendment to the Constitution, the Fourteenth, which constituted the second Radical plan of Reconstruction, and which was sent to the states for approval in the early summer. Section 1 of the amendment declared that all persons born or naturalized in the United States were citizens of the United States and of the state of their residence. This clause, which set up for the first time a national definition of citizenship, was followed by a statement that no state could abridge the rights of citizens of the United States or deprive any person of life, liberty, or property without due process of law or deny to any person within its jurisdiction the equal protection of the laws. Section 2 provided that if a state denied that suffrage to any of its adult male inhabitants, its representation in the House of Representatives and the Electoral College should suffer a proportionate reduction. Section 3 disqualified from any state or federal office persons who had previously taken an oath to support the Constitution and later had aided the Confederacy — until Congress by a two-thirds vote of each house should remove their disability. Johnson himself advised Southerners to defeat the amendment. Only Tennessee, of the former Confederate states, ratified it, thus winning readmittance. The other ten, joined by Kentucky and Delaware, voted it down. The amendment thus failed to receive the required approval of three-fourths of the states and was defeated — but only temporarily.

Public acceptance of the Radical program was strikingly manifested in the elections of 1866. This was essentially a contest for popular support between Johnson and the Radicals. The Radicals could point to recent events in the South — bloody race riots in which Negroes were the victims — as further evidence of the inadequacy of Johnson's policy. Johnson did his own cause no good by the intemperate, brawling speeches he made on a stumping tour from Washington to Chicago and back. The voters returned to Congress an overwhelming majority of Republicans, most of them of the Radical variety.

The Congressional Plan of 1867

After compromising differences among themselves and with the Moderates, the Radicals formulated their third plan of Reconstruction in three bills that passed Congress in the early months of 1867. All three were vetoed by Johnson and repassed.

This plan was based squarely on the principle that the seceded states had lost their political identity. The Lincoln-Johnson governments were declared to have no legal standing, and the ten seceded states (Tennessee was now out of the Reconstruction process) were combined into five military districts. Each district was to be put in the charge of a military commander, supported by troops, who was to prepare his provinces for readmission as states. To this end, he was to have made a registration of voters, which was to include all adult Negro males and white males who were not disqualified for participation in rebellion. The whites who were excluded were those coming under the disability of the Fourteenth Amendment; but each voter had to swear a complicated loyalty oath, and the registrars were empowered to reject white men on

the suspicion that they were not acting in good faith.

After the registration was completed in each province, the commanding general was to call on the voters to elect a convention to prepare a new state constitution that had to provide for Negro suffrage. If this document were ratified by the voters, elections for a state government could be held. Finally, if Congress approved the constitution, if the state legislature ratified the Fourteenth Amendment, and if this amendment were adopted by the required number of states and became a part of the Constitution — then the state was to be restored to the Union.

By 1868 six of the former Confederate states — Arkansas, North Carolina, South Carolina, Louisiana, Alabama, and Florida — had complied with the process of restoration outlined in the Reconstruction Acts and were readmitted to the Union. Delaying tactics by the whites held up the return of Mississippi, Virginia, Georgia, and Texas until 1870. These four laggard states had to meet an additional requirement, which with the existing requirements constituted the fourth and final congressional plan of Reconstruction. They had to ratify another constitutional amendment, the Fifteenth, which forbade the states and the federal government to deny the suffrage to any citizen on account of "race, color, or previous condition of servitude."

The great majority of the Northern states still denied the suffrage to Negroes at the time when the Reconstruction Acts granted it to Negroes in the Southern states. Attempts to give the vote to Northern blacks by amending the state constitutions had met with practically no success. Hence an amendment to the federal Constitution seemed necessary. Its sponsors were motivated by both idealistic and practical considerations. They would be consistent in extending to the Negro in the North a right they had already given to him elsewhere. At the same time they would be putting into the Constitution, where it would be safe from congressional repeal, the basis of Republican strength in the South. They were also concerned with the party's future in the North. In several of the Northern states the Negro vote, though small, would be large enough to decide close elections in favor of the Republicans.

A number of the Northern and border states refused to approve the Fifteenth Amendment, and it was adopted only with the support of the four Southern states that had to ratify it in order to be readmitted to the Union. In the case of both the Fourteenth and Fifteenth amendments, the Southern states were deemed capable of ratifying even while they were not otherwise recognized as states and had no representation in Congress.

The President Impeached

To curb the President, Congress passed the Tenure of Office Act (1867), which forbade him to remove civil officials, including members of his cabinet, without the consent of the Senate. Its principal purpose was to protect the job of Secretary of War Edwin M. Stanton, who was cooperating with the Radicals in his command of military units in the South.

Early in 1867 the Radicals began searching for evidence that Johnson had comitted crimes or misdemeanors in office, the only legal grounds for impeachment, but they could find nothing upon which to base charges. Then he gave them a plausible reason for action by deliberately violating the Tenure of Office Act. He suspended and then dismissed Secretary of War Stanton.

In the House of Representatives the elated Radicals framed and presented to the Senate eleven charges against the President. The first nine accusations dealt with the violation of the Tenure of Office Act. The tenth and eleventh charged Johnson with making speeches calculated to bring Congress into disrespect and of not faithfully enforcing the various Reconstruction Acts. In the trial before the Senate (March 25 to May 26, 1868) Johnson's lawyers maintained that he was justified in technically violating a law in order to force a test case and that the measure did not apply to Stanton anyway: it gave tenure to cabinet members for the term of the President by whom they had been appointed, and Stanton had been appointed by Lincoln. The House managers of the impeachment stressed the theme that Johnson had opposed the will of Congress. They implied that in doing so he was guilty of crimes and misdemeanors. They brought terrific pressure upon all the Republican senators, but seven Republicans joined the twelve Democrats to vote for acquittal. On three of the charges the vote was identical, 35 to 19, one short of the required two-thirds majority. Thereupon the Radicals called off the proceedings.

The Reconstructed States

In the ten states of the South that were reorganized under the congressional plan, approximately one-fourth of the white men were at first excluded from voting or holding office. The voter registration of 1867 enrolled a total of 703,000 black and 627,000 white voters. The Negro voters constituted a majority in half the states—Alabama, Florida, South Carolina, Mississippi, and Louisiana—though only in the last three of these states did the blacks outnumber the whites in the population as a whole. However, once new constitutions had been made and new governments launched, most of these permitted nearly all whites to vote (though for several years the Fourteenth Amendment continued to keep the leading ex-Confederates from holding office). This meant that in most of the Southern states the Republicans could maintain control only with the support of a great many Southern whites.

These Southern white Republicans, whom their opponents derisively called "scalawags," consisted in part of former Whigs who, after the break-up of the Whig organization in the 1850s, had acted with the Southern Democrats but had never felt completely at home with them. Some of the scalawag leaders were wealthy (or once wealthy) planters or businessmen. Such men, having long controlled the Negroes as slaves, expected to control them also as voters. Many other Southern whites who joined the Republican party were farmers living in areas where slavery had been unimportant or nonexistent. These men, many of whom had been wartime Unionists, favored the Republican program of internal improvements, which would help them get their crops to market.

White men from the North also served as Republican leaders in the South. Opponents of Reconstruction referred to them as "carpetbaggers," thus giving the impression that they were penniless adventurers who had arrived with all their possessions in a carpetbag (a then common kind of valise covered with carpeting material) in order to take advantage of the Negro vote for their own power and profit. In fact, the majority of the so-called carpetbaggers were veterans of the Union army who had looked upon the South as a new frontier, more promising than the West, and at the war's end had settled in it as hopeful planters or business or professional men.

THE NATURE OF RECONSTRUCTION

Where Historians Disagree

Historical writing on Reconstruction, even more controversial than that on the Civil War, similarly reflects the patterns of thought that have prevailed from time to time. The first professional historian of Reconstruction, William A. Dunning, who taught at Columbia University from the 1880s to the 1920s, carried on his work during a period when scholars generally held that certain racial and ethnic groups were inherently superior to others. Dunning assumed that Negroes were inferior and hence unfit to receive the vote. Many of his students wrote books dealing with Reconstruction in particular states, and he himself provided a general account, *Reconstruction, Political and Economic* (1907), which for many years was accepted as authoritative. According to Dunning and the members of the "Dunning school," the Republicans imposed their Radical program upon the South mainly to keep their party in power. (Some later writers, notably Howard K. Beale, added an economic motive – to protect Northern business interests.) Under the Radical plan, the Southern states suffered the agonies of "bayonet rule" and "Negro rule," when with army support the blacks and their unscrupulous white accomplices plundered the people in an unbelievable orgy of corruption, ruinous taxation, and astronomical increases in the public debt.

The first historian seriously to challenge the Dunning interpretation was the Negro scholar William E. B. Du Bois. In an article in the *American Historical Review* (1910) Du Bois pointed out that the misdeeds of the Reconstruction state governments had been exaggerated and their achievements overlooked. These governments were expensive, he explained, because they undertook to provide public education and other public services on a scale never before attempted in the South. In a long book, *Black Reconstruction* (1935), Du Bois described Reconstruction politics in the Southern states as an effort on the part of the masses, black and white, to create a true democratic society. Writing under the influence of Marxism, he assumed a class consciousness for which few other historians could find much evidence.

By the 1940s the attitudes toward race, on the part of scholars at least, had drastically changed. Since that time a new generation of historians has arisen – among them C. Vann Woodward, John Hope Franklin, Eric McKitrick, and John and La Wanda Cox – who assume that the freedmen of the 1860s and 1870s, despite the handicaps of their previous servitude, were by nature quite capable of participating in self-government. According to the new historians, the Radical Republicans were motivated less by partisan or economic interests than by a determination to guarantee basic rights to the former slaves and thus to secure the war aims of reunion and freedom. There was little if anything in the South that could properly be called either military rule or Negro rule, and the Negro, carpetbagger, and scalawag politicians were at least as honest and capable as others of their time. The mistake in Reconstruction was not the attempt to confer civil and political rights upon blacks, but the failure to provide an adequate economic and educational basis and sufficient governmental protection for the assurance of those rights. The recent views are ably synthesized in Kenneth M. Stampp, *The Era of Reconstruction* (1965).

The most numerous Republicans in the South were the freedmen, the vast majority of whom had no formal education and no previous experience in the management of affairs. Among the Negro leaders, however, were well-educated, highly intelligent men, most of whom had never been slaves and many of whom had been brought up in the North or abroad. The blacks quickly became politically self-conscious. In various states they held their own conventions, the one in Alabama announcing (1867): "We claim exactly *the same rights, privileges and immunities as are enjoyed by white men* – we ask nothing more and will be content with nothing less."

Negroes served as delegates to the conventions that, under the congressional plan, drew up new state constitutions in the South. Then, in the reconstructed states, Negroes were elected to public offices of practically every kind. All together (between 1869 and 1901) twenty of them were sent to the House of Representatives in Washington. Two went to the United States Senate, both of them from Mississippi. Hiram R. Revels – an ordained minister of the African Methodist Episcopal Church and a former North Carolina free Negro who had been educated at Knox College in Illinois – took the Senate seat (1870) that Jefferson Davis once had occupied. Blanche K. Bruce, who had escaped from slavery in Virginia and studied in the North, was made a senator in 1874 (he was the only Negro to be elected to a full term in the Senate until the election of Edward Brooke, of Massachusetts, in 1966).

Yet no such thing as "Negro rule" ever existed in any of the states. In the South as a whole the number of Negro officeholders was less than proportionate to the number of Negroes in the population. Nor did the state governments show much if any favoritism toward blacks as a group. Constitutions or statutes prohibited, on paper, discrimination on the basis of color, but segregation remained the common practice. Only in New Orleans were there, for a time, a few integrated schools.

The record of the Reconstruction governments is many-sided. As some of the leaders in the convention that framed the new state constitutions were Northerners, they put into these documents the most advanced provisions in those of the most progressive Northern states – provisions embodying the latest advances in local government, judicial organization, public finance, and poor relief.

The financial program of the Republican governments was a compound of blatant corruption and well-designed, if sometimes impractical, social legislation. State budgets expanded and state debts soared. In large measure, the corruption in the South was a phase of a national phe-

nomenon, with the same social force – an expanding capitalism eager to secure quick results – acting as the corrupting agent. Included in the spending programs of the Reconstruction governments were subsidies for railroads and other internal improvements, some of which materialized and some of which did not – because the promoters and the politicians pocketed the subsidies.

The state expenditures of the Reconstruction years seem huge only in comparison with the niggardly budgets of the conservative governments of the prewar era. The reconstructed governments undertook public education, public-works programs, poor relief, and other services that cost money. If there were thieving and foolish spending there were also positive and permanent accomplishments, particularly in education. One example is offered by South Carolina, which in 1860 had only 20,000 children in public schools; by 1873 some 50,000 white and 70,000 Negro students were enrolled.

A Soldier in the White House

At the end of the war both parties had angled to make General Grant their candidate, and he could have had the nomination of either party. As he watched the congressional Radicals triumph over President Johnson, he concluded that the Radical Reconstruction policy expressed the real wishes of the people. He was receptive when the Radical leaders approached him with offers of the Republican nomination.

The Republicans endorsed Radical Reconstruction and Negro suffrage for the South, but declared that in the North the question of Negro voting should be determined by each state. (Thus during the campaign the Republicans opposed the suffrage amendment, the Fifteenth, which they were to pass soon after the election.)

Unwisely the Democrats decided to meet the Republican challenge. Their platform also emphasized Reconstruction, denouncing in extravagant terms the Radical program and demanding restoration of "home rule" in the South. Thus the Democrats chose to fight the campaign on an issue that was related to the war and its emotions – an issue that enabled their opponents to associate them with rebellion. They did, however, attempt to inject a new question of an economic nature into the contest. In 1868 approximately $356 million of the Civil War greenbacks were in circulation, and Middle Western Democrats wanted to keep the paper currency and use it when legally possible to pay off the national debt. Behind this so-called "Ohio idea" was the larger question of retaining the greenbacks as a permanent part of the money supply. This proposal appealed to the debtor farmers of the West and also to many hard-pressed businessmen of the East. The Westerners succeeded in writing the Ohio idea into the platform, but the party nominated Horatio Seymour of New York, a gold or "sound money" man, who repudiated the currency plank.

After a bitter campaign revolving around Reconstruction and Seymour's war record as governor of New York (he had been a Peace Democrat), Grant carried twenty-six states and Seymour only eight. But Grant got only 3,012,000 popular votes to Seymour's 2,703,-000, a scant majority of 310,000, and this majority was due to Negro votes in the reconstructed states of the South.

Ulysses S. Grant was the second professional soldier to be elected to the Presidency (Zachary Taylor having been the first), and the last to be chosen until Dwight D. Eisenhower was selected in 1952. Grant had little knowledge of political issues or political ways, and he was naïve in choosing men to help him, often appointing rascals or mediocrities. His greatest defect was that he did not understand his function as President. He regarded the Presidency as a cermonial and administrative office and failed to provide real leadership in trying times.

Successes in Foreign Affairs

In foreign affairs the Grant administration achieved its most brilliant successes, as the Johnson administration also had done. These were the accomplishments of two outstanding Secretaries of State: William H. Seward (1861–1869) and Hamilton Fish (1869–1877).

An ardent expansionist and advocate of a vigorous foreign policy, Seward acted with as much daring as the demands of Reconstruction politics and the Republican hatred of President Johnson would permit. By exercising firm but patient pressure, he persuaded Napoleon III of France to abandon his Mexican empire, which was established during the war when the United States was in no position to protest. Napoleon withdrew his troops in 1867, his puppet Emperor Maximilian was executed by the Mexicans, and the validity of the Monroe Doctrine was strikingly reaffirmed.

When Russia let it be known that she would like to sell Alaska to the United States, the two nations long having been on friendly terms, Seward readily agreed to pay the asking price of $7.2 million. Only by strenuous efforts was he able to induce the Senate to ratify the treaty and the House to appropriate the money (1867–1868). Critics jeered that the secretary had bought a useless frozen wasteland – "Seward's Icebox" and "Walrussia" were some of the terms employed to describe it – but Alaska, a center for the fishing industry in the North Pacific and potentially rich in such resources as gold, was a distinct bargain. Seward was not content with expansion in continental North America. In 1867 he engineered the annexation of the tiny Midway Islands west of Hawaii.

The United States had a burning grievance against Great Britain which had originated during the Civil War. At that time the British government, according to the American interpretation, had violated the laws of neutrality by permitting Confederate cruisers, the *Alabama* and others, to be built and armed in English shipyards and let loose to prey on Northern commerce. American demands that England pay for the damages committed by these vessels became known as the "Alabama claims." Although the British government realized its diplomatic error in condoning construction of the cruisers (in a future war American-built *Alabamas* might operate against Britain), it at first hesitated to submit the issue to arbitration.

Seward tried earnestly to settle the Alabama claims before leaving office. Secretary Fish continued to work for a solution, and finally in 1871 the two countries agreed to the Treaty of Washington, one of the great landmarks in international pacification, providing for arbitration of the cruiser issue and other pending controversies. The Alabama claims were to be laid before a five-member tribunal appointed by the governments of the United States, England, Italy, Switzerland, and Brazil. In the covenant Britain expressed regret for the escape of the *Alabama* and agreed to a set of rules governing neutral obligations that virtually gave the British case away. In effect, this meant that the tribunal would have only to fix the sum to be paid by Britain. Convening at Geneva in Switzerland, the arbitrators awarded $15.5 million to the United States.

The Evils of "Grantism"

Through both his foreign and his domestic policies, President Grant antagonized and alienated a number of prominent Republicans, among them the famous Radical, Charles Sumner.

Sumner and other Republican leaders joined with civil-service reformers to criticize Grant for his use of the spoils system, his reliance on ruthless machine politicians. Republican critics of the President also denounced him for his support of Radical Reconstruction. He continued to station federal troops in the South, and on numerous occasions he sent them to the support of Negro-and-carpetbag governments that were on the point of collapsing. To growing numbers in the North this seemed like dangerous militarism, and they were more and more disgusted by the stories of governmental corruption and extravagance that came up from the South. Some Republicans were beginning to suspect that there was corruption not only in the Southern state governments but also in the federal government itself. Still others criticized Grant because he had declined to speak out in favor of a reduction of the tariff. The high wartime duties, used as a means of paying off the war debt, remained substantially unchanged.

In 1872, hoping to prevent Grant's reelection, his opponents bolted the party. Referring to themselves as Liberal Republicans, they proceeded to set up their own organization for running presidential and vice-presidential candidates. For the Presidency they named Horace Greeley, veteran editor and publisher of the New York *Tribune*. The Democratic convention, seeing in his candidacy the only chance to unseat the Republicans, endorsed him with no great enthusiasm. Despite his recent attacks on Radical Reconstruction, many Southerners, remembering Greeley's own Radical past, prepared to stay at home on election day. Greeley carried only two Southern and four border states.

During the campaign the first of a series of political scandals had come to light. Although the wrongdoing had occurred before Grant took office, it involved his party and the onus for it fell on his administration. This scandal originated with the Crédit Mobilier construction company that helped build the Union Pacific Railroad. In reality, the Crédit Mobilier was controlled by a few Union Pacific stockholders who awarded huge and fraudulent contracts to the construction company, thus milking the Union Pacific, a company of which they owned a minor share, of money that in part came from government subsidies. To avert a congressional inquiry into the deal, the directors sold at a discount (in effect gave) Crédit Mobilier stock to key members of Congress. A congressional investigation revealed that some high-placed Republicans had accepted stock, including Schuyler Colfax, now Grant's Vice President.

One dreary episode followed another during Grant's second term. Benjamin H. Bristow, secretary of the treasury, discovered that some of his officials and a group of distillers operating as a "Whiskey Ring" were cheating the government out of taxes by means of false reports. Among the prominent Republicans involved was the President's private secretary, Orville E. Babcock. Grant defended Babcock, appointed him to another office, and eased Bristow out of the cabinet. A House investigation revealed that William W. Belknap, secretary of war, had accepted bribes to retain an Indian-post trader in office. Belknap resigned with Grant's blessing before the Senate could act on impeachment charges brought by the House. Lesser scandals involved the Navy Department, which was suspected of selling business to contractors, and the Treasury, where John D. Sanborn, a special agent appointed to handle overdue taxes, collected $427,000 and retained a 50 percent commission for himself and the Republican bigwigs who had placed him in the job. Not to be left out of the picture, Congress passed an act doubling the annual salary of the President from $25,000 to $50,000 (the first increase since George Washington's time), and raising the salaries of members of Congress from $5,000 to $7,500 a year. The increases were justifiable, but the country was enraged to learn that its representatives had also voted themselves two years of back pay. Bowing before a storm of denunciation, the next Congress hastened to repeal the so-called "Salary Grab."

The Greenback Question

Meanwhile the Grant administration along with the country as a whole had suffered another blow when the Panic of 1873 struck. It was touched off by the failure of a leading investment banking firm, Jay Cooke and Company, the "financier of the Civil War," which had done well in the handling of government war bonds but had sunk excessive amounts in postwar railroad building. Depressions had come before with almost rhythmic regularity—in 1819, 1837, and 1857—but this was the worst one yet. It lasted four years, during which unemployment rose to 3 million, and agricultural prices fell so far that thousands of farmers, unable to meet mortgage payments, went more deeply into debt or lost their farms.

Debtors hoped the government would follow an inflationary, easy-money policy, which would have made it easier for them to pay their debts and would have helped to stimulate recovery from the depression. But President Grant and most Republicans preferred what they called a "sound" currency, which was to the advantage of the banks, money-lenders, and other creditors.

As a relief measure after the Panic of 1873, the Treasury increased the amount of greenbacks in circulation. For the same reason Congress, in the following year, voted to raise the total again. Grant, responding to pressures from the financial interests, vetoed the measure. In 1875 the Republican Congress enacted the Resumption Act, providing that after January 1, 1879, the government would exchange gold dollars for greenbacks and directing the government to acquire a gold reserve for redemption purposes. The law had its intended result: with the specie value of greenbacks assured, they were equal in worth to gold. The fundamental impact of the law was to produce deflation and thus protect the interests of the creditor classes, but at the same time, the debtor groups could take some comfort in the retention of the greenbacks.

Southern Republicans Lose

The period of Republican control in the South varied from state to state. In a few states the Democrats (or Conservatives) got into power as soon or almost as soon as restoration occurred. The longest that Republican rule lasted in any of the states was about ten years. It was ended in Virginia, North Carolina, and Georgia in 1870; in Texas in 1873; in Alabama and Arkansas in 1874; in Mississippi in 1875; and in South Carolina, Louisiana, and Florida in 1877.

In the states where the whites constituted a majority—the upper South states—overthrow of Republican control was a relatively simple matter. The whites had only to organize and win the elections. Their success was facilitated by the early restoration of the suffrage to those whites who had been deprived of it by national or state action. Presidential and congressional pardons returned the privilege to numerous individuals, and in 1872 Congress, responding to public demands to forgive the penalties of the war, enacted the Amnesty Act, which restored political rights to 150,000 ex-Confederates and left only 500 excluded from political life.

In other states, where the Negroes were in the majority or the population difference between the races was small, the whites resorted to intimidation and violence. Secret societies that were frankly terroristic appeared in many parts of the South—the Ku Klux Klan, the Knights of the White Camellia, and others. They attempted to frighten or physically prevent Negroes from voting. To stamp out these societies, Congress passed two Force Acts (1870–1871) and the Ku Klux Klan Act (1871), which authorized the President to use military force and martial law in areas where the orders were active.

More potent than the secret orders were the open semimilitary organizations that operated under such names as Rifle clubs, Red Shirts, and White Leagues. After the first such society was founded in Mississippi, the idea spread to other states, and the procedure employed by the clubs was called the Mississippi Plan. Briefly stated, the plan called for the whites in each community to organize and arm, and to be prepared, if necessary, to resort to force to win elections.

Perhaps an even stronger influence than the techniques practiced by the armed bands was the simple and direct weapon of economic pressure. The war had freed the Negro, but he was still a laborer—a hired worker or a tenant—dependent upon the whites for his livelihood. The whites readily discovered that this dependence placed the Negro in their power. Planters refused to rent land to Republican Negroes, storekeepers refused to extend them credit, employers refused to give them work.

Certainly the Negro's political position was hopeless without the continued backing of the Republican party and the federal government. But he was losing the support of people in the North, even of many humanitarian reformers who had worked for emancipation and Negro rights. After the adoption of the Fifteenth Amendment (1870), most of the reformers convinced themselves that their long campaign in his behalf at last was over, that with the vote he ought to be able to take care of himself.

When the depression came in 1873, the hard times aggravated political discontent both North and South. In the congressional elections of 1874 the Democrats gained a majority of the seats in the national House of Representatives. After 1875, when the new House met, the Republicans no longer controlled the whole Congress, as they had done since the beginning of the war. And President Grant, in view of the changing temper of the North, no longer was willing to use military force to save from violent overthrow the Republican regimes that were still standing in the South.

The Compromise of 1877

In 1876 the Republican managers, seeking to reunite the party, secured the nomination of Rutherford B. Hayes, governor of Ohio and a symbol of honest government. The Democrats nominated Samuel J. Tilden, governor of New York and also a symbol of honest government. Between the two candidates there was little difference. Both were conservative on economic issues and both were on record as favoring the withdrawal of troops from the South.

The November election revealed an apparent electoral and popular majority for Tilden. But disputed returns had come in from three Southern states, Louisiana, South Carolina, and Florida, whose total electoral vote was nineteen. In addition, there was a technical dispute in Oregon about one elector. Tilden had for certain 184 electoral votes, one short of a majority. The twenty votes in controversy would determine who would be President.

With surprise and consternation, the public now learned that no measure or method existed to determine the validity of disputed returns.

The Constitution stated: "The President of the Senate shall, in the presence of the Senate and House of Representatives, open all the certificates and the votes shall then be counted." The question was how and by whom? The Senate was Republican and so, of course, was its president, and the House was Democratic. The country was threatened with crisis—and possibly with chaos.

Not until the last days of January 1877 did Congress act to break the deadlock. Then it created a special Electoral Commission to pass on all the disputed votes. The Commission was to be composed of five Senators, five Representatives, and five Justices of the Supreme Court. Because of the party lineup, the Congressional delegation would consist of five Republicans and five Democrats. The creating law named four of the judicial commissioners, two Republicans and two Democrats. The four were to select their fifth colleague, and it was understood that they would choose David Davis, an independent Republican, thus ensuring that the deciding vote would be wielded by a relatively unbiased judge. But at this stage Davis was elected to the Senate from Illinois and refused to serve. His place on the Commission fell to a Republican. Sitting throughout February, the Commission by a partisan vote of eight to seven decided every disputed vote for Hayes. Congress accepted the final verdict of the agency on March 2, only two days before the inauguration of the new President.

But the findings of the Commission were not final until approved by Congress, and the Democrats could have prevented action by filibustering. The success of a filibuster, however, depended on concert between Northern and Southern Democrats, and this the Republicans disrupted by offering the Southerners sufficient inducement to accept the Commission's finds. They promised to the Southerners control of federal patronage in their states, generous internal improvements, federal aid for a Southern transcontinental railroad, and withdrawal of federal troops from the South. The Southerners accepted the package, and the crisis was over.

The withdrawal of the troops, which President Hayes effected soon after his inauguration, was a symbol that the national government was giving up its attempt to control Southern politics and to determine the place of the Negro in Southern society.

The controversy between the sections that finally erupted in civil war is treated in a number of general studies. Among the best of these are Allan Nevins, *Ordeal of the Union* (2 vols., 1947), and *The Emergence of Lincoln* (2 vols., 1950); A. O. Craven, *The Growth of Southern Nationalism, 1848–1861* (1953); A. C. Cole, *The Irrepressible Conflict, 1850–1865* (1934); R. F. Nichols, *The Disruption of American Democracy** (1948); and E. B. Smith, *The Death of Slavery, 1837–1865** (1967). Special aspects of the sectional quarrel are treated in Louis Filler, *The Crusade Against Slavery** (1960), and Holman Hamilton, *Prologue to Conflict** (1964), the Compromise of 1850. Lincoln's role in the developing crisis is subjected to searching analysis in D. E. Fehrenbacher, *Prelude to Greatness** (1962). On the ideas motivating Republicans there is Eric Foner's *Free Soil, Free Labor, Free Men: The Ideology of the Republican Party before the Civil War* (1970).

Some of the biographies cited in the immediately preceding section, especially those of Calhoun, Webster, and Clay, are useful for the decade of the fifties. Other good studies are Holman Hamilton, *Zachary Taylor, Soldier in the White House* (1951); G. F. Milton, *The Eve of Conflict* (1934), Stephen A. Douglas; David Donald, *Charles Sumner and the Coming of the Civil War* (1960); A. D. Kirwan, *John J. Crittenden* (1962); P. S. Klein, *President James Buchanan* (1962); and S. B. Oates, *To Purge This Land with Blood* (1970), John Brown. The critical events of 1860–1861 are related in D. M. Potter, *Lincoln and His Party in the Secession Crisis** (1942); K. M. Stampp, *And the War Came* (1950); and R. N. Current, *Lincoln and the First Shot** (1963).

The literature on the Civil War is so vast as to defy summary. Excellent bibliographies appear in the convenient survey by J. G. Randall and David Donald, *The Civil War and Reconstruction* (1961). There is the massive survey of Allan Nevins, *The War for the Union* (4 vols., 1959–1972). See also Bruce Catton, *This Hallowed Ground* (1956). Informative for the Southern side are Clement Eaton, *A History of the Southern Confederacy** (1954), and C. P. Roland, *The Confederacy** (1960).

On special aspects of the North at war see T. H. Williams, *Lincoln and the Radicals** (1941), and H. L. Trefousse, *The Radical Republicans* (1969), which offer somewhat contrasting views; Wood Gray, *The Hidden Civil War** (1942), the opposition to the war; F. L. Klement, *The Copperheads in the Middle West* (1960); B. I. Wiley, *The Life of Billy Yank** (1952), the common soldier; Dudley Cornish, *The Sable Arm** (1956), the Negro soldier; Benjamin Quarles, *The Negro in the Civil War* (1953); J. M. McPherson, *The Struggle for Equality* (1964), the abolitionists in the war; and P. W. Gates, *Agriculture and the Civil War* (1965). For Northern diplomacy see G. G. Van Deusen, *William Henry Seward* (1967). On the South at war consult B. I. Wiley, *The Life of Johnny Reb** (1943); F. E. Vandiver, *Rebel Brass* (1956), Southern command; A. B. Moore, *Conscription and Conflict in the Confederacy* (1924); and F. L. Owsley, *States Rights in the Confederacy* (1925), and *King Cotton Diplomacy* (1931, 1959).

Civil War biographies are many but vary in quality. There is no good life of Jefferson Davis. On Lincoln see B. F. Thomas, *Abraham Lincoln* (1952), and J. G. Randall, *Mr. Lincoln* (1957), distilled by R. N. Current from Randall's four-volumed *Lincoln the President*. See also R. N. Current, *Old Thad Stevens* (1942); Fawn Brodie, *Thaddeus Stevens* (1959), which presents a contrasting view; and David Donald, *Charles Sumner and the Rights of Man* (1970). A classic Confederate item is D. S. Freeman, *R. E. Lee* (4 vols., 1934–1935), abridged to one volume by Richard Harwell, *Lee* (1951).

Of the shelves of books treating Civil War campaigns, begin with J. B. Mitchell, *Decisive Battles of the Civil War** (1955); T. H. Williams, *Lincoln and His Generals** (1952); and Bern Anderson, *By Sea and By River* (1962), the navies. Eventually any serious student will have to get into D. S. Freeman, *Lee's Lieutenants* (3 vols., 1942–1944).

The older but now questioned view of Reconstruction appears in W. A. Dunning, *Reconstruction, Political and Economic** (1907), and W. L. Fleming, *The Sequel to Appomattox* (1919). It was first challenged by W. E. B. DuBois in *Black Reconstruction* (1935). Later and more telling challenges came in E. L. McKitrick, *Andrew Johnson and Reconstruction** (1966); J. H. Franklin, *Reconstruction** (1965); and David Donald, *The Politics of Reconstruction* (1965). Representative of a number of books treating the role of the Negro is Joel Williamson, *After Slavery* (1966). On the New South see C. V. Woodward, *Origins of the New South, 1877–1913** (1951), and *The Strange Career of Jim Crow** (1953). The best overall account is K. M. Stampp's *Era of Reconstruction* (1965).

* Titles available in paperback.

Modern America Emerges

"With a stride that astonished statisticians, the conquering hosts of business enterprise swept over the continent; twenty-five years after the death of Lincoln, America had become, in the quantity and value of her products, the first manufacturing nation of the world," the historians Charles and Mary Beard have written. "What England had accomplished in a hundred years, the United States had achieved in half the time."

The rate of industrial growth increased so rapidly in the postwar decades that these came to constitute a new age of industrialization. It was also an age of urbanization, in which cities assumed a greater and greater importance. The tremendous increase in the output of goods – and the multiplication of conveniences that city life afforded – made possible a higher and higher average level of living and increasing real income for most Americans. But the people did not share equally in the benefits of the industrial system. There were gross inequalities, and these provoked severe criticism of the system and sometimes violent attempts to bring about a redistribution of income.

Opportunities for individual success seemed to be shrinking with the near disappearance of good free land in the West. The census report for 1890 noted that the unsettled areas of the West had been "so broken into by isolated bodies of settlement" that a continuous frontier line could no longer be drawn. Three years later a young historian from the University of Wisconsin, Frederick Jackson Turner, startled the American Historical Association with a memorable paper, "The Significance of the Frontier in American History." The roots of the national character, Turner asserted, lay not so much in the East or in Europe as in the West. As he saw it, "the existence of an area of free land, its continuous recession, and the advance of settlement westward explain American development." This experience, by stimulating individualism, nationalism, and democracy, had made Americans the distinctive people that they were. "Now," Turner concluded ominously, "four centuries from the discovery of America, at the end of a hundred years of life under the Constitution, the frontier has gone, and with its going has closed the first period of American history."

Actually, long before 1890, the city had come to substitute for the frontier as the place of opportunity in America. The great folk movement of the time was from the country to the city, not the other way around. But American values had long been shaped by the rural background in which most of the people were brought up. Only slowly and with considerable stress did these values change in response to the more and more pervasive influence of the urban environment. Change they nevertheless did, and by the end of the nineteenth century the culture of the city predominated in American civilization.

Political leaders were slow to respond to the challenges of the time – to the serious problems arising out of the development of big business, the organization of labor and the resulting industrial conflict, the decline of agricultural prices and the worsening position of the farmer, and the economic instability that brought collapse in 1873 and again in 1893. With the politicians the object was to win power and jobs. In many cities and states a political boss headed a machine (organization) that operated as an "invisible government" controlling the official government of the city or state. The machine bought votes and sold governmental favors. The national parties looked to the boss and the machine to provide the votes with which to win elections. The parties depended for support not only on the patronage of government but also on contributions from business. It took the assassination of a President to shock the politicians into accepting a partial reform of the spoils system. After that, the parties had to depend more and more on corporation gifts.

By the early 1890s a tide of protest was swelling and dashing against politics as usual. It was headed by discontented farmers, but it included other dissatisfied groups whose numbers were increased by the onset of the depression. It encountered the forces of conservatism and partially recoiled before them but recovered to reach a roaring climax in the election of 1896. Thereafter the protest movement receded, as the economic system demonstrated its capacity to enlarge the general well-being, and the political system showed its ability to absorb dissenters into the traditional two parties.

Opening the two-party system to new groups and concerns in the first decades of the twentieth century was a new political impulse that came to be known as "progressivism." Those who thought of themselves as "progressives" saw with great concern the nation's rapid technological development and growing involvement in international affairs. They wanted to make sure that the United States, as an industrial giant and a world power, held on to the democratic ideals that it had inherited from the past.

There were many wrongs to be righted, and the progressives differed among themselves in both their aims and their methods. To some, the main evil was monopoly; to others, corruption in city government; to still others, the unequal status of women. And so it went. Various groups combined and cooperated, or they divided and worked against one another, on certain issues. For example, some favored and others opposed imperialism. Thus progressivism may be considered as an aggregate of causes rather than a single movement. Still, most progressives had in common the following convictions: (1) "the people" ought to have much more influence in government, and the "special interests" much less, and (2) government ought to be much stronger, more active, and more efficient in serving the public welfare.

In certain respects, progressivism was a continuation of Populism. Progressives advocated some (though not all) of the reforms that the Populists had proposed, and some of the former Populists joined the progressive movement. But progressivism and Populism differed in important respects. The People's party members had been mostly distressed farmers of the Southern and the Great Plains and Rocky Mountain states. The progressive ranks included men and women from all parts of the country, but especially from the Northeast and the Midwest, and prominent among the progressives were persons of the urban middle class. The progressives had a broader concept of both "the people" and the public welfare than the Populists had had.

A third party did take the name "Progressive," but the movement was too broad to be confined by party lines. Active in it were both Republicans and Democrats, though the Republicans were the more numerous. For most of them, regardless of party, the path of reform led from the city hall to the state capitol, and from there to the chambers of Congress and the White House. Many conspicuous evils of the time, incapable of cure by local or state authorities, required action by the federal government. Prominent figures of both major parties brought progressivism into national politics. Among the leading Republicans were Robert M. La Follette and Theodore Roosevelt; among the Democrats, William Jennings Bryan and Woodrow Wilson. From 1901 to 1916, politics and government largely reflected the opinions and ambitions of these men—especially Roosevelt and Wilson—and their respective followings.

Meanwhile the United States took a new direction in foreign affairs when it began to acquire possessions overseas. From the very beginning, of course, the republic had been expansionist. As the American people moved relentlessly westward across the continent, their government from time to time acquired new lands for them to occupy. Almost all these acquisitions—the fruits of what might be called the old Manifest Destiny—were contiguous with existing territories of the United States. Desired mainly as places of settlement for Americans seeking farms, these acquisitions represented a kind of agricultural imperialism. And they were expected to be organized as territories and ultimately as states. But the expansionism of the 1890s, the new Manifest Destiny, was in some respects different. It meant acquiring island possessions, some of which were already thickly populated, were unsuitable for settlement by migrants from the United States, and were expected to be held indefinitely as colonies, not as states or even territories. The new expansion was motivated largely (though not entirely) by considerations of trade. Thus it represented a kind of commercial imperialism. By 1900 the United States had finally become an empire. It was now recognized as a "world power," though in fact it had been one of the great nations of the world for some time.

After 1900 Americans clung to the old idea of keeping out of Europe's quarrels, but the nation drifted toward the twentieth-century maelstrom of world conflict. The industrial developments in Europe and America had brought, along with increased material abundance, a heightened competition for markets, sources of raw materials, places for investment, and sheer national prestige. To the great powers came not only social gains but also military ambitions, with an arms race that grew more and more frightening as Europe divided into two hostile alliances.

As the foremost of all industrial nations, the United States could scarcely remain unaffected by world events for long. Its emergence from the Spanish-American War with Pacific and Caribbean colonies intensified the risks of involvement. So did certain phases of the progressive spirit itself, which stimulated increased activity in foreign affairs. Some progressives aspired not only to revitalize democracy at home but also to extend it abroad. Finally, World War I brought the greatest challenge in a hundred years to the time-honored policy of neutrality and diplomatic independence.

For three years, from 1914 to 1917, the United States remained at peace, and then it joined in the hostilities. Its entrance hardly meant that the traditional policy had failed, for strict neutrality had not been tried. The American people had closer ties of kinship and commerce with one set of European belligerents than with the other. The prosperity of this country had come to depend on swollen wartime trade with the one side, which needed supplies to continue the war. Both groups of warring countries attempted to cut off the other's imports, and both used methods that were contrary to international law as the United States had long interpreted it. But now the American government drew a sharp distinction between the violations of neutral rights on the one side and those on the other. In the one case—the case of the side with the closer American ties—this government protested long-windedly and perfunctorily. In the other, it took a stern and threatening stand, demanding a "strict accountability."

According to this country's constitutional system, one man has the ultimate responsibility for war or peace—the President. In 1917 President Woodrow Wilson made the decision for war. He saw it as a war to end war, to bring about an international organization for keeping the future peace, and thus to "make the world safe for democracy." Wilson thereby took progressivism abroad; America's decision to enter World War I was a decision to wage progressivism by the sword.

Chapter 17. INDUSTRIAL AND URBAN AMERICA, TO 1900

The Rise of Big Business

Between 1865 and 1900 the American economy experienced a sensational expansion. This was most apparent in industry—in these years America became the first manufacturing nation of the world. Its rise to eminence rested on firm bases: the inventive and organizational skills of its people, its possession of unparalleled national resources, and its ever growing population that constituted a vast interior market and source of labor. Among the inventions and innovations of the period were the telephone, the typewriter, the adding machine, the cash register, and the use of electricity as a source of light and power.

In these same years business developed new and larger forms of organization. Before the Civil War business had employed such forms as the single proprietorship, the partnership, and the corporation, which was owned by a number of shareholders. After the war the corporate arrangement came into increasing use, and the corporations became larger in every way. The corporation, however, was not the ultimate form of organization. Even larger were forms combining a number of corporations—pools, trusts, and holding companies. A pool was an informal organization of several corporations in the same business. A trust came into being when the stockholders of a number of corporations transferred their stock to a directing board of trustees. A holding company was born when the directing company actually bought the stock of competing corporations.

Behind the movement toward concentration were powerful economic forces. The expanded number of business units intensified competition and the scramble for profits. More potent was the fact that between 1865 and 1897 prices declined steadily, forcing businessmen to consider every device that might cut costs. Equally powerful was the economy's increasing instability, which led businessmen to search for ways of making their world more predictable. Organization into larger units would eliminate competition, lower costs, and increase profits.

Thus American industry moved with unconscious purpose toward concentration. Fewer and fewer companies produced more and more of the nation's goods. By 1900 less than 2 percent of the manufacturing establishments were turning out almost 50 percent of all the manufactured goods in the country.

Bigness in Specific Industries

Steel is a basic material in an industrial and urban society, and the steel industry was one of the first to experience the impact of bigness. In this period the industry was concentrated in western Pennsylvania and eastern Ohio, although it drew its ore supplies from as far away as the Mesabi range in Minnesota. The profits to be made in steel tempted consolidation, and inevitably a master consolidator appeared, Andrew Carnegie, a Scottish immigrant boy who had worked his way up in the railroad industry and then had gone into steel. Gradually he built up his company to dominance in the industry, buying out or forcing out competitors and integrating the processing of steel from mine to market. In 1901 his Carnegie Steel Company and other concerns were combined in a gigantic holding company, United States Steel.

The modern petroleum industry also came into being during this period. Production was centered in Pennsylvania, Ohio, and West Virginia, the region where oil had first been discovered. Relatively little capital was required to drill for oil or to refine it, and a host of small companies, particularly refineries, competed savagely for business. But soon there appeared to bring order to the industry the greatest consolidator of the time. John D. Rockefeller was a comparatively young Cleveland businessman who decided that his future lay with oil. He and various associates built the Standard Oil Company of Ohio to a position of dominance. They bought up competing companies or forced them out of existence with price wars and formed the Standard Oil trust in 1882. More importantly, they also set up an integrated system of production, controlling both the refining and marketing of oil.

Other expanding industries owed their rise to the growing demands of an urban society. The meat-packing industry, centered in Chicago, supplied its products to a national market. So also did the flour-milling industry in Minneapolis. The prepared-foods industry, concentrating on the canning of vegetables, changed the eating habits of all Americans. When these industries expanded, they, like the steel and petroleum industries, underwent integration and consolidation. And with these new industries moving into areas other than the Northeast, it was no longer true that economic sectionalism divided the nation.

The Railroad Network

American industry could serve a national market because of the country's railroad system. The railroads had been the first giant American industry, and after the Civil War they continued to expand. Their trackage figure doubled every decade, and by the turn of the century the United States had the most extensive transportation system in the world.

In the years between 1865 and 1900 four important developments affected the railroad system. First, the railroads of the Northeast were consolidated into four major roads: the New York Central, the Pennsylvania, the Erie, and the Baltimore and Ohio. These lines then established connections with the Western market at Chicago. Second, in the South railroads damaged by the war were rehabilitated and an outburst of new construction occurred. Third, the roads in the Mississippi Valley expanded their facilities and began to push westward towards the Great Plains.

But it was the fourth development that caught the popular imagination, the building of the great "transcontinental" lines. During the Civil War, Congress had acted to make the dream of a road from the Mississippi Valley to the Pacific coast a reality. It had chartered two railroad corporations, the Union Pacific and the Central Pacific. The Union Pacific was to build westward from Omaha, Nebraska, and the Central Pacific eastward from Sacramento, California, until they met.

To provide the financial aid deemed necessary

to initiate the roads, Congress donated a right of way across the public domain and offered the companies special benefits: for each mile of track a company laid, it would receive twenty square miles of land in alternate sections along the right of way and a thirty-year loan of $16,000, $32,000, or $48,000, depending on whether the construction was in plains, foothill, or mountain country. In addition, the government accepted a second mortgage on the loans, and permitted the companies to issue first mortgage bonds up to the amount of the official loan. By the terms of the war legislation, the Union Pacific and the Central Pacific stood to receive approximately 20 million acres of land and $60 million in loans.

The companies started work in 1865. Appalling obstacles faced the builders—mountains, deserts, hostile Indians. In addition, supplies and labor had to be brought in from distant points. The Central Pacific imported several thousand Chinese laborers, while the Union Pacific hired thousands of Irish immigrants. Nevertheless, the job was pushed on, and in the spring of 1869 the nation was linked by rail from the Atlantic to the Pacific. The event set off a national celebration.

Other promoters now came forward with proposals for other transcontinental lines, and Congress responded with charters that provided for land grants but no financial subsidies. Some of the projected roads were not completed but others were. At the end of the century five transcontinental systems were in operation. All but one were built with some form of assistance from the national government or from state governments.

As the network of rails covered the country, it became evident that the railroad industry was being overbuilt and overextended; many railroad corporations, including some of the largest ones, were afflicted with impossible debt burdens. Moreover, many roads were looted and wrecked by their own directors. In some areas of the country certain railroads enjoyed monopolies, but wherever competition existed, it was savage and sustained. Competing roads fought ferocious rate wars and struggled for business by offering rebates to big shippers. The inevitable effects of overexpansion, fraudulent management, and cutthroat competition were apparent in the depression of the seventies, when 450 roads went into bankruptcy. Twenty years later, in the hard times of the nineties, 318 companies controlling 67,000 miles fell into the hands of receivers.

After the economic crises of 1873 and 1893, railroad capitalists moved to curb competition by creating larger systems and to enhance stability by introducing more efficient management. Reorganizing the railroads required huge sums of cash and credit, which could be supplied only by the big New York investment banking houses. The investment bankers, led by J. P. Morgan, were eager to finance consolidation in order to stop the railroads, with their wild financing and frenzied speculating, from ruining the investment business. But the bankers, as the price for their aid, insisted on being given a voice in the management of the roads, a condition that the railroad promoters had to accept. By the end of the century a few major railroad systems controlled over half the mileage in the country, and these systems were wholly or partially controlled by two banking houses.

Business Philosophy and Its Critics

The economic revolution produced a new ruling class among businessmen. They were a class with little tradition of culture and little concept of social responsibility beyond that dictated by the marketplace. In their view, they had won their wealth by work and merit, and they would do with it as they pleased. Their philosophy was epitomized by a much quoted statement of one of them: "Can't I do what I want with my own?" They were often crude and sometimes ruthless. But they have to be placed in a historical perspective.

They were, without realizing it, building the basis of a great economic society. Although some magnates could not resist the temptation to amass wealth quickly, more were interested in plowing back earnings into plants, equipment, and research. Some crushed competitors, but many produced better and cheaper products by integrating production and otherwise cutting costs. They were opening the way to economical mass production.

They were not clearly aware of what they were doing, but they felt that they had to explain it, if not to their critics, then to themselves. To a few businessmen, the formula of Social Darwinism seemed to explain both their own success and the nature of the society in which they operated. Social Darwinism was Charles Darwin's law of evolution applied to social organization. As expounded by the Englishman Herbert Spencer, it taught that struggle was a normal human activity, especially in economic life. The weak went down, the strong endured and became stronger, and society was benefited because the unfit were eliminated and the fit survived.

According to Social Darwinism, all attempts by labor to raise its wages by forming unions and all endeavors by government to regulate economic activities would fail, because economic life was controlled by a natural law, the law of competition, which could not be superseded by human restraints. This aspect of Darwinism coincided with another "higher law" that seemed to justify business practices and business dominance: the economic law of supply and demand as defined by Adam Smith and the classical economists. According to the economists, the economic system was like a great machine functioning by natural and automatic rules. The most basic of these rules was the law of supply and demand, which determined all economic values—prices, wages, rents, interest rates—at a level that was just to all concerned. Businessmen justified themselves by this economic theory even though the combinations they were creating threatened to undermine the foundations of the free competitive market. However, for those businessmen requiring ideological reassurance, most compelling was a popular "gospel of success," which held that the acquisition of a material fortune was a sure measure of divine blessing.

The beliefs of businessmen were not shared by all Americans. Many books—a whole literature of protest—questioned or denounced various aspects of the economic system. Henry George's angrily eloquent *Progress and Poverty,* published in 1879, was an immediate success; reprinted in successive editions, its worldwide sales reached millions. George addressed himself to the question of why poverty existed amidst the wealth created by modern industry. "This association of poverty with progress is the great enigma of our times," he wrote. He blamed poverty on monopoly, and he proposed a remedy, a "single tax" on unimproved land. An increase in the value of such land resulted from the growth of society around it. Thus when land

LEADERS OF BIG BUSINESS

Where Historians Disagree

Reflecting the division of public opinion, contemporary writings about late nineteenth-century business leaders usually were either flattering or denunciatory. In the "muckraking" years of the early twentieth century, denunciation came to predominate. Thus Ida M. Tarbell, *The History of the Standard Oil Company* (1904), presented John D. Rockefeller as a predatory character who drove smaller oilmen out of business by unscrupulous means. Gustavus Myers, *The History of the Great American Fortunes* (1907), undertook to show that other successful businessmen had also amassed their wealth by crushing competitors and corrupting politicians, not by practicing the old-fashioned American virtues of honesty, thrift, and hard work.

The treatment of these businessmen became more favorable during the prosperous 1920s. In *The Rise of American Civilization* (1927) Charles and Mary Beard described them as "captains of industry" who contributed to industrial development through their remarkable powers of organization. During the depression of the 1930s, however, the pioneers of big business again fell into disrepute. Matthew Josephson gave them a name that most historians accepted in his popular book *The Robber Barons* (1934). Josephson compared them to feudal lords who got rich by preying on legitimate commerce.

Allan Nevins challenged the Josephson view in *John D. Rockefeller: The Heroic Age of American Enterprise,* which was originally published in 1940 and republished with revisions and elaborations in 1953. Nevins depicted Rockefeller as an industrial statesman who brought order and efficiency to the oil business. The Nevins interpretation reflected the changed attitude that came with World War II and the cold war, when it seemed to many Americans that the industrial greatness of the United States made possible a successful effort to save the world from totalitarianism.

Meanwhile, from the 1920s on, historians at the Harvard Business School and elsewhere were writing business history without moral judgments. These "entrepreneurial historians," among them Thomas C. Cochran, Alfred D. Chandler, Jr., and Kenneth W. Porter, were primarily interested in techniques of management, in the kinds of decision-making that had led particular companies to success or to failure. Such writers looked for object lessons in the past that might be of value to business managers in the present.

increased in value, George argued, the private owner had not earned the increment, and the community should receive the increase. Such a tax supposedly would destroy monopolies, distribute wealth more equally, and eliminate poverty. Single-tax societies sprang up in many cities, and in 1886 George, backed by labor and the Socialists, narrowly missed being elected mayor of New York.

Rivaling George in popularity was Edward Bellamy, whose *Looking Backward,* published in 1888, became a best seller within a few years and eventually topped the million mark. Bellamy's book was a novel, a romance of a socialist Utopia. It described the experiences of a young Bostonian who in 1887 went into a hypnotic sleep from which he awakened in the year 2000. He found a new social order, based on collective ownership of property, where want, politics, and vice were unknown, and where people were incredibly happy. Shortly, over 160 "Nationalist Clubs" sprang up to propagate Bellamy's ideas, and the author devoted the remainder of his life to championing Utopian socialism.

Also calling for a larger role for government in controlling the economy was Henry Demarest Lloyd's *Wealth Against Commonwealth,* published in 1894. A tremendous if not always accurate attack on the Standard Oil trust, it contended that competition in industry had disappeared. Therefore industry would have to submit to strict government regulation, or perhaps to government ownership.

Labor Organizes

As business became big, consolidated, and national, inevitably labor attempted to create its own organizations that would match the power of capital. The economic revolution changed the worker from an artisan who owned his own tools to a factory laborer who operated machines owned by an employer more powerful than any individual worker. To counter corporate power, labor formed unions that sought to bargain collectively with employers. During the Civil War, twenty craft unions were formed, and by 1870 the industrial states counted thirty such organizations, nearly every one of which represented skilled workers. The first attempt to federate separate unions into a single national organization came in 1866, when, under the leadership of William H. Sylvis, the National Labor Union was founded. Claiming a membership of 640,-000, it was a polyglot association that included, in addition to a number of unions, a variety of reform groups having little direct relationship with labor.

The trade unions experienced stormy times during the hard years of the 1870s and after the panic of 1873 the National Labor Union disintegrated and disappeared. Their bargaining power weakened by depression conditions, unions faced antagonistic employers eager to destroy them, and a hostile public that rejected labor's claim to job security. Several of the disputes with capital were unusually bitter and were marked by violence, some of it labor's fault and some not, but for all of which labor received the blame. A near-hysteria gripped the country during the railroad strikes of 1877. The trouble started when the principal Eastern railroads announced a 10 percent slash in wages. Immediately railroad workers, whether organized or not, went out on strike. Rail service was disrupted from Baltimore to St. Louis, equipment was destroyed, and rioting mobs roamed the streets of Pittsburgh and other cities.

The strikes were America's first big· labor conflict and a flaming illustration of a new reality in the American economic system: with business becoming nationalized, disputes between labor and capital could no longer be localized but would affect the entire nation. State militia were employed against the strikers, and finally, and significantly, federal troops were called on to suppress the disorders. The power of the various railroad unions was seriously sapped by the failure of the strikes, and the prestige of unions in other industries was weakened by similar setbacks.

Meanwhile, another national labor organization appeared on the scene, the Noble Order of the Knights of Labor, founded in 1869 under the leadership of Uriah S. Stephens. Instead of attempting to federate unions, as the National Labor Union had done, the Knights organized their association on the basis of the individual. Membership was open to all who "toiled," and the definition of toilership was extremely liberal: the only excluded groups were lawyers, bankers, liquor dealers, and professional gamblers. The amorphous masses of members, including many unskilled workers, were arranged in local "assemblies" that might consist of the workers in a particular trade or a local union or simply all the members of the Knights in a city or district. Presiding laxly over the entire order was an agency known as the General Assembly. Much of the program of the Knights was as vague as the organization. Although they championed an eight-hour day and the abolition of child labor, the leaders were more interested in long-range reform of the economy than in the immediate objectives of wages and hours, which appealed to the trade unions.

Under the leadership of Terence V. Powderly, the order entered upon a spectacular period of expansion that culminated in 1886 with the total membership reaching 700,000. With a large membership, the order now included many militant elements that could not always be controlled by the moderate leadership. Against Powderly's wishes, local unions or assemblies associated with the Knights proceeded to inaugurate a series of strikes. In 1885 striking railway workers forced the Missouri Pacific, a link in the Gould system, to restore wage cuts and recognize their union. Although this victory redounded to the credit of the Knights, it was an ephemeral triumph. In the following year a strike on another Gould road, the Texas and Pacific, was crushed, and the power of the unions in the Gould system was broken. By

1890 the membership of the Knights had shrunk to 100,000, and within a few years the order was a thing of the past.

Rise of the AFL

Even before the Knights had begun their decline, a rival organization, based on an entirely different organizational concept, had appeared. In 1881 representatives of a number of craft unions formed the Federation of Organized Trade and Labor Unions of the United States and Canada. Five years later this body took the name it has borne ever since, the American Federation of Labor. Under the direction of its president and guiding spirit, Samuel Gompers, the Federation soon became the most important labor group in the country. As its name implies, it was a federation or association of national trade unions, each of which enjoyed essential autonomy within the larger organization. Rejecting completely the idea of individual membership and the corollary of one big union for everybody, the Federation built on the principle of the organization of skilled workers into craft unions.

The program of the Federation differed as markedly from that of the Knights as did its organizational arrangements. Gompers and his associates accepted the basic concepts of capitalism; their purpose was to secure for labor a greater share of capitalism's material rewards. Repudiating all notions of fundamental alteration of the existing system or long-range reform measures or a separate labor party, the AFL concentrated on labor's pressing objectives: wages, hours, and working conditions. While it hoped to attain its ends by collective bargaining, the Federation was ready to employ the strike if necessary.

As one of its first objectives, the Federation called for a national eight-hour day, to be attained by May 1, 1886, and to be obtained, if necessary, by a general strike. On the target day, strikes and demonstrations for a shorter workday took place all over the country. Although the national officers of the Knights had refused to cooperate in the movement, some local units joined in the demonstrations. So did a few unions that were dominated by anarchists — European radicals who wanted to destroy "class government" by terroristic methods — and that were affiliated with the so-called Black International. The most sensational demonstrations occurred in Chicago, which was a labor stronghold and an anarchist center.

At the time, a strike was in progress at the McCormick Harvester Company; and when the police harassed the strikers, labor and anarchist leaders called a protest meeting at the Haymarket Square. During the meeting, the police appeared and commanded those present to disperse. Someone — his identity was never determined — threw a bomb that resulted in the death of seven policemen and injury to sixty-seven others. The police, who on the previous day had killed four strikers, fired into the crowd and killed four more people. The score was about even. News of the Haymarket affair struck cold fear into Chicago and the business community of the nation. Blinded by hysteria, conservative, property-conscious, middle-class Americans demanded a victim or victims — to demonstrate to labor that it must cease its course of violence. Chicago officials finally rounded up eight anarchists and charged them with the murder of the policemen on the grounds that they had incited the individual who hurled the bomb. In one of the most injudicious trials in the record of American juridical history, all were found guilty. One was sentenced to prison and seven to death. Of the seven, one cheated his sentence by committing suicide, four were executed, and two had their penalty commuted to life imprisonment.

Although some of the blame for the Haymarket tragedy was unloaded on the AFL, most fell on the Knights, who had had almost nothing to do with the May demonstrations. In the public mind the Knights were dominated by anarchists and Socialists. The Knights never managed to free themselves from the stigma of radicalism as the AFL did and 1886 marked the eclipse of the Knights by the AFL.

The Homestead Strike

Some of the most violent strikes in American labor history occurred in the nineties. Two of the strikes, the one at the Homestead plant of the Carnegie Steel Company in Pennsylvania and the one against the Pullman Palace Car Company in the Chicago area, took place in companies controlled by men who prided themselves on being among the most enlightened of American employers: Andrew Carnegie, who had written magazine articles defending the rights of labor, and George M. Pullman, who had built a "model town" to house his employees.

The Amalgamated Association of Iron and Steel Workers, which was affiliated with the American Federation of Labor, was the most powerful trade union in the country. It had never been able, however, to organize all the plants of the Carnegie Steel Company, the largest corporation in the industry; of the three major steel mills in the Carnegie system, the union was a force only in one, the Homestead plant. In 1892, when the strike occurred, Carnegie was in Scotland, visiting at a castle that he maintained as a gesture of ancestral pride, and the direction of the company was in the hands of Henry Clay Frick, manager of Homestead and chairman of the Carnegie firm. Carnegie was, nevertheless, responsible for the company's course. Despite his earlier fine words about labor, he had decided with Frick before leaving to operate Homestead on a nonunion basis, even if this meant precipitating a clash with the union.

The trouble began when the management announced a new wage scale that would have meant cuts for a small minority of the workers. Frick abruptly shut down the plant, and asked the Pinkerton Detective Agency to furnish 300 guards to enable the company to resume operations on its own terms. (The Pinkerton Agency was really a strikebreaking concern.)

The hated Pinkertons, whose mere presence was enough to incite the workers to violence, approached the plant on barges in an adjacent river. Warned of their coming, the strikers met them at the docks with guns and dynamite, and a pitched battle ensued on July 6, 1892. After several hours of fighting, which brought death to three guards and ten strikers and severe injuries to many participants on both sides, the Pinkertons surrendered and were escorted roughly out of town. The company and local law officials then asked for militia protection from the Pennsylvania governor, who responded by sending the entire National Guard contingent, some 8,000 troops, to Homestead. Public opinion, at first sympathetic to the strikers, turned abruptly against them when an anarchist made an unsuccessful attempt to assassinate Frick. Slowly workers drifted back to their jobs.

The Pullman Strike

A dispute of greater magnitude and equal bitterness, although involving less loss of life, was the Pullman strike in 1894, a depression year that saw over 700,000 workers throughout the country out on strike. Near Chicago were the works of the Pullman Palace Car Company. This corporation leased sleeping and parlor cars to most of the nation's railroads; it also manufactured and repaired its own cars and also freight and passenger cars. Over 5,000 workers were employed in the various shops and factories of the company. At the instigation of George M. Pullman, inventor of the car that bore his name and president of the firm, the company had built the 600-acre town of Pullman, containing dwellings that were rented to the employees, churches, schools, parks and playgrounds, a bank, and a library — all owned and operated by the company. Pullman liked to exhibit his town as a model solution of the industrial problem and to refer to the workers as his "children"; his attitude was completely feudalistic and patronizing.

Nearly all of the workers were members of a union, a very militant one, the American Railway Union; this association had recently been organized by Eugene V. Debs, a sincere and idealistic labor leader formerly active in the Railroad Brotherhoods. Becoming disgusted with the brotherhoods' lack of interest in the lot of the unskilled workers, he had formed his own union, which soon attained a membership of 150,000, mainly in the Middle West.

The strike at Pullman began when the company during the winter of 1893–1894 slashed wages by an average of 25 percent. With revenues reduced by depression conditions, there was some reason for the company's action, but the cut was drastic, and several workers who served on a committee to protest to the management were discharged. At the same time, Pullman refused to reduce rentals in the model town. The strikers appealed to the Railway Union for support, and that organization voted to refuse to handle Pullman cars and equipment.

The General Managers' Association, representing twenty-four Chicago railroads, prepared to fight the boycott. Switchmen who refused to handle Pullman cars were summarily discharged. Whenever this happened, the union instructed its members to quit work. Within a few days thousands of railroad workers in twenty-seven states and territories were on strike, and transportation from Chicago to the Pacific coast was paralyzed.

Ordinarily, state governors responded readily to appeals from strike-threatened business, but the governor of Illinois was different. John P. Altgeld had pardoned the Haymarket anarchists remaining in prison. Business was not likely to appeal to such an executive for aid, and Altgeld was not the man to employ militia to smash a strike.

Bypassing Altgeld, the railroad operators besought the national government to send regular army troops to Illinois. At the same time federal postal officials and marshals were bombarding Washington with information that the strike was preventing the movement of mail on the trains. President Grover Cleveland was inclined to gratify the companies and so was his Attorney General, Richard Olney, a former railroad lawyer and a bitter foe of labor. Cleveland and Olney decided that the government could employ the army to keep the mails moving, and in July 1894 the President, over Altgeld's strident protest, ordered 2,000 troops to the Chicago area.

At Olney's suggestion, government lawyers obtained from a federal court an order restraining Debs and other union officials from interfering with the interstate transportation of the mails. This "blanket injunction" was so broad in scope that it practically forbade Debs and his associates to continue the strike. They ignored the injunction and were arrested, tried for contempt of court (without a jury trial), and sentenced to six months in prison. With federal troops protecting the hiring of new workers and with the union leaders in a federal jail, the strike quickly collapsed.

It left a bitter heritage. Labor was convinced that the government was not a neutral arbiter representing the common interest, but a supporter of one side alone. Debs emerged from prison a martyr, a convert to socialism, and a dedicated enemy of capital.

The Worker's Gains

Despite all the organizations that were formed and all the strikes and demonstrations that were so hopefully launched, the labor movement accomplished relatively little in the years between 1865 and 1900. Its leaders could point to a few legislative victories: the abolition by Congress in

1885 of the Contract Labor law; Congressional closing of Chinese immigration in 1882; the establishment by Congress in 1868 of an eight-hour day on public works and in 1892 of the same work period for government employees; and a host of state laws governing hours of labor and safety standards, most of which were not enforced. But an overwhelming majority of employers still regarded labor as a force to be disregarded when possible and to be crushed when practicable, and the American public in overwhelming numbers considered unions to be alien and dangerous elements in the national economy.

Labor's greatest weakness was that only a small part of its vast strength was organized. The American Federation, with its some half million members, and the Railroad Brotherhoods (engineers, conductors, firemen, trainmen) represented the skilled workers, but the mass of laborers, both skilled and unskilled, were not enrolled in any union. All told, less than 3 percent of the nation's workers were union members at the turn of the century. Big Business was firmly entrenched; Big Labor awaited the future.

Ironically, however, real wages earned by manufacturing workers increased by more than 50 percent between 1865 and 1897, while the number of hours an average worker toiled declined steadily. By 1890 the average laborer in industry worked 60 hours while skilled tradesmen had attained a 50-hour week. Moreover, the distribution of income in the nation's cities tended to become more uniform, favoring skilled workers in particular. These very significant gains were far less a result of union activity than a consequence of a labor-scarce economy. That economy encouraged laborers, especially skilled workers in large cities, to change employment to obtain the highest possible wages and induced employers to offer workers monetary incentives for increased productivity. Indeed, this successful labor market contributed directly to the sluggishness of the organized labor movement.

The Newer Immigrants

During the years of industrial expansion the population of the United States more than doubled, increasing from about 31 million in 1860 to almost 76 million in 1900. The fertility of the

American population as a whole declined. Instead, a rising tide of foreign immigration led the increase: some 14 million aliens entered the country during these years. Most of the immigrants settled in the industrial cities, causing the urban population to increase sixfold, three times as rapidly as the total population.

Up to 1880 the great majority of the immigrants had originated in the countries of western and northern Europe: England, Ireland, Germany, and the Scandinavian countries. Although there had always been friction between these people and "native" Americans, most of the newcomers were in culture and outlook essentially similar to those among whom they settled, and they were eventually assimilated. But in the eighties the immigrant stream began to flow from another source — southern and eastern Europe. Among the new ethnic stocks were Austrians, Hungarians, Bohemians, Poles, Serbs, Italians, Russians, and Jews from Poland and Russia. They came for the reasons that had always brought immigrants to the United States: the desire to escape unfavorable economic and political conditions at home; the advertising propaganda of railroads, which in their eagerness to dispose of their landholdings painted an alluring picture of America; knowledge of the opportunities in America gained from friends and relatives who had already crossed the Atlantic; and the demand for cheap labor by industry.

To natives of whatever national background, the new arrivals seemed strange indeed. They had different cultural and economic standards and spoke diverse languages (the British and Irish who composed the bulk of the previous immigration had presented no language dissimilarity). The new immigrants were in overwhelming numbers Catholics in a predominantly Protestant country, and their influx called into existence a short-lived nativist organization, the American Protective Association, which was vaguely but bitterly anti-alien and anti-Catholic. Many native-born laborers were incensed by the willingness of the immigrants to accept lower wages and to take over jobs of strikers.

The later immigrants flocked to the industrial cities of the East and became unskilled laborers. They did not have the capital to begin farming operations in the West; they had to have immediate employment, and this was offered them by the meat packers, railroads, coal producers, and steel manufacturers, hungry for cheap labor; and in a strange land the immigrants felt the need for association with their fellows, which only city life could give.

Crowded into slums and patronized by natives, the aliens seemingly offered prime material for the recruiters of reforms. The leaders of the extreme left, the anarchists and socialists, expecting a ready response, directed their appeals squarely to the immigrant masses. Some newcomers did support the anarchists, but the great bulk of the newcomers were repelled by their justification of violence. The doctrines of socialism were only slightly more attractive. The Socialist Labor party, founded in the seventies, fell under the leadership of Daniel De Leon, an immigrant from the West Indies; other party chiefs hailed from eastern Europe. Although De Leon aroused something of a following in the industrial cities, his party never succeeded in polling over 82,000 votes.

The new immigrants, like the old ones, came with high hopes to what they expected to be a land of opportunity. Needy families, both native and foreign-born, could look to private charitable societies for assistance, but generally these were run by middle-class humanitarians who insisted on middle-class standards of morality. Such societies operated on the belief that poverty was more commonly due to laziness and vice than to misfortune. After careful investigation they confined their help to the "deserving poor." In 1879, a year after its founding in London, the Salvation Army began its work in American cities, but at first it concentrated on religious revivals rather than on the relief of the homeless and hungry. Social workers established settlement houses in the foreign neighborhoods to entice the aliens from the saloons and streets and bring them under religious influences. The most famous of the houses were the Henry Street Settlement in New York, founded by Lillian D. Wald, and Hull House in Chicago, directed by Jane Addams. By 1900 fifty such centers were operating in American cities.

For most of the urban poor, especially the foreign-born and their families, the main welfare agency was the political machine, headed by a boss, who himself was typically of foreign birth or parentage, most commonly Irish. To maintain his power, the boss needed votes, and in exchange for these he offered favors of various kinds. He provided the poor with occasional relief, such as a basket of groceries or a bag of coal. He stepped in to save from jail those arrested for petty crimes. When he could, he found work for the unemployed. Most important, he rewarded his followers with political jobs, with opportunities to rise in the party organization.

With the mounting of the alien tide, the first demands for immigration restrictions rose in the land. In 1882, besides excluding the Chinese, Congress passed a general immigration law denying entry to certain undesirables—convicts, paupers, idiots—and placed a tax of 50 cents on every person admitted. Later legislation of the nineties enlarged the proscriptive list and increased the tax. These measures reflected rising American fears that continued unlimited immigration would exhaust the resources of the nation and endanger its social institutions. The laws kept out only a small number of aliens, however, and were far from fulfilling the purposes of the extreme exclusionists. The exclusionists worked for a literacy test, a device intended to exclude immigrants from eastern and southern Europe. Congress passed a literacy law in 1897, but President Cleveland vetoed it.

The Urban Scene

The fast-growing American cities were places of violent contrast—of poverty and wealth, of palatial homes and dingy slums. They were also places faced by many perplexing problems, most of them the result of a suddenly expanded population.

The urban masses had to have a means of rapid and cheap transportation. Before the Civil War some cities had experimented with streetcars drawn by horses, and after 1865 horsecar lines appeared in all the metropolitan centers. Richmond, Virginia, introduced an electric railway system in 1887, and soon other cities followed suit. New York opened its first elevated railway (with steam locomotives) in 1870, and in 1897 Boston, putting the streetcars underground, completed the first American subway.

Another urgent urban problem was disease. In the dark and dirty slums, where families were huddled in single rooms with inadequate toilet and sanitary facilities, thousands died annually of epidemics. From the slums, disease spread into other sections. At the time of the Civil War, most cities took no precautions to guard the pu-

rity of their water supply and no satisfactory measures to dispose of their sewage and garbage. A common practice was to empty sewage into nearby rivers, sometimes into the stream from which the city secured its water; in other cases the sewage was dumped into open ditches within the city limits. Garbage was customarily placed on the streets, where it might remain indefinitely.

Out of the urban environment arose the first American public health movement. First cities and then states created boards of health empowered to correct slum conditions, enforce sanitation measures, and improve sewage and garbage disposal. Covered sewers were installed in many cities, and in others sewage was dumped at sea. Garbage was collected on regular schedules and was burned in furnaces or fed to hogs, an unfortunate practice that spread disease. Many cities built reservoirs and pressed water-purification programs. At the turn of the century the life of the urban dweller was still dangerous from the medical standpoint, but it was immeasurably safer than it had been.

Such improvements in urban services were engineered politically by the city bosses. While the bosses personally profited from the bribes extracted for the granting of public contracts, those contracts provided urban centers with needed streets, sewers, public buildings, reservoirs, parks, and playgrounds. Boss rule was made possible by the weakness of existing city government. Within the government, no single official held decisive power. Power was divided among a number of officeholders—the mayor, the aldermen, and others—and was limited by the state legislature, which had ultimate authority over municipal affairs. Centralizing power in his own hands, the boss together with his machine formed a sort of "invisible government" that made up for the inadequacy of the regular government. From time to time middle-class reformers sought to overthrow a boss. But they succeeded only when they had support from powerful, dissident elements within the machine who believed that the boss had abused his power and taken exorbitant graft. Such an instance was the overthrow of New York City's William M. Tweed and the "Tweed Ring" in 1871. The system of boss rule continued to flourish in New York and other large cities because the conditions that produced it remained essentially unchanged.

Chapter 18. THE GILDED AGE

The Last West

During the late nineteenth century, at the same time the industrial revolution was accelerating, a dramatic transformation of the American scene was occurring west of the Mississippi River. There, in the vast area stretching from the middle valley to the far western highlands, a propulsive movement of population settled the last frontier in America. By the turn of the century practically every part of the region had been organized into states or territories.

The last frontier was made up of three distinct natural, or physiographic areas: the Great Plains, the Rocky Mountains, and the Basin and Plateau region between the Rockies on the east and the Sierra Nevada-Cascade range on the west. The settlers who entered this "west" found an environment utterly different from the lands behind them. The Great Plains were largely level, thinly timbered, and mostly arid. The rugged Rockies had only small patches of arable land and suffered from a deficiency of rainfall. Also rugged and dry was the Basin-Plateau area. The last two regions were, however, rich in gold, silver, and other minerals.

The lure of minerals drew the first settlers to the last West. They began to come on the eve of the Civil War, came even during the war, and entered in larger numbers after its close. The mining frontier had a brief but brilliant existence, beginning around 1860, flourishing until 1880, and then abruptly declining. The settlement of the region followed a pattern. News of a gold or silver strike in some part of it—Colorado, Nevada, South Dakota—would bring a stampede of prospectors. These men, using pan and placer mining, exploited and quickly exhausted the shallower deposits of ore and then moved on to other places. Next corporations moved in to engage in lode or quartz mining of the deeper deposits. But even these resources eventually thinned or ran out, and though commercial mining might continue on a restricted basis, the population of a typical mining area declined. It would not rise until agriculture was developed to give the region a more stable economy.

Soon after the mineral empire burst into being, another great economic province took shape, the cattle kingdom of the Great Plains. Like the mining frontier, it had a brief and brilliant existence, from about 1865 to 1885. The rise of the cattle kingdom was directly related to the developing industrial society of urban America—the concentration of population in cities created a new market for meat and other foods. Two factors enabled the cattle industry to spread from Texas over the West. First, the open range, the unclaimed grasslands of the public domain, provided a vast area where the cattlemen could graze their herds free of charge. Second, the ever expanding railroads gave the cattlemen access to the Eastern markets. To various towns on these roads, Sedalia, Abilene, and others, ranchers drove their herds, sometimes numbering in the thousands, in the famous "long drives."

The profits to be made in the cattle industry were tremendous and inevitably tempted more investors into it. The ranges became overstocked, and prices fell drastically. As abruptly as it had risen, the cattle kingdom fell. Cattlemen turned to more modest operations, acquiring title to lands, fencing in their tracts, and becoming settled ranchers.

The Western Indians

The settlers of the last frontier had to advance against a determined and sustained Indian resistance. The Indian population of the region was perhaps 240,000, divided into numerous tribes of varying sizes. The two principal nations were the Sioux of the northern plains and the Apache of the southwest highlands. They were also the most warlike of the tribes. Mounted on their horses, they were a formidable foe, whether armed with a bow, spear, or rifle. They possessed a mobility enjoyed by no previous Indians, and students of war have ranked them among the best light cavalry in military history.

There were almost incessant Indian wars from the sixties to the eighties. The fighting on the part of the whites was done by cavalry of the regular army, of which two regiments were Negroes. In the end the army and superior white technology triumphed. The army had better weapons than the Indians, the railroads facilitated quick troop concentrations, and the telegraph reported instantly the movements of hostile bands.

As the Indians were supressed, the government moved them into specified areas known as reserves. It also acted to break down the tribal structure that was the cornerstone of Indian culture, to force the Indian to become, in effect, a white man. The Dawes Severalty Act of 1887 provided for the gradual abrogation of tribal ownership of land and the allotment of tracts to individuals; it conferred citizenship on adult owners but forbade them to alienate their property for twenty-five years. The Indians, however, were not ready for a change from collectivism to individualism, particularly since the reserves afforded them little economic opportunity. Congress sought to facilitate the transition with the Burke Act of 1906, which deferred citizenship for twenty-five years but permitted Indians who had proved their adaptability to secure both citizenship and land ownership in a shorter time. Full rights of citizenship were finally conferred on all Indians in 1924.

The Farming Frontier

Some farmers had drifted into the last frontier during its first stages of settlement. More came in the late seventies, and a rush of them in the eighties. They gradually converted the area to an agricultural economy.

Most of the farmers settled on the Great Plains, although some went to valleys in the Rockies or the Basin-Plateau region. Wherever they stopped, they had to contend with problems not encountered in any previous region. The most acute one was the lack of water. The rainfall was not, except in rare years, sufficient to sustain crops. Of various expedients proposed to provide water, the most practical one was irrigation. But large-scale irrigation obviously called for government planning. The national government tried to hand the issue to the states, turning over to them in the Carey Act (1894) several million acres of public land to be reclaimed. The states made little progress, largely because the problems of reclamation cut over

state lines. In the Newlands Act (1902) the national government finally accepted the responsiblity for an irrigation program.

The Farmer's Grievances

One of the great agricultural changes of the nineteenth century reached its culmination in the years after 1865 – the change from subsistence, or self-sufficient, farming to commercial farming. In commercial farming, the producer specialized in a cash crop, sold it in an outside market, and in the same market bought the household supplies he had previously made. This kind of farming, when it was successful, raised the farmer's living standards. But it also made him more dependent on other factors and groups in the economy. He had become a businessman, but unlike many large manufacturers, he could not regulate his production or control his prices.

Impelling economic forces had dictated the shift to commercial farming – an expanding national and world demand for farm products. In answer to this demand, the farmers of America increased their output, putting huge new areas of land under cultivation, especially in the West; utilizing labor-saving machines – the reaper, thresher, and others; and going into debt to finance purchases of land and machinery. But while farmers were going more deeply into debt they faced declining prices – a result of the failure of the money supply to keep up with the pace of production between the Civil War and the late 1890s. Like all debtor capitalists, including most small businessmen during the period, the farmers found their debts increasing as prices declined; they encountered severe difficulty in paying off those debts during the depressions of the 1870s and 1890s. The farmers were too numerous and their interests too diverse to unite in restricting production to raise prices.

The farmers were painfully aware that something was wrong and first turned their attention and anger to the middlemen with whom they dealt. Farmers contended that the banks charged too-high interest rates, sometimes as much as 10 to 25 percent, and were reluctant to lend to farmers. Also, they accused speculators and bankers of conspiring to fix prices to benefit themselves. Farmers also believed that there was a conspiracy to fix the prices of supplies. The most burning grievance was against the railroads. The farmers believed that the roads charged high and discriminatory rates to small producers while favoring large shippers. They were also convinced that the railroads controlled the elevator-warehouse facilities in buying centers and levied arbitrary storage rates. The anger of the farmers at the railroads shook them out of their traditional individualism and caused them to turn for the first time to organized action.

In the South the farmer had additional problems of his own, especially if he was black.

The Southern Negro

The men who came to power in the South after 1877 were not in the old agrarian, planter tradition. Known as Bourbons or Redeemers, they preached the industrialization of the South through the importation of Northern capital and a policy of low taxes to attract business. Controlling state governments through the medium of the Democratic party, which as a result of Reconstruction was virtually the only party in the section, they practiced a program marked by economy in government and few social services. They did not attempt to abolish Negro suffrage but instead used the Negro vote to maintain their power. Negroes continued to vote after the return of white rule, but in reduced numbers and usually as directed.

Not until the 1890s did the Southern states pass laws to disfranchise the Negroes, and then because of pressure by the white farmers. The farmers demanded disfranchisement because they were opposed for racial reasons to Negro voting and because they objected to the Negro vote being used against them. The rich whites, deciding to placate the farmers, acquiesced.

In devising laws to disfranchise the Negroes, the Southern states had to take care to evade the intent of the Fifteenth Amendment, to exclude Negroes without seeming to do so because of color. Two devices were widely employed before 1900. One was the poll tax or some form of property qualification. The other was the literacy and understanding test, which required a voter to demonstrate an ability to read and to interpret the Constitution. Many states passed so-called "grandfather laws," which permitted white men who could not meet the literacy and property qualifications to be admitted to the suffrage if their ancestors had voted before 1867 or some date before Reconstruction began.

The Supreme Court proved compliant in ruling on the various Southern laws. Earlier, in the Civil Rights Cases of 1883, it had held that while the Fourteenth Amendment prohibited states from imposing segregation because of color, it did not enjoin such private institutions as railroads or hotels. Then in *Plessy* v. *Ferguson* (1896), a case involving separate seating arrangements on railroads, it affirmed that a state could enforce segregation if the separate arrangements were equal. The separate but equal principle was shortly applied to education.

The Court was equally cooperative in accepting the disfranchising laws. Although it voided the grandfather laws, it validated the literacy tests and manifested a general willingness to let the Southern states define suffrage standards — provided the evasions of the Fifteenth Amendment were not too glaring. As the turn of the century approached, the South seemed to have won a complete victory over the outside influences that had sought to disturb its way of life.

The "New South"

With relative rapidity, the South recovered from the effects of war and restored its economic life. Since it was an agricultural society, its productive powers rested on the basis of land, and the land had survived the war. The chief problem was to get the plantations and farms under cultivation again. Work began at once (crops were raised in 1865), and progress was steady. The demands of industry for cotton remained strong and by 1879 the cotton crop exceeded that of 1860, part of the increase resulting from the opening of new growing areas west of the Mississippi, in Texas and Arkansas.

The rehabilitation of the South's agrarian economy was accomplished with relatively few changes in the nature of Southern agriculture. There was something of a shift in the distribution of land ownership, in the direction of an increase in the number of small holders, but the plantation system, although modified, survived.

During the Reconstruction period, perhaps a third or more of the farmers in the South were tenants, and most of them, black and white, were poor despite the continued profitability of cotton production. In place of slavery there arose the share-crop system, in which produce and labor took the place of money. The sharecroppers, most of whom were Negroes, worked a strip of land on a large unit. The landlord provided the cropper with tools, seed, and a house and arranged credit facilities for him at the local store. The cropper, for his part, agreed to consign from one-third to one-half of his crop to the landlord. Moreover, the storekeeper, the source of credit, protected his interest by taking a mortgage or lien on the tenant's share of the crop.

The dreams of the leaders of the New South for an industrial economy were only partially realized. On the surface it seemed that an astonishing advance was made. By 1880 the region boasted 80 percent more manufacturing plants than in 1860. Important expansion had occurred in railroads, textiles, and other industries. But the appearance of industrial growth was deceptive. Expansion in the other sections proceeded at an even faster rate, and in the economy as a whole the South had a smaller percentage of industrial activity than in 1860.

The Pragmatic Approach

While the farmer's prestige declined, the urban environment increasingly made its influence felt upon the entire nation, despite the persistence of stereotypes from the rural past. The city's influence was spread through the educational system, which was being broadened and extended, and through the publishing industry, which centered in New York and reached out for a wider and wider readership.

Along with the economic and social changes of the time, there was a change in the philosophical assumptions of thinking Americans. This came about largely in response to the doctrine of evolution—the thesis that all living things had evolved from earlier forms and that the various species had resulted from a process of natural selection.

Here was a doctrine that apparently challenged almost every tenet of the American faith. If Darwin and the scientists were right, man was not endowed with a higher nature, but was only a biological organism, another form of animal life—the highest form, it was true, but still like the other animals that had had their day in past ages. Instead of history being the working out of a divine plan, it was a random process dominated by the fiercest or luckiest competitors.

All over the United States Darwinism became a subject of popular interest and an issue of debate. By 1900 the evolutionists had carried the day, except in the South and parts of the rural Midwest. Many Protestant ministers, especially those in urban centers, had managed a reconciliation between religion and science. Particularly in the cities and larger towns, more and more people accepted the basic principles of evolution. Science was enshrined in the university and college curriculums.

Out of the controversy over Darwinism there arose finally a new philosophy that was peculiarly American and peculiarly suited to America's changing material civilization. The name of the philosophy was pragmatism, and its principal formulators were Charles Peirce and William James in the period before 1900, and John Dewey later.

Pragmatism is difficult to define, partly because its advocates differed as to its meaning, but mainly because it avoided absolutes and dealt with relative standards. According to the pragmatists, who accepted the idea of organic evolution, the validity of human institutions and actions should be determined by their consequences. If the ends of an institution or the techniques of a group did not satisfy social needs, then a change was in order. In blunt terms, the pragmatists applied one standard: Does it work? They employed the same test to truth. There were no final truths or answers, they contended, but a series of truths for each generation and each society. Truth, like institutions, had to be validated by consequences. Said James: "The ultimate test for us of what a truth means is the conduct it dictates or inspires."

Toward Universal Schooling

Mary Antin, a Russian girl who came as an immigrant to the United States, had heard that in America everything was free. Best of all: "Education was free. That subject my father had written about repeatedly, as comprising his chief hope for us children, the essence of American opportunity, the treasure that no thief could touch, not even misfortune or poverty." Education in America after the Civil War was indeed free or in the process of becoming so—free, public, and almost universal. Education was becoming the central means for transmitting democratic virtue, for providing a skilled labor force, and for acculturating immigrants.

In 1860 there were only 100 public high schools in the country, but by 1900 the number had reached 6,000; their total enrollment, however, was not more than 200,000. The most spectacular expansion occurred at the elementary grade school level. Below the elementary level appeared the kindergartens, the first of which was established in St. Louis in 1873. By 1900 compulsory school attendance laws were in effect, although not always enforced, in thirty-one states and territories. In the expansion of school facilities, the Northeast led, the Middle West followed, and the South trailed behind. Between 1860 and 1900 the share of the nation's resources devoted to education had doubled.

In the 1880s a number of innovations in educational methods began to make their influence felt. New, more up-to-date textbooks were introduced, and the curriculum was expanded to include more science and practical or vocational courses. At the same time German educational doctrines, stressing the necessity of arousing the student's desire to learn, stirred the attention of American educators. Among those impressed by the German theories was John Dewey, one of the pragmatic philosophers and a member of the faculty of the school of education of the University of Chicago. In lectures and essays in the 1890s, Dewey proposed that education should be considered as a part of the social process, that its purpose should be to prepare students to live in modern society, and that pupils should learn by doing instead of by the traditional rote or drill method. His program of progressive education had its greatest impact after 1900.

Powerfully stimulating the expansion of higher learning were huge new financial resources made available by the national government and private benefactors. The national government, by the Morrill Land Grant Act of the Civil War period, donated land to states for the establishment of colleges to teach, among other subjects, agriculture and mechanical arts. After 1865, particularly in the West and the South, states began to exploit the possibilities of the act to strengthen existing institutions or to found new ones. In some cases the proceeds went to a single state university with an agricultural and mechanical division, and in other cases

to a separate college for the practical arts. In all, sixty-nine "land grant" institutions came into existence, among them the universities of Wisconsin, California, Minnesota, and Illinois.

Supplementing the resources of the government were the millions of dollars contributed by business and financial tycoons, who endowed private institutions. The motives of the magnates were various: they were influenced by the gospel of wealth; they thought that education would blunt class differences; they realized that the demands of an industrial society called for specialized knowledge—or they were simply vain. Men like Rockefeller and Carnegie gave generously to such schools as Harvard, Chicago, Northwestern, Syracuse, Yale, and Columbia. Other philanthropists founded new universities and thereby perpetuated their family names—Vanderbilt, Johns Hopkins, Cornell, Tulane, and Stanford.

Two groups in American society—women and Negroes—did not receive the full benefits of higher education. Before the Civil War, girls had been generally admitted on an equal basis to elementary and secondary schools, but the doors of most colleges were closed to them. A few private colleges for women had been founded, and a very few schools (three, to be exact) admitted women to study with men. After the war a number of additional women's colleges came into existence, generally as the result of donations from philanthropists: Vassar, Wellesley, Smith, Bryn Mawr, and Goucher. In addition, some of the largest private universities established on their campuses separate colleges for women. But the greatest educational opportunities for women opened in the Middle West, where the state universities began to admit women along with men.

Negroes reaped the fewest advantages from the educational renaissance. In the South, and also in most parts of the North, they attended segregated elementary and secondary schools that were nearly always poorer than the white schools. Negroes desiring a higher education were almost universally barred from white institutions and had to attend one of the colleges established for their race by Northern philanthropy: Howard University, in Washington; Fisk University, in Nashville; Straight University, in New Orleans; or Shaw University, in Raleigh. Some Negro leaders were disturbed by the tendency of their people to seek a "classical" education that did not fit them for the economic position they occupied in the South. For the transitional period after emancipation, these leaders believed that an industrial education, stressing vocational training and the dignity of labor, was preferable. The result of their thinking was the establishment, with aid from private sources, of the Hampton Normal and Industrial Institute in Virginia and the Tuskegee Institute in Alabama, the latter presided over by Booker T. Washington, the most influential Negro leader of his times.

The Publishing Business

Newspapers and magazines provided the reading matter for most Americans. During the period 1870–1910 the circulation of daily newspapers had a nearly ninefold increase (from less than 3 million to more than 24 million), which was over three times as great as the increase in population.

Meanwhile, journalism changed in various ways: (1) Newspapers became predominantly news organs, while editorial opinion and the editorial page declined in importance. (2) The nature of news changed. Politics received less attention, and there was an increasing emphasis on what was called the "human-interest" story. (3) Journalism became a recognized and respected profession. Salaries of reporters doubled. Able, educated men and women were attracted to the profession, and schools of journalism were begun on university campuses. (4) With the passing of personal journalism, newspapers became corporations, impersonal business organizations similar to those emerging in industry, their worth often reckoned in millions of dollars. At the same time, they tended to become standardized. The press services furnished the same news to all their subscribing papers, and syndicates came into existence to provide their customers with indentical features, columns, editorials, and pictures. By the turn of the century there were several newspaper chains, harbingers of a development that would become stronger in the future. Thus the newspapers conformed to and reinforced the trend toward uniformity that characterized American society as a whole. (5) There was a distinct improvement in the physical appearance of newspapers. The traditional pages of poorly and closely printed columns,

each with its own headlines, disappeared; in their place came something resembling the modern paper, complete with varied make-up, pictures, cartoons, and imaginative advertising.

Book publishing became a business, and, in line with the trend in industry, a big business. The corporation replaced the individual publisher, and publishing became more impersonal and increasingly commercial. For approximately twenty years after the war most publishing houses sold books only by subscription. But gradually this type of organization was supplanted by the large firm that sold its products to book stores and reached the public through advertising techniques. By 1900 most of the big publishing houses were centered in New York City, the recognized publishing capital of the country and also the largest literary market. The passage by Congress in 1891 of an International Copyright Law prevented American publishers from pirating foreign books without payment (and also prevented foreign pirating of American books). The result was that publishers had to rely more on American authors and pay them better.

Reflections in Literature

In a novel, *The Gilded Age* (1873), Mark Twain and Charles Dudley Warner satirized the men and manners of industrial society and thus provided a name that is sometimes applied to the last decades of the nineteenth century. The novel deals with greedy men and their get-rich-quick schemes. It suggests that American life, though showy on the surface, was essentially acquisitive and corrupt. Its authors thus reflected the economic and social changes of the time. Different writers responded to these changes in a variety of ways. Some faced up to the realities of the industrializing and urbanizing trend; others sought a vicarious escape for themselves and for their readers.

Though New York City was the publishing center, the production of literature – the actual writing – was done all over the country. A literary renaissance began in the West and the South as well as the East. Writers in each section, describing their home scenes in local-color stories, found a national market for their wares.

Writers of the local-color school thought of themselves as realists. Rebelling against the sentimentality of the tear-jerking popular novelists like Mary Jane Holmes (whose thirty-nine novels sold more than 2 million copies), they insisted on careful reporting, real people and real plots, and an honest rendition of such things as dialect, dress, food, and manners. Usually, however, they were content with an accurate surface description that did not come to grips with fundamental problems, and on occasion some of them wrote sentimental nonsense.

Mark Twain (born Samuel Clemens) began his career on a newspaper, and he long considered himself to be a journalist. The public long insisted on regarding him as merely a humorist, but he was probably the greatest American novelist in the era between 1865 and 1900. His first important success, *The Innocents Abroad* (1869), a tale of American tourists in Europe, was a loud and scornful laugh at Old World decay and hypocrisy—and also at American worship of European institutions. His literary fame, however, rests primarily on *The Adventures of Tom Sawyer* (1876) and *The Adventures of Huckleberry Finn* (1885), sensitive and sympathetic accounts of life in rural mid-America.

Not all the writers were concerned with departing cultures. Some viewed with misgiving the culture of their own times, and deplored its materialism and economic inequalities. Gradually there developed a literature of protest, expressed chiefly in the medium of the problem novel. The dissenters attacked their targets from many and varied angles. A few, like Henry Adams in *Democracy* (1880) and John Hay in *The Breadwinners* (1884), spoke for the old aristocracy, the former ruling class; in criticizing the crassness of the new rich, they merely expressed the resentment of their group at being dethroned. No novelist of stature voiced the aspirations of labor, although Stephen Crane in *Maggie: A Girl of the Streets* (1893) described slum conditions and urban poverty with somber realism. For rural America and its small towns, Hamlin Garland and Edgar W. Howe grimly performed a similar descriptive job. Garland, smashing the traditional idyllic picture of pastoral culture, exposed in *Main-Travelled Roads* (1891) the ugliness, isolation, and drudgery of farm life, and Howe in *The Story of a Country Town* (1883) starkly painted the narrow, provincial nature of the American village.

A few literary critics of the American scene retreated from its vigor and materialism and found refuge in Europe. Preeminent among them was Henry James, who studied and described his country from England. In such novels as *The American* (1876), *An International Episode* (1878), and *Daisy Miller* (1879), he detailed the psychological impact of Europe's ancient culture upon visiting Americans. In his coldly realistic volumes, the Americans are usually frustrated or defeated by Europe, but nearly always they appear more noble than the civilization they cannot understand. During his later years, James confessed he wished he had remained in America.

The greatest realistic novelist of the period, ranking second only to Twain in the hierarchy of letters, was William Dean Howells. His realism was confined to the common and the average; shunning the abnormal, he was the most painstaking literary historian of what was normal in the America of his age. In *The Rise of Silas Lapham* (1884), he portrayed shrewdly and in not completely flattering terms the psychology of the self-made businessman. His later novels, written during the social upheaval and labor strife of the nineties, dealt with social problems and social injustices.

New Uses of Leisure

Many Americans, especially those of the urban middle and professional classes, found that they had more leisure at their command, and they had incomes sufficient to gratify their demands for pleasure. Even the workers had more free time, and they too sought satisfactory forms of recreation. The late nineteenth century marked the expansion and specialization of urban entertainment industries. The circus, vaudeville, burlesque, popular theater, and the legitimate stage evolved as distinct forms. Saloons, beer gardens, houses of prostitution, dance halls, and billiard parlors flourished. Rapid-transit companies, in conjunction with suburban amusement parks, provided new opportunities for weekend outings. Most dramatic was the rise of organized spectator sports, such as horse racing, prize fighting, and baseball; by 1900 sports had become a business.

Most popular of all the organized sports and well on its way to becoming the national game was baseball. Its origins probably stretched back to 1839, when Abner Doubleday, a civil engineering student, laid out a diamond-shaped field at Cooperstown, New York, and attempted to standardize the rules governing the playing of such games as town ball and four old cat, the ancestors of baseball. By the end of the Civil War, interest in the game had grown rapidly. Over 200 teams or clubs existed, some of which toured the country playing rivals; they belonged to a national association of "Baseball Players" that had proclaimed a set of standard rules. These teams were amateurs or semi-professionals, but as the game waxed in popularity, it offered opportunities for profit, and the first professional team, the Cincinnati Red Stockings, appeared in 1869. Other cities soon fielded professional teams, and in 1876 the present National League was organized chiefly by Albert Spalding. Soon a rival league appeared, the American Association. Competition between the two was intense, and in 1883 they played a postseason contest, the first "world's series." The American Association eventually collapsed, but in 1900 the American League was organized.

The second most popular game, football, arose in the colleges and universities. At first football had been played by rival student groups at the same school. Then in 1869 occurred the first intercollegiate game in this country, between Princeton and Rutgers, with twenty-five men on each side. Soon other Eastern schools fielded teams, organized a conference, the American Intercollegiate Football Association, and attempted to standardize the rules.

As football grew in popularity, it spread to other sections, notably to the Middle Western state universities, soon destined to overthrow the Eastern schools as the powers of the game. It also began to exhibit those taints of professionalism that have marked it ever since. Some schools employed as players "ringers," tramp athletes who were not even registered as students. In an effort to eliminate such abuses, Amos A. Stagg, athletic director and coach at the University of Chicago, led the formation of the Western Conference, or Big Ten, in 1896.

A game that would eventually become one of the great spectator sports, basketball, was invented in 1891 at Springfield, Massachusetts, by Dr. James A. Naismith. It is the only major sport that is completely American in origin.

Boxing did not become a respectable sport until the 1880s. Before that time prize fights were illegal in practically every state, and bouts had to be conducted in isolated places beyond the reach of law officials. The existing rules were few and encouraged brutality. Contestants fought without gloves, a round ended when one man was knocked down, and a fight continued until one of the participants was unwilling or unable to go on. In the 1870s the Marquis-of-Queensberry rules were introduced in England and later in the United States. By these regulations, fighters were required to wear padded gloves, a round was limited to three minutes, and certain rough practices and types of blows were ruled out.

Before 1900 golf and tennis were almost completely participant rather than spectator sports. The first modern golf course in the United States was laid out at Yonkers, New York, in 1888, and the first golf tournament in the country was played at Newport, Rhode Island, six years later. The only courses were at exclusive private clubs, and until after 1900 the game was restricted to the rich. Much the same was true of tennis, first played at Eastern resorts, frequented by the wealthy. The United States Lawn Tennis Association was organized in 1881 to standardize the rules and encourage the game, and in 1897 American tennis players engaged an English team in the first international match.

The nineties saw the birth of the bicycle craze. Bicycling was both a recreation and, for many people in urban areas, a convenient method of transportation. The bicycle in the 1880s, with a high wheel in front, often pitched the rider over the handlebars for a "header" in the dirt. It was too dangerous for practically everyone except the most daring young men. The "safety" bicycle of the 1890s, with two wheels of equal size and with pneumatic tires, invited riders of both sexes and all ages. By 1900 an estimated 10 million Americans, mostly adults, were riding bicycles. While it lasted, the mania had some influence on American life. It brought into being a new industry for the manufacture of the vehicles. The cyclists, organized in the League of American Wheelmen, spurred local governments to improve highways. And cycling changed clothing styles as many young women put on blouses and moderate-length skirts in place of the former dragging street dresses.

Chapter 19.   AGRARIAN PROTEST, 1865–1900

The Politics of Complacency

In 1873 depression struck the country and farmers began to voice their grievances with unprecedented fervor.

They began to stress the necessity of eliminating middlemen and curbing the monopolistic practices of the railroads. They flocked to the organization called the National Grange of the Patrons of Husbandry and launched the first major cooperative movement in the United States. In the political action area, the Grangers labored to elect to state legislatures candidates who pledged to bring the railroads under social control. Usually operating through the Republican and Democratic parties, they won majorities in Illinois, Iowa, Minnesota, and Wisconsin. The legislatures of those states, between 1870 and 1874, enacted laws to regulate railroads and warehouse and elevator facilities. These "Granger laws" authorized maximum rates for freight and passenger traffic, provided rules and rates for the storing of grain, and prohibited a number of alleged discriminatory practices. They were to be administered and enforced by special state commissions.

The railroads contested the legality of the laws, and eventually fought them from the state courts up to the United States Supreme Court. In 1877 the Court handed down a decision in the first of the "Granger cases," *Munn* v. *Illinois*. It concerned the right of a state to regulate storage rates for warehouses and formed the basis for other decisions involving railroads. The Court rejected the argument of the plaintiffs. It held that a state in the exercise of its police power could regulate private property devoted to public use and could regulate interstate commerce in the absence of national regulation; it dismissed "due process" with the observation that it was not intended to restrict the police power.

The railroads, however, continued to contest the laws and eventually succeeded in destroying their effectiveness. The process by which this was accomplished involved intricate questions of law and came about after new justices friendly to property rights and unfriendly to state power ascended to the Supreme Court.

Under pressure of successful railroad challenges in the courts, the farmers turned to a demand for national regulation, and in 1887 Congress, responding to an increasing national demand, enacted the Interstate Commerce Act. The measure prohibited various discriminatory practices by railroads and provided that rates in interstate commerce should be "reasonable and just." The act was to be administered by the Interstate Commerce Commission, which had the power to hear complaints from shippers and, if it thought a complaint was justified, to order a carrier to lower its charges. If the road refused, the Commission had to take its case to the courts and prove the fairness of its order, a cumbersome procedure that militated against effective regulation. The law failed immediately to force rates down, but it was still a landmark measure, the first major American regulatory act.

The rumblings of agrarian discontent made little impression on the political leaders of the years between 1877 and 1890, a transitional period in politics. The politicians were not unaware of the new economic problems that were emerging, but they were complacent about the need for economic reform. They were primarily concerned, when they became disturbed, with improving the processes of government.

The politics of the era was exemplified in the administration of Rutherford B. Hayes, who became President after the disputed returns of 1876–1877 were settled. Hayes was an intelligent and high-minded man, but his administration was only partially successful. His failure to accomplish a more positive record was not entirely his fault. His party was divided between two vigorously competing factions. The Stalwarts, led by Senator Roscoe Conkling of New York, stood frankly for machine politics and the allocation of spoils to the victors. The Half-Breeds, captained by James G. Blaine of Maine, also believed in machine politics but were less blatant in admitting it; they paid lip service to civil service and governmental efficiency. Hayes tried to work with both factions but generally sided with the Half-Breeds.

Hayes took up the problem of governmental reform. Long an advocate of civil service reform, he instructed cabinet heads and other officials to award appointments on the basis of merit. Some of them complied, but others ignored or evaded his wishes. The spoils system was so embedded in the government that not even a President could uproot it. Hayes had even less luck with Congress. Despite his repeated appeals, the legislators refused to appropriate money to renew the civil service commission created under Grant.

On economic questions that emerged during his administration Hayes evinced a conservative attitude. In Congress a coalition of Western Democrats and Republicans from the farming states introduced a free silver measure that would commit the government to buying and coining all the silver offered to it. Their objective was to expand the nation's money supply and thereby halt the downward movement of prices. They were forced, however, to accept a compromise, the Bland-Allison Act, which provided that the government each month would purchase a specified amount of silver and coin it into dollars at the ratio of sixteen-to-one (the silver dollar would have sixteen times as much silver as the gold dollar had gold). The specter of price inflation horrified Hayes, who vetoed the bill. Congress, however, repassed it. The silver forces had won a partial victory.

By the time of the election of 1880 the Republicans had achieved at least a surface unity. At their convention they nominated a veteran member of the House of Representatives from Ohio, James A. Garfield. As Garfield was known as a Half-Breed, the convention gave the second place on the ticket to a Stalwart, Chester A. Arthur of New York. The Democrats, lacking a strong leader, finally settled on Winfield Scott Hancock, who had been a secondary general in the Civil War. The November election, coming after a bitter personal campaign, showed that Garfield had won a decisive electoral but narrow popular victory.

Garfield, on becoming President, gave evidence that he intended to conduct a moderate Half-Breed administration. But it is impossible to say what kind of President he would have made. Four months after his inauguration he was shot by a deranged office seeker. For over two months more he lingered in pain before dying.

Arthur now took over the Presidency, and observers feared that he would preside over a spoils-ridden administration. But Arthur, as though dignified by the office, reversed his past political course. He pursued an independent course between Stalwarts and Half-Breeds and pushed zealously for civil service. The public, shocked by Garfield's assassination, was more favorably disposed toward civil-service reform, and in 1883 Congress passed the Pendleton Act. By its terms a limited number of federal jobs were to be "classified": applicants for them were to be chosen on the basis of competitive written examinations. At first only about 14,000 of some 100,000 offices were placed on the classified list. But the act provided that future Presidents might by executive order enlarge the list. Every President thereafter extended the list, primarily to "blanket" his appointees into office. By this piecemeal process civil service was finally achieved by the 1940s.

Return of the Democrats

The election of 1884, with its absence of national issues and its emphasis on the personal qualities of the candidates, epitomized the politics of the era of complacency. The Republicans nominated their most popular man, James G. Blaine, known to his admirers as "the plumed knight." He was also their most vulnerable candidate because of an alleged involvement in a railroad scandal. His selection split the party. The reform element, now known as the Mugwumps, announced that they were prepared to support an honest Democrat. Rising to the bait, the Democrats nominated Grover Cleveland, the reform governor of New York. The platforms of the two parties were almost identical on the tariff, trusts, and other issues.

With no real issues between the parties, the campaign developed into a mudslinging contest as to the personal fitness of the candidates. The Democrats exposed Blaine's none too savory past record. The Republicans unearthed a story that Cleveland as a young man had been accused of fathering an illegitimate child. Cleveland did not specifically deny the charge, and so sex became an issue in the contest. In the November election Cleveland won a narrow electoral victory and a bare popular plurality.

Cleveland was the ablest President of the Gilded Age. He was honest and courageous and had fair mental abilities. Uninterested in economic issues, Cleveland was absorbed with plans to improve the efficiency and honesty of government. He enlarged the civil service list, although not as much as the reformers wished. He vetoed a number of "pork-barrel" appropriations and Civil War pension bills. He sponsored two major bills in Congress. The Electoral Court Act, passed with the election of 1876 in mind, stipulated that Congress was to accept the returns certified by the government of each state. The Presidential Succession Act, designed to ensure a safer succession to the chief office, provided that after the Vice President the heads of cabinet departments were to succeed in the order of the establishment of their agencies.

Despite Cleveland's preoccupation with political reform, economic issues obtruded into his administration. The Interstate Commerce Act was passed in 1887, and he signed it. He himself instigated one economic issue. He decided that the high tariff rates were responsible for the Treasury surpluses that tempted Congress to reckless appropriation bills. Therefore in December 1887 he asked Congress to lower the rates — but not to such a point that the interests of industry would be endangered.

The Democrats, who controlled the House, responded to the President's leadership by passing the Mills Bill, which provided for moderate tariff reductions. But the Republicans, who controlled the Senate, rejected the Mills Bill and offered as an alternative a protective measure. Action was thus deadlocked, and the tariff became an issue in the election of 1888.

The Democrats nominated Cleveland and pledged support to his tariff policy. The Republicans, meeting the challenge, endorsed protection, and nominated Benjamin Harrison of Indiana. The election was the first one since the Civil War that was fought out on a definite issue. Curiously, the November results revealed that the voters had not registered a definite decision. Harrison had a small electoral majority, but Cleveland led slightly in the popular vote. Harrison would take office as a new wave of protest burst on the country.

Rise of the Populists

As prices continued to decline during the 1880s, farmers more embittered and frustrated than the Grangers turned to militant forms of organization. A multitude of farm societies sprang into existence, but by the end of the decade they had united into major organizations: the National Farmers' Alliance, centered in the prairie states west of the Mississippi and usually known as the Northern Alliance, and the Farmers' Alliance and Industrial Union, largely restricted to the South and known as the Southern Alliance. Loosely associated with the Southern order was a Negro branch, the Colored Farmers' Alliance. Although the latter group functioned separately, Southern Alliance leaders preached that the farmers of both races faced the same problems and had to work together.

Almost immediately the Alliance leaders in both sections turned to politics as a means of saving the farmer. Departing from the techniques of the Grangers, they decided that farm problems would have to be solved by national rather than state legislation and that this legislation could not be secured from the Democrats or the Republicans. Therefore farmers had to form their own party. Alliance candidates first ran in state and Congressional elections in 1890, appearing under diverse party labels in the West and usually as Alliance Democrats in the South.

The farm forces surprised conservatives and probably themselves with their success in 1890. They won control of the legislatures in eight Southern and four Western states and elected six governors, three United States Senators, and some fifty Congressmen. The sweep of the vote encouraged the Alliance leaders, who now laid plans to form a national third party. In July 1892 delegates from the farm states gathered at Omaha, Nebraska, to proclaim the new party and its principles. The party already had by common consent a name, the People's or Populist party. The delegates almost ignored such traditional issues as civil service or the tariff. "We believe that the power of government . . . should be expanded," they announced, "to the end that oppression, injustice, and poverty shall eventually cease in the land."

The Populist platform demanded national government ownership and operation of the railroad, telephone, and telegraph systems; a flexible national currency issued by the govern-

THE MEANING OF POPULISM

Where Historians Disagree

The historical literature on Populism is of comparatively recent origin. The first scholarly study of the movement appeared in 1931, when J. D. Hicks published *The Populist Revolt*. It is still the only general treatment of Populism, and as a full and factual account it remains the standard work.

The book's viewpoint is summarized in Hicks' statement that Populism represented "the last phase of a long and perhaps a losing struggle – the struggle to save agricultural America from the devouring jaws of industrial America." Hicks wrote at a time when scholars tended to see certain evils in American industrial society and definite virtues in the older agrarian America of the previous century; inherent in his pages was an assumption that the reforms proposed by the Populists were good. He seemed to lament the failure of the Populist dream, and yet he conceded that parts of the dream eventually became reality when, in later years, many Populist proposals were enacted into law.

This favorable view of the Populists prevailed for over twenty years. Then, in 1955, Richard Hofstadter put forth a different thesis and unleashed an attack on the Populists in *The Age of Reform*. Hofstadter represented a new school of history, one having its roots in an urban society and having certain doubts about the older rural order. He argued that important aspects of Populism had been overlooked by Hicks and previous writers. Thus Populism had a soft side. It was essentially romantic and did not face up to the hard problems of a modern society. It proposed simple solutions and favored returning to an older and simpler America. Moreover, it had a dark side. Many Populists denounced international bankers, some of whom were Jewish, and therefore the movement displayed anti-Semitic tendencies. Other writers expanded this charge to say that Populism possibly reflected a fascist psychology.

The Hofstadter view was challenged almost immediately. In *The Populist Response to Industrialism* (1962), Norman Pollack argued that the Populists had a sophisticated and mature view of society, that they accepted the modern world and proposed sensible ways of dealing with its problems. And W. T. K. Nugent, in *The Tolerant Populists* (1963), refuted the charge of religious or ethnic bias.

Today some journalists and scholars apply the term "populist" to a great variety of politicians – to men as different as Jimmy Carter, George McGovern, and Joseph McCarthy. Such loose usage makes the term virtually meaningless.

---

ment and not by the banks; the free and unlimited coinage of silver; government-operated postal savings banks; a graduated income tax; and the subtreasury plan, an arrangement whereby farmers could deposit nonperishable produce in government warehouses and borrow in United States treasury notes up to 80 percent of the current value of their commodities, thus enabling farmers to withhold crops from sale until the price was right. Bidding for the support of labor, the platform also demanded shorter hours for workers and restrictions on immigration, and denounced the employment of private detective agencies as strikebreakers in labor disputes.

Other planks called for new political techniques to place government more directly under democratic control: the Australian, or secret, ballot; the popular election of United States Senators (instead of election by the state legislatures); the initiative, a device whereby state legislation could be introduced or enacted by the voters; and the referendum, a method whereby the voters could veto actions of state legislatures.

The new party was launched, but its appearance of strength was somewhat illusory. Its popular vote was restricted to the South and the prairie West, the one-crop regions where agricultural distress was most acute, and the Rocky

Mountain states, where its advocacy of free silver appealed to the mining interests. The Populists aroused little response in the old Granger states of the Middle West, now converted to diversified farming and a new prosperity and a new conservatism. The Populists also failed to attract the forces of urban protest. The Knights of Labor endorsed the new party, but the Knights were a dying organization. The rising but still small American Federation of Labor was interested primarily in wages and hours and felt no communion of interests with the farmers. The mass of laborers, whether organized or not, noted the Populist emphasis on free silver and concluded that expansion of the currency would raise prices and hence their cost of living.

The Populists came increasingly to stress the free silver issue. In large part, the strategy was forced on them. Currency expansion was a simple matter to explain to the voters, much easier than extolling the benefits of government ownership of key industries. Moreover, it was already a popular issue with debtor farmers, who were correct in believing that price inflation would lighten their burdens and that free silver would produce inflation. The Populists badly needed money to finance their campaigns, and the only source of help was the silver-mine owners, who insisted on an elevation of the money question. Lastly, many Populist leaders were professional politicians and had a natural desire to win office, and free silver seemed to offer the best promise of achieving that objective. This concentration on an immediate reform could, however, lead to another result. One of the major parties might seek to absorb the Populists by taking over free silver for itself.

President Harrison

Benjamin Harrison, the victor in the election of 1888, assumed the Presidency the following year in the nation's centennial inauguration. Just forty-eight years before, his grandfather, William Henry Harrison, had entered the same office and died almost immediately. Benjamin Harrison served out his term, but he left behind a slight record of accomplishment. Not a strong leader, he left the framing of a legislative program to the party leaders in Congress. They were content to push for bills for more generous internal improvements and pensions.

Public opinion, however, forced Congress to consider legislation affecting broad areas of the economy, and in 1890 important measures were enacted dealing with big business, the "trusts," and the tariff. The public was most stirred by the issue of the trusts, demanding that they be curbed. In response, Congress passed the Sherman Antitrust Act. Based on the power of Congress to regulate interstate commerce, the measure declared that any "combination" in restraint of trade between the states was illegal. The language was general but could mean that any company big enough to influence the price of a commodity in interstate trade was illegal. But for over a decade after its passage, the government made little effort to enforce the Sherman Act. It brought few suits in the courts against trusts and lost nearly every one it brought. The public, however, was satisfied, seeming to think the trusts had disappeared — while all the time they were becoming more numerous.

Having blunted the movement against big business, the Republicans next had to turn back a new demand for currency inflation by the silver forces in the party. These groups wanted free silver, but instead they had to accept a compromise, the Sherman Silver Purchase Act. This measure directed the Treasury to buy each month 4,500,000 ounces of silver, an amount estimated to be the maximum domestic production, and to pay for the bullion in treasury notes. Inflationists denounced the act as a sham, while creditors demanded a return to a single gold standard.

From bills they had to enact, the Republicans turned with anticipation to framing a higher tariff. In 1890 they passed the McKinley Tariff Act, which raised the rates on imported goods to the highest level yet in history. Many voters assumed that the increases had raised the cost of living, and in the elections of 1890 they turned a large number of Republicans out of Congress.

In the presidential election of 1892 Harrison was again the Republican nominee and Cleveland the Democratic one. Once more the platforms of the two parties were almost identical except for the tariff, with the Republicans upholding protection and the Democrats pledging reduction. Only the Populists, offering their first presidential candidate, James B. Weaver, emphasized economic reform. The result of the election indicated that the people desired some kind of change. Cleveland was elected, and the Democrats won a majority of both houses of Congress. Weaver polled twenty-two electoral votes and over a million popular votes, and the Populists elected at least a dozen candidates to Congress.

Cleveland Again

As Cleveland began his second term in 1893, a severe depression struck the country. Brought on by an overexpansion of productive facilities and exacerbated by a sharp contraction of the money supply, it lasted until almost the end of the decade. Thousands of business concerns and banks failed, farm prices tumbled, and a million workers, 20 percent of the laboring force, were thrown out of jobs.

The behavior of the unemployed workers should have warned conservatives that new forces of protest were loose in the country. In previous depressions the unemployed had accepted the common opinion that such debacles were naturally caused and could not be cured: they had to be endured by all classes until they worked themselves out. But now workers demanded that the national government should provide jobs for them. The most specific proposal for a federal relief program was advanced by Jacob S. Coxey, an Ohio Populist, who tried to dramatize his plan by organizing a march of the unemployed on Washington. Only 500 of "Coxey's army" were able to make their way to Washington, and these were barred from the Capitol and herded into camps on the pretext that their presence endangered public health.

Cleveland, however, continued to be concerned solely with the effect of the panic on the government's monetary system. Its onset, coupled with the threat to the gold standard posed by the Populists, caused holders of greenbacks and silver certificates to present their notes to the Treasury and demand redemption in gold, and soon the reserve sank below the level necessary to maintain the gold standard. Cleveland had always disliked the Sherman Silver Purchase Act and now he could point out that it was a major factor draining gold from the Treasury.

In one of his rare moods of leadership, the President summoned Congress into special session and demanded the repeal of the Sherman Act. He worked his way but only by swinging the patronage lash hard on recalcitrant Democrats and enlisting the support of Eastern Republicans. Western and Southern Democrats fought repeal to the last and in defeat were incredibly bitter.

Repeal slowed but did not stop the drain on the Treasury, however, as persons with treasury notes continued to present them for redemption. Cleveland, in desperation, went for help to the most powerful source of power he knew—the big New York bankers. A syndicate headed by J. P. Morgan agreed to take up a $65 million bond issue and to use the influence of the financial community to check the flow of gold to Europe. As a result, confidence in the ability of the government to maintain the gold standard was renewed, the stampede to redeem notes ended, and the depression eased. But to agrarian Democrats and to Populists it seemed that Cleveland had sold out to Wall Street, perhaps for personal profit. Actually, no corruption was involved, although the bankers turned a large profit. In the absence of a central banking system (like the Federal Reserve System) only the international bankers had power sufficient to resolve the monetary crisis.

The fight over the money issue revealed a dangerous division within Democratic ranks, and this split was deepened by the party's course on the tariff. After the silver question was disposed of, Cleveland called on his party to redeem its campaign pledge to lower the existing tariff rates. A bill was introduced in the House providing for moderate downward revision while retaining adequate protection for domestic producers. To get the support of Populist and Populist-minded Democrats, the bill contained an income tax of 2 percent on incomes over $4,000. When the bill reached the Senate, over 600 amendments were added to it. Most of them were made by Eastern Democrats and had the effect of raising the duties. Strong pressure from the Democratic leadership induced the House to accept the Senate version, which became law as the Wilson-Gorman Tariff. Cleveland stigmatized it as a violation of the party's platform but allowed it to become law without his signature.

The measure reduced the general scale of duties only 10 percent and was denounced by Western and Southern Democrats and Populists as a sham. Even the one crust thrown to the agrarians, the income tax, was shortly snatched away by the Supreme Court. In a case testing the right of the government to levy an income tax (*Pollack* v. *The Farmer's Loan and Trust Co.*), the court declared in a five-four decision that a tax on incomes was a "direct" tax and hence had to be apportioned among states according to population. Since an income tax, by its very nature, would be effective only if applied on a basis of individual wealth, the Court had made it impossible to levy such a tax. The decision was bitterly condemned in agrarian circles as another concession to big business. The lines were being drawn for the election of 1896.

The Choice of 1896

As the election approached, the Republicans were confident of victory. The recent Democratic years had been ones of depression and dissension, and some Republicans boasted that the party could elect any man it nominated. But one leader was determined that the party should put up a safe candidate. This was Senator Marcus A. Hanna of Ohio, a wealthy industrialist who was emerging as the boss of the party. Hanna had picked out his candidate — former Ohio Congressman William McKinley, author of the tariff of 1890, and now governor of his state. On every occasion Hanna presented his man as "Bill McKinley, the advance agent of prosperity."

By the time the convention met, Hanna had lined up enough delegates to nominate McKinley on the first ballot. The platform endorsed the protective tariff, ignored completely such issues as the income tax and railroad and trust abuses, and opposed the free coinage of silver except by international agreement with the leading commercial nations. As these countries were unlikely to abandon the gold standard, the Republicans were in reality supporting gold.

The Democrats met amid scenes of drama seldom equaled in American political history. The Southern and Western delegates, a majority, came to the convention determined to seize control of the party from the Easterners. To counter the rise of Populist strength in their sections, they intended to write free silver and other planks of the third party into the platform and to nominate a silver candidate.

The resolutions committee presented to the convention two reports. The majority platform demanded tariff reduction, endorsed the principle of the income tax, denounced the issue of currency notes by the national banks, condemned the use of injunctions in industrial disputes, pledged a "stricter control" of trusts and railroads, and — this was the issue that headlined the platform — called for free silver. The minority resolution opposed the free coinage of silver except by international agreement, a stand identical to that of the Republicans.

Various speakers then debated the two platforms before the convention. Last to appear was a young Nebraskan, only thirty-six years of age, William Jennings Bryan. His political experience was limited to two terms in the House of Representatives, but he was widely known in the plains country as a magnetic orator and he had been mentioned as a possible nominee of the party. He delivered one of the great speeches in American political history.

He devoted most of his remarks to a plea for free silver. But he also called for the Democratic party to steer a new course — to represent the "struggling masses" and to support national legislation to better the life of the masses. He ended with a peroration that brought the delegates and the spectators to their feet in thunderous applause: "You shall not press down upon the brow of labor this crown of thorns; you shall not crucify mankind upon a cross of gold." The majority platform was quickly adopted, and on the following day Bryan was nominated on the fifth ballot. The agrarians had found a cause and a leader.

The action of the Democratic convention placed the Populists in a quandary. They had expected both of the major parties to adopt conservative platforms and nominate conservative candidates. But now the Democrats had taken over part of the Populist program, such as free silver and the income tax, while ignoring such demands for fundamental change as government ownership of key industries. Some Populists argued that the party should retain its identity and fight for broad reform. Others contended that endorsement of Bryan offered the party a chance to get some of its ideas adopted. The Populists at their convention finally voted to support Bryan, and the party thereby lost its identity.

The campaign of 1896 had drama, excitement, and a clean-cut issue. The Republicans, amply financed by business and banking and directed by "Mark" Hanna, presented McKinley as the champion of stability, prosperity, and order.

They also stigmatized Bryan as a dangerous radical, as, in the words of one campaign document, "an apostle of atheism, repudiation, and anarchy."

Bryan, breaking with precedent, embarked on a stumping tour of the country, traveling 18,000 miles and addressing an estimated 5,000,000 people. His reception frightened the Republicans, who in the closing days of the campaign resorted to the weapon of economic pressure. Employers told their workers not to report for work in case of a Democratic victory, for all industry would be taken over by the government. There were banks that let it be known that farmers supporting the Democrats would have their mortgages foreclosed or at least not renewed. But the crucial source of Republican votes was the honest worry of urban workers over tariff reductions and monetary expansion.

The election results recorded a decisive victory for the Republicans in both the electoral and popular vote. Bryan carried the Confederate South plus Missouri, swept the plains and mountain states with the exception of North Dakota, but lost California and Oregon on the Pacific coast. In short, he won only the mining regions and the areas where staple farming was predominant and agricultural prices were lowest. The appeal of the Democrats and Populists had been too narrowly agrarian to win a national election.

The Gold Standard

As the Republicans had fought the campaign on the gold issue, it might be expected that on coming to power in 1897 they would immediately enact legislation protecting the gold standard.

McKinley and his advisors, however, were disposed to proceed cautiously on the issue. The Western wing of the party contained many silverites, and impulsive action might divide the victors in their hour of triumph. Instead, the leaders turned to an issue on which Republicans were agreed, higher tariff rates. A special session of Congress enacted the Dingley Tariff, which raised the duties to 57 percent, the highest level yet attained. Not until 1900 did Congress deal with the money question. Then it passed the Gold Standard Act, which declared gold to be the legal standard and enlarged the redemption fund.

And so the "battle of the standards" ended in a victory for gold. Economic developments after 1898 seemed to prove that the supporters of gold had been right. Prosperity returned to America. Business entered another cycle of booming expansion. Farm prices shot up because of crop failures in Europe. Actually, the adherents of silver had a point. The world supply of money had not kept pace with the expansion of the world economy. It so happened that the supply was greatly increased after the Republicans came into power. A new technique for extracting gold from low-content ores, the cyanide process, made it possible to work mines previously considered marginal, and huge new gold deposits were discovered in Alaska, South Africa, and Australia. Within a few years the currency supply was expanded far beyond the level proposed by Bryan and that expansion halted the prolonged price decline of the late nineteenth century. In the glow of prosperity Americans did not pause to analyze economic subtleties; instead, they turned their eyes to the expanding economy.

Chapter 20. THE PROGRESSIVE MOVEMENT, 1900–1917

The Automobile

Americans, as they greeted the twentieth century, were perhaps most proud of the enormous technical achievements that had advanced the United States to a preeminent position as an industrial nation. The achievements were indeed impressive: the introduction of countless machines that saved labor, the use of electricity in industrial production as well as in many homes, and a revolution in communications marked by business and domestic utilization of the telephone.

A new transportation revolution also was beginning. Since the introduction of railroads, men had been intrigued with the idea of installing some kind of engine in carriages or cars that would run on roads. Throughout the nineteenth century, inventors had experimented with engines driven by steam or electric power, but the vehicles thus propelled all demonstrated impossible mechanical drawbacks. In the 1870s designers in France, Germany, and Austria began to develop the internal-combustion engine using the expanding power of burning gas to drive pistons, and the gasoline engine soon supplanted all other types. France seized the lead in the early automotive industry; from French dominance come such terms as "garage," "chassis," and the word "automobile" itself.

Meanwhile, in the United States inventors were busily designing their own models—the Duryea brothers (Charles E. and J. Frank), Elwood Haynes, Ransom Olds, and Henry Ford. In 1893 the Duryeas built and operated the first gasoline-driven motor vehicle in the United States. Three years later Ford produced the first of the famous cars that would bear his name, a two-cylinder, four-horsepower affair. Other "firsts" followed in rapid succession. In 1898 the first automobile ad in the country appeared in the *Scientific American;* its headline read: "Dispense with a horse." The first automobile salesroom was opened in New York in 1899, and the next year the first automobile show was held at Madison Square Garden. In 1901 Ransom Olds built 1,500 curved-dash Oldsmobiles, thus becoming the first mass-producer of automobiles.

In 1900 the several automobile companies turned out over 4,000 cars, a trifling production compared to what would shortly come. A number of factors held back production. For one thing, the country's roads were not adequate for automobile transportation. Only 150,000 miles, 7 percent of the total mileage, were improved with gravel, oil, shell, or other forms of surfacing; by contrast, there were over 2,000,000 miles of dirt roads. The greatest deterring force was the expense involved in the manufacturing process, which resulted in cars priced too high for the mass market. The first builders had to order their parts from many sources, including sewing-machine and bicycle companies, and then begin the job of assembling, but soon they turned to assembly-line techniques and mass-production methods. The day of the automobile was at hand.

There had been only four automobiles on the American highways in 1895; by 1917 there were nearly five million, and the automobile was beginning to remake American life. Automobiles then had become commonplace among upper-middle-class families, just as telephones were almost essential in middle-class homes.

Not yet at hand was the day of the airplane. In 1903 at Kitty Hawk, North Carolina, Orville and Wilbur Wright became the first men to fly in a motor-driven machine heavier than air. Their plane and later models could stay aloft only a short time, but the experiments were obviously successful. But because of manufacturing expense and public apathy the airplane did not quickly become a familiar feature in American life.

Mass Production

American industrialists increasingly brought scientists and engineers into their plants to engage in research for new tools and products. A few years earlier any industrialist who established a laboratory would have been looked upon as a crackpot. Now laboratories became accepted, partly because of the phenomenal success of some of the pioneering ones. There was, as every schoolboy could proudly cite, the industrial laboratory of Thomas A. Edison at Menlo Park, New Jersey, out of which had come the incandescent lamp, the phonograph, the motion picture, and scores of other devices. By 1913 Bell Telephone, Du Pont, General Electric, Eastman Kodak, and about fifty other companies had established laboratories with budgets totaling hundreds of thousands of dollars per year.

With new methods and machines, mass production flourished. Precision manufacturing made possible interchangeability of parts, even in assembling a machine as complicated as the automobile. Ford began with stationary assembly, earlier used in manufacturing guns, clocks, and the like, then gradually changed by 1914 to the moving assembly line. This revolutionary technique cut the time for assembling a chassis from twelve and a half hours to one and a half. While Ford raised the wages and lowered the hours of his workers, he cut the base price of his Model T car from $950 to $290. Other industrialists, following his example, soon took over the assembly line and mass production for their plants also.

By 1914 American manufacturers were producing 76 percent more goods than in 1899. They were doing so with only 36 percent more workers, and 13 percent more establishments. The greater output of goods reflected the rising living standards and the growth of population at home far more than the growth of the foreign market.

Social and Cultural Advances

In other areas as well, the United States took giant strides into the twentieth century. Medical advances helped continue the marked improvement in public health that had begun in the late nineteenth century. The Caribbean adventures of the United States led to great discoveries in tropical medicine. In 1900 Dr. Walter Reed and his associates proved conclusively the hypothesis of a Cuban doctor that a striped variety of mosquito transmitted yellow fever. During the digging of the Panama Canal (1904–1914), Major William C. Gorgas applied the new knowledge and eradicated the mosquitoes so thoroughly that not one case of yellow fever originated there, and malaria was virtually eradicated.

Utilizing newly discovered chemicals and vaccines, doctors made encouraging progress in combating venereal diseases, typhus, typhoid, and diphtheria. Sanitariums and a national association successfully combated tuberculosis. Campaigns against mosquitoes and flies, improved sanitation, milk inspection, and, beginning in 1908, the chlorination of water supplies reflected new vigor of the state and municipal boards of health. To cap the entire program, the old marine hospital service expanded in 1902, and in 1912 became the United States Public Health Service. The death rate dropped from 17 per thousand in 1900 to 13.2 in 1920; life expectancy increased from 49 years in 1901 to 56 in 1920.

The number of public high schools nearly doubled between 1900 and 1914; the number of students increased two and a half times. In higher education, enrollment more than doubled, going to over 200,000 undergraduates, while professional and graduate schools were greatly strengthened. In many fields, American universities at last rivaled those of Europe. Still much remained to be accomplished in some areas of education. In 1900 the average elementary school term was only 143 days, of which a child was likely to attend half the time. Both the term and the attendance figures had risen by 1900, but even then most children went to school only an average of slightly more than six years. However, by 1917 effective compulsory education laws were in force and had begun to reduce the number of child workers.

The literary pioneers of the period, the so-called naturalists, drew for inspiration upon the French writer Emile Zola and European literary movements, but presented American realities harshly, in the spirit of rural and urban revolt. Theodore Dreiser's blunt, powerful *Sister Carrie* (1900) dealt so frankly with sex that it was suppressed by its publisher; it was not until 1911 when the public attitude had changed that his next novel appeared. Then in *The Financier* (1912) and *The Titan* (1914) he portrayed a ruthless Chicagoan who destroyed his business competitors. Frank Norris also wrote of unscrupulous businessmen, California railroad barons, in *The Octopus* (1901) and Chicago grain speculators in *The Pit* (1903).

The new poets either extolled the common

man or wrote about him with realism. Carl Sandburg in free verse applied the themes of Walt Whitman to Chicago; Vachel Lindsay composed chants like *The Congo,* full of mysticism and rhythm. Robert Frost, writing in a quiet, almost vernacular way about the rural folk and nature of New England, failed at first to find an audience. In 1915 he returned from England, where he had published two books, to take his place as an accepted poet. Closer to European movements than American, Ezra Pound, an expatriate from Idaho, proclaimed the techniques of the Imagists. Among them were Amy Lowell of Boston and later T. S. Eliot of St. Louis, who in 1914 moved permanently to London. The Imagists discarded rhyme from their work as an obstacle in the way of creating a pure image of everyday life.

A similar ferment stirred other branches of the arts. A group of young American artists painted the urban life as Crane and Dreiser wrote about it. Conservatives dismissed these realists as the "Ash-Can School," but were even more shocked by the Armory Show of 1913, which exhibited the American moderns and brought French postimpressionism to America.

Americans in the larger cities could enjoy stage plays and vaudeville skits that were booked out of New York City by a national syndicate. But most Americans found their entertainment in the newly developed motion picture. The first film telling a continuous story was a melodrama, *The Great Train Robbery,* produced in 1903. In 1915 the lengthy, impressive feature film arrived with *The Birth of a Nation.* It was as significant in marking the coming of age of a new art form as it was deplorable in its glorification of the Ku Klux Klan. Its popularity revealed that racial prejudice abounded in all sections of the country. By 1914 motion pictures had become a multimillion dollar industry and were moving into large and impressive theaters.

High Noon of Wealth

Most Americans were aware that "big business" dominated the economy—and was getting bigger. By 1904 there were 318 so-called trusts with a capitalization of over seven billion dollars. These combinations included basic industries like copper, oil, and steel, and industries directly affecting the consumer like sugar and tobacco. Six financial groups controlled 95 percent of the nation's railway mileage. The vital steel industry operated in the shadow of the nation's first billion-dollar corporation, United States Steel. It was able to set standard prices for steel everywhere in the United States—prices from which none of the smaller steel companies dared to deviate.

Whatever pride Americans might have felt over the emergence of these industrial giants and the wealth they created was mingled with serious misgivings. For millions of Americans the economic system meant personal poverty and misery. There was a dramatic disparity between the incomes of the wealthy few and the poor multitudes. One percent of the American families owned nearly seven-eighths of the physical assets; 99 percent of the families owned only one-eighth. While a fifth of the families were comfortable or even rich, four-fifths lived on modest or marginal incomes. A careful estimate in 1904 indicated that about one-eighth of the people, or a total of ten million, lived in poverty.

At the top, Carnegie had earned an estimated $23 million from his steel company alone in the one year 1900. It had paid him an average of $10 million a year during the previous five years. On none of this did he have to pay a cent of income tax. Carnegie lived comparatively modestly and devoted his millions to worthy causes, but many of the very rich created sensational headlines through their ostentatious living. The Vanderbilts, like a clan of feudal barons, maintained, in addition to their many country estates, seven mansions in seven blocks on Fifth Avenue.

These wealthy few often spent incredible sums on parties, accounts of which fascinated but also angered readers of yellow journals. The most notorious was the ball upon which Mrs. Martin Bradley spent $250,000; it created such a furor that she and her husband fled to exile in England. A less exceptional dinner, served on gold plates at the old Waldorf-Astoria in 1899, cost $10,000 for forty people, or $250 apiece. At this time, $250 was six months' wages for the average workingman.

Ranking particularly low in the wage scale were women. One woman in five worked, and often for wages as low as $6 or $8 per week. Unless a girl lived at home, it was almost impossible for her to exist upon these wages. Advocates of a minimum wage law to protect women created a sensation in Chicago by bringing several women to a hearing to testify that low pay and poverty had driven them to prostitution. Nevertheless, the Illinois legislature failed to enact the desired law.

Child labor was becoming an increasingly serious problem by the early 1900s. At least 1,700,000 children under sixteen were employed in factories and fields. Ten percent of the girls between ten and fifteen, and 20 percent of the boys, were gainfully employed. At least thirty-eight states had laws to protect children, but these typically applied only to children employed in factories, and set a minimum age of twelve years and a maximum work day of ten hours. Sixty percent of the child workers were employed in agriculture, which could mean a twelve-hour day picking or hoeing the fields. In the cotton mills of the South, children working at the looms all night were kept awake by having cold water thrown in their faces. In canneries, little girls cut fruits or vegetables sixteen hours a day. Some children worked at dangerous machines without safety devices.

Labor and Immigration

For most laborers – men, women, children – working conditions were dangerous. Only a few states had laws requiring safety devices in factories or provided for inspection of facilities. But there was little effective enforcement of the laws, if indeed personnel for enforcement existed. In American factories and mines, and on the railroads, the accident rate was higher than in any other industrial nation in the world. As late as 1907 an average of twelve railroad men a week were killed. In factories, little had been done to prevent occupational diseases such as phosphorus and lead poisoning.

Nor was there much economic incentive for employers to improve working conditions. Under the common law, if an accident was due, even in part, to the negligence of an employee himself or a fellow employee, the employer bore no responsibility. Even if the employer were liable under the common law, the courts were slow, and often too expensive for the maimed worker or his widow. Until 1911 there were almost no state workmen's compensation laws.

Working conditions appeared to worsen and responsibility for that was often laid to the heightened pace of immigration. While the flow of the "old immigrants" from northern and western Europe continued, a new flood, comprising about 72 percent of the total between 1900 and 1910, poured in from southern and eastern Europe. For the most part they were Italians, Slavs, and Jews. In the single year 1905, over 1,250,000 arrived. In most big cities of the North, immigrants and their children outnumbered the native-born. Bewildered at being thrust into an alien culture, living under conditions far below the level of native Americans (except Negroes), they filled most of the backbreaking unskilled jobs in the new heavy industries, on the railroads, and around the cities. The Jews, many of whom brought their skill with the needle, went into the garment trade, but often under just as wretched circumstances.

The American Federation of Labor (whose president, Samuel Gompers, was himself an immigrant) fought to cut off this flood of cheap, unskilled foreign labor, which was said to keep wages down and hamper unionization. Many Americans were susceptible to the popular dogma of Anglo-Saxon superiority, and joined in the anti-immigration movement. They feared the high birthrate among immigrants as compared with the low birthrate among natives in the higher-income groups. They feared the spread of disease from urban ghettos. They blamed the squalor of the slums and the power of the political bosses largely upon the immigrants, and felt that through restriction could come improvement. As a result of their agitation, the United States government negotiated in 1907 a "gentlemen's agreement" with Japan that stopped the immigration of Japanese laborers to the Pacific Coast. A series of restrictive laws prohibited various undesirables, ranging from ex-convicts to alcoholics, from entering the United States. In 1917, over the veto of President Wilson, Congress passed a law setting up a literacy test as a means of reducing the number of immigrants.

For millions of people crowded in the great urban centers life was hard and dreary. Municipal governments and individual reformers had effected some progress in eradicating slums and providing parks and playgrounds. But in most cities substandard housing conditions still existed. In New York City, two-thirds of the city's three and a half millions lived in tenement houses. Most of them were by no means slum dwellings but nevertheless had direct light and air in only four rooms of the fourteen on each floor.

Origins of Progressivism

It was against this social and economic background that a new political movement developed — the progressive movement. Progressives were concerned at the social ills they saw in America, and were disturbed by the growing economic and political power of big business.

Progressive leaders were chiefly from the urban middle class, to a remarkable extent college-educated self-employed professional men or small businessmen, of native-born Protestant background. For the most part they were about forty years old, financially secure civic leaders who had earlier been McKinley Republicans.

Following these leaders was a middle class, like them still clinging to the traditional agrarian values, but caught up in the social whirlpool of the new industrial age. The older segment of the middle class, the independent professional and business men, somewhat more than doubled between 1870 and 1910. This meant it grew as rapidly as the population as a whole, which increased about two and a third times. The working class (including farm laborers) trebled; farmers and farm tenants doubled. But there was another group, a new middle class of white-collar workers — the clerks, sales people, and technicians who worked for corporations or service enterprises. It increased almost eight times, from 756,000 to 5,609,000 people, thus reaching a number almost double the size of the older middle class.

While members of this new white-collar class did not provide leadership for the progressive movement, they did help to provide it with voting strength. Political action was their only outlet for economic protest, since they did not belong to unions or trade associations. And basically, like the older middle class, they were urbanites who still expressed the emotions of their rural roots. These two groups, the white-collar class and the older middle class, combined to form the respectable element of the towns and cities who, along with many of the more successful farmers and some of the laborers, were ready to accept the new progressive creed.

Middle-class people were frightened by urban political bosses, not only because of their corrupt ties with the industrial moguls but also because of their hold over the laboring masses (often largely immigrants) of the cities. Moreover, these middle-class people had some fear of the new rising labor unions. Populist farmers had shared the suspicions of the moguls and the masses. One of the Populist papers had said the purpose of the party was to serve as a "bulwark against the anarchy of the upper and lower scums of society."

The motivation of a typical progressive was revealed by Theodore Roosevelt, who became a leader in the movement. Roosevelt, a member of the older rich class, was told by associates that politics was a cheap affair of saloon keepers and horsecar conductors, which gentlemen should shun. "I answered," Roosevelt wrote, "that if this were so it merely meant that the people I knew did not belong to the governing class, and that the other people did — and that I intended to be one of the governing class."

A Variety of Reformers

Progressives were not a cohesive group. Reflecting the political situation in their cities or states, some were Republicans and some were Democrats. Often they had divergent goals. To one progressive, regulation of trusts might be the great end; to another, clean municipal government; to a third, equal rights for women; to a fourth, restriction of immigration. Sometimes progressives would coalesce to attain common objectives; occasionally they would even oppose each other. Thus some progressives favored imperialism while others fought it bitterly. Out of all these varying drives there emerged two great streams of progressivism — the movement for social justice and the demand for political reform, which dominated progressivism until World War I.

The social-justice movement was already well advanced by the turn of the century. It had its roots in European, especially English, reform movements. Almost every prominent English reformer visited the United States, and conversely almost every American progressive leader fell under the influence of the British. Young Jane Addams had worked at the newly established Toynbee Hall in the Limehouse section of London; in 1889 she returned to the

THE NATURE OF PROGRESSIVISM

Where Historians Disagree

The first historians of the progressive movement were men who had lived through it and enthusiastically hailed its achievements. Sometimes in their writings they fell little short of some progressive memoirists who remembered the movement as the coming of the millennium.

One of the first and best interpretations, sympathetic but balanced, was that of Charles and Mary Beard, who in a notable chapter of *The Rise of American Civilization* (1927) linked Populism and progressivism as a single heroic surge toward social democracy. In the *Quest for Social Justice* (1931), Harold U. Faulkner embellished this theme. "To many thoughtful men in the opening years of the twentieth century it seemed that America in making her fortune was in peril of losing her soul," wrote Faulkner. "Crude and chaotic as was this civilization in many respects, its essential soundness became manifest in the next decade and a half as the rising social consciousness of the people directed the national energy into fresh and nobler channels."

This optimistic, and rather agrarian-based view of progressivism as a triumph of the Jeffersonian tradition dominated academic thinking into the 1940s. It persisted even as, in the depression years of the thirties, several disillusioned popular writers, especially John Chamberlain, whose *Farewell to Reform* appeared in 1932, began to attack progressivism as a basically conservative exercise in futility. Chamberlain went so far as to assert that progressivism had been "preparing the ground for an American Fascism."

The economic determinist views of Chamberlain and others preceded skeptical scholarly appraisals of progressivism, which began to appear after World War II. George Mowry and Richard Hofstadter emphasized the middle-class urban background of the progressive leaders. In *The Age of Reform* (1955), Hofstadter suggested that these leaders were drawn to progressivism as a means of regaining the political status and power that had been draining away from their class, and that rising prices created a consumer consciousness that "gave mass appeal and political force to many Progressive issues and provided the Progressive leaders with a broad avenue of access to the public."

A succeeding group of historians, members of the New Left, believed, on the contrary, that progressivism meant no more than a successful maneuver on the part of businessmen to obtain government regulation that would further their own economic interests. The most vigorous of these historians, Gabriel Kolko, in *The Triumph of Conservatism* (1963), wrote: "Progressivism was initially a movement for the political rationalization of business and industrial conditions, a movement that operated on the assumption that the general welfare of the community could be best served by satisfying the concrete needs of business."

Richard H. Wiebe, in *The Search for Order, 1887–1920* (1971), agreed that progressivism was a quest for a more stable society; he argued that support for that quest was spread throughout middle- and upper-class America.

Historians have used the term "progressive" to describe such a vast array of politicians and reforms that some have suggested abandoning the term.

United States to establish Hull House, a slum relief center, in Chicago. Settlement houses, slum clearance programs, and a great variety of other English reforms quickly developed counterparts in the United States.

The Salvation Army, which had recently come to the United States from England, by 1900 boasted a corps of 3,000 officers and 20,000 privates. It offered aid as well as religion to the dregs of the cities. So did ministers, priests, and rabbis who by the nineties were working in the slums; these men were united in their determination to improve the existence of the miserable people around them in addition to saving their souls. "One could hear human virtue cracking and crushing all around," Walter Rauschenbusch wrote of Hell's Kitchen in New York City. Thus many an American Protestant minister arrived at the "social gospel." Catholics like Father John Augustine Ryan joined in the fight for social justice under the authority they found in Pope Leo XIII's encyclical *Rerum Novarum.* It declared that "a small number of very rich men have been able to lay upon the masses of the poor a yoke little better than slavery itself. . . . No practical solution of this question will ever be found without the assistance of religion and the church."

Close behind the ministry were middle-class and upper-class women. In the 1890s many of them had seemed restless and discontented, taking more schooling and reading more widely than their husbands or brothers, joining literary circles and women's clubs. By the early 1900s these clubs were beginning to display a remarkable growth; the General Federation of Women's Clubs, from a membership of 50,000 in 1898, grew to over 1,000,000 by 1914. In the new era, the members of the clubs were quick to take up the fight for the ballot and legal equality for themselves, and for a wide array of reforms on behalf of children and working women.

Another small but mighty social-justice group consisted of those who gathered careful data and statistics on the need for reform. They were often social-welfare workers or crusaders working for federal or state agencies. In many a state before 1900 there were bureaus of labor that could and did, as in the case of Illinois, compile great quantities of data on deplorable working and living conditions. But research alone could not gather a great force of public opinion behind the progressive movement. That was the task of a group of men and women called by a critic the "muckrakers."

The muckrakers were the many journalists who dramatized the need for reform by writing exposés of the unsavory in business and government. The muckraking writers found a huge national audience in the new popular magazines, selling for 10 cents or 15 cents, which were then building mass circulation. *McClure's,* already a magazine of broad appeal, began publishing Ida Tarbell's series on Standard Oil. The publisher, S. S. McClure, sent a new editor, Lincoln Steffens, out to see the country first-hand; this experience led Steffens to begin a series on municipal corruption. At the same time, Ray Stannard Baker contributed an article belaboring a union for wrongdoing during a coal strike.

At the height of the muckraking movement, ten journals with a combined circulation of about three million were devoting considerable space to the literature of exposure. In addition, some newspapers, such as the New York *World* and the Kansas City *Star,* featured articles by muckrakers. Even in fiction the technique of exposure appeared. Upton Sinclair's *The Jungle,* which depicted conditions in the meat-packing industry, became an immediate bestseller, and gave impetus to a rising demand for federal inspection of the packing plants.

Reform in the Cities

The Shame of the Cities was the title Lincoln Steffens gave to his notable series of exposés, which first appeared in *McClure's,* and shame was what civic-minded progressives felt. They tried to wrest control of their city governments away from the machines, reorganize the governments scientifically, and use them as instruments of economic and social reform.

Arrayed in the opposition were the bosses, and behind them those interests so abhorrent to the progressives, the saloons and brothels, and various businesses that could gain more from the bosses than from clean government. Allied with the bosses were some newspapers that ridiculed the progressives as either killjoys or scoundrels. Finally, there was the great constituency of city working people, mostly of immigrant origins. To them the bosses were friends who could be counted upon to help them when they ran afoul of the law in some minor way, or were in need of jobs or food. Progressives, on the other hand, seemed to be do-gooders who were trying to take away the saloon, the poor man's club, and to deprive him of his amusements from prize-fighting to Sunday baseball.

Many progressives, finding it difficult to grasp the relationship between the bosses and their constituents, saw the problem in simple moral and legal terms. Bad government, they thought, came from bad charters. Reformers should seize the municipal governments and, by remaking the charters, usher in the urban millennium.

Municipal reform began in response to a tragedy in Galveston, Texas, where the old, ineffective government broke down in the wake of a tidal wave. The citizens replaced it with a commission of five, whose members by 1908 were jointly enacting ordinances and were singly running the main city departments. In 1907 Des Moines adopted the commission plan with modifications to make it more democratic, and other cities followed. Another variation was the city-manager plan which placed a trained expert, similar to the manager of a business, in charge of the city, and made him responsible to the commission or the mayor and council. Staunton, Virginia, hired a city manager in 1908; the new device attracted national attention when Dayton, Ohio, adopted it in 1913 to speed rehabilitation from a serious flood. By the end of the progressive era some 400 cities were operating under commissions, and another 45 under city managers.

Progressives fought also to destroy economic privilege on the municipal level. They favored municipal ownership of streetcar and other franchises; if the franchises were privately owned, progressives battled to force the often high rates down. The most notable of the reform mayors was Tom Johnson of Cleveland, who had invented the streetcar fare box. He was a "traction magnate" (a street-railway entrepreneur) converted to the ideas of Henry George. As mayor, Johnson fought to raise the ridiculously low assessments upon railroad and utility property, introduce city planning, and above all, lower streetcar fares to 3 cents. After his defeat and death, his brilliant aide, Newton D. Baker, was elected mayor and helped maintain Cleveland's position as the best governed American city.

Many of the urban gains of progressivism were permanent, but in some cities, as soon as progressives relaxed, the old forces recaptured the city hall. In other municipalities, state control over city government made reform almost impossible. Cities derived all of their powers from the state, and many a state legislature granted new charters only reluctantly, or controlled a large city within the state through special legislation.

Statewide Reforms

Sometimes progressives tried to obtain state laws allowing cities to write their own charters. More often, urban progressive leaders moved into state politics, running for governorships and trying to control legislatures. They wanted to help their cities, but also to establish progressivism on a larger scene.

At the state level, progressives enacted a wide array of legislation to increase the power of crusading governors, give the people more direct control over the government, and decrease the functions of legislators. These ill-paid, relatively inconspicuous men found themselves exposed by muckrakers as the villains in many a state. William Allen White wrote of Missouri: "The legislature met biennially, and enacted such laws as the corporations paid for, and such others as were necessary to fool the people, and only such laws were enforced as party expediency demanded." This view of the legislatures led progressives to circumscribe and circumvent them in almost every conceivable way. The most important of the devices, the initiative and the referendum, were first enacted in Oregon in 1902 as a result of the quiet but persistent advocacy of the secretary of several voters' organizations, William S. U'Ren. The initiative enabled voters to short-circuit the legislature and vote upon measures at general elections; the referendum forced the return of laws from the legislature to the electorate. By 1918 twenty states had adopted these schemes.

Progressives also believed that elective government would be more honest if placed more directly under popular control. Hence they supported the direct primary, a device whereby the voters of a party instead of a machine-dominated convention would nominate the party's candidates. By 1915 every state had adopted some form of the direct primary.

The most controversial of the progressive reforms was the recall, which made possible the removal of officials at a special election to be called after sufficient numbers of the electorate had signed petitions. Many states enacted recall laws, but because of the difficulty of obtaining the required number of signatures the device was little used.

Aided by the new devices and supported by public opinion, progressive leaders won control of a number of states. Robert M. LaFollette in Wisconsin pushed through firm regulation of railroads, compensation for workmen injured in industrial accidents, and graduated taxation of incomes. Charles Evans Hughes in New York obtained a commission to regulate public utilities. When Woodrow Wilson, fresh from the presidency of Princeton University, became governor of New Jersey in 1911, he obtained from the legislature a substantial array of measures to transform the state into one of the progressive leaders.

Nevertheless, much social-justice legislation came only late and after great struggle. New York failed to enact factory-safety legislation until it was shocked into action by the Triangle Shirtwaist Factory fire in New York City in 1911, in which 148 people, mostly young women, were helplessly trapped and killed in a few minutes. But eventually in some urban states, New York and others, the city machines joined the progressives in supporting factory legislation. The bosses found that such measures won them votes among their working-class constituents.

Throughout the era, progressive legislators ran the risk that the Supreme Court would invalidate their handiwork. The Court made one great, although temporary, shift toward progressivism. This came in 1908 when Louis D. Brandeis argued in support of an Oregon law to limit women workers to a ten-hour day. He presented a brief in which he devoted only 2 of 104 pages to the legal precedents and the remainder to proofs that Oregon's police power was necessary to protect the health and general welfare of the mothers, and thus of all mankind. The Supreme Court accepted this argument and thus moved toward a "sociological jurisprudence" which adjusted "principles and doctrines to [the] human conditions they are to govern rather than to assumed first principles."

As a final measure in their program to place government more directly under popular control, progressives sought to eliminate the election of United States Senators by state legislatures and to substitute popular election. They charged that too many legislatures were influenced by corporations and elected men chosen by the corporations.

By 1902 the House of Representatives had already five times passed resolutions for a constitutional amendment for direct election of Senators; each time the Senate blocked the amendment. Impatient progressives in various states provided in effect for direct election by means of preferential votes for Senators; the legislatures were obligated to choose the candidate whom the voters preferred. By 1912 twenty-nine states had adopted these devices. Finally the Senate in 1912 passed the Seventeenth Amendment, for the direct election of Senators, and by 1913 the requisite number of states had ratified it. The new amendment did not startlingly modify the nature of the Senate, since most progressive states had already elected Senators of a new mettle.

Neither did another progressive reform measure, the preferential presidential primary, have much consequence. This was begun in Oregon in 1910 and spread to twenty states by 1920, but it by no means eliminated the maneuvering in conventions. Its main effect was to provide a series of state-wide popularity contests among leading candidates in the months before the convention.

Women's Causes

Women took an active part in many of the progressive reforms, such as those for the protection of female employees, who by 1910 included approximately 25 percent of all women over the age of fifteen. Women were especially important in the furthering of two causes that long antedated the progressive period but received new impetus from the reform spirit of the time. These two were temperance and woman suffrage.

Since 1874 the Woman's Christian Temperance Union, whose greatest leader was Frances E. Willard, had worked through schools and churches to arouse public opinion against strong drink. The Anti-Saloon League, containing both men and women, joined the crusade in 1893. For many years the cause gained publicity from the one-woman campaign of Carry Nation, who took out after the saloons in her home state of Kansas with a hatchet.

Since 1880 Kansas had had an antiliquor law, but it was poorly enforced. The temperance crusaders undertook to get antiliquor legislation in other states and also to obtain a national prohibition amendment. By 1917 more than half of the states had banned liquor sales, and several others had permitted counties or municipalities to do so (through "local option"). In 1917 Congress approved an amendment prohibiting the manufacture, sale, or transportation of intoxicating beverages throughout the country. This, the Eighteenth Amendment, went into effect in 1920.

Of all the rights that women sought, the most important was the right to vote, for this would enable them to secure their other rights. So it seemed, at least, to feminist leaders of the late nineteenth and early twentieth centuries. A great many women contributed to the suffrage movement, but the two who had the most to do with its ultimate success were Susan B. Anthony (born in North Adams, Massachusetts, in 1820) and Carrie Chapman Catt (born in Ripon, Wisconsin, in 1859).

As early as 1868, Miss Anthony and her friend Elizabeth Cady Stanton had persuaded a congressman to introduce a constitutional amendment to enfranchise women, but nothing came of it. At that time the demand for woman suffrage was a response to the proposal of Negro suffrage. Miss Anthony and like-minded feminists called for "educated suffrage irrespective of sex and color." They objected to the Fifteenth Amendment, since it removed only race and not sex as a bar to voting. When black men began to vote, Miss Anthony voted and was arrested for doing so. In 1878 the suffragists introduced another amendment in Congress, and they reintroduced it in every session after that for more than forty years.

While urging the federal government to act, Miss Anthony also carried her campaign to the state legislatures. But before the 1890s gains were minimal, limited to the granting of suffrage to women for certain school elections in nineteen states. After taking over the leadership of the movement in the 1890s, Mrs. Catt decided to concentrate on state action, so as to produce enough "suffrage states" to compel the federal government to go along. When Wyoming entered the Union, in 1890, it was the only state with equal suffrage, having adopted it as a territory in 1869. During the 1890s the neighboring states of Colorado, Utah, and Idaho followed the example of Wyoming. By 1914 a total of eleven states, all but one of them west of the Mississippi River, allowed women the same voting privileges as men. In 1916 the women voters of Montana helped to elect the first woman to serve as a member of Congress, Jeannette Rankin.

Progress with state action was so slow that, in the meantime, Mrs. Catt and most of the feminists had returned to the earlier emphasis on federal action. They disagreed, however, on the methods they should use. One leader, Alice Paul, favored imitating the "nuisance tactics" of radical English suffragettes who smashed windows, destroyed mailboxes, and disrupted public meetings to get attention for the cause. American suffragettes did march in parades and picket the White House, but Mrs. Catt and the majority of the leaders in the United States preferred the more conventional methods of persuasion and political pressure.

Resistance was strong. Antifeminists formed the Association Opposed to Woman Suffrage and chose a woman to head it. They had the support of the "liquor interests," who feared that women with the vote would hasten the day of national prohibition. The opponents also had the support of "preparedness" advocates, who argued that woman suffrage would weaken the nation in the face of possible war. And much of the South joined in opposition, fearing that enfranchisement of women might lead to enfranchisement of blacks.

Congresswoman Rankin did, indeed, oppose the declaration of war in 1917 (and she was to be the only member of Congress to vote against it in 1941). But Mrs. Catt, though herself a pacifist, believed that the cooperation of women in the war effort would help them to gain the vote. She was right. Women, suffragettes among them, contributed to victory in World War I by working on farms and in factories, assisting in the sale of war bonds, and joining in other patriotic activities on the home front. In 1919, more than half a century after the introduction of the first woman suffrage proposal, Congress finally endorsed the Nineteenth Amendment, which made it unconstitutional to deny or abridge the right to vote "on account of sex." This was ratified in time for the election of 1920.

The Neglected Negro

The Negro was the forgotten man of the progressive era. He made few gains except in literacy—between 1900 and 1910 the percentage of Negroes who could read and write increased from about 65 to 70. In the South, despite the "separate but equal" theory, his schools were far inferior to the whites'. In the nation as a whole there were, as late as 1910, only some 8,000 Negroes attending high school.

In some respects the plight of black Americans worsened, and progressives themselves were largely to blame for this in the Southern states. Progressive leaders there concluded that political reform was hopeless so long as the Negro remained a potential voter, for their opponents could argue that the progressive movement, by dividing the whites and disrupting the Solid South, would lead to "Negro domination." Hence progressives joined in the popular demand to remove the Negro, finally and completely, from politics. Already most Southern Negroes were kept from the polls by intimidation or other means. Between 1895 and 1907 every state of the former Confederacy except Tennessee took steps, by law or constitutional amendment, to exclude all Negroes from the suffrage.

Meanwhile Negroes suffered more and more at the hands of lynching mobs in the South and rioters in both the South and the North. In 1908, while the city's leaders were planning a 1909 celebration of the centennial of Abraham Lincoln's birth, a bloody race riot broke out in Springfield, Illinois, Lincoln's home town. This event led directly to the rise of the first effective nationwide organization for Negro rights.

The emerging leader in the cause was William E. Burghardt Du Bois, a Negro historian and sociologist with a Harvard Ph.D. Du Bois openly challenged Booker T. Washington as the spokesman for their race. Washington taught Negroes that they must be patient and submissive until they had proved their worth, and thus he "tended to make the whites, North and South, shift the burden of the Negro problem to the Negro's shoulders and stand aside as critical and rather pessimistic spectators," Du Bois charged, "when in fact the burden belongs to the nation, and the hands of none of us are clean if we bend not our energies to righting these great wrongs."

At first Du Bois and a group of like-minded reformers, Negro and white, met from time to time in a fellowship known as the Niagara Movement. Then, on Lincoln's Birthday in 1909, they organized the National Association for the Advancement of Colored People. White men were named to most of the offices of the NAACP, but Du Bois as its director of publicity and research remained the guiding spirit. From 1909 on, the NAACP worked slowly but steadily for equal rights, mainly through legal strategy, through filing and winning one lawsuit after another in the federal courts.

T. R. and the Trusts

Progressivism appeared first in cities, then shifted to state government, and finally and inevitably developed into a national movement. In the years between 1900 and 1917 most Americans accepted in one form or another the faith of progressivism. It was important to the movement that in its early years the man who was President was sympathetic to its ideals. Theodore Roosevelt, probably the most popular American of the era, was, in part, a progressive.

Roosevelt, elected Vice President in 1900, became President in the following year when McKinley died at the hands of an assassin. The new chief executive was young, only forty-two years of age, dynamic, and sensitive to the growing desire for reform. But he felt that he had to proceed cautiously. Conservative Republicans controlled the party machinery in Congress and throughout the country, and they would look coldly on a too-ambitious accidental President. Hence Roosevelt devoted his first major effort to gaining control of the party organization. But at the same time he let it be known that he was on the side of the progressives.

In his first annual message to Congress, December 3, 1901, he set forth his basic policy toward trusts: "There is a widespread conviction in the minds of the American people that . . . trusts are in certain of their features and tendencies hurtful to the general welfare. This . . . is based upon sincere conviction that combination and concentration should be, not prohibited, but supervised and within reasonable limits controlled; and in my judgment this conviction is right."

Specifically, Roosevelt asked for legislation to give the government the right to inspect and examine the workings of great corporations, and subsequently to supervise them in a mild fashion, rather similar to the regulation of banks. What he desired first was the power to investigate trusts and publicize their activities; on the basis of these data, Congress could later frame legislation to regulate or tax the trusts. Consequently he requested the establishment of a Department of Commerce and Labor, containing a Bureau of Corporations to carry on investigations. Congress set up such a department in 1903.

The establishment of a great railroad monopoly in the Northwest, after a bitter and spectacular stock-market battle in 1901, gave Roosevelt an opportunity to begin prosecution under the Sherman Anti-Trust Act. And so he did, even though his avowed purpose had been to regulate, not destroy, and to stamp underfoot only "malefactors of great wealth," while sparing large corporations that were benign. The new Northern Securities Company had emerged out of the struggle for control of the Northern Pacific between E. H. Harriman of the Union Pacific on the one side, and James J. Hill of the Great Northern and J. P. Morgan on the other. In the eyes of progressives, these men were malefactors.

When the Supreme Court in 1904 dissolved the Northern Securities combine, it in no material way injured Harriman, Hill, or Morgan. But it did convince progressives that Roosevelt, however cautious his avowed policies might be, was a heroic "trust-buster."

Trust-busting was popular and proceeded apace. Roosevelt's attorneys obtained twenty-five indictments altogether and instituted suits against the beef, oil, and tobacco combinations. In these, the government was ultimately successful, but the Supreme Court instituted a "rule of reason," declaring in effect that the Sherman Act prohibited only unreasonable restraints upon trade. The end result of the trust-busting policy was disappointing. Instead of forming trusts, business consolidators increasingly engaged in simple merger. As one critic said, trust-busting was like trying to unscramble eggs. But Roosevelt's campaign probably slowed the pace of business concentration.

Government and Labor

Roosevelt foresaw an active role for government as *neutral* regulators of relations between capital and labor. Presidential intervention in labor disputes was nothing new — there had been, for example, the Pullman strike — but the government had usually acted as a strikebreaker for the captains of industry. Now Roosevelt was ready to make the government an impartial arbiter instead. He found an opportunity to demonstrate his views when in 1902 a strike broke out in the anthracite coal mining industry, which was controlled by eight railroads under the domination of the Morgan banking house. The United Mine Workers, led by John Mitchell, demanded an eight-hour day, a 20 percent wage increase, and recognition of the union. Mitchell so effectively presented the miners' claims, and George F. Baer, spokesman for the operators, was so truculent, that public sympathy was aligned with the strikers. Roosevelt toyed with schemes to send federal troops to take over the mines. In the end he persuaded Morgan to force arbitration upon the operators. The miners after their long strike failed to gain union recognition but did obtain a 10 percent wage increase.

These first years of progressivism constituted a "honeymoon" period between capital and labor. Some big business concerns preferred to negotiate with labor rather than risk a strike. Some labor leaders, such as Samuel Gompers, preached that labor could cooperate with capital. One result of the new mood was that union membership more than doubled, reaching a figure of over two million.

Roosevelt, despite some setbacks, was satisfied with his administration — but wanted another in his own right. He could not be denied the Republican nomination, although some conservatives were disturbed by his progressive gestures. The Democrats, as though playing for the conservative vote, nominated a virtual unknown, Cleveland's former law partner, Alton B. Parker. After a dull campaign Roosevelt swept to a resounding electoral and popular victory in November.

Regulation and Conservation

Roosevelt interpreted the election as a mandate to continue his program of moderate progressive reform. His course alienated some of the businessmen who had contributed money to his campaign. Henry Clay Frick, the steel magnate, complained: "We bought the —— and he didn't stay bought." He equally offended the advanced progressives of the Middle West with his undisguised disdain for "the La Follette type of fool radicalism."

Some progressives urged Roosevelt to move for tariff reduction, but he showed little interest in this issue. He was primarily interested in obtaining more effective railroad rate reductions by strengthening the Interstate Commerce Act of 1887. By a series of intricate maneuvers, Roosevelt managed to force a new regulatory law through Congress. At one point he seemed to join Senator La Follette in demands for really drastic regulation of railroads. La Follette wished to give the ICC power to evaluate railroad property as a base for determining rates. He felt betrayed when Roosevelt abandoned him, but Roosevelt had been intent only upon obtaining a moderate law. Although the Hepburn Act of June 1906 was in La Follette's eyes only half a loaf, it was at least the beginning of effective national railroad regulation. It empowered the ICC to put into effect reasonable rates, subject to later court review; extended its jurisdiction to cover express, sleeping car, and pipeline companies; separated railroad management from other enterprises such as mining; prescribed uniform bookkeeping; and forbade passes and rebates.

Although Roosevelt continued to press suits against trusts, he, as well as other progressives, turned increasingly to regulation as the remedy for the problems of an industrial society. The President worked with progressives in Congress to secure the enactment of the Meat Inspection Act and the Pure Food and Drug Act. Passed largely because of public anger at the unsanitary practices of the meat packers, the laws provided for federal inspection of certain products destined for interstate commerce. They were not as immediately effective as their sponsors hoped, but their mere passage was significant—two additional industries had been brought under federal regulation.

In line with the regulatory pattern was Roosevelt's policy on conservation of natural resources. The President had long believed that the United States should develop great national forests like those of the European countries, and now he became convinced that the government should act to conserve other resources for the public good. By executive order he withdrew practically all remaining forests in the public domain from exploitation by private interests, and then all the remaining coal lands. He also prepared the way for a new government policy on electric power by reserving water power sites that expanding private utility companies wanted to obtain.

Finally, Roosevelt was instrumental in establishing a national irrigation system. Earlier he had supported the Newlands Reclamation Act, which provided that money from the sale of Western lands should go into a revolving fund to undertake irrigation projects too large for private capital or state resources. Eventually, the government built huge dams for the development of power and storage of water, and extensive systems of canals to carry the water to arid lands. By 1915 the government had invested $80 million in twenty-five projects, of which the largest was the Roosevelt Dam on the Salt River of Arizona. The principle of government aid in irrigation and power development in the West had become firmly established.

At the end of his second administration Roosevelt could look back at a record of varied achievement. The trust-busting policy on which he had set such great store had had disappointing results. But the regulatory measures of the administration had been more successful—they marked the direction in which progressivism would go.

Taft and the Progressives

On the night of his election in 1904 Roosevelt had announced that he would not seek another term. He kept his word, but as the election of 1908 approached he was determined that the Republicans should nominate a man of his choosing, one who would carry on the Roosevelt policy of moderate progressivism. His choice fell on his Secretary of War, William Howard Taft of Ohio, who had a long and solid record of service in state and national government. The Republican convention obediently nominated Taft, while the Democrats named William Jennings Bryan, now running for a third time. Both candidates advanced progressive ideals during the campaign, but between the two, most businessmen preferred Taft. So did the voters in November, but although Taft's electoral majority was substantial, his popular lead over Bryan was only half the size of Roosevelt's plurality in 1904. The vote portended that many progressives were not sure Taft was one of them.

Taft was a progressive but he lacked Roosevelt's political skills. The result was that during his administration a division between progressives and conservatives split the party. Such a division had threatened under Roosevelt, but T. R. had been able to face it down. Taft, who did not subscribe to the principle of strong presidential leadership, sat back while the split widened. To progressives it seemed that he was betraying their cause—and Roosevelt.

The first of these seeming betrayals occurred when Taft called Congress into special session to redeem the Republican platform pledge to revise the tariff downward. The revision that progressives had in mind would have accomplished only a moderate reduction, but even this was not acceptable to conservative Republicans and high-tariff Democrats. They added over 800 amendments to the tariff bill that had been introduced, and the Payne-Aldrich Act that finally emerged was on the whole a protective measure. Taft gave the progressives no help in their fight to lower the rates, and then infuriated them by signing the bill, which he declared to be the "best" tariff the Republicans had ever passed.

The most important betrayal came in the Ballinger-Pinchot controversy. Richard Ballinger had been appointed by Taft to be Secretary of the Interior. As the head of this office, he had charge of government lands containing natural resources; he was known to favor a policy of permitting private interests to exploit these lands. Gifford Pinchot was in charge of the Forestry Service in the Department of Agriculture, a Roosevelt appointee and zealous conservationist. Pinchot precipitated the controversy by charging that Ballinger was conniving to turn over valuable coal lands in Alaska to a private syndicate in return for a financial consideration. Taft stood by his Secretary and discharged Pinchot for insubordination. Although the President correctly judged that Ballinger was personally honorable, he had placed himself in the position of supporting an anti-conservationist. Progressives cried that Taft was scuttling the Roosevelt conservation program.

A third issue of division arose in the "revolt against Cannon." Progressives had long resented the domination of the House of Representatives by conservative Speaker Joseph Cannon. They would have liked to oust him, but failing that, they set out to shear him of his powers. After a fierce fight they succeeded in "democratizing" the rules of the House. Cannon was removed from the important Rules committee and all committees were made elective. The progressives had won but they had received no help from Taft.

In their mounting anger at Taft the progressives overlooked the fact that he had followed a partly progressive course. In his one administration the government brought twice as many antitrust suits as Roosevelt had in two administrations. And Taft supported the Mann-Elkins Act of 1910, which extended the authority of the ICC over railroads and brought two additional industries, the telephone and the telegraph, under national regulation.

A Rift in Republican Ranks

Roosevelt, after seeing Taft inaugurated, had departed for Africa to hunt big game and then traveled through Europe. Arriving home in 1910, he was met by indignant progressives who told him they were ready to oppose Taft's renomination at the Republican convention. Some of them were supporters of Senator La Follette, but most of them hoped that Roosevelt himself could be persuaded to run. At first he said that he wished only to unify the party. Being T. R., he could not stay out of a fight. "My hat is in the ring," he announced finally. He also announced his platform, which he called the New Nationalism. Abandoning trust-busting, it proposed that the government should regulate the economy in the public interest. Boldly Roosevelt declared that the advocate of property rights "must now give way to the advocate of human welfare, who rightly maintains that every man holds his property subject to the general right of the community to regulate its use to whatever degree the public welfare may require it."

Roosevelt's enormous popularity led many progressives to flock immediately to his standard. In the states that chose delegates to the convention in primary elections he defeated Taft. But in most states the delegates were selected by the state organizations, which were often under the influence of the administration and picked representatives pledged to Taft. When the convention convened in Chicago, the Taft forces were in firm control and demonstrated their strength by denying seats to a number of delegates supporting Roosevelt. T. R., breaking with tradition, had come in person to Chicago to direct his followers. But when his delegates were denied admission, he angrily announced that he was bolting the party. He left the city, and left the convention to Taft, who was nominated.

Before leaving, Roosevelt had discussed with associates the desirability of forming a new party. Quickly the Progressive party came into being, and it convened in Chicago shortly after the Republican convention adjourned. In an almost religious atmosphere the delegates nominated Roosevelt and adopted a platform embodying the ideals of the New Nationalism. T. R., in agreeing to run, declared he was fit as a bull moose, thus giving the new party a symbol.

Woodrow Wilson Wins

Between the Progressive bolt of the Republican convention and the nomination of Roosevelt, the Democrats met in Baltimore, exultant with the heady knowledge that, though they were a political minority, they almost certainly were nominating the next President. The two leading contenders for the nomination were Governor Woodrow Wilson of New Jersey and Speaker Champ Clark of Missouri. Wilson's reform record in New Jersey made him the favorite of progressive Democrats, while Clark had the support of conservatives and most of the bosses. Clark led on the early ballots, but the forces of Wilson and other aspirants stood firm, preventing the Missourian from attaining the necessary two-thirds majority. Finally, on the forty-sixth ballot, the convention turned to Wilson. His aspiration had always been to become a political leader, but when he had found the road rough as a beginning lawyer in Atlanta, he had taken a Ph.D. degree at Johns Hopkins, had become a Professor of Political Economy, and then served as president of Princeton University.

Both as president of Princeton and as governor of New Jersey, Wilson demonstrated the courageous strength and alarming weaknesses that would characterize his Presidency. He had the vision to inspire multitudes but was dogmatic and distant with individuals. He could lecture the opposition in high moral terms, but his sense that he and he alone was absolutely right prevented him from stooping to necessary political negotiations.

The Democratic platform had emphasized trust-busting as the solution to the problems of an industrial society. This older strategy of progressivism appealed to Wilson, who had his own program, which he called the New Freedom. He believed that the federal government should create an economic climate in which competition could flourish. Roosevelt's New Nationalism, Wilson charged, would mean the federal licensing of the juggernauts of big business to crush the American people. In contrast, Wilson proclaimed his New Freedom as the fight for emancipation of the small businessman, the "man on the make." He proclaimed: "If America is not to have free enterprise, then she can have freedom of no sort whatever."

In November, because of the three-cornered contest, Wilson won an overwhelming electoral victory. Roosevelt trailed far behind and Taft was a poor third. But the combined popular vote of Roosevelt and Taft exceeded that of Wilson, who garnered less than 42 percent of the total. Still the result revealed that the country was in a progressive mood. All three candidates were in varying degree progressive, and in 1913, the year that Wilson took office, two amendments to the Constitution backed by progressives were ratified: the Sixteenth, authorizing Congress to levy an income tax, and the Seventeenth, providing for the direct election of United States Senators.

Enacting the New Freedom

In his inaugural address Wilson called for action on three broad fronts: tariff revision, banking and currency reform, and antitrust legislation. He immediately demonstrated that he was going to be a President who would try to influence what Congress did. Summoning the legislators into special session, he appeared before them in person to read his message, thus breaking a precedent in effect since Jefferson's time. He demanded as a first priority a reduction of the tariff.

Responding to the President's leadership, the Democratic majority pushed through the Underwood-Simmons Tariff. The reductions still retained protection for domestic manufacturers, but they represented the first substantial lowering of duties since before the Civil War. One section of the measure provided for a graduated income tax. This first modern income tax imposed upon individuals and corporations a tax of 1 percent on all income of $4,000, and an additional surtax of 1 percent on income over $20,000, ranging up to a maximum of 6 percent on income over $500,000. It was the beginning of a change in the American tax structure; the United States was beginning to place upon those of large income a proportionately greater share of the cost of the government.

Rather than lose momentum, President Wilson held Congress in session through the sweltering summer, to begin work on banking reform. In 1911 he had declared: "The great monopoly in this country is the money monopoly. So long as that exists, our old variety and freedom and individual energy of development are out of the question." A House investigating committee headed by a Democrat, Arsene Pujo, early in 1913 published frightening statistics to back Wilson's accusation. Thus the Morgan-Rockefeller empire held "in all, 341 directorships in 112 corporations having aggregate resources or capitalization of $22,245,000,000." This was in 1913, when the entire national wealth was estimated at less than ten times this figure.

To President Wilson, evidence like this indicated a need to break the money trust. At the same time, one of the serious ills of the American banking system was its decentralization and independence, except through the loose tie of urban clearing houses. This meant that in time of financial crisis and deflation, banks lacked adequate reserves to meet all their obligations. In a crisis, banks would call in their loans, thereby worsening the contraction. Reform was obviously necessary, but Wilson and most progressives rejected the idea of a central bank or too great a degree of government control over the banking system. Instead they favored a federated system under loose federal regulation. Their concepts were embodied in the Federal Reserve Act of 1913.

This measure created central banks for each of twelve regions. Each bank was to serve and be owned by the banks of its district. The Federal Reserve bank would rediscount their notes, issue a new type of paper currency, Federal Reserve notes, and fulfill other banking functions for member banks and the government. The act required National Banks to become members, and encouraged other banks to do so. Although the American Bankers' Association

had criticized the legislation, nearly half the nation's banking resources were represented in the system within its first year of operation, and four-fifths by the late 1920s. Bankers had no cause to fear the Federal Reserve Board, which governed the system, and to which Wilson appointed conservative, sympathetic men.

The Federal Reserve system provided the federal government with the means to create currency or bank reserves in periods of crisis. It did not destroy the so-called money trust, but it did mark a significant start toward government management of the money supply in the United States.

Last on Wilson's agenda was the trust problem. Several measures aimed at bigness were introduced, but progressives tended to favor one known as the Clayton bill. To the surprise of many progressives, Wilson showed little interest in the proposal but seemed to veer toward a regulatory approach.

He gave his strong support to a bill prohibiting unfair trade practices and establishing a Federal Trade Commission to prohibit unfair methods of competition such as price discrimination or exclusive dealing contracts. The Commission would police business through cease-and-desist orders, engaging in prevention as well as punishment. Thus Wilson intended to restrict practices that might lead to monopoly.

Congress did, however, pass the Clayton Anti-Trust Act, although much modified. Conservatives in Congress put qualifying clauses around the sections outlawing interlocking directorates or stockholdings and exclusive selling contracts, so that the clauses, as a progressive Republican Senator complained, did not have enough teeth to masticate milk toast. As a concession to labor, the act stated that labor was not a commodity and declared that unions were not conspiracies in restraint of trade. President Gompers of the AFL chose to hail the Clayton Act as "Labor's Magna Carta," and insist that organized labor was now exempted from antitrust prosecution.

The passage of his program seemed to satisfy Wilson that enough reform had been accomplished. But after his reelection in 1916 he returned to the attack. In part he was responding to pressure from progressive Democrats for additional legislation, but he also saw that stronger measures were necessary. In his second administration he accepted a farm-loan bank system in the Federal Farm Loan Act. At the urging of progressives, he applied pressure on the Democratic leaders in the Senate to obtain a workmen's compensation system for federal employees, and the first federal child-labor law. The child-labor law, the Keating-Owen Act of 1916, prohibited the shipment in interstate commerce of products manufactured by underage children. It marked not only a significant reversal on the part of Wilson but also a new assumption of federal control over manufacturing through the commerce clause. When the Supreme Court invalidated the law by a five to four decision in 1918, Congress passed an act levying a heavy tax on the products of child labor. This too President Wilson signed, and this too the Supreme Court ultimately invalidated, with Taft as Chief Justice writing the decision. He also signed the Adamson Act which provided a maximum eight-hour day for railroad workers.

The legislation of the second Wilson Administration completed the reform impulse generated in 1912. It also demonstrated that progressives, whether or not they wanted to, were moving away from the negative policy of trust-busting to the positive solution of regulation.

Chapter 21. EMERGENCE OF A WORLD POWER

The New Manifest Destiny

In the years following the Civil War the American people were little interested in foreign affairs. Occupied with domestic problems — Reconstruction, the growing pains of the economy — they seemed to have forgotten the expansionist impulse that had led their forebears to sweep across the continent. By the 1890s the American people were ready to resume the course of expansion that in the forties had been characterized as Manifest Destiny.

Various forces shaped the new national mood. The rapid settlement of the last frontier shifted popular attention from the continental limits to lands beyond. The bitter class strife of the nineties alarmed many leaders, who thought that a more aggressive foreign policy might divert the popular mind from domestic dissensions. The swelling value of foreign trade directed American interests to foreign markets — and to the possible necessity of securing foreign colonies. Finally, America was influenced by the imperialism of the powers of Europe, who had partitioned most of Africa between them and were turning eager eyes on Asia. America "must not fall out of the line of march," one leader cried.

A philosophic justification for expansionism was provided by historians, professors, clergymen, and other intellectuals, who found a basis for imperialism in Charles Darwin's theories. These thinkers contended that among nations or "races," as well as biological species, there was a struggle for existence and only the fittest could survive. If the strong dominated the weak, that was in accordance with the law of nature.

The Hawaiian Islands

The first area into which the United States directed its imperialist impulse after the Civil War was the vast Pacific Ocean region.

The islands of Hawaii in the mid-Pacific had been an important stopover station for American ships in the China trade since the early 1800s. The first American settlers to reach Hawaii were New England missionaries, who advertised the economic possibilities of the islands in the religious press. Soon other Americans arrived to become sugar planters and to found a profitable new industry. Eventually, officers of the growing navy looked longingly on the magnificent natural base of Pearl Harbor on the island of Oahu.

The American residents of Hawaii came to dominate the economic life of the islands and also the political policies of the native ruler. A reciprocity treaty signed in 1875 permitted Hawaiian sugar to enter the United States duty-free, and bound Hawaii to make no territorial or economic concessions to other powers. In 1887 a new treaty renewed the existing arrangements and granted the United States exclusive use of Pearl Harbor as a naval station. The course of events was rendering outright political union almost inevitable.

Spurred by the favorable provisions of the treaties, sugar production in Hawaii boomed, and prosperity burgeoned for the American planters. Then the McKinley Tariff of 1890 dealt the planters a bad blow; by removing the duty on foreign raw sugar and giving domestic producers a bounty, it deprived Hawaii of its privileged position in the American sugar market. Annexation seemed the only alternative to economic strangulation. At the same time there ascended to the throne a new ruler, Queen Liliuokalani, who was determined to eliminate American influence in the government.

The American residents decided to act at once. They started a revolution (1893) and called on the United States for protection. At a critical moment the American minister, John L. Stevens, an ardent annexationist, ordered 160 marines from a warship in Honolulu harbor to go ashore to aid the rebels. The Queen yielded her authority, and a delegation representing the triumphant provisional government set out for Washington to negotiate a treaty of annexation. They found President Harrison highly receptive, but before the resulting treaty could be acted on by the Senate he was succeeded by Cleveland.

Cleveland had old-fashioned reservations about taking other people's property. Suspicious of what had happened in Hawaii, he withdrew the treaty and sent a special representative to the islands to investigate. When this agent reported that the American element and Stevens had engineered the revolution, Cleveland endeavored to restore the Queen to her throne. But the Americans were in control of the kingdom and refused to budge. Reluctantly the President had to accord recognition to their government as representing the "republic" of Hawaii. Cleveland, however, had only delayed the inevitable. In 1898, with the Republicans again in power, Hawaii was annexed by joint resolution of both houses of Congress.

The Samoan Islands

Three thousand miles to the south of Hawaii, the Samoan Islands dominated the sea lanes of the South Pacific and had long served as a way station for American ships in the Pacific trade. As American commerce with Asia increased, certain business groups regarded Samoa with new interest, and the navy eyed the harbor of Pago Pago on the island of Tutuila. In 1878 a native prince was brought to Washington, where he signed a treaty, which was approved by the Senate, providing for an American naval station at Pago Pago and binding the United States to employ its "good offices" to adjust any differences between a foreign power and Samoa. This was not a protectorate but it clearly indicated that this country meant to have a voice in anything happening in Samoa.

Controversy over Cuba

Not all the territory falling to the rising imperialist republic was obtained by annexation agreements with native rulers. A substantial area was wrenched from Spain by war in 1898.

The immediate background of the Spanish-American War lay in the Caribbean island of Cuba, which with nearby Puerto Rico comprised nearly all that was left of Spain's once extensive Latin American empire. The Cubans had long resented Spanish rule and several times

had tried unsuccessfully to throw it off. In 1895 they rose again in revolt.

This revolution immediately took on aspects of ferocity that shocked Americans. The Cubans, determined to win this revolution, deliberately devastated the island to force the Spaniards to leave. Just as determined to repress the insurrection, the Spanish resorted to extreme methods of coercion. General Valeriano Weyler — or "Butcher" Weyler, as he soon came to be known in the American press — in an effort to stamp out the Cuban guerrilla forces ordered the entire civilian population in certain areas confined to hastily prepared concentration camps, where, not surprisingly, they died by the thousands, victims of disease and malnutrition.

The American public was enraged at the actions of the Spanish. The reaction was caused by the way the situation in Cuba was reported in the American press, reported so as to give the impression that all the atrocities were being committed by the Spaniards.

The Cuban revolt came when Joseph Pulitzer with his New York *World* and William Randolph Hearst with his New York *Journal* were revolutionizing American journalism. This new "yellow press" specialized in lurid and sensational news; when such news did not exist, editors were not above creating it. To Hearst and Pulitzer, engaged in a ruthless circulation war, the struggle in Cuba was a journalist's dream. Both sent batteries of reporters and illustrators to Cuba with orders to provide accounts of Spanish atrocities. "You furnish the pictures," Hearst supposedly told a too scrupulous artist, "and I'll furnish the war."

The mounting storm of indignation against Spain left President Cleveland unmoved. Convinced that both sides in Cuba were guilty of atrocities and that the United States had no interests justifying involvement in the struggle, he issued a proclamation of neutrality. When Congress, in a state of excitement, passed a resolution favoring recognition of Cuban belligerency, he ignored the action. His only concession to the demands for intervention was to offer America's good offices to mediate the conflict, a proposition Spain declined.

When McKinley took over the Presidency in 1897, he renewed the American mediation offer, which was again refused. Taking a stronger line than his predecessor, he protested to Spain against her "uncivilized and inhuman" conduct.

The Spanish government, alarmed that McKinley's course might forebode American intervention in Cuba, recalled Weyler, modified the concentration policy, and took steps to grant the island a qualified autonomy. At the end of 1897, with the insurrection losing ground, it seemed that war might be averted.

If there was any chance of a peaceful settlement, it was extinguished by two dramatic incidents in February 1898.

A Cuban agent in Havana stole a private letter written by Dupuy de Lôme, the Spanish minister in Washington, and thoughtfully turned it over to the American press. First published in Hearst's New York *Journal,* the minister's letter described McKinley as a weak man and "a bidder for the admiration of the crowd." Popular anger was intense, and Dupuy de Lôme resigned before the outraged McKinley could demand his recall.

While the excitement was still at fever pitch, even more sensational news hit the front pages: the battleship *Maine* had been blown up in Havana harbor with a loss of over 260 lives. This vessel had been ordered to Cuban waters in January on a "friendly" visit, but the real reason for its presence was to protect American lives and property against possible attacks by Spanish loyalists. Many Americans jumped to the conclusion that the Spanish had sunk the ship—"an act of dirty treachery," Theodore Roosevelt announced—and the imperialists and the jingoists screamed for war. This opinion seemed confirmed when a naval court of inquiry reported that an external explosion by a submarine mine had caused the disaster. As war hysteria swept the country, Congress unanimously appropriated $50 million for military preparations. "Remember the *Maine*" became a national chant for revenge.

After the *Maine* episode there was little chance that the government could keep the people from war. In March 1898 McKinley asked Spain to agree to an armistice, with negotiations for a permanent peace to follow, and an immediate ending of the concentration system. After a slight delay, Spain essentially accepted the American demands on April 9. Two days later McKinley asked Congress for authority to use military force to end the hostilities in Cuba—in short, for a declaration of war. After reviewing the reasons that impelled him to recommend war ("in the name of humanity, in the name of civili-

zation, in behalf of endangered American interests") he mentioned only casually, at the end of the message, that Spain had capitulated to his requests.

It is doubtful whether any emphasis he might have given Spain's submission would have influenced Congress. That body, reflecting the people's will, was not going to be cheated out of a war by anything Spain might yield at the last minute. By huge majorities Congress passed a joint resolution declaring Cuba free and authorizing the President to employ force to expel the Spanish from the island. Added to the resolution, which was really a declaration of war, was the Teller Amendment, disclaiming any intention on the part of the United States to annex Cuba.

The "Splendid Little War"

The Spanish-American War was, in the words of Roosevelt's friend John Hay, "a splendid little war." Indeed, to all Americans, with the possible exception of the enlisted men who fought it, it was almost an ideal war. It was the last small, short, individualistic war before the huge, protracted, impersonal struggles of the twentieth century. Declared in April, it was over by August. Newspaper readers easily and eagerly followed the campaigns and the heroic exploits of American soldiers and sailors. Only 460 Americans were killed in battle or died of wounds, but some 5,200 perished of disease: malaria, dysentery, typhoid, and other ills.

Blithely and confidently the United States embarked on a war it was not prepared to fight. The regular army, numbering only 28,000 troops and officers scattered around the country at various posts, was a tough little force, skilled at quelling Indian outbreaks, but with no experience in anything resembling large-scale war. Hastily Congress directed the President to increase the army to 62,000 and to call for 125,000 volunteers. It was expected that the National Guard, the state militia, would furnish the bulk of the volunteers, and in addition the President was authorized to accept directly into the national service three volunteer cavalry regiments. The services of supply, manned by elderly bureaucratic officers, proved incapable of meeting the modest wants of the forces raised during the war.

The Spanish army numbered almost 130,000

troops, of whom 80,000 were already in Cuba at the beginning of the war. Despite its imposing size, it was not an efficient army; its commanders seemed to be paralyzed by a conviction of certain defeat. The American navy, fifth largest in the world, was far superior to the Spanish in ships, gunnery, and personnel.

No agency in the American military system was charged with strategic planning, and on the eve of the war only the navy had worked out an objective. The commander of the Asiatic Squadron, Commodore George Dewey, had received instructions that when war came, he was to attack the Spanish fleet in the Philippines. Immediately after war was declared, Dewey left the China coast and headed for Manila, where a venerable Spanish fleet was stationed. He destroyed the enemy with no damage to his ships. But the Spanish still held Manila City, and Dewey could not dislodge them. While he waited, the government assembled an expeditionary force to relieve him. The Americans, aided by native insurgents, were soon able to take Manila. The men who gave Dewey his orders may have meant only to strike a blow at Spanish power. But whatever the case, the purpose of the war had been changed. It had begun as a war to free Cuba. Now it was becoming a struggle for colonies.

But Cuba was not to be left out of the war picture. Late in April it was known in the United States that a Spanish fleet under Admiral Pascual Cervera had sailed for the west, presumably for a Cuban harbor. Dispatched as a gesture to national honor, Cervera's antique armada was no match for the powerful American Atlantic Squadron commanded by Admiral William T. Sampson. It was thought in America that Sampson would be able to intercept and destroy Cervera before he reached his destination. But Cervera eluded pursuit and slipped into Santiago harbor on the southern coast of Cuba, where he was not discovered by the Americans until ten days after his arrival. Immediately the Atlantic fleet moved to bottle him up.

While the navy was monopolizing the first phases of the war, the War Department was trying to mobilize and train an army. The volunteer and National Guard units were collected near Chattanooga, Tennessee, while the regulars were assembled at Tampa, Florida, under the command of General William R. Shafter. The entire mobilization process was conducted with remarkable inefficiency. There were appalling shortages of arms, ammunition, food, clothing, and medical supplies.

The army's commanding general, Nelson A. Miles, veteran of the Civil War, had planned to train the troops until autumn, then to occupy Puerto Rico and in conjunction with the Cuban rebels attack Havana. But with a Spanish naval force at Santiago, plans were hastily changed. It was decided to send Shafter with his force of 17,000 to take Santiago. The embarkation was accomplished amidst scenes of fantastic incompetence, but it was efficiency itself compared to the landing. Five days were required to put the army ashore, and this with the enemy offering no opposition.

Once landed, Shafter moved his army toward Santiago, planning to surround and capture it. On the way he fought and defeated the Spaniards at two battles, El Caney and San Juan Hill. Shafter was now before Santiago, but his army was so weakened by sickness that he feared he might have to abandon his position. When he besought Sampson to unite with him in a joint attack on the city, the admiral answered that mines in the harbor made it too dangerous to take his big ships in.

At this point disaster seemingly confronted the Americans, but unknown to them the Spanish government had decided that Santiago was lost. On July 3 Cervera, acting under orders from home, broke from the harbor to attempt an escape that he knew was hopeless. The waiting American squadron destroyed his entire fleet. Shafter then pressed the Spanish army commander to surrender, and that official, after bargaining Shafter into generous terms, including free transportation back to Spain for this troops, turned over Santiago on July 16. While the Santiago campaign was in its last stages, an American army landed in Puerto Rico and occupied it against virtually no opposition.

Spain was whipped and knew it. Through the medium of the French ambassador in Washington Spain asked for peace, and on August 12 an armistice ended the war.

Decision for Imperialism

In agreeing to a preliminary peace, the United States had laid down terms on which a permanent settlement must be based: Spain was to relinquish Cuba, cede Puerto Rico to the United States, cede also to the victor an island in the Ladrones, midway between Hawaii and the Philippines (this turned out to be Guam), and permit the Americans to hold Manila pending the final disposition of the Philippines. The American demands showed how quickly the war to free Cuba had assumed an imperialist character. Aroused by the excitement of military victory and a heady sense of mastery, the American government and people were disposed to keep what American arms had won.

In October 1898 commissioners from the United States and Spain met at Paris, France, to determine a permanent peace. With little protest Spain agreed to recognize Cuba's independence, to assume the Cuban debt, and to cede Puerto Rico and Guam to the victor. Then the American commissioners, acting under instruction from McKinley, startled the conference by demanding the cession of all the Philippines. Stubbornly the Spanish resisted the American demand, although they realized they could retain the islands only by resuming the war. They yielded to the inevitable when the United States offered a money payment of $20 million. The Treaty of Paris was signed on December 10, 1898, and sent to the United States for ratification by the Senate.

When the treaty was submitted to the Senate, it encountered immediate and fierce criticism and occasioned in that body and throughout the country one of those "great debates" that frequently precede a departure in American foreign policy. The chief point at issue was the acquisition of the Philippines, denounced by many, including prominent Republicans, as a repudiation of America's high moral position in the war and a shameful occupation of a land that wanted to be free. Favoring ratification were the imperialists, the big navy lobby, the Protestant clergy, who saw in a colonial empire enlarged fields for missionary enterprise, and most Republicans. Business, which had opposed the war, swung over to support the treaty, converted by the notion that possession of the Philippines would enable American interests to dominate the Oriental trade. In the forces opposing the treaty were old-fashioned Americans who objected to their country's annexing other people against their will, traditionalists who feared that a colonial empire would necessitate large armaments and foreign alliances, a majority of the

intellectuals, economic interests like the sugar growers who foresaw colonial competition, and most Democrats.

After weeks of bitter wrangling, the treaty was ratified February 6, 1899, but only because it received an unexpected assist from William Jennings Bryan, who expected to be his party's candidate in the election of 1900. He persuaded a number of Democratic Senators to vote for ratification. It has been charged that he was looking for a campaign issue, and in his defense it has been said that he thought the question of the Philippines should be decided by a national referendum: if the Democrats won in 1900 they would free the islands. Whatever his reasoning, it was faulty. The Philippines, once grasped, would not be easily loosed, no matter who carried the election.

Bryan was the Democratic standard-bearer in 1900, running against McKinley again, the principal issue was imperialism, and Bryan went down to a crushing defeat. The Republicans claimed, with some justification, that the result constituted a mandate for imperialism.

The Colonial Empire

The new colonial empire was extensive enough to warm the heart of the most ardent imperialist. Stretching from the Caribbean to the far reaches of the Pacific, it embraced Puerto Rico, Alaska, Hawaii, a part of Samoa, Guam, the Philippines, and a chain of minor Pacific islands.

Immediately, the nation faced the problem of how to govern its dependencies. Did Congress have to administer the colonies in accordance with the Constitution? In a phrase that pleased the public fancy, did the Constitution follow the flag? The Supreme Court pointed to a solution in the Insular Cases (*De Lima* v. *Bidwell, Downes* v. *Bidwell,* and others, 1900–1904), involving duties on colonial trade. In a series of decisions the Court distinguished between "incorporated" and "unincorporated" territories. In legislating for the latter—the insular possessions—Congress was not bound by all the limitations in the Constitution applicable to incorporated territories, although some restrictions did apply. What the Court was saying was that the Constitution followed the flag only if Congress so decided and that the government could administer its colonies in almost any way it saw fit.

Three of the dependencies, Hawaii, Alaska, and Puerto Rico, were given territorial status as quickly as Congress considered them ready for it. For Hawaii, with its large American population and close economic ties with the United States, a basis for government was provided by an act of 1900. This measure granted American citizenship to all persons who were citizens of the Hawaiian republic, authorized an elective two-house legislature, and vested executive authority in a governor appointed from Washington. By the terms of an act of 1884 Alaska was governed by appointed civil officials. The discovery of gold in 1896 caused the first substantial influx of Americans, and in 1912 Alaska received territorial status and a legislature, and its inhabitants were given the rights of citizenship. Because Puerto Rico's population readily accepted American rule, military occupation of the island was ended in 1900, and civil government was established by the Foraker Act. The governor and upper house of the legislature were to be appointed from Washington, while only the lower house was to be elected. The act did not declare the Puerto Ricans to be American citizens, this privilege being deferred until 1917. Lesser possessions in the empire were dealt with more arbitrarily. Such places as Guam and Tutuila were placed under control of naval officials, and many of the small islands, containing only a handful of inhabitants, experienced no form of American government at all.

American military forces remained in Cuba until 1902, the occupation being protracted to enable American administrators to prepare the island for the independence promised in the peace treaty of 1898. The vigorous occupiers built roads, schools, and hospitals, reorganized the legal, financial, and administrative systems, and introduced far-reaching sanitary reforms.

Then a convention assembled to draft a constitution for independent Cuba. To the disappointment of the American government, the document contained no provisions concerning relations with the nation responsible for Cuba's freedom. The United States was quite willing to relinquish Cuba, but, with its expanding interests in the Caribbean, it expected to exercise some kind of control over the island republic. The nature of this control was spelled out by Congress in 1901 in the Platt Amendment, a rider to an army appropriation bill, which Cuba was pressured into incorporating in her constitu-

tion. The Platt Amendment stated that Cuba should never impair her independence by treaty with a foreign power (this was equivalent to giving the United States a veto over Cuba's diplomatic policy), that the United States had the right to intervene in Cuba to preserve its independence and life and property, and that Cuba must sell or lease to the United States lands for naval stations. The amendment left Cuba only nominally independent. It was in fact, if not in name, an American appendage.

Alone among the possessions in the imperial system, the Philippines offered resistance to American rule. The Filipinos, rebellious against Spain before 1898, had hailed Dewey and the expeditionary force sent to Manila as their deliverers from tyranny, but they soon realized that American altruism for a free Cuba did not include them. When the hard fact sank in that the Americans had come to stay, the Filipinos resolved to expel the new invaders. In 1899 they resorted to war (by the American definition, rebellion) and, ably led by Emilio Aguinaldo, they fought the army of occupation from island to island until 1901. In the end the Americans repressed the uprising, but only after employing methods unpleasantly reminiscent of Weyler's tenure in Cuba, including the use of concentration camps. Civil government began taking over from the military in 1901, and the Filipinos, with great adaptability, began the process of adjusting to American culture. Thus they started on the long road that would lead, in 1946, to the independence that they so ardently desired.

The Open Door

The acquisition of the Philippines made the United States an Asian power, necessarily interested in anything that happened in the area and particularly in its largest nation, China. At the same time other nations were casting covetous eyes on China. By the turn of the century the great European imperialistic powers — England, France, Germany and Russia — and one Asian power, Japan, were beginning to partition China into "spheres of influence." One nation would force the Chinese government to grant it "concessions" to develop a particular area; another would use pressure to secure a long-term lease to a region. In some cases the outside powers even asserted ownership to territory. The process, if continued, threatened to destroy American trade with China. More ominous still, if one of the powers came to dominate China, American possession of the Philippines might be endangered.

The situation posed a delicate problem for the men directing American foreign policy. Knowing that public opinion would not support any use of force, they had to find a way to protect American interests in China without risking war. McKinley's Secretary of State, John Hay, attempted an audacious solution. In September 1899 he addressed identical notes to England, Germany and Russia, and later to France, Japan, and Italy, asking them to approve a formula that became known as the "Open Door." It embodied three principles: (1) each nation with a sphere of influence was to respect the rights and privileges of other nations in its sphere; (2) Chinese officials were to continue to collect tariff duties in all spheres (the existing tariff favored the United States); and (3) each nation with a sphere was not to discriminate against other nations in levying port dues and railroad rates.

The nations addressed replied that they accepted the idea of the Open Door but could make no commitment to support it. Apparently the United States had met a humiliating rebuff, but Hay boldly announced that since all the powers had accepted the principle of the Open Door, his government considered their assent to be "final and definitive." Although the American public applauded his diplomacy, Hay had won little more than a theoretical victory. The United States could not prevent any nation that wanted to violate the Open Door from doing so — unless it was willing to resort to war.

Almost immediately after the diplomatic maneuvering over the Open Door ended, a secret Chinese society known as the Boxers instigated an uprising against foreigners in China. The movement came to a blazing climax when the Boxers and their supporters besieged the entire foreign diplomatic corps in the British embassy in Peking. At this point the powers with interests in China decided to send an international expeditionary force to rescue the diplomats. The situation seemed to offer a perfect excuse to those nations with ambitions to dismember China.

The United States contributed 2,500 troops to the rescue force, which in August 1900 fought its way into Peking and broke the siege. McKinley and Hay had decided on American participation in order to secure a voice in the settlement of the uprising and to prevent the partition of China. Again Hay sent a note to the powers. This time he called for the Open Door not only in the spheres of influence but in "all parts of the Chinese Empire." He also called for the maintenance of China's "territorial and administrative integrity." He persuaded England and Germany to approve his views, and then with their support he induced the participating powers to accept a money indemnity as satisfaction. The sum allotted to the United States amounted to almost $25 million, which greatly exceeded damages, and later the American government reduced the obligation and even remitted an unpaid balance. China gratefully used part of the remission to educate Chinese students in the United States.

T. R. and World Politics

The United States moved into the twentieth century as a world power. The foremost industrial nation, it profited from a growing world trade, and American capital was beginning to flow into other countries to finance that trade. The United States was also an imperial power. Its colonies stretched from the Caribbean Sea of the Atlantic Ocean across the Pacific to the Philippine Islands on the fringes of Asia. This new American position brought with it new commitments. In addition to upholding the pledge of the Monroe Doctrine, the American government felt an urge to support the economic activities of its citizens abroad, and it believed it had to maintain control of its colonies, including the distant Philippines. Not all Americans understood that the recent commitments might necessitate a change in the time-honored policy of diplomatic isolation. One American who did understand the necessity was Theodore Roosevelt, who played an even more active role in foreign affairs than in domestic policy.

Roosevelt's concept of the role of the United States in world politics emphasized sea power. Now that the United States had colonies, it needed to build a navy powerful enough to keep the sea lanes open to them. It also needed to build an Isthmian canal so that naval units could sail quickly from one ocean to another. In addition it needed to protect the Caribbean approaches to the canal from encroachment. All this predicated a strong naval policy at a time when the key to strength in the world was a powerful fleet. This meant a navy second only to that of Great Britain.

At the same time Kaiser Wilhelm's Germany was launching upon a gigantic naval race with Great Britain. The German fleet laws of 1898 and 1900 committed Germany too to a navy second only to England's, and set forth plans for one that could even challenge England. As Britain in 1905 picked up the gauntlet by beginning construction on the first dreadnought, both Germany and the United States embarked upon an intensive naval race, amidst increasing alarms of war.

Under the strong urging of President Roosevelt, who was himself the most effective of naval lobbyists, Congress between 1902 and 1905 voted for ten battleships and four armored cruisers. These were far stronger than the relatively light vessels of the nineties; they were no longer being built primarily to defend the American coastline. By 1906 the American navy was second only to the British but in the next few years was surpassed by the German.

Roosevelt liked to quote an African proverb: "Speak softly and carry a big stick." This certainly characterized his action in the Far East, as well as in the Caribbean.

The Asian Balance

In the East, Roosevelt thought that it was vital to the Open Door policy to block Russian expansion in Manchuria. Therefore he encouraged Japan to oppose the Russian drive. When the Japanese made a surprise attack upon the Russian fleet at Port Arthur, Manchuria, in 1904, he was inclined to cheer, as were most Americans. He warned the French and Germans against aiding Russia, but he did not wish to see the Japanese totally victorious, since this might "possibly mean a struggle between them and us in the future."

The Japanese, however, even after winning a series of spectacular victories, faced such serious financial difficulties that they asked Roosevelt to mediate. He agreed and called a peace conference at Portsmouth, New Hampshire, in the summer of 1905. But Roosevelt lost Japan's good will by opposing her demand for an enormous indemnity, even though he approved her territorial gains at the conference — her control over Korea and South Manchuria and her annexation of the southern half of Sakhalin Island, which had belonged to Russia.

Japanese-American relations, thus suddenly made worse, were not much improved by a secret Japanese-American agreement effected at the time of the Portsmouth conference. President Roosevelt had dispatched Secretary of War Taft from Manila to Tokyo to reach a Far Eastern understanding with the Japanese. In the resulting Taft-Katsura executive agreement of July 1905 the Japanese acknowledged American sovereignty in the Philippines, and the United States recognized the suzerainty of Japan over Korea.

Shortly another issue fanned anger between the United States and Japan. In 1906 the San Francisco school board ordered the segregation of Oriental school children. This step was taken in response to the feelings of Californians against the 500 to 1,000 Japanese immigrants coming in each year, feelings which were intensified by lurid "Yellow Peril" articles in the Hearst and other newspapers. Resentment in Japan flared high, and jingoes in each country fanned the flames still higher.

Roosevelt worked skillfully to douse the flames. He persuaded San Francisco to desegregate its schools, and in return in 1907 he negotiated a "gentlemen's agreement" with Japan to keep out agricultural laborers. Then, lest the Japanese government think he had acted through fear, he launched a spectacular naval demonstration. He sent sixteen battleships of the new navy, "the Great White Fleet," on an unprecedented 45,000-mile voyage around the world. It gave the navy invaluable experience in sailing in formation while demonstrating the danger of dependence on foreign-owned coaling stations. Most important, the Japanese invited this formidable armada to visit Yokohama and gave it a clamorous welcome. Thus Roosevelt felt that through brandishing the big stick he had helped the cause of peace.

For the moment, the United States had demonstrated sufficient naval strength to restore an unsteady balance in Asian waters. In 1908, before the fleet had returned home, Japan and the United States negotiated the comprehensive Root-Takahira Agreement. Both countries agreed to support the Open Door in China. The

United States tacitly seemed to give Japan a free hand in Manchuria (where rivalry with Russia continued) in return for an explicit guarantee of the status quo in the Pacific.

The Panama Canal

Roosevelt's preoccupation with the American strategy of defense in the Caribbean — especially his almost obsessive fear of German penetration — betrayed him into becoming an iron-fisted neighbor toward small countries to the South. He first used his might impetuously to start work on a canal in Panama.

Even before Roosevelt became President, the McKinley administration was negotiating with England to remove an old obstacle, an 1850 treaty agreeing that the two countries would jointly construct a canal. In 1901 the British, eager to court American friendship, consented in the Hay-Pauncefote treaty to exclusive American construction — and fortification — of a canal.

The next question was where to build the canal. There were two possible routes. The shortest one would be across the Isthmus of Panama, but the rights there were owned by a French company, the successor of an earlier company which had tried and failed to dig a canal. The French company wanted $109,000,-000 for its franchise, which would make a Panama canal more expensive than a Nicaraguan one. Consequently a commission, Congress, and President Roosevelt all favored the Nicaraguan route. But the French company had expert agents in Philippe Bunau-Varilla, its chief engineer, and William Nelson Cromwell, an attorney who had contributed heavily to the Republican campaign fund in 1900. Hastily they cut the price of their rights to $40,000,000; unless sold to the United States and sold quickly, the rights would be worthless, for they would expire in 1904. This price cut — and able lobbying — caused Congress and the President to change their minds.

Impatient to begin digging the canal, Roosevelt put pressure upon Colombia, which owned Panama, to conclude a treaty authorizing the United States to dig a canal. In 1903 Secretary of State Hay signed one with the Colombian chargé d'affaires Tomás Herrán, which was most unfavorable to Colombia. It authorized the United States to construct a canal in return for a payment of only $10,000,000 and an annual rental of $250,000. The Colombian Senate rejected the treaty.

Roosevelt was furious. Fuming that the Colombians were "inefficient bandits," he considered seizing Panama through twisting a technicality in an 1846 treaty with Colombia (then New Granada) guaranteeing the neutrality and free transit of the Isthmus. Roosevelt's intended seizure became unnecessary, because Bunau-Varilla helped organize a Panamanian revolution. There had been many such revolutions, all failures. But at the outset of this one, the United States landed troops from the U.S.S. *Nashville,* and, invoking the 1846 treaty obligation to maintain order, prevented Colombian troops from putting down the revolution. Three days later the United States recognized the new republic of Panama and, soon after that, negotiated a treaty paying Panama the sum Colombia had rejected, in return for the grant of a zone ten miles wide. The minister from Panama who arranged the treaty was Bunau-Varilla.

Work on the canal proceeded smoothly and efficiently. The elimination of tropical diseases in the area, the digging of the tremendous cuts, and the installation of huge locks at a total cost of $375,000,000 filled Americans with patriotic enthusiasm. The achievements demonstrated that the United States, like other imperial nations, could undertake enormous projects in the tropics. The canal opened in 1914.

The "Roosevelt Corollary"

Meanwhile, in 1902 and 1903, Roosevelt had to deal with an apparent German grab at Venezuela. That country had not honored its debt to a group of German, English, and Italian bankers, and Germany responded by blockading and bombarding Venezuela's principal port. Roosevelt, fearing that the German intervention might lead to establishment of a naval base, took a firm line. He later said he had warned the German ambassador that the United States would use force if Germany tried to acquire territory anywhere in the area.

The Germans, wishing to avoid an incident, quickly agreed to arbitration. The episode seemed, nevertheless, to confirm American fears that the Germans were scheming to get a foothold in the Caribbean. There was, in particular, a persistent fear that the Germans might try to acquire the Danish West Indies. In 1902 the Senate ratified a treaty for their purchase, but the Danish parliament rejected it. Finally in 1917 the United States acquired the poverty-stricken islets, which were then renamed the Virgin Islands, for an exorbitant $25,000,000. Their value was purely defensive: the United States wanted to make sure they were not in the possession of any potentially hostile power.

The Venezuela incident led to a new Caribbean policy usually called the "Roosevelt corollary" to the Monroe Doctrine. Roosevelt declared that if the Latin American nations could not meet their obligations to outside creditors, the United States reluctantly would police them and collect debt payments from them in order to forestall European intervention. In effect, Uncle Sam would act as a bill collector for European bankers. Roosevelt declared to the Congress in 1904 that the United States might be forced "however reluctantly, in flagrant cases of . . . wrongdoing or impotence, to the exercise of an international police power."

The occasion for putting the "Roosevelt corollary" into operation was the defaulting of Santo Domingo on about $22,000,000 of its debt to European nations. France and Italy threatened to intervene. In effect, the United States established a receivership, taking over Dominican customs, paying 45 percent of the receipts to the Dominican government, and paying the rest to foreign creditors.

As a part of an American strategy of defense, Roosevelt's Caribbean policy was doubtless successful. As a means of securing the support and cooperation of nations to the south, it left much to be desired. Roosevelt's tactics inspired fear rather than friendship.

Taft and Dollar Diplomacy

President Taft was neither so vigorous nor so able as Roosevelt in exercising leadership in foreign affairs. He and his Secretary of State, Philander C. Knox, made no real effort to maintain a balance of power in Europe or Asia. Rather, they promoted expansion of American business and banking activities to enhance American political power overseas. This policy became known as "dollar diplomacy."

The makers of American policy argued that in the Far East dollar diplomacy was the financial expression of the Open Door, that it would make "a guaranty for the preservation, rather than the destruction of China's integrity." Taft, therefore, was ready to ignore Roosevelt's tacit arrangement with Japan that the United States would stay out of Manchuria, and to support the right of Americans to invest both there and in China. When British, French, and German bankers formed a consortium to finance railroads in China, Secretary Knox insisted that Americans should also participate. In 1911 they were admitted. Then Knox proposed that an international syndicate purchase the South Manchurian Railroad in order to neutralize it. This led the rivals Russia and Japan to sign a treaty of amity in 1910, thus closing the Manchurian door in Taft's face.

In the Caribbean, dollar diplomacy resulted in a series of interventions going far beyond Roosevelt's limited ones, to establish firm military and political control over several unstable republics to the south. Advocates of this program argued that American investors must be invited in to replace European investors, who otherwise might in time bring about European intervention. A perhaps inevitable step had been taken beyond the Roosevelt corollary.

With the active support of the government, American bankers acquired holdings in Honduras, Haiti, and other countries. The government even sent marines to Nicaragua to protect revolutionaries, sponsored by an American mining company, who were fighting to overthrow a hostile dictator. Knox negotiated a treaty with the new friendly government giving the United States financial control, but the United States Senate failed to approve it. However, American bankers accepted Knox's invitation to move in. By 1912 the new pro-American government was so unpopular that revolution broke out. Taft sent marines to crush the uprising, and some of them remained as late as 1925.

Wilsonian Intervention

President Wilson brought to the determination of foreign policy a flair for idealistic pronouncements. He was never unsure of his moral position but was often uncertain how to reach it. He disapproved of the crasser aspects of dollar diplomacy, but at the same time felt an urge to use American force to uplift the nations to the south. He also convinced himself that an American-sponsored stability in the Caribbean was vital to national defense.

The Wilson administration not only regularized through treaty the continuing occupation of Nicaragua, but also initiated new interventions in Santo Domingo and Haiti. In spite of American customs control, revolution after revolution had swept through and impoverished Santo Domingo. The United States took over all Dominican finances and the police force, but the Dominicans would not agree to a treaty establishing a virtual protectorate. In 1916 Wilson established a military government. During the eight years that it continued, the United States forcibly maintained order, trained a native constabulary, and promoted education, sanitation, and public works.

On the other end of the island of Hispaniola, the Negro republic of Haiti was even more revolution-wracked. Wilson again sent in the marines, established another military government, and began the task of improving living conditions in Haiti. The marines demonstrated their efficiency in 1918 when they supervised an election to ratify a new American-sponsored constitution.

Making Mexico Behave

American business interests had invested about a billion dollars in Mexico during the regime of a friendly dictator, Porfirio Díaz. They owned over half the oil, two-thirds of the railroads, and three-fourths of the mines and smelters. Popular though Díaz was in the United States, he came to be hated in Mexico because, while he encouraged foreigners to amass huge profits, he suppressed civil liberties and kept the masses in peonage. In 1910 the aged Díaz was overthrown by a democratic reform leader, who in turn was murdered and succeeded by the reactionary Victoriano Huerta just before Wilson took office. Wilson turned a deaf ear to American investors who saw in Huerta's presidency an opportunity to return to the "good old days." Rather, he refused to recognize "the government of butchers."

Wilson hoped that, by refusing recognition to Huerta's government, he could bring about its collapse and the development of constitutionalism in Mexico. He offered to mediate between Huerta and the opposing Constitutionalists of Venustiano Carranza, but both sides refused.

Wilson was in a dilemma: he might have to choose between recognizing Huerta, stronger than ever, or intervening with armed force, which could mean war against all the Mexican factions. An unforseen incident gave Wilson a way out. The commander of one of the American naval vessels hovering off the coast of Mexico gave some of his men permission to go ashore at Tampico. One of Huerta's officers promptly arrested them; a superior officer quickly released them and apologized. But the American admiral demanded in addition a twenty-one gun salute to the United States flag. At this Huerta balked. Wilson, deciding to back the admiral, sent all available warships to Mexican waters and asked Congress for authority to take drastic action. But before Congress could act, Wilson ordered the navy to seize Vera Cruz. It did so, but not in the bloodless way that Wilson had anticipated. Both sides sustained substantial casualties.

At this difficult point, Argentina, Brazil, and Chile offered to mediate. With relief, Wilson accepted, and sent his delegates to confer with Huerta's at Niagara Falls, Canada. As the negotiations went on and on, the Carranzists advanced on Mexico City, finally bringing the result Wilson wished, the abdication of Huerta.

Under Carranza's presidency, the Mexican muddle did not clear up but got worse. By 1914 civil war was again devastating Mexico, as a former general of Carranza's, Francisco ("Pancho") Villa, tried to overthrow him. In 1915 the United States gave de facto recognition to Carranza's government.

This antagonized Villa, who was still roaming northern Mexico. He tried to bring about a war between the United States and Mexico by shooting sixteen Americans he seized from a train. When that failed he raided Columbus, New Mexico, just across the border, killing nineteen more Americans. Wilson retaliated by ordering a punitive expedition under Brigadier General John J. Pershing to hunt down Villa. Wilson tried not to offend Carranza, but as Villa drew the American forces 300 miles into Mexico, two skirmishes occurred with Mexican troops which almost led to a war. In 1916 Carranza suggested the appointment of a Joint High

Pershing 1916–1917
1. Dolphin Incident 1914
2. U.S. Seizure 1914
3. 16 Americans Murdered 1916
4. Villa's Raid 1916
5. Troops Clash 1916

0   200 400 600 800 mi.

The U.S. in Mexico   1914–1917

Commission to consider the problem. After long debate the commission broke up without establishing a basis for the withdrawal of American troops. By then the United States was so close to war with Germany that it nevertheless withdrew the troops and in 1917 gave de jure recognition to Carranza's government.

War in Europe

At the outset of his administration, Wilson was preoccupied with domestic reform. "It would be the irony of fate," he had remarked shortly before his inauguration, "if my administration had to deal chiefly with foreign affairs."

Wilson and other American leaders ignored the tense situation that had developed in Europe. There most of the nations, big and small, had become aligned in two potentially hostile diplomatic blocs. On one side was the Entente, led by England, France, and Russia; on the other was the Central Alliance, represented by Germany and Austria-Hungary. Economic and power rivalries between the two blocs exploded into war in the summer of 1914 following the assassination of an Austrian Archduke by a young man of Serbian antecedents. The conflict eventually involved so many nations that it became known as the World War.

Bewildered Americans congratulated themselves that at least the explosion could not extend to their shores; the New World was still secure. A minority of Americans, mainly those of German descent, sympathized with the Central Powers. But the great majority, bound by cultural or sentimental ties to England and France, sympathized with the Entente nations, now known as the Allies. They were pro-Allies without being at all sure what the war was about. None of them in August 1914 envisaged American entrance into the war.

Neutral Trade and Neutral Rights

At the outbreak of the war Wilson issued a proclamation of neutrality in which he asked the American people to be impartial even in their thinking. But it soon became evident that there were problems involved in being a neutral. As a maritime nation, the United States was in a position to take over the carrying trade of the nations at war. These nations, however, were not disposed to permit neutral trade with the enemy. Great Britain particularly, the greatest naval power in the world, was determined to wage economic warfare against Germany. She established a naval blockade of Germany and stopped and searched American ships for "contraband" goods that might aid the enemy. Wilson protested these acts but not too vigorously because of American sympathy for England and her allies.

On the whole, the British blockade proved to be no economic handicap for the United States, since by early 1915 heavy war orders were arriving from Britain and France. While trade with the Central Powers almost came to an end, that with the Allies jumped between 1914 and 1916 from $824,000,000 to $3,214,000,000—a staggering figure for that time. In March 1915 the government relaxed its regulations so as to allow the Allies to float huge loans in the United States for financing their purchases. In effect the United States, embarking upon the greatest boom in its history, was becoming the great banker and arsenal for the allies.

This the Germans could not permit. During the first weeks of the war they imposed no blockades but concentrated upon trying to win a decision in France. The German armies drove deep but were halted short of Paris in the Battle of the Marne in September 1914. Although on the Russian front great armies continued to move back and forth for several years, in the west the war turned into grinding attrition of trench combat along lines extending from the North Sea to Switzerland. As a relative stalemate developed along the Western Front, Germany turned toward the relatively new weapon of the submarine as a possible means of breaking the British blockade. Submarines had the advantage of surprise but were so vulnerable to attack by an armed ship that they could scarcely follow the accepted rules of international law. These rules called for visit and search of enemy merchantmen and allowed sinking only if provision were made for the safety of passengers and crew. The sinking of merchant vessels without warning seemed to Americans to add a new and frightful dimension to warfare.

Beginning in 1915, this was what Germany set out to do. She announced that she would sink enemy vessels in a broad zone around the British Isles. This policy, the Germans explained, was in retaliation for the British food blockade, which they claimed would starve women and children in Germany. President Wilson declared on February 10 that he would hold Germany to "strict accountability" for unlawful acts.

A serious crisis developed when a submarine fired a torpedo without warning into the Cunard liner *Lusitania*. The ship went down in eighteen minutes, drowning 1,198 people, among them 128 Americans.

Shortly before, the Germans had launched against the Allied lines at Ypres a new weapon of frightfulness, poison gas. On May 13 American newspapers carried lengthy excerpts from an official British report on almost unprintable alleged German atrocities in Belgium. This report contained fabrications, yet few Americans questioned its authenticity, for by this time most people were ready to believe almost anything against Germany. Even in their revulsion, however, they were not ready to fight.

Wilson came close to the point of coercion over the *Lusitania* incident, in an exchange of notes with Germany. In his first note he virtually demanded that Germany end its submarine blockade. When the Germans sent an argumentative reply, he drafted a still stronger second note. Apparently Wilson was ready to risk war rather than surrender to Germany what he considered to be American maritime rights, even

though he had said: "There is such a thing as a man being too proud to fight."

New trouble developed in the early months of 1916 when the Allies began arming merchantmen and ordering them to attack submarines. Germany gave notice that it would sink them without warning. Wilson reiterated his doctrine of "strict accountability," and when the channel steamer *Sussex* was torpedoed, he threatened to break off diplomatic relations if Germany did not abandon its unrestricted submarine campaign. He made the threat at a time when Germany still lacked sufficient submarines to maintain a tight blockade and did not wish to bring the United States into the war. Consequently the German Foreign Office pledged that submarine commanders would observe rules of visit and search. The President had won a diplomatic victory, and relations with Germany became less tense during the eight months that followed.

The Preparedness Program

With the outbreak of war, the leaders of the military establishment and civilian advocates of a larger military machine began to advocate a preparedness program. Leading the agitation were "big navy" men who declared that despite its expansion in the T. R. era the navy was not strong enough to take on a first-rate foe.

The army was much less ready than the navy to fight a major war. The establishment of the General Staff and other administrative reforms had come into effect in the Roosevelt administration, but the older officers were still antagonistic toward such changes. The quartermaster corps in 1913 was thinking about using trucks, but as yet not seriously testing them. The air force, consisting of seventeen planes, was part of the signal corps; its 1913 appropriation was $125,000. The army numbered less than 80,000 men, a large part of whom were required to maintain the posts within the United States. The National Guard was somewhat larger, but was scarcely professional.

President Wilson opposed new armaments, and so did public opinion, until the crisis over submarine sinkings frightened the nation into preparedness. In November 1915 the President proposed a long-range program which by 1925 would give the United States a navy second to none and would reorganize the army and provide a reserve force of 400,000 men. This proposal touched off a hot debate in Congress and throughout the country. Progressives in the House fought the program vigorously. Throughout the country, the pleas of peace organizations strongly appealed to farmers and workingmen. Wilson took the issue to the country in a series of speeches, but the House would not budge.

Wilson ultimately got part of what he wanted. Congress passed legislation providing for substantial increases in the army, the navy, and merchant shipping. The Merchant Marine Act of 1916 established the United States Shipping Board, which was empowered to own and operate vessels and regulate shipping.

Conservatives wished to finance the defense expenditures through bonds, but the administration proposed new, heavier taxes. Progressives denounced the tax proposals as falling too heavily upon the masses, and in Congress fought through a tax measure frankly aimed at making the wealthy, whom they blamed for preparedness demands, pay the bill. The Revenue Act of 1916 levied heavy income and inheritance taxes upon the rich for the first time in American history.

In 1916 Democrats and Republicans fought the presidential campaign over the issue of foreign policy before a seriously divided people.

The Democrats renominated Wilson and adopted as their slogan "He kept us out of war." They went into the campaign in a strong position. Many of the ex-Bull Moosers, Republican farmers in the Midwest, and workers who had once voted for a full dinner pail now favored the Democrats. They did so because of Wilson's progressive domestic policy but still more because of their hope that the President could continue to keep the country out of the war.

As for the Republicans, they persuaded Charles Evans Hughes, who had an impeccable progressive record, to resign from the Supreme Court and accept the nomination. Primarily because of the whooping of Roosevelt and others on the sidelines, the Republicans gradually began to look like the war party, and Hughes was made to seem like a war candidate.

The people's wish to keep out of war was disclosed in the election returns. Wilson received 3 million more popular votes than he had in 1912, although his electoral majority was narrow. The Democrats also retained a thin majority in Congress.

Leading the People to War

So far as elections can be regarded as national plebiscites, Wilson had received a narrow mandate to continue along the path of progressivism and peace. Undoubtedly he intended to follow such a course.

Even before the war began, he had tried to bring an end to the armaments race. Since the outbreak of the war he had repeatedly sought means to bring the warring nations into a peace conference. But both sides had invested too heavily in the conflict, and were still too hopeful of realizing gain upon their investment, to talk of a negotiated peace.

Immediately after the election, Wilson renewed negotiations looking toward a settlement. The Germans, successful on the eastern front, for a while appeared to be receptive. But the top German generals did not want any conference because they believed they could win a decisive victory. Early in 1917 Wilson spread his plan before the Senate, calling for a lasting peace that the American people would help maintain through a league of nations. It would be a peace with freedom of the seas, disarmament, national self-determination for subject peoples, and equality among nations. "Peace among equals" — a lasting peace — could come only through "peace without victory."

But the military leaders of Germany had decided upon one final cast of the iron dice. They had resolved to return to unrestricted submarine warfare even though it would bring the United States into the war. They hoped that they could crush France on land and starve Britain from the sea before America could make its weight felt. Consequently Germany announced that, beginning the following day, submarines would sink all ships, enemy or neutral, in a broad zone around the British Isles.

President Wilson now faced a dilemma of his own making. Earlier he had issued what amounted to an ultimatum to Germany — the demand that American citizens and vessels had the right to travel on the high seas in time of war — and he had threatened Germany with war if she should disregard the demand. He now had to take the step made inevitable by his policy. He broke off diplomatic relations with Germany, knowing this was probably a prelude to hostilities.

Events now carried Wilson and the country

THE CAUSES OF AMERICAN ENTRANCE INTO WORLD WAR I

Where Historians Disagree

In the 1920s, as soon as historians began to write about American entrance into World War I, they divided into two schools of interpretation. One stressed (as this chapter does) the complex problems that the policy decisions of the belligerents created for the Wilson administration, which was trying to defend the neutral rights of the United States. This group of historians also considered the larger elements of world politics.

Paying scarcely any attention to the actions of other nations, the other school focused upon economic factors within the United States. These factors, they asserted, were critical in bringing about an unnecessary and unwise American involvement in the struggle. This economic determinist view was widely popularized in the 1930s and became an important historical factor in molding the neutrality legislation intended to keep the nation out of World War II, which was clearly imminent. Walter Millis, a journalist, expressed this view in a best seller, *Road to War, 1914–1917* (1935). Millis emphasized the effectiveness of British propaganda and the emotional ties of Wilson and much of the public with Britain and France as well as the machinations of bankers and munitions makers as factors leading to the misguided decision to intervene. The most vehement scholarly argument along these lines was that of Charles C. Tansill in *America Goes to War* (1938). In more recent years, sophisticated historians critical of Wilson have put less emphasis on economic factors: instead they stress the President's misplaced concern for moral and legal questions rather than for the basic national interest. This was the view of George F. Kennan, a diplomat-turned-historian, and of the political scientist Hans J. Morgenthau, author of *In Defense of the National Interest* (1951). But another political scientist, Edward H. Buehrig, disagreed. In *Woodrow Wilson and the Balance of Power* (1955) he contended that Wilson and his advisers were concerned with the problem of restoring the world balance of power and thus maintaining American security.

Wilson also has had persuasive defenders among historians. Wilson's foremost biographer, Arthur Link, in *Wilson the Diplomatist* (1957) and in numerous other writings since World War II, stressed that Wilson was realistic as well as idealistic and that by 1917, when Germany began her unrestricted submarine warfare, Wilson had few or no alternatives to war. Ernest E. May, in *The World War and American Isolation* (1959) agreed. May believed that "in nearly every case requiring a decision by the President [from 1914 to 1917], there were present considerations of law, morality, power, national prestige, and domestic politics, all of which had to be taken into account." The ultimate responsibility for war, May implied, was the German government's, not Wilson.

rapidly toward war. The British turned over to the American government an intercepted note from the German Foreign Secretary, Arthur Zimmerman, proposing that in the event of war, Mexico should attack the United States and receive in return her lost provinces north of the border. Americans were infuriated. At about the same time, the Russian revolution eliminated one of the moral problems in Wilson's mind by replacing a despotism among the Allies with a constitutional monarchy. (This government lasted only until November 1917 when Lenin and the Communists came into power.) It seemed increasingly clear to Wilson—despite the horrors and losses of war, and the way in which it would bring brutality even at home and damage progressive reforms—that American participation would be worthwhile. He had faith that, at the conference table, the United States could bring about a just and lasting peace.

In 1917 news came that submarines had torpedoed three American ships. Thereupon the cabinet unanimously advised the President to ask Congress for a declaration of war.

On the evening of April 2, 1917, President Wilson delivered his war message to Congress. After enumerating the German transgressions of American neutral rights, he declared: "It is a fearful thing to lead this great peaceful people into war, into the most terrible . . . of all wars. . . . But the right is more precious than peace, and we shall fight for the things which we have always carried nearest our hearts — for democracy, . . . for the rights and liberties of small nations, for a universal dominion of right by such a concert of free peoples as shall bring peace and safety to all nations and make the world itself at last free."

Four days later, Congress passed the war declaration and the President signed it. The American people had yet to learn what this would entail, and to realize the broad aims for which they were struggling. No people had ever embarked upon a crusade more reluctantly.

SELECTED READINGS

Politics in the years following the Civil War is treated in a variety of works. Two convenient surveys are Matthew Josephson, *The Politicos, 1865-1898** (1938), and E. F. Goldman, *Rendezvous with Destiny** (1951), emphasizing reform movements. The movement for civil service receives attention in Ari Hogenboom, *Outlawing the Spoils* (1961). On the money issue see Irwin Unger, *The Greenback Era* (1964), and W. T. K. Nugent, *Money and American Society* (1968). Good biographies are W. B. Hesseltine, *Ulysses S. Grant, Politician* (1935); Allan Nevins, *Hamilton Fish* (1936), strong on foreign policy; and Harry Barnard, *Rutherford B. Hayes and His America* (1954). Standard on the election of 1876 and its aftermath is C. V. Woodward, *Reunion and Reaction** (1951).

Politics in the age of protest is analyzed in H. U. Faulkner, *Politics, Reform and Expansion** (1959); J. R. Hollingsworth, *The Democracy of Cleveland and Bryan* (1963); and Richard Hofstadter, *The Age of Reform** (1955). Also useful are several biographies. Allan Nevins, *Grover Cleveland* (1932), is massive; shorter on Cleveland but informative is H. S. Merrill, *Bourbon Leader* (1957). See also P. W. Glad, *The Trumpet Soundeth* (1960), on Bryan; and H. W. Morgan, *William McKinley and His America* (1963). Standard on the farm uprising is J. D. Hicks, *The Populist Revolt** (1931).

For the Progressive period convenient surveys are G. E. Mowry, *The Era of Theodore Roosevelt, 1900-1912** (1958); S. F. Hays, *The Response to Industrialism 1885-1914** (1957); Russell Nye, *Midwestern Progressive Politics* (1959); R. H. Wiebe, *The Search for Order, 1877-1920* (1967); and O. L. Graham, Jr., *The Great Campaigns: Reform and War in America, 1900-1928** (1971). A critical view of progressivism is registered in Gabriel Kolko, *The Triumph of Conservatism* (1963). On the ambitions of the Negro in this and earlier years see August Meier, *Negro Thought in America, 1880-1915* (1968).

The nature of progressivism is revealed also in biographies. Good on Roosevelt are W. R. Harbaugh, *Power and Responsibility** (1961), and J. M. Blum, *The Republican Roosevelt** (1954). See also Belle and Fola La Follette, *Robert M. Lafollette* (2 vols. 1953). For Taft see Henry Pringle, *William Howard Taft* (2 vols., 1939). On Wilson's first years in the presidency, go to A. S. Link, *The Road to the White House** (1947), and *Woodrow Wilson and the Progressive Era, 1900-1917** (1954); and J. M. Blum, *Woodrow Wilson and the Politics of Morality** (1956).

The industrial revolution in America has received detailed attention from historians. A survey is found in W. E. Brownlee, *Dynamics of Ascent: A History of the American Economy* (1974). A critical account of big business is Matthew Josephson, *The Robber Barons** (1934). Aspects of business thought are treated in I. V. Wyllie, *The Self-Made Man in America** (1954), and Richard Hofstadter, *Social Darwinism in American Thought** (1944). On labor see Norman Ware, *The Labor Movement in the United States, 1860–1895** (1929).

A number of good works deal with American society and thought, but only representative items can be listed. Recommended are M. G. White, *Social Thought in America** (1949); H. W. Morgan, ed., *The Gilded Age** (1963); Justin Kaplan, *Mr. Clemens and Mark Twain* (1966); J. D. Hart, *The Popular Book** (1950); L. A. Cremin, *The Transformation of the School** (1961); H. F. May, *The Protestant Churches and Industrial America* (1949); J. T. Ellis, *American Catholicism** (1956); Neil Harris, *The Artist in American Society* (1966); F. L. Mott, *American Journalism* (1950); Andrew Tully, *The Era of Elegance** (1947); F. R. Dulles, *America Learns to Play* (1950); J. B. Rae, *The American Automobile* (1965); H. F. May, *The End of American Innocence* (1959); R. E. Spiller, *et al.*, *American Perspectives* (1961); H. U. Faulkner, *The Quest for Social Justice* (1931); Morton White, *The Age of Analysis** (1955); Alfred Kazin, *On Native Grounds** (1942); and Barbara Rose, *American Art Since 1900** (1967).

There are several textbook treatments of the West. Good but not necessarily the best is R. A. Billington, *Westward Expansion* (1960). A classic regional study is W. P. Webb, *The Great Plains* (1931). On the public domain see R. M. Bobbins, *Our Landed Heritage** (1942), and H. N. Smith, *Virgin Land** (1957).

The rise of the cities is depicted in Blake McKelvey, *The Urbanization of America* (1963). Also useful on urban reform is H. H. Quint, *The Forging of American Socialism** (1953). Several good books deal with immigration. Among them are Oscar Handlin, *The Uprooted** (1951), and John Higham, *Strangers in the Land** (1955).

On the women's movement see Eleanor Flexner, *Century of Struggle: The Woman's Rights Movement** (1959); Aileen Kraditor, *The Ideas of the Woman Suffrage Movement, 1880–1920** (1965); and William O'Neill, *Everyone was Brave: The Rise and Fall of Feminism in America** (1969).

On foreign policy and the imperialist urge there are a number of good works. Typical are Dexter Perkins, *A History of the Monroe Doctrine** (1955); E. R. May, *Imperial Democracy** (1961); and Walter LaFeber, *The New Empire** (1963). A vivid account of the war with Spain is Frank Freidel, *The Splendid Little War* (1958).

On foreign policy and American entrance into the World War see G. F. Kennan, *American Diplomacy, 1900–1950** (1951); H. K. Beale, *Theodore Roosevelt and the Rise of America to World Power** (1956); Richard Leopold, *Elihu Root and the Conservative Tradition** (1954); A. S. Link, *Wilson the Diplomatist** (1957), and *Wilson: The Struggle for Neutrality* (1968); Walter Millis, *The Road to War* (1935); Ernest May, *The World War and American Isolation* (1959); N. G. Levin, *Woodrow Wilson and World Politics* (1958); and E. H. Buehrig, *Woodrow Wilson and the Balance of Power* (1955).

* Titles available in paperback.

From Total War Through Depression

In a real sense America did not enter the twentieth century until 1917. Among the hallmarks of the twentieth century have been total war, economic calamity, and a vast expansion of centralized government. In contrast, the nineteenth century was far more an era of peace, economic stability, and diffused, weak governmental authority. The intervention of 1917 launched America into the mainstream of the twentieth century.

When Americans accepted the idealistic statement of war aims set down by Woodrow Wilson, they proceeded to build an enormous war machine commensurate with their moral obligation to the war effort. The creation and operation of more than 5,000 government war agencies involved an unprecedented amount of planning and regimentation in American life. Although most of these agencies were abandoned after the war, they showed that the federal government could meet a national emergency through a coordinated, centrally directed effort. This lesson would be remembered in the 1930s.

One government power tested by the mobilization effort was that of manipulating public opinion through propaganda. To win the full support of Americans for the war the Wilson administration persuaded newspaper and magazine editors to engage in voluntary self-censorship; disseminated tons of literature; and enlisted the services of 150,000 writers, lecturers, actors, and artists. Much of the message was idealistic, directly reflecting Wilson's own aims, but much appealed to fear and hate as well. A consequence of the propaganda and the insecurity of a public disturbed by war and social change was a campaign for 100 percent Americanism that sought to suppress dissent and deviant social behavior. The making of the peace at Versailles only enhanced American insecurity as it tragically brought into question Woodrow Wilson's assumption that world peace and stability would logically result from American participation in the war. An embittered public viewed with even more enthusiasm the national crusade for conformity that included not only the Red Scare of 1919 but enactment of prohibition and later the drastic restriction of immigration.

To find relief from Wilsonian idealism the American public turned to Warren G. Harding and elected him President in 1920. He said that "America's present need is not heroics, but healing; not nostrums, but normalcy" and thereby captured the electorate and provided a catch phrase for the period following World War I. The American people, or at least the majority of them, were tired of legislation, tired of wartime restrictions, tired of progressive reforms. They wanted a return to "normalcy," to the good old days, to the days that never had existed except in nostalgic reverie.

The days that were to come in the 1920s were old in some respects but new in others. They were old—like those of the late nineteenth century—in respect to the position of big business, which again dominated both government and society. Indeed, business was more sanctified than ever. "The business of America is business," said Calvin Coolidge, who succeeded Harding in the Presidency. In *The Man Nobody Knows* (1925), a best seller of the period, Bruce Barton described Jesus Christ as "a startling example of business success," the author of "the most powerful advertisements of all time," and "the founder of modern business."

But much was new in the decade of the twenties. This was the time when the automobile came into its own, with production increasing from 1.5 million cars in 1921 to 4.75 million in 1929, by which year the automotive industry was responsible, directly or indirectly, for the employment of more than 3 million persons. It was the time of the coming of numerous household gadgets: the radio, the refrigerator, the vacuum cleaner, and many others. It was an age when the federal government sought to impose a species of morality by prohibiting the manufacture, sale, or transportation of intoxicating beverages — and an age of what seemed to many like unprecedented license in speech and behavior, the age of "flaming youth" and of unrestrained dances like the "bunny hug" and the "Charleston."

From 1923 to 1929 it was also a time of remarkable prosperity and economic stability. The people generally assumed — and experts in business, economics, and government told them — that this was veritably a new era in human history. The country had reached a "permanent plateau" of prosperity and need never worry again about the possibility of a serious slump. But prosperity, like "normalcy," proved to be only temporary. Eventually the country fell into much the worst economic depression it had ever known.

During 1917 and 1918 the government of the United States, in order to win a war, had undertaken to control nearly all aspects of the economy. But never before the 1930s had the government intervened in so many ways to overcome a depression. Between 1933 and 1938, under the leadership of President Franklin D. Roosevelt, the government launched a bewildering variety of programs and set up a jumble of "alphabetical agencies" — AAA, NRA, TVA, and so on — to administer them. Some of these were intended to provide immediate relief for people facing a loss of income or property. Others were expected to stimulate economic activity and bring about recovery from the depression. Still others were designed to reform the economic system in order to reduce poverty and insecurity and avoid future depressions. Some of the programs served two or all three of these aims. All together, the series of measures constituted the New Deal.

The "three Rs" of the New Deal were Relief, Recovery, and Reform. Its conservative critics, among them former President Hoover, contended that it involved also a "fourth R," namely, Revolution. Certainly the New Deal, which at first was rather cautious, emphasizing short-term measures of relief and recovery, gradually became somewhat more daring and placed greater emphasis on lasting reforms. All along, however, the programs were directed toward patching up and preserving, not destroying, the political and economic institutions that President Roosevelt and the American people had inherited. The programs were mostly improvisations that were drawn up to meet the needs of the moment. They were based on previous American experience. A precedent for practically every one of them can be found in something that had been proposed or tried out earlier.

The New Deal was revolutionary only in the sense that it embodied a large number of undertakings at one time and carried them to greater lengths than comparable movements, such as the New Freedom, had done.

The New Deal failed to bring about complete recovery; not until after 1941 did war, the greatest of public works, take up the slack in the employment of human and other resources. But the New Deal did produce a very rapid rate of recovery from the exceptionally depressed conditions of 1933. And the relief measures enabled both the people and the economic system to survive the depression; the reform measures made significant and enduring changes in the system itself. The role of government in economic life was vastly increased (and was to be increased still further by the ensuing war). The nation had become a welfare state. Henceforth the principle was to be generally accepted – though not always completely realized – that it was the government's duty to "provide for the general welfare" by controlling business and agriculture, maintaining full employment, and assuring at least a basic level of economic security to all members of society.

Having fought a war to end war and make the world safe for democracy, Americans of the 1920s were generally optimistic about the prospects whenever they gave thought to international affairs. True, the United States had failed to join the League of Nations, the organization that was intended to keep the peace. But this country took the lead in bringing the nations of the world to renounce war in the Kellogg Pact (1928), which many people hailed as the sign of a warless future. Henceforth, said admirers of the pact, aggressive war was illegal.

Optimism faded after the great depression struck. During the 1930s, Japan under fanatical militarists, Germany under Hitler and the Nazis, and Italy under Mussolini and the Fascists each launched programs of domestic tyranny and foreign conquest. Opposed to these aggressive nations were the contented powers of Europe – Great Britain, France, and the Soviet Union – which disagreed on many things but had a common interest in maintaining the status quo.

The American government faced a choice between two broad lines of policy. On the one hand, the United States might back Great Britain, France, and the Soviet Union (if they could manage to get together themselves) in the hope that all somehow could and would provide for their "collective security," enforce the Kellogg Pact, prevent aggression, and maintain peace – though in this there was the real risk of hastening a general war. On the other hand, the United States might follow a policy of so-called "isolation." That is, this country might strengthen its position in the Western Hemisphere and concentrate on keeping out of war instead of preventing it.

Most of the American people favored the second of these alternatives. They were preoccupied with the depression and were determined to set their own country to rights, regardless of what might go on in the rest of the world. They were disillusioned about their earlier effort to bring peace through war – more than 70 percent of them, according to an opinion poll in 1937, thought it had been a mistake to go to war in 1917 – and they were in no mood to go on a second crusade.

Ever regardful of public opinion, President Franklin D. Roosevelt hesitated to come out openly and clearly in favor of collective security even after the long-expected war had broken out in Europe in 1939. He continued to talk the language of isolationism, representing his policy as one of keeping out of war, while he committed the country to greater and greater support of Great Britain and her allies. The issues became more and more confused as the debate between "interventionists" and "isolationists" grew hotter. On December 7, 1941, the debate was stilled.

1917–1941

Chapter 22.   THE WAR TO END WAR AND ITS AFTERMATH, 1917–1920

Mobilizing Men and Resources

The World War was a total war. The nations that fought it had to mobilize their entire resources, human and material, to wage the struggle. As the United States had entered the conflict largely unprepared, it had to mobilize its resources hurriedly. It performed the task, sometimes clumsily, but in the end with impressive results.

Both the President and the Congress realized that the mass armies required in this war could not be raised using only volunteers. Soon after war was declared, Congress enacted the Selective Service Act, which required that all males between the ages of eighteen and forty-five register for military service. Nearly three million men were inducted under the act. With the existing regular army and National Guard, the United States eventually had an army of three and a half million men, of whom two million were sent overseas. (Negroes were drafted along with whites and for the second time, the Civil War being the first, blacks served in large numbers in an American conflict — but in segregated units.)

It was also necessary to mobilize the country's vast economic resources. Indeed, it was thought at first by the Allies that America's greatest contribution to the war effort would be in furnishing supplies. To accomplish the task, the War Industries Board was established by executive order. When it seemed unable to do the job, Wilson asked Congress to delegate to him almost unlimited power over the economy. Congress responded with the Overman Act, which authorized the Board to fix priorities on raw materials, standardize products, and set prices. Under the chairmanship of Bernard Baruch, a shrewd Wall Street broker, the Board used its great powers to achieve what was called "the miracle of production."

In addition to arms and munitions, it was expected that the United States would provide food for its allies as well as itself. "Food will win the war" became a popular slogan. To increase production, Congress authorized the creation of the Food Administration. Administered by Herbert Hoover, an able mining engineer, this agency persuaded consumers to conserve food by observing meatless and wheatless days. But it did not rely on voluntary appeals to convince farmers to increase production — it set prices and set them high. As an example of the results of its work, wheat acreage jumped from 45 million acres to 75 million acres. A similar agency was the Fuel Administration, which was authorized to increase coal production by offering high prices to mine operators.

Increased industrial and agricultural production would be useless unless the supplies could be delivered to Europe. The chaotic railroad system was unable to deliver raw materials to factories or munitions and men to embarkation ports. Consequently the lines were put under the control of a single agency, the Railroad Administration, and operated as a unit. As compensation, the roads received a rental equivalent to their average earnings between 1914 and 1917.

The supplies still had to be transported to Europe, and this called for the creation of what was called a "bridge of ships." The Shipping Board was authorized to increase the merchant marine by building new vessels or buying or leasing existing ones. It too accomplished a miracle of production, and the ships crossed the Atlantic in great convoys guarded by the navy. During the war the navy experienced a spectacular expansion, numbering at the end over 2,000 ships of all types and counting a personnel of over half a million men.

To prevent industrial disputes from impeding production, the War Labor Board was established. Made up of representatives from organized labor and business, it discouraged strikes and sought to mediate disputes. At the same time it recognized that labor had the right to bargain collectively and deserved a fair wage. As a result, wages rose faster than prices, and the unions almost doubled their membership.

The great American war effort was extremely costly, and the task of financing it fell to Secretary of the Treasury William G. McAdoo. He sought to raise as much of the money as possible through taxes but opposition to the war limited

250

his success. Only a third of the total cost, $32 billion, was raised through taxes. The War Revenue Act imposed a variety of excise taxes, raised income tax rates to a new high, and imposed heavy corporation and excess profits duties. The remainder was secured through loans. Banks provided some of the loans, but the government also asked ordinary men and women to lend money by buying Liberty Bonds. It was an early example of attempted mass financing of a war. All of the loans were facilitated by the decision of the Federal Reserve system to allow the money supply and credit to expand dramatically during the war.

Altogether nearly 5,000 special agencies operated during the war. They brought the American economy and people under a regulation not previously known.

Mobilizing Opinion

In this total war the government acted to mobilize minds as well as men and materials. Congress created a special agency to rally opinion behind the war, the Committee on Public Information, headed by progressive journalist George Creel. The Committee published tons of propaganda designed to demonstrate that America and her allies were fighting a war for democracy and justice; much of it was written by volunteers: authors, professors, and others. The Committee also commanded the services of thousands of volunteer speakers from all walks of life all over the country who at a minute's notice would defend the purposes of the war.

Much of the Committee's material was idealistic in nature and was undoubtedly needed, for many Americans, especially those of German descent, were sympathetic to the Central Powers or indifferent to the war. On the other hand some of the publications preached hatred of the enemy, especially Germany, and inevitably the result was to arouse in this country hatred of German-Americans, pacifists, or any individuals who opposed the war or even criticized its conduct. Eventually a mood of hysteria gripped the country. German books were removed from some libraries and the teaching of the German language was dropped from some schools. In some cities and states patriots enforced their own repression on dissenters by tarring and feathering or hanging.

The government gave official approval to a policy of repression with the Espionage Act and the Sedition Act. The Espionage Act prescribed severe penalties of fine and imprisonment for anyone who interfered with the draft or encouraged obstruction of the war effort. The Sedition Act, even more sweeping, imposed the same penalties for anyone who spoke, wrote, or printed any "disloyal language." Over 1,500 persons were arrested under these laws, and some of them were sentenced to prison terms for as long as twenty years. President Wilson had feared that in the stress of war the American people might lose their sense of tolerance, and events seemed to be proving that he had been right.

The AEF in France

The World War was truly global in extent. It was fought in Europe, Asia, Africa, and on the oceans. Shortly after the United States entered the war, it seemed that Germany and her allies were on the point of achieving victory. In the fall of 1917 Germany in effect knocked Russia out of the war. The government of the Tsar fell and was briefly replaced by a constitutional democracy. This government was in turn replaced by a Communist regime that concluded peace with Germany. At the same time the Germans and Austrians inflicted a near-fatal blow to the Italians. Relieved of pressure on its eastern border, Germany was able to give almost its full attention to the war on the Western Front in France.

Across France the contending armies, German on the one side and French and British on the other, faced each other in complex lines of trenches. The Germans had struck into France in 1914 but after an initial successful advance had been stopped. In this war new weapons gave the defense an advantage – improved small arms, quick-firing artillery, and above all the machine gun. An attacking army in the cramped space of France could make only a limited advance and suffered appalling casualties. The war had settled down to one of position rather than maneuver.

Although the Allies desperately needed manpower, they at first regarded with doubts the arriving American Expeditionary Force under General John J. Pershing. The American troops had had only a brief training, and the British and

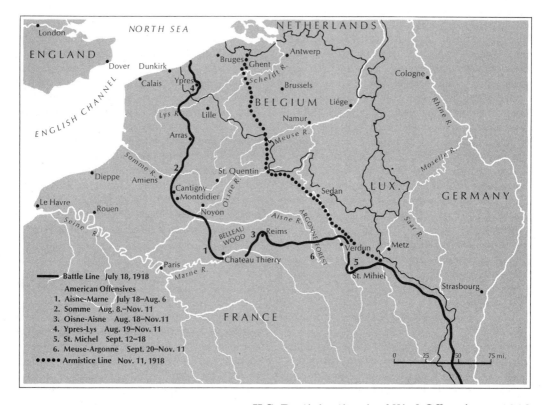

U.S. Participation in Allied Offensives   1918

French generals did not feel that this green army could be relied on. They therefore proposed that the Americans be mixed in with their more experienced units. Pershing, however, insisted that his force should operate as a separate army and was backed up by President Wilson. The Allied Supreme War Council had to agree, but the Americans were stationed on a relatively quiet sector of the front.

In the spring of 1918 the Germans launched a great offensive that they hoped would end the war. All along the line they surged forward and at first scored impressive gains. The shaken Allies for the first time appointed a commander in chief, the French Marshal Ferdinand Foch, and threw in everything they had to resist the Germans. In the crisis Pershing permitted some of his troops to be brigaded with allied units. Fighting mixed or separately, the Americans surprised the French and British by their efficiency, performing with particular brilliance at Château-Thierry, only fifty miles from Paris. By

July the German offensive was contained. At this time reinforcements had brought the AEF up to over a million men.

Almost immediately the Allies went over to the offensive. The Americans, forming the southern wing of the attack, first erased a German salient that jutted into the Allied line at St. Mihiel. Then by Foch's command they were turned northward in the great Meuse-Argonne offensive that lasted for forty-seven days and carried the AEF toward the German border. In other sectors the Allied thrusts were equally successful, and the Germans knew they would have to sue for peace. Envoys from the German government asked Foch for an armistice and received terms so stiff that a resumption of hostilities would be impossible. Nevertheless the Germans signed the armistice on November 11, 1918. The German imperial government fell and was replaced by a democratic regime, and the resistance of Germany's allies collapsed. The war was in effect over.

The United States had played an important part in achieving the victory. The success of the Allied offensive rested on the accession of American manpower (and also on the introduction of a new weapon by the British, the armored tank). But in comparison to her allies the United States had suffered light losses. The total American dead and missing were only something over 100,000. The French lost 1,385,000 men and the English 900,000. A frightful war had ended. Now it remained to make a peace.

Preparing for Peace

President Wilson intended that he and his country should play a large role in determining the nature of the peace. In various public pronouncements Wilson set forth the outline of what he thought the peace should be like—a peace of idealism, a "peace without victory." In January 1918 he became more specific in an address to a joint session of Congress. He laid down as a basis for a settlement his Fourteen Points. The most important ones proposed "open covenants of peace openly arrived at," freedom of navigation on the seas, removal of tariff barriers, reduction of armaments, adjustment of colonial claims with consideration being given to the wishes of the colonial peoples, and a League of Nations to preserve peace. In the meantime he had learned that the Allied powers had made secret treaties among themselves to divide up the colonies of the enemy and to take other spoils. But he convinced himself that he could persuade the heads of these governments to adopt a more lofty and disinterested attitude at the peace conference that was to convene at the palace of Versailles in Paris early in 1919.

Wilson announced that he would go to Paris as the head of the American delegation. His decision was unprecedented—that a President should leave the country—and was widely criticized. But the conference was what would be later called a summit meeting, and Wilson had reason to go. The heads of the other principal allied governments planned to be at Paris— Premier Georges Clemenceau of France, Premier Vittorio Orlando of Italy, and Prime Minister David Lloyd George of England. They, with Wilson, would comprise what came to be known as the Big Four.

Wilson did, however, commit two serious tactical errors. On the eve of the congressional elections of 1918 he asked the voters to return a Democratic majority as a vindication of his foreign policy. The people responded by electing a Republican majority to both houses. Thus in a sense Wilson went to Paris repudiated at home. His second mistake was in not taking on the American delegation a ranking Republican, especially a Republican Senator, since Republican votes would be required in the Senate to muster the required two-thirds majority to ratify the treaty coming out of the conference. He was accompanied only by a Republican career diplomat. To many people it seemed that the making of the peace had become too much a partisan process.

Wilson at Versailles

During the negotiations for an armistice, the Germans had asked for an agreement based on the Fourteen Points. The Allies had seemed to agree but had made certain reservations, one being that Germany had to pay financial reparations for damages committed by her on Allied civilian populations. Despite the reservations, and his knowledge of the secret treaties, Wilson arrived in Paris confident that the peace would be based on the Fourteen Points.

At Paris all the nations that had declared war on Germany were represented whether or not they had contributed much to the war effort. It was soon discovered that such a large assemblage could not conveniently arrive at agreements. Therefore the Big Four took to meeting secretly and then transmitting their decisions to the other delegates. One of the Fourteen Points, open covenants openly arrived at, had gone by the board already.

At the outset Wilson had to struggle to prevent a division of spoils under the secret treaties. He tried to block the Japanese from obtaining permanently the German treaty rights in the Shantung Peninsula of China and the former German islands north of the Equator in the Pacific, which could be Japanese strongholds. He had to give way, however, to the insistence of the British that they honor the treaty promises with which they had lured the Japanese into the war. Wilson with more success persuaded the Allies to hold former German colonies and Turkish territories on a basis of trusteeship responsible to the League of Nations. This was the new and unprecedented "mandate" system.

Simultaneously, Wilson worked on the drafting of the League Covenant. He insisted that it form the first part of the treaty, and be inseparable from it, and he labored long and hard fabricating it in meticulous detail. In the League Covenant he saw the one possible way of overriding the vengeful selfishness that seemed dominant among the victorious nations. Whatever imperfections and inequities there were in the Treaty he thought could be rectified through the League: through it and it alone, the world could avoid future wars. In the League he envisaged a potentially powerful (but not armed) international organization through which the nations of the world could share responsibility in maintaining the security of all against any aggressor.

Opposition to the League

At the end of February 1919, as Congress prepared to adjourn, Wilson came home to sign bills. He brought with him the League Covenant, determined that he would force the Senate to accept it without compromise. He was convinced that public sentiment was overwhelmingly behind him. When a friend warned him he must be prepared to compromise with the Senate, he retorted: "I have found that you get nothing in this world that is worth-while without fighting for it."

But strong resistance was taking shape. Senator Henry Cabot Lodge of Massachusetts produced a round robin signed by thirty-nine Senators, a number sufficient to block the treaty, announcing they would not accept the Covenant in its existing form. Wilson, about to re-embark for Paris, retorted angrily. But back at the Conference he did obtain some of the reservations for the United States upon which the Senate would obviously insist. These provided that a nation need not accept a mandate against its will, that a member could withdraw with two years' notice, that the League would not regulate immigration and other internal matters, and that it would not infringe upon the Monroe Doctrine. To obtain these, Wilson had to trade concessions with the Allies. He made little progress toward conciliating the Republican Senators.

Many of them saw in the struggle over the Covenant a means of embarrassing Wilson, stripping him of some of his glory, and developing a winning issue for the campaign of 1920.

The Versailles Treaty

While Wilson was obtaining revision of the Covenant, the Conference was also grappling with the critical problem of Germany and the remaking of the European map. Together with Lloyd George, Wilson resisted the French proposal to break up western Germany into buffer states. He did sanction the return to France of Alsace-Lorraine, and the establishment of a strong Poland and Czechoslovakia on Germany's borders, all in keeping with the national self-determination clauses of the Fourteen Points. He also supported German demilitarization, long-term Allied occupation of the west bank of the Rhine, and an Anglo-French-American mutual defense pact (which was never ratified). If maintained, these security provisions should have prevented the resurgence of Germany as a military menace to the West.

Elsewhere the remapping of Europe proceeded rather fitfully. Italy obtained the Brenner Pass area in which 200,000 Austrians lived, then was outraged at not also receiving Fiume, which Wilson felt must be a port for the new nation of Yugoslavia. In this region and others, the economic needs of nations and the principle of national self-determination of peoples often conflicted.

Wilson's most important departure from the Fourteen Points was his acceptance of British and French demands for heavy reparations from the Germans. Even before the armistice, he had partly accepted their demands that Germans must make payment for civilian damages, although such a proposal ran counter to his negotiations with the Germans. At the Conference, he permitted these demands to cover even pensions for veterans; the astronomical sum was to be set later by a reparations commission. Meanwhile, although Wilson himself for years had taken an economic-determinism view of the origins of the war, the other powers insisted that Germany must accept sole responsibility for starting it. The "war guilt" clause and reparations stuck in the craw of Germans. Even in the United States, the harsh peace meted out against Germany disillusioned many liberals and alienated them from Wilson. They regarded the treaty as a "hell's brew" that would ultimately lead to another war.

Defeat in the Senate

Wilson returned to the United States confident that the Senate, despite the difficulties Lodge was stirring up, would ratify the treaty. On July 10, 1919, when he presented it to the Senate, he asked rhetorically: "Dare we reject it and break the heart of the world?"

Through a combination of coercion and compromise he might have brought about ratification. But he was suffering from hardening of the arteries and while in Paris had been so ill that he may have been close to a stroke. His physical condition robbed him of his political suppleness; instead of using patience and tact, he was more likely to shower his opponents with self-righteous anger.

Wilson's opponents in the Senate were men of varied motives. The fourteen "irreconcilables" were men of conscience, of Middle Western or Far Western progressive tradition, like Republicans Borah of Idaho, Johnson of California, and La Follette of Wisconsin, and Democrat James Reed of Missouri. They acted from a deep conviction that their nation could best be served by staying out of the League. Other opponents with less conviction were more concerned with constructing a winning issue for the Republicans in the 1920 election than they were with the future of the world. Senator Lodge, applying all his brilliant intellect to his loathing of Wilson, was ready, as chairman of the Senate Foreign Relations Committee, to use every possible tactic to obstruct, delay, and defeat the treaty. Public sentiment seemed to favor ratification, and Lodge needed time to marshal forces against it. Consequently, he spent the first two weeks after it reached the committee reading aloud every word on its nearly three hundred pages. Next, he held six weeks' of public hearings, listening to the complaints of every disgruntled minority.

The strongest objection of opponents was to Article X of the League Covenant, the collective security section designed to prevent aggression. It provided that the League Council, in the unlikely event it should agree, could impose economic sanctions on an aggressor nation; or the Council could recommend to member nations that they take military action against the aggressor. To many Senators it seemed that this provision would involve the United States in countless wars. Wilson was told that he would have to accept a modification of this article and other reservations if he wished to obtain ratification. He replied: "Never! Never! . . . I'll appeal to the country!"

So Wilson, at the end of his physical resources, against the stern warnings of his physician, undertook a cross-country speaking tour, writing his speeches as he went along, delivering them night after night. In twenty-two days he traveled over 8,000 miles, giving thirty-six speeches averaging an hour in length. At first the halls were not entirely filled nor were his speeches always well polished. As the tour proceeded, he gained larger and more enthusiastic audiences and grew more eloquent in his moral fervor. Had it been possible to sway the United States Senate through public opinion, the tour might have been a success. But Wilson became more and more frail. Finally after speaking at Pueblo, Colorado, September 25, he suffered such acute headaches that he had to cancel the tour and return to Washington.

Then he suffered an acute stroke that partially paralyzed his left side. For two weeks he was close to death, and for six weeks more so seriously ill that he could attend only to what little business his devoted wife and doctor thought would not unduly upset or fatigue him. The country was in effect without a President.

At this critical period the Senate Foreign Relations Committee finally reported the treaty, recommending forty-five amendments and three reservations. Lodge managed to marshal the Republican Senators so well that in November he obtained adoption of fourteen reservations. By this time Wilson had recovered sufficiently to give stern directions to the Democratic minority: they must vote only for the treaty without any reservations whatsoever. Although none of the Lodge reservations would have devitalized the League, Wilson preferred no ratification of the treaty to ratification with reservations. While he was by no means his old self, he was able to exert power enough to maintain discipline over the loyal Democrats. When the vote came, November 19, 1919, forty-two Democrats joined with the thirteen Republican irreconcilables to vote down the treaty with reservations. Next, the Senate voted on ratification of the treaty without reservations. There were thirty-eight Senators, all but one of them a Democrat, who voted for it; fifty-five voted against it.

On the day of the final vote, March 19, 1920, when the Senate considered the treaty with fifteen reservations, it came within seven votes of receiving the requisite two-thirds. By this time, President Wilson looked to the campaign of 1920 as the opportunity for a "solemn referendum" on the League issue.

Demobilization

Wilson and his wartime planners had been highly successful in converting a peacetime society to one that could conduct a total war. But, perhaps preoccupied with the Versailles treaty, they made a shambles of the reconversion to peace. They allowed virtually all of the wartime agencies to shut down almost immediately after the conclusion of hostilities. Moreover, they paid little attention to the fact that the dropping of wartime controls and the continued stimulation of the money supply by the Federal Reserve (to ease the financing of the Treasury Department's 1919 borrowing) produced overexpansion of the economy and soaring prices during 1919 and much of 1920. While prices had increased 12 percent during 1918, they rose 29 percent during 1919. By May 1920 (when a very sharp depression ensued, lasting until July 1921), prices were almost three times as high as they had been only six years earlier. The sharply rising cost of living particularly hurt white collar workers and other middle-class people. There was little way they could take out their resentment except at the polls, and they became bitter against not only the Wilson administration but organized labor as well.

Union workers tried to preserve their wartime economic gains by striking for higher wages to compensate for the rise in living costs, but came to be castigated as subversives. A great wave of strikes spread across the country, involving in 1919 some 4 million workers. Many were successful, but they alienated much of the public which accepted the industrialists' protests that higher wages were responsible for higher prices and that the strike leaders were radicals. The outbreak of a steel strike in September 1919 brought antilabor feeling to a boil. The griev-ances of the workers were serious. They were working an average of nearly sixty-nine hours a week for bare subsistence wages. United States Steel was able to swing public sentiment away from the strikers by claiming that the leaders were Communists; William Z. Foster, the main organizer, was to emerge in 1924 as the presidential candidate of the Communists. The company also tried to stir up trouble between Italian and Serb strikers, and brought in Negro strikebreakers. By January 1920 the workers were starved out. Steel remained unorganized for another decade and a half.

Public opinion turned even more firmly against organized labor when a police strike broke out in Boston. The policemen were working long hours on prewar salaries under unpleasant conditions. They struck when the police commissioner dismissed the leaders of a union they were organizing. Citizens were horrified when rowdies took over the streets of Boston; troops quickly restored order. When President Gompers of the AFL appealed to Governor Coolidge to permit the reemployment of the policemen who had gone on strike, Coolidge wired: "There is no right to strike against the public safety, anywhere, anytime." No strikers were ever rehired, and this one telegram made Coolidge a formidable contender for the Republican presidential nomination in 1920.

Red Scare and Reaction

In Washington, Attorney General A. Mitchell Palmer was becoming a leading contender for the Democratic nomination through his war on both labor and radicals. By obtaining Federal court injunctions, he smashed the strike of John L. Lewis' United Mine Workers in November 1919. He attracted even more attention with his crusade against Reds. Throughout the country the violent suppression of pro-German persons during the war had been continued in the persecution of the IWW, the Socialists, and all other leftwingers. A series of bombing outrages in 1919–1920 intensified the public revulsion against radicals and encouraged Palmer's repressive tactics. On January 1, 1920, he conducted a great Red roundup, jailing some 6,000 suspects. Communists who were United States citizens he turned over to the states for prosecution under their criminal syndicalist laws. The aliens came under the jurisdiction of the Labor Department, which gave them fair treatment. Only 556 proved Communists were deported.

In Massachusetts a payroll robbery and murder in April 1920 led to the trial and conviction of two anarchists, Nicola Sacco and Bartolomeo Vanzetti. Numerous believers in civil liberties insisted that the two men were being prosecuted more on the basis of their radicalism than on criminal evidence, but in August 1927 Sacco and Vanzetti were executed. Their case was the cause célèbre of the 1920s.

Intolerance at the beginning of the 1920s led to the persecution of not only radicals and labor organizers, but also aliens, Catholics, Jews, and Negroes.

No group suffered more severely than the Negroes. For hundreds of thousands of them, the war had offered an opportunity to break out of the narrow caste structure of the South. Some 400,000 served in the army, half of them in Europe, which drew no color line. Several hundred thousand more moved into the industrial North, where there was less discrimination against them than in the South. Even in the North, however, they suffered from wretched housing, low pay, and the animosity of unskilled white workers who feared their competition. Many Negroes in the North and South alike began to follow the militant leadership of the National Association for the Advancement of Colored People, which demanded larger economic opportunities and greater civil rights for Negroes.

In both North and South, Negroes faced explosive resentment against them. To intimidate Negroes back into their old subservience, Southerners resorted to the terrorism of the Ku Klux Klan, which grew by 1919 to a membership of 100,000, and to lynchings, which increased from 34 in 1917 to more than 70 in 1919. Terrible race riots broke out, beginning in July 1919, in twenty-six towns and cities. Hundreds of persons were killed or wounded, and millions of dollars worth of property was destroyed.

These terrors led as many as a half-million Negroes to follow a leader of magnetic appeal, Marcus Garvey, founder of the Universal Negro Improvement Association. In return for their contributions he promised to take them home to an African empire. Garvey, appealing particularly to poorer Negroes, helped arouse their racial pride. Du Bois and the NAACP attacked Garvey's scheme as "bombastic and impracticable." Garvey badly handled the funds poor Negroes invested with him, and in 1923 was convicted of using the mails to defraud and sentenced to federal prison. Negro nationalism nevertheless persisted.

Progressivism Turns Sour

The strains of demobilization, which followed so rapidly the disruptions of war and disillusionment with Wilson's idealistic war aims, produced a movement on behalf of "100 percent Americanism" — a crusade to control or destroy all that seemed alien to American society. As a consequence, progressives who had been interested in using the powers of the government to enhance efficiency, rather than to promote social justice, came to the fore and found widespread support, not only for an anti-Red campaign, but for prohibition and for immigration restriction.

In December 1917 Congress had adopted and sent to the nation the Eighteenth Amendment authorizing federal prohibition of the manufacture, sale, and transportation of alcoholic beverages. The amendment was approved in January 1919, and in October 1919, over President Wilson's veto, Congress passed the drastic Volstead Act to implement the amendment. It prohibited all liquors containing more than 0.5 percent of alcohol, rather than permitting the sale of weak beer, which might have appeased millions of city-dwelling opponents of prohibition. To jubilant members of the Anti-Saloon League and the Women's Christian Temperance Union, this meant the enforcement of morality; to opponents it meant an unjustifiable infringement on their personal liberties.

During 1920–1921, as a new flood of immigration from Europe developed, labor leaders, such as Samuel Gompers, and progressives who had been hostile to immigration found that they now had great support; they quickly induced Congress to pass an emergency immigration act. That act established a quota system cutting the number of immigrants from 800,000 in the year ending June 1921 to about 300,000 in the next twelve months. Opponents of immigration were still not satisfied, so in 1924 Congress enacted the National Origins Act. This measure completely banned the people of East Asia, thus abrogating the Gentlemen's Agreement with Japan and incensing the Japanese people. It set a quota of 2 percent for Europeans, on the basis of the 1890 census, thus cutting the total inflow to 164,000 a year, heavily weighted in favor of those from northeastern Europe. The great flood of diverse peoples from Europe had been cut to a few drops.

The approval of the women's suffrage amendment (the Nineteenth) was related to the enactment of prohibition and immigration restriction. The cause of women's suffrage had won many new adherents during World War I as women expanded their participation in American society and as women's organizations became increasingly militant in seeking the vote. But the critical link to success appeared when supporters of prohibition and immigration restriction decided that women would be valuable allies in protecting and expanding their programs. Ironically, women achieved full participation in the American democracy only when the nation was in a mood for the restriction of rights. Congress ratified the suffrage amendment in June 1919, and the last state ratified it in August 1920—just in time for women to vote in the presidential election.

Harding's Election

Domestic tensions made it impossible for the election of 1920 to serve as the "solemn referendum" on the League of Nations that President Wilson had hoped for. Rather, the Red scare and the rising cost of living almost guaranteed in advance a Republican victory, making it unnecessary for Republican politicians to choose a strong, popular candidate such as Herbert Hoover. Rather, when the two leading contenders, General Leonard Wood and Governor Frank O. Lowden of Illinois, deadlocked at the nominating convention, they turned to the amia-

ble, pliable Senator Warren G. Harding of Ohio. As his running mate, the delegates chose the hero of the Boston police strike, Calvin Coolidge. These thoroughly conservative candidates ran on a thoroughly conservative platform.

The Democrats assembled at San Francisco rather confused because President Wilson, who could have designated a candidate, seemed to be waiting with pathetic coyness to be renominated for a third term. After thirty-eight ballots, the urban bosses stepped in and secured the nomination of an antiprohibition candidate who might salvage their city tickets for them—the former progressive Governor of Ohio, James M. Cox. As a gesture toward the Wilsonians, Assistant Secretary of the Navy Franklin D. Roosevelt was nominated for Vice President. Cox and Roosevelt campaigned arduously to try to make the election the referendum on the League that Wilson wished it to be, but faced the hostility of foreign-born city voters, and the indifference elsewhere of all but small groups of intellectuals.

Harding, following the advice of his managers, made few speeches and took few positions on the issues except to promise a return to what he earlier had called "normalcy." On the League he at first gave the impression that he favored joining, then as city resentment against it flared, gave the impression that he was against it. Thirty-one distinguished Republicans stated that a vote for Harding was a vote to enter the League with reservations.

The landslide exceeded even the expectations of the Republicans. Harding received 16,143,407 popular votes, 61 percent of the total, and carried every state outside of the Solid South. He won even Tennessee. Cox received only 9,147,000 popular votes. Debs, running on the Socialist ticket while in the Atlanta penitentiary, received 920,000 votes. The sweep brought in a Republican majority of 22 in the Senate and 167 in the House.

Chapter 23. FROM NORMALCY TO DEPRESSION, 1920–1933

The Tragedy of Harding

The Presidency of Warren G. Harding symbolized the mixture of solid achievement and tragic human failure that characterized the 1920s. Harding was an attractive, well-meaning President who sincerely wished to surround himself with the best qualified men. And in part he succeeded. He placed Herbert Hoover, the friend of small enterprise and expert on efficiency, in charge of the Commerce Department. Andrew W. Mellon represented big business as Secretary of the Treasury. When Harding was persuaded that his friend Albert B. Fall was not of a caliber to be Secretary of State, he appointed the distinguished Charles Evans Hughes. But Harding placed Fall, a notorious anti-conservationist, in charge of the Interior Department, and made some equally disastrous appointments to other offices. Despite good intentions, Harding's lack of executive ability and his poor choice of political friends proved his undoing.

Into 1923 the public saw only the work of the able men, who seemed to be carrying out Harding's campaign slogan, "Less government in business and more business in government." The relatively mild depression beginning in 1920 hurt the Republicans in the 1922 congressional elections, but the return of prosperity soon afterwards heightened their popularity. Harding occasionally was even conspicuous in his humanity. On Christmas Day 1921 he pardoned the Socialist Eugene V. Debs, and at the urging of Hoover, he pressured the steel companies into granting an eight-hour day to their workers.

Behind the façade, rot had set in. The poker-playing and drinking companions whom Harding had placed in positions of trust betrayed him and the American people. Probably Harding never knew in detail how shockingly they were looting the government, but he knew enough to be heartsick. One of the "Ohio Gang," Attorney General Harry Daugherty's friend, Jesse Smith, had been engaging in large-scale "fixing" in the Department of Justice. After Harding ordered him out of Washington, he committed suicide.

The Director of the Veterans' Bureau, Charles R. Forbes, engaged in such colossal thievery that the total loss ran to nearly $250 million. The most spectacular fraud involved Secretary of the Interior Fall, who leased rich naval oil reserves at Teapot Dome, Wyoming, and Elk Hills, California, to Harry F. Sinclair and Edward L. Doheny. Fall, who had been in financial straits, suddenly became affluent; he had received over $400,000 in loans and a herd of cattle for his ranch. In 1929 Fall was convicted of bribery, fined $100,000 and sentenced to a year in a federal penitentiary.

In the summer of 1923 Harding journeyed to Alaska. Tired and depressed, he responded wanly to the cheering throngs. He never had to face the coming storm, for upon his return, in San Francisco he died of a heart attack. In the months that followed, as exposure after exposure crowded the headlines, his reputation collapsed.

Keeping Cool with Coolidge

It was the singular good fortune of Vice President Calvin Coolidge to become President of the United States at the only time since the 1890s when his largely negative custodial approach to the Presidency could bring him popularity rather than disaster. He came to be Chief Executive through a curious mixture of luck, political regularity, and Yankee shrewdness. Unlike Harding, he had a clear-cut conservative philosophy; he always cooperated wholeheartedly with the big interests because he believed in them, and fought unwaveringly for what he believed.

To the older circle in Washington, Coolidge's personality was not especially appealing; Alice Roosevelt Longworth remarked that he had been weaned on a dill pickle. To the American public, however, there was an infinite appeal and security in his folksy virtues, so lavishly detailed and praised in the nation's press. Coolidge reinforced this appeal with little homilies drawn from his Vermont boyhood – exhortations (in which he fervently believed) to thrift, hard work, and respect for business.

Under this comforting moral leadership, the men of power in the United States could take a calm and even incredulous view of the Harding scandals as one by one they came to light in the winter of 1923–1924. Indeed, the respectable press showered indignation less upon the corrupt officials than upon those pressing the investigations.

The Coolidge administration seemed so patently incorruptible that the exposures appeared if anything to backfire against the exposing Democrats. Ultimately Coolidge forced Attorney General Daugherty to resign and helped clean up the scandals. There was no possibility that they would be repeated; and as the election of 1924 approached, they seemed to be doing no appreciable harm to the Republican party. The nation appeared ready to heed the party's campaign slogan: "Keep cool with Coolidge."

In 1924 the Democratic party was badly split between its rural and urban wings. Democrats outside the big cities were in favor of prohibition and fearful of Catholicism; their candidate was William Gibbs McAdoo, who had been Wilson's Secretary of the Treasury. Big-city Democrats, holding quite reverse views, ardently supported the competent governor of New York, Alfred E. Smith, the son of Irish immigrants, a Catholic, and a "wet." The two contenders deadlocked at the Democratic convention until, on the 103rd ballot, when the nomination had become meaningless, they gave way to a compromise candidate, John W. Davis, a wealthy and able corporation lawyer.

While the Democratic convention dragged on, insurgent Republicans and allied representatives of organized labor held a third convention to organize a Progressive party and nominate Robert M. La Follette. Here, apparently, was a real contrast to the Republican and Democratic tickets, and it served as a made-to-order target for the Republicans. They urged the electorate to choose Coolidge as the only alternative to the "red radicalism" of La Follette. Before election day, labor became lukewarm toward La Follette and Republican farmers, as crop prices rose, decided to stay within the party. In its last thrust the old Middle Western insurgency carried only Wisconsin and secured but 16.5 percent of the popular vote throughout the country. Coolidge

polled 54 percent, and Davis only 28.8 percent.

In his inaugural, March 4, 1925, President Coolidge, declaring that the nation had achieved "a state of contentment seldom before seen," pledged himself to the maintenance of things as they were. During the prosperous years of the Coolidge era, as revenues came pouring in, the federal government did not greatly enlarge its services. It spent nothing in such areas as public housing, and little on public works or to aid depressed agriculture. Arms expenditures were a relative pittance. Consequently the budget varied little between 1923, when it was $3.25 billion, and 1929, when it was $3.3 billion. Meanwhile the national debt dropped by nearly a quarter, from $22.4 billion to $17 billion.

Business Is Business

Big business had a special friend in the government during the 1920s. Andrew Mellon, the Pittsburgh aluminum baron who served as Secretary of the Treasury from Harding's inauguration into the Hoover administration, was widely hailed as the greatest Secretary of the Treasury since Hamilton. His prime mission seemed to be to promote tax cuts. Cartoonists routinely pictured Mellon slicing a tax melon. So far as he could, as a matter of principle, he divided these among wealthy individuals and large corporations to encourage them to become more productive.

Smaller businessmen also had a strong champion in the government, Secretary of Commerce Hoover. In his own spectacular rise as an international mining engineer, Hoover epitomized the self-made businessman. He made Commerce the most spectacular of the departments, as he sought to aid small business in becoming as efficient and profitable as big business. The National Bureau of Standards, one of the important agencies in the department, performed innumerable scientific services for industry, such as setting simplified standards and eliminating waste.

The most significant of Hoover's aids to small business was the sponsorship of voluntary trade associations similar to the committees of the War Industries Board. By 1921 some 2,000 were in operation. These associations, free from government regulation, could establish codes of ethics, standardize production, establish efficiency, and make substantial savings. They could also, contrary to Hoover's wishes, arrive indirectly at higher standard prices that would bring them better profits. Their real value to highly competitive smaller businesses was to eliminate competition through setting up standard schedules of quality (and prices).

Voluntarism was at the heart of all Hoover's projects. As the new field of commercial radio broadcasting began to develop, Hoover fostered voluntary self-regulation for it. Only when the efforts to keep stations off each other's wavelengths completely broke down did he move toward compulsory government regulation through the Federal Radio Commission, established in 1927. In the same way, the Department of Commerce finally took over regulation of commercial aeronautics through the Air Commerce Act in 1926.

On the whole, business thrived during the New Era. In part, this was due to benign governmental policies: Hoover's laudable efforts to bring about increased standardization and efficiency enhanced business stability and profits. Secretary Mellon's tax policies increased productivity and profits. The tendency of the courts to frown upon trade-association price schedules helped stimulate mergers.

Beginning in the mid-1920s a new wave of mergers swept through American business, carrying 8,000 mining and manufacturing companies into mergers with other companies. The firms that made the most fervent efforts to promote mergers were those that experienced the most rapid growth of production during the 1920s, the manufacturers of automobiles, chemicals, and household appliances. Their strategies were to acquire greater control over prices, to diversify into new products, and to find the capital necessary to make their plants and equipment more productive. The manufacturers who made the most rapid strides in productivity were those who applied scientific information to production and pursued innovations that allowed full mechanization of their activities, in particular techniques for mass production and the electrification of factories.

Consumers and Workers

The growing productivity of business was a major source of the real prosperity American consumers and workers enjoyed during the 1920s. Per capita income increased almost 20 percent during the 1920s, and although the evidence is incomplete, it appears that income became distributed more evenly as the end of immigration created a shortage of unskilled labor and a consequent increase in the relative wages of unskilled workers. The decade witnessed a dramatic rise in the consumption of automobiles, furniture, and electrical appliances. Through their governmental units, consumers spent three times more for education than before the war. Between 1921 and 1929 an unusual degree of price stability and an exceptionally low level of unemployment accompanied the high levels of income. The average annual rate of price increase was less than 1 percent, and unemployment dropped to an annual average of only 3.7 percent. That record was a significant improvement over that of the two preceding decades and has not been matched since.

The wage gains of the 1920s were achieved largely without the benefit of unions. Indeed, the living conditions of many factory workers improved sufficiently to make easier the drive of most employers against unions. The paternalistic policies of welfare capitalism, combined with a continued crusade against the open shop, led to a decline in union membership during the 1920s. Many companies greatly improved working conditions by installing safety devices and cafeterias, promoting athletic teams, and providing pension plans. Company unions through which workers could voice their grievances were effective safety valves. Through such devices, companies helped fend off unionism from the new mass-production industries like automobile manufacturing. Union membership declined from over 5 million in 1920 to 4.3 million in 1929.

The prosperity was, however, not uniform. Certain industries were depressed during the 1920s, and their problems would become even more severe during the 1930s. For example, the New England textile industry suffered from the movement of firms to the cheaper labor markets of the South. Railroads encountered stiff competition in freight and passenger service from publicly subsidized highways (including a trunk system initiated by the Federal Aid Road Act of 1916). Mining had experienced overexpansion as a result of wartime demands and was particularly depressed. In coal mining, an industry suffering competition from petroleum and natural gas, wages fell more than 10 percent between

1923 and 1929. The lumber industry was also paying the price of overexpansion, particularly in the Great Lakes states. What is most remarkable is that even in the face of these problems the economy as a whole enjoyed unmatched prosperity during the 1920s.

Thunder from the Farm Belt

The industry that suffered the greatest adversity during the 1920s was agriculture. The income of farmers drastically declined during the 1920s. In 1920 they lost their price supports at the same time that the bloated wartime European market contracted. At home, as machines released men from heavy manual labor, consumption of starches sharply dropped. Within agriculture, the shifting eating habits brought a doubling of truck farming and an increase by a third in dairying and citrus growing, together with profits for many of these farmers. At the same time, those who had moved on to marginal or submarginal land during the war suffered so acutely that in the five years after 1919 thirteen million acres were abandoned. These farmers were often heavily burdened with debts acquired at high wartime prices and unable to compete with new, expensive machinery, which especially helped contribute to the glut of wheat. These were the years when tractors almost completely replaced horses, releasing 35 million acres of land for additional crops. Only big operators could enjoy good incomes from producing staples. In the year ending June 30, 1927, the income of all the 6,300,000 farmers averaged only $548. Farm income in 1920 was 15 percent of the national total; by 1929 it was only 9 percent. It is not surprising that the agricultural population dropped three million between 1921 and 1928.

Those who remained on their farms began to agitate militantly for relief. The radical Non-Partisan League, first organized in North Dakota in 1915, evolved into the Farmer-Labor Party in the 1920s, but could not win the support of farmers earning $1,000 to $4,000 a year. This middle 40 percent of the farmers rather sought through the Farm Bureau Federation or the Grange to obtain federal price supports. In 1921 Midwestern congressional leaders from both parties organized a farm bloc to support these demands.

One price-raising scheme came to dominate the farmers' thinking. Behind the tariff barrier, the American protected price for crops should be raised to a "fair exchange value" based on the price of the crop during ten prewar years, compared with the general average of all prices during the same period. This price concept was called "parity." The government should obtain parity prices for farmers by buying up the surplus at the high American price and selling it abroad for whatever it would bring. To make up for the loss an equalization fee or tax should be imposed upon the participating farmers.

Between 1924 and 1928 Senator Charles L. McNary of Oregon and Representative Gilbert Haugen of Iowa promoted this scheme in Congress. In 1924 the McNary-Haugen bill covered only grain, and was defeated in the House, but in 1926 the addition of cotton, tobacco, and rice brought Southern support. In 1927 Congress passed it, but President Coolidge coldly vetoed it as being preferential legislation contrary to the principles of laissez-faire and, quite correctly, as legislation that would increase surpluses without improving the farmers' income. But farmers remained unconvinced. A year later, the McNary-Haugen bill was again passed and vetoed.

The U.S. and the World

The problem of developing Republican alternatives to the Wilsonian foreign policy fell largely on the shoulders of Secretary of State Charles Evans Hughes. Hughes' policies involved first of all ending the war with Germany by an act of Congress, which was signed July 2, 1921, then the negotiation of separate peace treaties to obtain for the United States the benefits of the Paris treaties without the responsibilities. He persuaded President Harding in 1923 to recommend that the United States join with reservations the World Court, an almost powerless body. When Harding's recommendation (and that of each succeeding President through Franklin D. Roosevelt) came before the Senate, irreconcilable isolationists defeated it.

Secretary Hughes' most notable substitute for American entrance into the League was the Washington Arms Conference of 1921-1922, intended to fend off a three-way naval construction race among the United States, Great Britain, and Japan. In the negotiations, Japan agreed to limit her capital ships to a total of approximately 300,000 tons compared with 500,000 tons each for the United States and Great Britain. Thus the Five Power Pact of February 6, 1922, provided a ratio of 5:5:3 for the United States, Great Britain, and Japan, and 1.75:1.75 for France and Italy. Two other treaties aimed at guaranteeing the status quo in the Far East. The Nine Power Pact pledged a continuation of the "Open Door" in China. Afterwards Japan restored to China full sovereign rights in the Shantung Peninsula and promised to withdraw Japanese troops from Siberia. The Four Power Pact, among the United States, Great Britain, France, and Japan, was a mutual guarantee of insular rights in the Pacific. Upon its ratification, Japan relinquished her alliance with Great Britain.

For nearly a decade these Washington treaties lowered the tension between the United States and Japan. Their one unfortunate result was that the United States relinquished the physical force with which to impose its will in the Far East but retained its moral, economic, and political presence in the area.

The United States participated in other activities intended to prevent war, but without making any collective security arrangements. Public opinion within the country was such that no administration dared to make any international commitment that could conceivably lead to the use of armed force. Thus the United States took an important part in disarmament discussions at Geneva and London, and signed a multilateral treaty (usually referred to as the Briand-Kellogg Pact of 1928) solemnly condemning war as an instrument of national policy, but providing no machinery whatever for enforcement. Almost every nation signed.

Toward Latin America, the United States moved away from the progressive policy of intervention and tried wherever possible to substitute the nonrecognition of undesirable governments, even though during the Coolidge years, new troubles in Nicaragua and difficulties with Mexico over the rights of oil companies threatened a reversion to old policies.

In European affairs the big issues were reparations and war debts. The League Reparations Commission, in the absence of Americans, set astronomically high sums for Germany to pay. Reparations payments depended to a considerable degree upon American private loans to Germany; war-debt payments from the Allies to the United States depended almost entirely upon reparations. The American public insisted that the Allies should repay the $10 billion the United States had loaned during the war. The United States pressured the former Allies to negotiate long-term schedules of debt payments. American private loans to Germany were largely what kept the system going in the 1920s.

The United States was pouring out goods throughout the world and building huge investments abroad, yet through a protective tariff it was slowing down the reciprocal flow of goods into this country. Such a system of trade and finance could function only so long as prosperity continued, if indeed that long. As soon as the Republicans came into power in the spring of 1921 they enacted an emergency tariff measure to raise the low Underwood rates. In 1922 they raised the rates again in the Fordney-McCumber Act. Other nations followed the American lead in economic nationalism; by 1928 some sixty countries had raised their tariffs.

The Jazz Age

For those who shared in the prosperity, it was a wonderful era. The national wealth of the United States was almost as great as that of all of Europe. The average middle-class American family owned an automobile. There were 23,000,000 cars in use by 1929, and on Sundays it seemed as though they were all out on the new concrete highways. At home, people listened to the radio. The first commercial station, KDKA, broadcast the news of Harding's election in November 1920; by 1924 the National Broadcasting Company had organized a nationwide network of stations. Household appliances were supplanting the housemaid and the hired girl. Food and clothing accounted for only 44 percent of the family expenditures, compared with 58 percent in 1899 — a clear indication of the rising living standards.

New ways of life, alarming to the older generation, swept America. Women seemed to have lost their modesty as they bobbed their hair, applied lipstick, donned short skirts and silk stockings, and unblushingly began using words previously reserved for males. Younger people talked frankly and openly about sex. Some of them further flouted the older moral standards by drinking bootleg beer or cocktails, listening to jazz, and dancing the Charleston. Many critics thought that Gertrude Stein had correctly labeled this the "lost generation"; they would not have believed that these young rebels in time would mature into censorious middle age.

Motion pictures flamboyantly heralded the new moral code and helped fabricate false stereotypes of the period. An estimated 50,000,000 people a week went to theaters to see the "it" girl, Clara Bow, the glamorous Rudolph Valentino, the comedian Charlie Chaplin, gangster pictures, westerns, and great spectacles like *The Ten Commandments*. These helped standardize American habits, and not always in the most edifying way. Further, since at this time nine-tenths of the world's motion pictures were made in the United States, they brought to other countries curiously distorted notions of American culture. In 1927 a revolution struck the motion picture industry when successful talking pictures were produced—and American speech was heard in movie houses throughout the world.

The prosperity of the twenties spilled over into the educational system. The per capita expenditure per pupil jumped from $24 in 1910 to $90 in 1930. Free elementary education had become established throughout the nation; illiteracy dropped from 7.7 percent to 4.3 percent. Enrollment in high schools increased 400 percent, and universities grew nearly as rapidly.

Writers and Musicians

American writers made themselves heard, and often impressively. Seldom has such a remarkable galaxy appeared. Sherwood Anderson, giving up his paint factory, wrote tart Freudian sketches of small-town America in *Winesburg, Ohio* (1919). Sinclair Lewis more spectacularly exploited the same vein in his satiric *Main Street* (1920). His onslaught against business Philistinism, in a long series of novels, at times verged close to caricature, but in time brought him a Nobel Prize. Theodore Dreiser came into his own in 1925 with *An American Tragedy,* which analyzed with compassion both the psychological and environmental factors that led a young man to consider drowning his mistress. The novelist who best embodied the jazz age in both his personal life and his writing was F. Scott Fitzgerald, catapulted to success with *This Side*

of Paradise (1920). Other young novelists appeared who helped set patterns for later decades. Above all, there were Ernest Hemingway and William Faulkner. The reaction against war was most vigorously stated in Hemingway's novel of disillusion, *A Farewell to Arms* (1929), which also helped set a new literary style. Faulkner, analyzing the South with morbid intensity in novels like *The Sound and the Fury* (1929) and *Sanctuary* (1931), developed an abstruse stream-of-consciousness technique that profoundly influenced other writers.

In the drama these were the golden years of Eugene O'Neill, who drew from Ibsen, Strindberg, and Freud to develop American plays that were both critical and popular successes. *The Emperor Jones* (1920), *Anna Christie* (1922), *Strange Interlude* (1928), and other plays won O'Neill three Pulitzer prizes in the decade. In poetry, two of the most significant writers were expatriates from the United States. These were T. S. Eliot in London, whose *The Waste Land* appeared in 1922, and Ezra Pound, who settled in Italy where he wrote *Cantos* and embraced Fascism. At home, Edna St. Vincent Millay typified the twenties with her hedonistic love poetry, while Robinson Jeffers turned to dark naturalistic themes.

In music the twenties were notable for the rise of jazz, "the most important musical expression that America has achieved." It had originated among Negro musicians in the South, particularly in New Orleans, who drew upon their African heritage in composing and playing tunes with improvised harmonies and a syncopated beat. Among the outstanding black creators of jazz were the guitar-playing singer Huddie Ledbetter ("Leadbelly") and the band-conductor William C. Handy, the "father of the blues," whose compositions include *St. Louis Blues* (1914). The new music first became widely known when jazzmen moved with the general black migration northward during and after World War I. The great trumpet-player Louis ("Satchmo") Armstrong, for example, went from New Orleans to Chicago in 1922 to join a band that helped spread jazz through phonograph recordings. Meanwhile, white musicians had begun to take up the new form, modify it, and make it increasingly popular and respected by treating it as serious music. Prominent among them were the composer George Gershwin, who incorporated jazz elements in his *Rhapsody in*

Blue, and the conductor Paul Whiteman, whose band presented a pioneering jazz concert in New York City in 1922.

A Search for Values

In letters, the arts, and learning, there was a seeking for values that would be something more than the advertising man's paeans to mass-production cultures. This seeking was the reason so many of the younger writers were reject-ing the popular values of the United States for those of Europe, which did not seem to them to be caught in the new commercial maelstrom. Others were trying to interpret the new society with the psychoanalytical approach suggested by Sigmund Freud, or the economic deter-minism stemming from Karl Marx.

Among ministers, publicists, philosophers, and economists seeking to interpret the new order, there was some confusion. The fun-damentalist ministers went on much as before; however, in some quarters they were subjected to ridicule in 1925 when their champion, William Jennings Bryan, matched wits with the agnostic Clarence Darrow in the famous Scopes trial in-volving a Tennessee law forbidding the teaching of evolution. Many ministers, not accepting fun-damentalism, concentrated upon the building of fine churches and the development of a sophis-ticated theology embracing the new psycholog-ical concepts.

A number of the most popular publicists were negative in their view of government. Henry L. Mencken, the editor of the sophisticated *Ameri-can Mercury,* launched some of his most scathing attacks against the American democratic sys-tem. The Socialist candidate for President in 1928, Norman Thomas, lamented, "The old reformer has become the Tired Radical and his sons and daughters drink at the fountain of the *American Mercury.*" Nevertheless, many of the most influential philosophers and social scien-tists, such as John Dewey, continued to write in modified progressive terms. Faith in reform was not extinct but latent until a more propitious time and leadership. Franklin D. Roosevelt, in 1925 a New York executive, reviewing Claude Bowers' *Jefferson and Hamilton,* declared: "Hamiltons we have today. Is a Jefferson on the horizon?"

Hoover Follows Coolidge

To many Americans, a simple and effective way of perpetuating the Coolidge prosperity after 1928 seemed to be to put the "Great Engineer," Herbert Hoover, in the White House. Hoover himself seemed to think that a continuation of the administrative policies of his predecessor would bring continued boom. "Given a chance to go forward with the policies of the last eight years," he promised, "we shall soon with the help of God be in sight of the day when poverty will be vanished from this nation." Instead, the stock market crashed in the fall of 1929 and the nation began to descend into its worst depres-sion.

A scramble for the Republican nomination had begun when President Coolidge announced: "I do not choose to run in 1928." Hoover was easily nominated on the first ballot. The platform emphasized prosperity and straddled the trou-blesome issues of farm relief and prohibition.

Among Democrats, the experienced politi-cians were still almost as badly divided as in 1924, but they saw no reason to turn their con-vention into another brawl when their candidate had no chance of winning against Republican prosperity. Even those who were ardently dry and Protestant raised no barrier against the wet, Catholic governor of New York, Alfred E. Smith. He was nominated on the first ballot to run on a platform not much more positive than that of the Republicans. It did, however, in-clude a plank offering the farmers McNary-Haugenism.

More important, Smith promised, despite a compromise plan on prohibition, that he would favor relaxing the Volstead enforcement act. This forced prohibition into the forefront of the campaign. There was little except that and re-ligion to campaign about.

Both Hoover and Smith were self-made men and proud of it. Hoover's path, from an Iowa farm through Stanford University, had been marked by a phenomenally successful rise as a business and government executive. Smith's path led from the East Side of New York through the Fulton Fish Market and the Tam-many hierarchy to the governorship of New York. There he had demonstrated a consum-mate political and administrative skill. He had reorganized the state government; fought to build schools, parks, and parkways; and struggled for public development of the great power sites. Both candidates were mild progressives dedicated to perpetuating the intimate ties between business and government.

This contest between two men of high character degenerated into one of the lowest mud-slinging campaigns in American history. Hoover himself stressed prosperity, which was popularly translated into the notion of a chicken in every pot and two cars in every garage. This left the political storms to sweep around Smith, who evoked more enthusiastic loyalty and venomous hatred than any candidate since Bryan. Millions of the urban masses, mostly of immigrant and Catholic background, saw in Smith their spokesman, their great hero. In the Protestant South belief in prohibition was still almost an act of faith, and the Ku Klux Klan was boisterous in its anti-Catholicism. Fiery crosses greeted Smith near Oklahoma City, where he courageously denounced the Klan. Smith had no effective defense against the religious and prohibition issues; they overrode rural Americans' disgust with Hoover's coldness toward their demands.

The Hoover landslide far exceeded expectations, with a popular vote of 21,391,000 to 15,016,000 for Smith.

Repeal of Prohibition

To some observers, the 1928 election seemed to be a great national referendum in favor of prohibition, yet prohibition was not to last much longer than prosperity. Though Hoover had referred to it as a "noble experiment," enforcement was breaking down so badly that Congress stiffened the penalties for violating the Volstead Act and authorized the new President to appoint a National Law Enforcement Commission. This comission, headed by a former Attorney General, George Wickersham, and including such distinguished members as Newton D. Baker and Roscoe Pound, ultimately reported in 1931 that prohibition was not only not being enforced but was virtually unenforceable.

It provided an opportunity for gangsters, who during the 1920s switched to the large-scale smuggling or manufacture and distribution of liquor. In Chicago, "Scarface" Al Capone built an underworld empire; based on beer and extending out into slot machines, laundries, and labor unions, it grossed about $60,000,000 per

year. He guarded it against interlopers with an army of 700 to 1,000 gunmen. Between 1920 and 1927 over 250 gangsters were killed in Chicago warfare alone. Capone miraculously survived both his rivals and the forces of the law, until finally in 1931 he was convicted of federal income tax evasion.

Rampant gangsterism and the open flouting of the law by millions of otherwise respectable citizens convinced many thoughtful Americans that prohibition was not worth its price in lawlessness. With the coming of the depression, some well-to-do people, already banded into antiprohibition organizations like the Crusaders, redoubled their efforts in the hope that repeal would bring lower income taxes and greater prosperity. In the campaign of 1932 prohibition, compared with the depression, evaporated as a serious issue, and the Democrats bluntly advocated repeal. In February 1933 Congress submitted to the states the Twenty-first Amendment repealing prohibition; by December it had been ratified, and the experiment was at an end.

Farm Relief and the Tariff

No problems more serious than prohibition and farm relief were on President Hoover's agenda as he took office in March 1929, presumably to bring the nation sane and scientific government.

Hoover's immediate positive step was to call Congress into special session in April 1929 to enact farm-relief legislation and raise the tariff. Hoover's program, embodied in the Agricultural Marketing Act of 1929, established, for the first time in peacetime, large-scale government programs to aid the farmer. The program, as Hoover insisted, was voluntary and did not include any of the price-fixing schemes for which farm organizations were lobbying. In keeping with Hoover's long-established ideas, it encouraged the voluntary combination of farmers to help themselves under government auspices. A Farm Board of eight members was set up to administer a revolving fund of $500,000,000. The Board could make loans to national marketing cooperatives or itself establish corporations to buy surpluses and thus raise prices. Within six months the depression precipitated farm prices toward new lows. Until the summer of 1931, the Wheat Stabilization Corporation and the Cotton Stabilization Corporation were able to keep prices a bit above world levels. By 1932 their funds were spent, their warehouses full, and grain prices at the lowest point since the reign of Queen Elizabeth I. The Board functioned well until 1931; thereafter the severity of the depression made it necessary for farmers to control production to raise prices. The Farm Board experiment thus prepared the way for a more drastic measure.

Congress, taking President Hoover's advice to raise agricultural tariffs, prepared an overall measure, the Hawley-Smoot bill, which contained seventy-five largely futile increases on farm products, and 925 on manufactured goods. It raised the average ad valorem duty from the 26 percent of the Fordney-McCumber Act to a new high of 50 percent. By the time it was ready for the President's signature in the spring of 1930, a thousand members of the American Economic Association had signed a petition urging him to veto it as an unwise piece of economic nationalism. He ignored such warnings and signed the measure. Other nations in reprisal placed high tariffs on American goods. In a time of world depression, rampant economic nationalism was perhaps inevitable, but it was unfortunate and unnecessary for the United States to have led the way.

The Wall Street Crash

As in the cases of farm relief and the tariff, almost every other action of the Hoover administration also revolved around the depression, which began in the summer of 1929.

The initial downturn occurred because manufacturers had grossly overestimated the ability of the consuming public to buy their products, particularly automobiles and appliances. The result was accumulating inventories, cutbacks in production, the laying-off of workers, and reduced incomes and buying power. At first, this downturn was a normal business contraction; the economy had tolerated many such episodes in the past without developing long periods of severe unemployment and extraordinarily low incomes. What helped make the post-1929 contraction unusually severe was the collapse of the stock market in October and November. From the latter part of 1927 on the New York Stock Exchange had been in a grotesquely inflated condition. Full of flaws, the stock market had be-

come for many speculators a great national gambling casino. By 1929 disaster became inevitable and the recession that began in the summer produced the pinprick of doubt that burst the bubble on October 21. Within three weeks, stocks had lost over 40 percent of their former value.

To Americans of all walks of life the stock market had become the symbol of national economic strength and the embodiment of a faith in big business. When the crash came, the public became deeply pessimistic about the future not only of the stock market but also of the economy. Thus, the impact of the crash was to sharpen and prolong the crisis of confidence, which grew worse as the depression dragged on. In a sense, the depression became self-feeding: the longer it continued, the more dismal the prospects for recovery, and expectations of extended depression inhibited the consumption and investment necessary to stimulate the economy.

Hoover Faces the Depression

President Hoover was far more energetic and imaginative than any previous American President in trying to develop a program to combat the depression. His secretary of the treasury, Mellon, remembering the panic of 1873, was ready to see the economy go through the wringer in the old laissez-faire fashion; he was a "leave-it-alone liquidationist" who thought a thoroughgoing cycle of bankruptcy and deflation would be healthy. Hoover did not agree; he pointed out that only 30 percent of the people lived on farms where they might weather such a depression by living on their own produce, compared with 75 percent in the 1870s. He determined that the government should intervene positively but in a very limited way, seeking the voluntary cooperation of business and labor. His philosophy and techniques were the same as they had been when he was Secretary of Commerce.

First, to restore confidence, Hoover declared: "The fundamental business of this country, that is, production and distribution of commodities, is on a sound and prosperous basis." Most of the business moguls echoed him. Next, he held a number of highly publicized meetings of business, farm, and labor leaders in an effort to rally the country to adopt a voluntary program. Business participants pledged themselves not to cut payrolls or production; labor leaders, not to ask for better wages or hours. In addition, Hoover used the government to fight deflation. He announced a significant tax cut and arranged for the Federal Reserve to provide liberal credit for business and for the Farm Board to prop up farm prices. He asked Congress for an increase of $423 million in public works—a huge sum for the period—and called upon mayors and governors to engage in the "energetic yet prudent pursuit" of them. Until 1931, it seemed as though these positive steps might be sufficient.

Democrats, finding in the growing depression the issue so conspicuously lacking two years earlier, campaigned vigorously in the fall of 1930. They won a bare majority in the House of Representatives and, with the aid of Republican progressives, took effective control of the Senate. From this point on, Congress began seriously to harass Hoover, demanding that he move from voluntary measures to large-scale federal relief and spending. Hoover refused to budge, and in the spring of 1931 conditions seemed to be improving. The depression up to this point had not been much more serious than that of 1920–1921; perhaps, Hoover and others thought, it was nearly over.

From Bad to Worse

Instead, the nation was dragged down into far worse conditions as the repercussions of European panic hit these shores. Since the flow of long-term American loans to central Europe had slackened several years previously, Germany and Austria had depended upon short-term credit. French bankers cut this off in March 1931 and by May the largest bank in Austria had collapsed. This disaster threatened to wreck the financial system of Germany and nations further west. Germany, appealing to the United States in June, obtained from President Hoover the proposal of a one-year moratorium on reparations and war debt payments, but France destroyed much of the good effect through her delay in accepting the plan. By September England and most other nations of the world went off the gold standard. The crisis in western Europe severely hit the United States in the spring of 1931 as European gold was withdrawn from American banks in anticipation of American abandonment of the gold standard; European holdings of American securities were

dumped on the market. As other nations devalued their currency in going off the gold standard, American trade with them declined disastrously.

In October 1931, because of the conviction that maintenance of the gold standard was essential to recovery from the depression, the Federal Reserve responded to the outward flow of gold by taking a series of actions designed to protect the dollar and to encourage a return of gold to American shores. By contracting the nation's money supply and raising short-term interest rates the Reserve succeeded in keeping the United States on the gold standard, but the monetary contraction was so severe (over 30 percent of the nation's money supply had disappeared by February 1932) that immediate economic recovery became impossible. Americans became further convinced that prices would continue to fall and even more insistent on increasing their holdings of cash, which were gaining in value. To make things worse, the monetary contraction made it difficult for banks to meet their obligations, and fearful depositors withdrew their savings. Consequently, instead of improving in 1931, the economy sank lower and lower. Security and commodity prices continued to fall; bankruptcies and bank failures multiplied; unemployment soared. By December 1931 when Congress met, conditions were so frightening that President Hoover abandoned his reliance upon voluntary measures and proposed direct governmental action of an unprecedented sort to combat the depression. The Republican progressives and Democrats in Congress were so slow to act that Hoover felt they were deliberately sabotaging his program, that they did not want to bring about recovery before the election of 1932. Slowly they passed some of his measures.

In January 1932 Congress created a giant loan agency, the Reconstruction Finance Corporation, which during 1932 loaned $1,500,000,000, mostly to banks, railroads, and other businesses. Hoover, trying to parry criticism that he had set up a bread line for big business, asserted that his purpose was to stop deflation and thus increase employment, mainly by helping relatively small companies.

President Hoover also obtained some reform of the Federal Reserve system and the establishment of home loan banks, together with further capital for existing loan banks, to help prevent mortgage foreclosures. On the issues of very large-scale public works and direct relief, he clashed bitterly with progressives and Democrats in Congress. In July 1932 he vetoed their bill as being impractical and dangerous; he felt that direct relief was a state and local responsibility. Subsequently, he signed a bill he had recommended, authorizing the RFC to lend $300,000,000 for relief, and another $1,-500,000,000 for self-liquidating public works.

Hoover believed that while people must not go cold and hungry, feeding them was a voluntary and local responsibility. "If we start appropriations of this character," he had declared, "we have not only impaired something infinitely valuable in the life of the American people but have struck at the roots of self-government." It was hard to impress the niceties of distinctions like this upon desperate people. Hoover, who for so many years had been one of the most popular of American heroes, became the scapegoat for the depression.

The People in Hard Times

As the depression deepened, there were surprisingly few signs of social disorder or outbursts of violence within the United States. Communists agitated, won a few converts among intellectual leaders, and made almost no impact upon the masses.

The chain reaction of unemployment slowly spread from 1930 into 1933. At first those in marginal or poorer jobs were hit hardest, as those who had been in better jobs moved downward. In time millions who had never been unemployed for any length of time were jobless and unable to find work of any sort. They were bewildered, for they had been brought up in the sturdy tradition of self-reliance and had accepted the doctrine of rugged individualism — that opportunities were limitless if only one had the ambition and energy to take advantage of them. Now these people were humiliated and baffled at not being able to provide for themselves and their families. As they remained idle for months and then years, they were in danger of losing their skills as well as their morale; physical and moral erosion threatened.

Care of the unemployed had always been a responsibility primarily of private charity, and for several years the President and governors exhorted citizens to contribute to the Red Cross or to emergency funds. But the task soon became far too great for private charity to handle. By 1931, the Red Cross could provide only 75 cents a week to feed each hungry family in southern Illinois.

Although several European nations had maintained unemployment insurance programs for decades, not a single state in the United States enacted such a law until January 1932 when Wisconsin passed one. Even as the distress grew, many magazines and newspapers proclaimed that any permanent system of direct unemployment relief like the British dole would bankrupt the government and undermine the moral fiber of the recipients. Not until September 1931 did the New York legislature at the insistence of Governor Franklin D. Roosevelt establish the first relief organization of any state, the Temporary Emergency Relief Administration, which became the model for other states and the prototype of the later federal relief agency.

To some of the unemployed who had recently moved to cities, the solution seemed to be to return to the farm; the migration away from farms was now reversed. But farm prices fell so low that once again, on parts of the plains, farmers burned corn to keep warm. A rancher sold seven lambs in the Denver livestock market and, after paying commissions and fees, received a check for 75 cents. In a railroad diner, two lamb chops cost the same amount. Prices of manufactured goods were relatively so high that it took ten bushels of wheat to buy a cheap pair of shoes. In drought areas farmers lacked even sufficient food.

This is what had happened to farm prices:

	Cotton per lb.	Corn and wheat per bushel	
1919	35.3¢	$1.51	$2.16
1929	16.7	.79	1.03
1932	6.5	.31	.38

Some bewildered farmers around Sioux City, Iowa, in 1932 embargoed milk bound into the city, because they were receiving 2 cents a quart and it retailed for 8 cents. Many more Iowa farmers participated in Milo Reno's militant Farmers' Holiday Association to block all farm products from the market until prices went higher.

Through the summer of 1932, some twelve to fourteen thousand unemployed veterans congregated in Washington to demonstrate for the immediate payments of their bonus for wartime service, not due until 1945. For weeks they lived in squalor in abandoned tenements and in shanties on the mud flats of the Anacostia River. After Congress failed to pass a bonus bill, about half of them, discouraged, went home. The continued presence of the rest alarmed Hoover and many Washingtonians. After a riot, the President called upon the army to oust the veterans. Under the personal command of General Douglas MacArthur, and his officers Dwight Eisenhower and George Patton, the army did so with tanks, gas masks, and fixed bayonets. "That was a bad looking mob," MacArthur declared. "It was animated by the essence of revolution."

The farmers' strike and the bonus march did not really threaten revolution. Even in this period of extreme despair, Americans were willing to depend upon the ballot box.

Hoover-Stimson Foreign Policies

The depression affected the conduct of foreign affairs as well as the course of domestic politics. For example, President Hoover found that eventually it influenced relations with Japan and threatened one of the objectives he had set forth in his acceptance address—the pursuit of peace. At that time he had declared: "We have no hates; we wish no further possessions; we harbor no military threats."

With respect to Latin America, Hoover continued the movement which under his successor became the "Good Neighbor" policy. Before his inauguration he toured much of the hemisphere, promoting good will; during his administration he prepared for the removal of marines from Haiti and did finally withdraw them from Nicaragua. He refused to intervene in Cuba, which was restless under a dictatorship. Throughout Latin America, as depression toppled about half the regimes, he recognized de facto rulers without questioning the means by which they had come into power. Even when several countries

defaulted on their obligations in October 1931 he did not press them to pay or threaten to seize their custom houses.

Toward Europe, American policies became increasingly important as economic conditions sagged. The moratorium on war-debt and reparations payments, begun in June 1931, helped temporarily. Secretary of State Henry L. Stimson wished it to lead to a general cancellation of these obligations but could not convince the President, who considered them sacred. Soon Germany ceased reparations payments, and nations owing the United States, except for Finland, began to default or make mere token payments.

In the Far East, policies were aimed at safeguarding American rights while preserving peace. As unstable conditions in China continued throughout the 1920s, the United States could do little to protect China from the encroachments of strong nations. As Russia became stronger, she built up her forces in eastern Siberia, and in 1929, when China tried to oust her from Northern Manchuria, fought an undeclared war to retain her foothold. Stimson tried to invoke the Kellogg-Briand pact outlawing war, and to bring about mediation; he failed, demonstrating the weakness of the pact.

Japanese military leaders, feeling that their treaty rights in Southern Manchuria were being threatened both by the Russians and by the Chinese Nationalists under Chiang Kai-shek, wrested the initiative from the Foreign Office in a manner little short of mutiny. In September 1931 they launched a large-scale military campaign in Manchuria at a time when the United States and Great Britain were preoccupied with the monetary crisis. For several weeks Stimson maintained a moderate attitude in the hope that the civilians in the Japanese cabinet could regain control; the British were even less disposed to pursue a strong policy. The Japanese Foreign Office engaged in conciliatory talk but was unable to alter events as the army plunged deeper into Southern Manchuria. By January 2, 1932, the conquest was complete.

As early as October 1931 Stimson had felt the United States might have to cooperate with the League of Nations in imposing economic sanctions against Japan even though these might lead to war. Hoover strongly opposed such action and in cabinet meetings discouraged Stimson by referring to the Washington treaties and the

Kellogg-Briand pact as scraps of paper. He learned from the British that they too opposed sanctions. Hoover was willing to allow Stimson to exert moral suasion against the Japanese, and suggested that he apply the doctrine of nonrecognition against territorial changes brought by force of arms. Stimson did so on January 7, 1932.

The American people were eager to see the United States assume moral leadership – and nothing more – against aggression. Their ideal was international disarmament, not policing. Hoover himself took the same view. In any case, the deepening depression weakened the nation's ability to apply economic sanctions.

After the Geneva Conference of 1927 had failed to extend quotas to destroyers, cruisers, and submarines, the United States had threatened to begin a substantial building program. Hoover, fearing a naval race, called a conference that opened in London in January 1930. There the United States, Great Britain, and Japan agreed not to build the capital ships authorized under the Washington treaty, and even to scrap some existing ships. They also agreed to ratios on smaller ships, to continue until 1936.

The United States participated vigorously in the World Disarmament Conference that opened under League sponsorship at Geneva in February 1932. With the Japanese attacking Shanghai, and Hitler daily winning new converts to his militaristic Nazi movement in Germany, the French firmly demanded an international army and compulsory arbitration rather than disarmament. In June 1932 Hoover tried to break the deadlock with a proposal to abolish immediately all offensive weapons, such as bombing planes and tanks, and to cut all land and naval forces approximately 30 percent. Despite much enthusiasm for the proposal, nothing came of it.

President Hoover's foreign policy was so acceptable to Democrats as well as Republicans (and so overshadowed by domestic issues) that it raised no debate in the campaign of 1932.

The Election of 1932

Republicans meeting in Chicago renominated Hoover in a spirit far from jubilant; they had little illusion about the outcome of the election. The Democrats, assembling later in an excited, expectant mood, saw almost certain victory after twelve years out of power. Almost anyone they nominated was sure to be elected.

Well over a majority of the delegates came pledged to vote for Governor Roosevelt of New York. Roosevelt astutely had been working for the nomination for years. To a considerable degree he bridged the gulf between the urban and rural Democrats. He was ready to emphasize economic issues and ignore the earlier divisions over prohibition and religion.

Breaking precedent, Roosevelt flew immediately to Chicago to deliver his acceptance address before the convention. He endorsed the Democratic platform, which except for a promise of prohibition repeal was not much bolder than that of the Republicans. He declared: "I pledge you, I pledge myself, to a new deal for the American people." Thus the Roosevelt program acquired a name before the electorate had more than the haziest notion of what it might embody.

Nor did the voters learn much during the campaign, for Roosevelt astutely confined himself to warm generalities that would offend few and yet would bring him the enormous vote of protest against Hoover. Through Roosevelt's speeches ran many of the old progressive themes, together with new suggestions for economic planning. An able team, largely of university professors under the leadership of Raymond Moley, helped devise policies and draft speeches for him. Newspapermen dubbed this group of advisers the "Brain Trust." At the Commonwealth Club in San Francisco, Roosevelt broke furthest from the past by insisting that the government must assist business in developing a well regulated economic system. Everyone, he said, had a right to a comfortable living; the nation's industrial and agricultural mechanism could produce enough for everyone with some to spare. If need be, to achieve this end, government must police irresponsible economic power. Roosevelt felt he was doing no more than to restate the objectives of Jefferson and Wilson in terms of the complexities of the thirties when he proposed that government should act as a regulator for the common good within the existing economic system. So far as Roosevelt explained the New Deal during the campaign, this was its essence.

President Hoover, tired and grim, took to the road in October to warn the populace that without his program things might be infinitely worse. His speeches, though earnest, were dull and dreary in both style and delivery compared with Roosevelt's breezy, optimistic performances. Hoover was the last of the Presidents to scorn the aid of speechwriters.

Some voters, disappointed because they could detect little difference between Roosevelt's program and Hoover's, turned to Norman Thomas and the Socialists or to William Z. Foster and the Communists. Yet, even in this year of despair, the Socialists polled only 882,000 votes, and the Communists only 103,000. Roosevelt received 22,822,000 popular votes, or 57.4 percent, to 15,762,000, or 39.7 percent, for Hoover; he carried the electoral college 472 to 92. The Democrats carried both houses of Congress by top-heavy majorities. Roosevelt had won an overwhelming mandate – but for what?

Actually, there had been discernible differences between the two candidates and their programs – besides the obvious difference that Hoover was a worn, discredited President, and Roosevelt a buoyant candidate. Hoover had seen the depression as world-wide in origin and development; he was ready to combat it internationally through currency stabilization. Roosevelt chose to regard the depression as domestic, specifically Republican, in origin. During the campaign Hoover had forced him to equivocate on the old Democratic low-tariff position; Roosevelt was ready (as both his record as governor and his speeches indicated) to move toward economic nationalism. Like Hoover, he believed in economy and a balanced budget, although these would run contrary to his advocacy of social and economic planning. Unlike Hoover, he was so far from being doctrinaire that inconsistencies in his program would bother him little.

The Interregnum

President Hoover faced an agonizing four months before Roosevelt would take office on March 4: Norris' Twentieth ("lame duck") Amendment to end this long carryover of a defeated President and Congress was not ratified until February 1933. As the economy plummeted once again, Hoover ascribed the drop to lack of business confidence in the incoming President. There was a brief economic upswing in the spring months of 1932, reaching a peak in July, as the Federal Reserve relaxed its policies. But then gold resumed its outward flow

because investors expected Roosevelt to devalue the dollar, and the Federal Reserve resumed a tight-money policy. Hoover felt he was bringing an end to the depression and that only the threat of unsettling measures from Roosevelt was preventing continued recovery. Hence, in a series of interchanges with Roosevelt during the winter of 1932–1933, he tried to bind the President-elect to economic orthodoxy.

The first negotiations were over the question of European debts. Both Hoover and Roosevelt opposed cancellation, but Hoover wished to use the debts as a lever to reestablish an international gold standard. Tied in with this was the proposed International Economic and Monetary Conference, which Hoover hoped would restore financial stability. Roosevelt would make no commitments.

By February 1933 an acute banking crisis had developed. Bank resources and deposits had been declining at an alarming rate. In the previous three years, 5,000 banks had failed, and now one after another was collapsing as depositors lined up to withdraw their deposits. To prevent failures, governors began proclaiming banking holidays in their states, beginning with Michigan on February 14. By March 4 banking was at a halt or drastically restricted in all states but one.

President Hoover penned a lengthy longhand letter to Roosevelt, charging that the crisis was due to "steadily degenerating confidence" in the President-elect, and calling upon him to give prompt public assurance that there would be no tinkering with the currency, no heavy borrowing, and a balanced budget. Roosevelt had not the slightest intention of adopting Hoover's views.

Sources of the Great Depression

The depression shook the faith of Americans in their economic system and convinced many, including most of the economists who came of age during the depression, that the economy contained fundamental flaws that, unless remedied, made serious depressions inevitable. However, their conviction reflected only the terrible contrast between the 1920s and the early part of the 1930s. The unusual severity of the depression resulted not from fundamental flaws but from the failure of government officials to use effectively the instruments of stabilization at their disposal, particularly those of the Federal Reserve system; from the public's primitive understanding of the economy, which focused almost exclusively on the vagaries of the stock market; and from the distortions that World War I had created in agriculture and the international economy. These were all serious problems, but they were not fundamental to the economy and therefore were problems that would yield to moderate reforms. Herbert Hoover had launched those reforms. But because he remained loyal to the Federal Reserve system and to the international gold standard and because he was unable to command public confidence and enthusiasm, he failed to move the nation decisively on the path of recovery. That role fell to Franklin Roosevelt.

F. D. R. Takes Command

When Roosevelt was inaugurated, on March 4, 1933, most of the nation's banks were closed. At least 13 million people were unemployed, some of them so close to starvation that they were scrabbling for food scraps on garbage dumps. Millions of farmers were on the brink of foreclosure; many others had fallen over the brink.

In his inaugural address, President Roosevelt spoke with vigor and confidence. "This great Nation will endure as it has endured, will revive and will prosper," he declared. "So, first of all, let me assert my firm belief that the only thing we have to fear is fear itself." Somehow these words, although they said nothing new, helped inspire the American people. From their depths of helplessness they were ready to be commanded, and in Roosevelt they saw someone ready to take strong leadership. Such leadership he promised. If Congress did not act, he announced, he would ask for "broad executive power to wage a war against the emergency, as great as the power that would be given to me if we were in fact invaded by a foreign foe."

Few Presidents have been better trained for the White House. Roosevelt had served in the New York state senate, been wartime assistant secretary of the navy, and had been twice elected governor of New York. He was skilled in both legislative and administrative techniques as well as in practical politics. As a youth he had spent much time in Europe and maintained a continuing interest in foreign affairs. Roosevelt's ideology was progressive, influenced by his wife's uncle, Theodore Roosevelt, whom he adored, and his former chief, Woodrow Wilson, whom he revered.

Neither he nor his advisers were clear-cut in their thinking. What was important was that Roosevelt, while basically rooted in the older economics and the social-justice tradition of the progressives, was ready to experiment. His program would be flexible, not doctrinaire; the new economic theories would grow from it, not it from the theories. When one of the brain trusters warned of perils ahead, Roosevelt declared:

"There is nothing to do but meet every day's troubles as they come."

With the banking crisis at its height, he might well have taken drastic steps, but the American people would not have long tolerated them. The background of Roosevelt was such that he resorted to only the mildest of expedients.

Cautious Beginnings

During his first days as President, Roosevelt seemed bent above all upon restoring the confidence of businessmen. His initial program differed little from what they had been advocating. He met the banking crisis in a manner pleasing to the banking community. He issued a proclamation on March 6, 1933, closing all banks and stopping transactions or exports in gold for four days until Congress could meet in special session. On March 9, he sent in a conservative bill that would bolster the stronger banks. It authorized the Federal Reserve system to issue notes against their assets, and the Reconstruction Finance Corporation to make them loans. The bill dealt a death blow to weaker banks; inspectors would deny them licenses to reopen. It stopped the ebb of gold from the Treasury and from the country through prohibiting hoarding and exportation. Congress passed the bill within four hours of its introduction.

On March 12, in the first of his "fireside chats" over the radio, the President, speaking in a warm, intimate manner, told the American people that the crisis was over. And so indeed it was; by this simple legislation and his confident leadership, Roosevelt had averted the threat to banks and the capitalist system. Three-fourths of the banks in the Federal Reserve system reopened within the next three days; a billion dollars in hoarded currency and gold flowed back into them within a month. During the next two years the RFC loaned a billion dollars to shaky banks; the Treasury Department refused to license another 1,772 of them. Practically all unsafe banks were out of business; altogether the crisis had closed a total of 2,352. There were

THE NATURE OF THE NEW DEAL

Denouncing the New Dealers, former President Herbert Hoover once said they professed the "three Rs" of Relief, Recovery, and Reform but secretly espoused the "fourth R" of Revolution. How revolutionary was the New Deal in fact? To what extent did it break with the American past? Historians have given a wide variety of answers to these questions.

Some authors maintained that the New Deal was more evolutionary than revolutionary, that in essence it was an extension of the progressive movement. In *The History of the New Deal* (1944) Basil Rauch made a distinction between a "first" and a "second" New Deal. The first (1933–1935), rather conservative, concentrated on recovery as the chief aim and gave aid mostly to big business and big agriculture. The second (1935–1938), relatively liberal, paid more attention to reform and provided more benefits to industrial workers and small farmers. In *Rendezvous with Destiny* (1952) Eric F. Goldman saw the first phase as similar to Theodore Roosevelt's New Nationalism, the second as reminiscent of Woodrow Wilson's New Freedom, though Goldman thought "there was something more to New Deal liberalism," since it included such unprecedented measures as social security. But William E. Leuchtenburg, in *Franklin D. Roosevelt and the New Deal, 1932–1940* (1963), felt that the extent of the leftward shift had been exaggerated.

Other writers emphasized the elements of change rather than those of continuity. Richard Hofstadter, *The Age of Reform* (1955), conceded that there were continuities from progressivism but insisted that, as a whole, the Franklin D. Roosevelt program was a "drastic new departure" and was "different from anything that had yet happened in the United States." Hofstadter pointed out that many old progressives, still living in the 1930s, opposed the New Deal. Carl N. Degler, *Out of Our Past* (1959), called the New Deal the "Third American Revolution" (the first two being the Revolution of 1776 and the Civil War) and said it "marked the crossing of a divide from which, it would seem, there could be no turning back."

All the foregoing historians thought of themselves as liberals and, though in some respects critical, were basically sympathetic with Roosevelt and his program. A conservative, anti-Roosevelt historian, Edgar E. Robinson, considered the New Deal a sharp break with the past but deplored it. In *The Roosevelt Leadership, 1933–1945* (1955) Robinson complained that Roosevelt, "an eloquent proponent of revolutionary change," moved the country toward "many of the primary leveling objectives of communism."

Young radicals of the 1960s took just the opposite view. Concerned about the unsolved problems of their own generation, they criticized the New Deal for having preserved too many of the evils of capitalism. "Many millions — businessmen, professionals, unionized workingmen, commercial farmers — had been given substantial help," the New Left historian Howard Zinn wrote in his introduction to *New Deal Thought* (1966). "Many millions more — sharecroppers, slum-dwellers, Negroes of North and South, the unemployed — still awaited a genuine 'new deal.'"

very few new failures in the years that followed.

On the morning after the passage of the Emergency Banking Act, Roosevelt further reassured business by sending Congress an economy bill, to balance the budget by cutting salaries of government employees and pensions of veterans as much as 15 percent. This bill too passed almost instantly, though pressure from veterans soon caused Congress to rescind the pension cuts. Roosevelt also induced Congress to legalize beer of 3.2 percent alcoholic content, pending repeal of the prohibition amendment. This, he felt, would stimulate recovery and bring in needed tax revenue. It would also rescue millions of law violators from the hazards of home-brew and gangster-made beer.

Thus far, the Roosevelt program had done little more than improve the confidence of bankers, businessmen, and the public generally. Roosevelt, political expert that he was, knew the psychological moment was at hand for pushing a more comprehensive program through Congress. He decided to keep Congress in session, and during the next hundred-odd days a remarkable array of laws came forth. The New Deal began to take form.

Emergency Relief

The first step was to feed the millions of hungry unemployed. While Roosevelt subscribed to his predecessor's maxim that relief was primarily the task of states and communities, he proposed that the federal government provide grants rather than loans to states. Congress established the Federal Emergency Relief Administration, and appropriated an initial half-billion dollars for it. Roosevelt appointed the director of the New York state relief agency, Harry Hopkins, whom he hardly knew as yet, to run the federal program. Hopkins was a dedicated social worker with a lively tongue and a keen sense of professional ethics. He ardently believed in work relief rather than direct relief, but in the spring of 1933 everyone hoped recovery was at hand so that relief would be needed only for a few months.

But recovery lagged, and some new way had to be found to care for the unemployed through the winter of 1933–1934. Relief administrator Hopkins persuaded the President to establish a temporary work relief program, the Civil Works Administration. Between November and April it put 4 million people to work at emergency projects. Sometimes it was made-work like leaf raking, to which critics applied an old Texas term, "boondoggling." Some of the projects, despite lack of funds for materials and tools, made substantial improvements. The output was of secondary importance; the work raised the morale

of the unemployed and increased their buying power by $950 million. The purchasing power thus injected into the economy contributed to the beginnings of recovery, as the index of production rose from 71 in November 1933 to 86 in May 1934. But soon Roosevelt capitulated to fierce conservative criticism and liquidated the program.

Congress also created an organization that reflected Roosevelt's keen interest in perserving natural as well as human resources, the Civilian Conservation Corps. It received a grant of $300 million to enroll 250,000 young men from relief families and 50,000 veterans and woodsmen, to work at reforestation and flood control. Ultimately the CCC enrolled 500,000 young men, but this was only a fraction of the unemployed youths in the nation.

Mortgage relief was a pressing need of millions of farm owners and home owners. Roosevelt quickly consolidated all farm credit organizations into a new Farm Credit Administration. Congress voted such large additional funds for it that within two years it had refinanced a fifth of all farm mortgages in the United States. The Frazier-Limke Farm-Bankruptcy Act of 1933 enabled some farmers to regain their farms even after the foreclosure of mortgages. But these measures came too late to save all farmers; by 1934 a quarter of them for one reason or another had lost their property. A comparable Home Owners' Loan Corporation, established in June 1933, in a three-year period loaned $3 billion to refinance the mortgages of over a million distressed householders. Altogether it carried about a sixth of the nation's urban mortgage burden. A year later Congress established a Federal Housing Administration to insure mortgages for new construction and home repairs — more properly a recovery than a relief agency. All these mortgage agencies not only rescued mortgage holders, but also eased the burden on banks and insurance companies, thus filling a recovery function.

Under the New Deal, the Reconstruction Finance Corporation continued to function as the key loan agency for relief to business. The Democratic Congress inveighed against the RFC policy of making large loans only to big businesses and not to individuals. Congress therefore broadened the RFC's lending power so that it could, and indeed did, also lend to small businessmen. Under the conservative management of a shrewd Texan, Jesse Jones, it continued to make most of its loans to large enterprises, including banks, and to governmental units, on sound security and with a high percentage of ultimate repayment.

The First AAA

The Agricultural Adjustment Administration, created in May 1933, marked the triumphant conclusion of the farmers' long struggle to get government aid for raising farm prices. Henceforth the farmers, who continued to be a declining fraction of the whole population, received preferential treatment from the government.

Roosevelt was mainly interested in the relatively substantial, more commercial farmers, such as the 300,000 who even in 1933 were paying dues of $10 a year or more to the Farm Bureau Federation. These and the Grange members desired a program to limit crops. Poorer members of other farm organizations like the Farmers Union and the National Farmers' Holiday Association opposed production cuts, seeking instead direct relief and, above all, inflation. Roosevelt hoped to develop a program that would fit the Farm Bureau formula and yet would not drive poorer farmers into new revolt. He let the various farm organization leaders devise their own plan. Fifty of them met in Washington early in March 1933 and drafted an omnibus bill that contained scraps and reworkings of most of the old schemes but it moved toward the production controls that had been lacking in both McNary-Haugenism and Hoover's schemes. It provided for a "domestic-allotment" system. Producers of seven basic commodities (wheat, cotton, corn, hogs, rice, tobacco, and milk and dairy products) were to receive benefit payments if they cut acreage or production. Funds for these payments would come from a tax upon the processing of commodities—for example, a tax on the milling of wheat. The tax would be added to the price of the flour or other product, and so it would be passed on to the consumer, who would thus indirectly pay the farmer for growing less. Farm prices were to be brought up to "parity," that is, a level that would provide the same price relationship of farm products to manufactured goods as during the period 1909–1914.

Because the 1933 farm season was well under way when the AAA began operations, large-scale destruction was necessary to cut surpluses. Six million pigs and 220,000 sows about to farrow were slaughtered. Nine-tenths of their weight was inedible and processed into fertilizer, but they nevertheless provided 100 million pounds of pork for needy families. Bad weather so drastically cut the wheat crop that the AAA did not have to intervene to reduce it. Cotton farmers plowed under a quarter of their crop—but it was the poorest quarter and they so intensively cultivated the rest that 30 million acres produced more than 36 million had done the previous year.

Despite continued high cotton production, a short textile boom sent the price up from 5.5 cents per pound to 10.6 cents in the summer. Then the price began to sag again and was held to 9.6 cents only through another device. A subsidiary of the AAA, the Commodity Credit Corporation, loaned 10 cents per pound to cotton farmers who would agree to take additional land out of production the next year. Since the loan was in excess of the market value of cotton, the government in effect was buying the crop at a premium price in return for the promise of drastic cuts in production. In this way cotton farmers received double the cash in 1933 than they had in 1931.

Farmers in other crop-reduction programs did not fare as well, although corn producers too could obtain commodity loans in the fall of 1933. Drought more than crop limitations reduced the output of wheat, corn, and hogs. Rising prices of manufactured goods canceled out most of the farmer's gain in real income. Yet on the whole his relative position improved somewhat.

The AAA actually hurt many of the farmers on the least productive farms, especially in the cotton belt. At times the AAA indirectly dispossessed them because planters, in reducing their acreage, sometimes evicted tenants and fired field hands. Unintentionally the AAA stimulated the great migration away from sharecropper cabins, at a time when city jobs no longer awaited the migrants. Rapid mechanization of farms and destructive wind storms on the Great Plains gave the great migration its impetus.

The NRA

Hard-pressed businessmen sought measures providing for government stabilization of business. Since 1931 leaders of the United States Chamber of Commerce and others had been urging an antideflation scheme that involved price fixing through trade associations. This plan would have necessitated suspension of the anti-trust laws. President Hoover, who earlier had given strong support to the trade association movement, indignantly opposed price-fixing schemes. His attorney general forced five leading trade associations to dissolve, and the Federal Trade Commission compelled revision of the trade association codes for sixty-two industries.

In the spring of 1933 businessmen sought from Roosevelt what Hoover had refused them. Many of them also demanded government enforcement of their agreements in order to raise prices and stabilize production. The New Deal was ready to give them what they wanted if they would accept wages-and-hours regulation and other concessions for labor. As a consequence of such an arrangement, prices and wages would go up but consumers' buying power might lag and thus defeat the scheme. Therefore the New Dealers drafting the great recovery bill added another ingredient for which there was much pressure: a large-scale public works spending program to prime the economic pump. This was the genesis of the National Industrial Recovery Act, which passed Congress in June 1933.

A new era of government alliance with business for the common good seemed to be opening. Roosevelt as he signed the act called it "the most important and far-reaching legislation ever enacted by the American Congress." On the same day, the President appointed as administrator the volatile, colorful General Hugh S. Johnson, who pictured himself as a sort of benign dictator presiding over the economy.

The President turned over the $3.3 billion for public works to Secretary of the Interior Harold L. Ickes, who slowly and methodically began to gather plans for projects, checking each carefully to make sure it would be really worthwhile. The need was for heavy spending in the next few months, but it was four years before Ickes' Public Works Administration pumped appreciable amounts of money into the economy.

President Roosevelt and NRA administrator Johnson called upon an excited nation to accept an interim blanket code, providing minimum wages of 30 cents or 40 cents an hour, maximum working hours of thirty-five or forty per week, and the abolition of child labor. Employers who agreed with the code were to display the NRA

blue-eagle symbol; consumers who cooperated were to sign pledges that they would buy only from blue-eagle establishments. In much the spirit of 1917, the nation participated in NRA parades and rallies. As Johnson began negotiating codes with big industries, recovery seemed really imminent.

By the beginning of September 1933, specific codes for most of the big industries were in operation. In the drafting of the codes, Johnson had tried to serve as arbiter to balance the conflicting interests of business, labor, and the consumer. All three were represented at the bargaining table and received some degree of protection. Nevertheless, the real power in drawing up the regulations went to the businessmen themselves, to the leaders within each industry. They flocked to Washington and in the urgency of the moment rewrote their old trade association agreements into new NRA codes. These codes often contained provisions that were difficult for small units in the industry to maintain. Most of them provided for limiting production and, though often in disguised form, for price fixing.

End of the NRA

Production, after a sharp rise, skidded downward during the fall of 1933, from an index figure of 101 in July to 71 in November, even as prices began to creep upward. The brave words and great NRA demonstrations of the spring and summer had not brought sustained recovery. The New Deal honeymoon was over, and as General Johnson had predicted, the dead cats began to fly.

In the spring of 1934 a National Recovery Review Board under the famous iconoclastic lawyer Clarence Darrow reported that the NRA was dominated by big business; he hinted that what was needed was socialism. In the ensuing storm of vituperation between Johnson and Darrow, the NRA lost still more prestige and, most critically, the confidence of Roosevelt.

A case involving the National Recovery Administration finally reached the Supreme Court. The constitutional basis for the NRA was the power of Congress to regulate commerce among the states, but the test case involved alleged code violations by the Schechter brothers, who were operating a wholesale poultry business confined to one locality, Brooklyn. Among the charges against them were the selling of poultry in poor condition and the unfair treatment of employees. The Court (1935) unanimously held that the Schechters were not engaged in interstate commerce, and that Congress had unconstitutionally delegated legislative power to the President to draft the codes.

The "sick chicken" decision outraged Roosevelt. Seeing in it a threat to the whole New Deal, he lashed out at the judges for thinking in terms of the horse-and-buggy era. Actually, the decision proved to be more a blessing than a catastrophe for the New Deal, since it ended the decrepit NRA code system with its tacit suspension of the antitrust laws. "It has been an awful headache," Roosevelt confessed privately.

TVA and Conservation

Increasingly New Dealers turned their attention to measures that would remedy conditions they felt had helped bring on the depression. Their indignation burned especially hot against the private power interests, which they felt had gulled investors and overcharged consumers. The spectacular collapse of the great Insull utility empire in the Middle West lent credence to their charges. Hence the first and most far-reaching of the New Deal reform measures was the creation of the Tennessee Valley Authority.

Through the twenties, millions of progressive Americans of both parties had shared the dream of Senator George Norris of Nebraska that the government might develop the nation's great water resources to provide cheap electric power. Millions of others accepted the educational program of the utilities companies, which spent $28 million to $35 million per year combating the idea of a national power program. The battle centered on the great dam that had been started at Muscle Shoals on the Tennessee River but had not been finished in time to provide nitrates during the war. Coolidge and the conservatives wished to sell it to Henry Ford for private development. Norris and his cohorts in Congress blocked them. Norris wished to make Muscle Shoals the center for developing the resources of the area and bringing abundance to millions of people living in poverty. His bill was vetoed by Coolidge and again by Hoover but was approved by Roosevelt in May 1933.

Basically, the TVA aimed to prevent the devastating floods that all too frequently had rolled down the rivers of the area, and to provide cheap, plentiful electricity as a yardstick for the measurement of private rates. More than this, the project became a great experiment in regional planning and rehabilitation.

Under a three-man board of directors with wide powers, the TVA in the next twenty years improved five existing dams and constructed twenty new ones. It stopped floods in the largest heavy-rainfall region in the nation and, by holding back the water, provided an inland waterway system with a nine-foot channel 652 miles long, soon heavy with traffic. From water power, and increasingly from steam plants, the TVA became the greatest producer of electricity in the United States. It also manufactured low-cost phosphate fertilizers. It taught farmers how to use them, how to restore the fertility of their soil, and how to end erosion by means of contour plowing and reforestation. TVA worked no miracles, but it did bring a higher living standard to the farmers of the area. It brought new light industry and increased business. When World War II came, the new power plants provided indispensable electricity for the production of munitions, aluminum, and plutonium.

In its "yardstick" function, TVA drove down the price of power in the area from 10 cents a kilowatt hour to 3 cents. Throughout the country, because of TVA and other pressures, the average residential rate dropped from 5.52 cents in 1933 to 3.67 cents in 1942. To private power companies the "yardstick" seemed grossly unfair, and they claimed that the TVA did not set its rates on the basis of true costs, including taxes. Its officials replied that its payments to local and state governments were comparable to the taxes assessed against private power companies.

Other great public power and irrigation developments were under way in the West during the same years. On the Colorado River, the Hoover Dam (begun during the Hoover administration) was finished in 1936, and on the Columbia River the Bonneville Dam was constructed in 1937 and the Grand Coulee Dam in 1942. In 1937 Norris proposed the creation of six additional regional authorities like the TVA; Congress failed to act, and the debate over public versus private development of power continued.

To combat drought conditions in the West, Roosevelt in 1934 by executive order set aside

$15 million to build a "shelter belt" of trees on the Great Plains, to break the wind, collect moisture, and harbor wildlife. Critics scoffed, but somehow the trees grew where no one had believed they would. A Soil Erosion Service (later Soil Conservation Service), using much Civilian Conservation Corps manpower, was active, especially in the West. Homesteading on the range, which meant dry-farming under almost insuperable difficulties, came to an end with the passage of the Taylor Grazing Act of 1934, which withdrew overgrazed land and set regulations for the use of public rangeland. Spoliation of Indian lands came to at least a temporary halt with the passage of the Indian Reorganization Act of 1934, intended to preserve the tribal domain, customs, and civil liberties of the Indians.

Money and Banking

Much of the early New Deal was aimed at raising prices as a means of stimulating recovery. One way was to cut down production, as the AAA tried to do for agriculture and the NRA for industry. Another way was to put money into circulation through government spending, as was done in the relief programs (though recovery was not the primary aim of these). Still another way was to increase the money supply.

As a result of a variety of programs the money supply increased at the rapid rate of almost 11 percent per year between April 1933 and March 1937. Many economists now see that expansion as the critical factor in explaining the exceptionally rapid rate of economic recovery that occurred during the same period. During those four years the annual rate of increase in gross national product was 12 percent; the nation has never had a four-year period during peacetime with such rapid growth of national product.

The New Deal's promotion of monetary expansion began as a program of banking reform. In June 1933, following the bank holiday and the Emergency Banking Act, Roosevelt signed the Glass-Steagall Act aimed at curbing speculation by banks. This bill also established the Federal Deposit Insurance Corporation, which for the first time insured depositors against bank collapse, making them more willing to put their funds in the custody of banks. With increased deposits banks were able to expand their loan

activities. To prevent the kind of errors by the Federal Reserve that had produced severe monetary contraction between 1931 and 1933, Roosevelt engineered passage of the Banking Act of 1935, which centralized control of the system in the hands of the Federal Reserve Board and moved the Board's locus of power from New York to Washington so that it would be more responsive to the desires of politicians. Chastened by the strength of their opponents, between 1933 and 1937 the Federal Reserve abstained from any actions that might restrict monetary expansion.

The restraint of the Federal Reserve system permitted Roosevelt to stimulate rapid monetary growth. In May 1933 Congress authorized the President to reduce the gold content of the dollar by as much as 50 percent. From November 1933 through January 1934 Roosevelt kept the announced price of gold, in terms of dollars, higher than the price abroad. The subsequent Gold Reserve Act of 1934 made his devaluation official by fixing a buying and selling price for gold of $35 an ounce rather than the $21 an ounce adhered to formerly. (Also, this act modified the gold standard by permitting the selling of gold only for foreign payments.) The new gold price provided a bonanza for foreigners holding gold and for world gold production because the pegged price was substantially higher than the world price. Consequently both gold production and the importation of gold into the United States soared, the stock in Fort Knox more than tripling between early 1934 and the end of 1940. Correspondingly, currency paid out for gold imports underwent a large increase, this provided a massive growth in the nation's money supply, which stimulated loan activity, encouraged the upward movement of prices, broke the deflationary psychology that had prevailed until 1933, and unleashed the forces of production. If Roosevelt and Congress had allowed the Federal Reserve to be independent in the 1930s and if the system had adhered to its earlier policies, it would have taken action to cut off the large influx of gold and thus forcefully inhibited economic expansion.

Expression and Escape

Both the depression and the government's efforts to combat it left a mark on the cultural life of the time. Unemployment left many people with unaccustomed leisure, which they used either to protest against or to escape from unpleasant realities. The federal government became a patron and promoter of culture on a scale it had never attempted before.

Even before the establishment of the Federal Art Project, which eventually enrolled 5,000 persons, the government had aided artists through an earlier relief project and the commissioning of extensive murals for new public buildings. Some of these artists expressed leftist themes comparable to those of the highly popular Mexican muralists. Many turned their attention, sometimes satirically, to the American scene. This was the heyday of Grant Wood, with his patterned Iowa landscapes and austere rural portraits, and of Thomas Hart Benton, who with dramatic sympathy portrayed sharecroppers and Negroes. In sculpture, responding to the new government aid and the resurgent nationalism, Gutzon Borglum finished the enormous heads of Washington, Jefferson, Lincoln, and Theodore Roosevelt that were carved on a rocky mountainside in the Black Hills. Altogether, thousands of artists and sculptors worked during the depression years; never before had America possessed so many who were competent and promising.

Appreciation of the arts took a strong upturn, partly through art classes sponsored by the Federal Art Project, partly through the opening of new art museums. In 1941, the National Art Gallery in Washington opened, displaying collections of European art valued at $35 million, the gift of Andrew W. Mellon. Samuel H. Kress added 400 Italian paintings. More people than ever before visited galleries and bought reproductions of the old masters and of the French impressionists, especially Vincent Van Gogh.

Although jazz more than held its own, interest in classical music increased. The Federal Music Project employed 15,000 persons. They brought concerts to 100 million people and gave free music lessons to over a half-million pupils, most of whom could have afforded neither concerts nor lessons. Much of the music they played was that of American composers, such as Roy Harris' Third Symphony, and Aaron Copland's *Music for the Theatre*. Through new high-quality radio receivers and recordings, many additional millions listened to fine music, especially the symphony broadcasts conducted by Arturo Toscanini and the Metropolitan Opera performances. In 1940 listeners contributed over $300,000 to help "save the Met." Many millions more mourned the death in 1937 of young George Gershwin, composer of *Porgy and Bess* and *Rhapsody in Blue*. To the great mass of Americans, music still meant either sweet popular songs played by bands like Guy Lombardo's, or jazz like Benny Goodman's, which came surging back into favor in 1934.

After depression and competition from motion pictures had thrown most actors and old vaudeville performers out of employment, the Federal Theatre Project found employment for 12,500 of them. It brought performances to millions who had never previously seen a stage production. Some of these were highly successful as entertainment, some were of an advanced experimental nature, and some were so far to the left that they kindled the wrath of Congress, which killed the project in 1939. Many of the Broadway playwrights, impervious to congressional hostility, also took a critical look at social problems, as did Lillian Hellman in *The Little Foxes*. Robert E. Sherwood, who illustrated another trend, stopped writing light comedies and dramatized the impotence of the intellectual (*The Petrified Forest*, 1936) and the menace of war (*Idiot's Delight*, 1936). Later, in the pressure of world events, he reversed themes, and glorified the intellectual fighting totalitarian aggression (*There Shall Be No Night*, 1940). Meanwhile, Thornton Wilder wrote *Our Town* (1938) and Eugene O'Neill, who in 1936 won a Nobel Prize, labored quietly on a long-continuing cycle of plays.

Novelists likewise divided into those who, like William Faulkner, seemed to be largely unaffected by the era, and others like Ernest Hemingway, who paralleled Sherwood's cycle from 1929 (*A Farewell to Arms*) to 1940 (*For Whom the Bell Tolls*). Thomas Wolfe richly and poetically portrayed the world swirling around him, in his *Of Time and the River* (1935) and his posthumous *You Can't Go Home Again* (1940). Many other novelists turned out proletarian themes from Marxist molds. John Steinbeck sentimentalized his suffering protagonists in his best-selling novel about the Oklahoman trek to California, *The Grapes of Wrath* (1939). The lure of romantic escape and the bargain of the sheer bulk helped make best-sellers of Hervey Allen's *Anthony Adverse* (1933) and Margaret Mitchell's *Gone With the Wind* (1936).

Reading was one of the most inexpensive pursuits of the depression years, and although libraries suffered from slashed funds, book circulation increased considerably. Depression likewise cut the cost of radios and enlarged the size of audiences. In 1929 12 million families owned radios; by 1940 28 million families, comprising 86 percent of the population, owned them. This in part explains why Roosevelt, the master of the radio "fireside chat," campaigned so successfully with at least 70 percent of the metropolitan newspaper circulation opposing him. A radio serial, *Amos and Andy,* was so popular that Huey Long took the name of one its characters, the Kingfish, as his sobriquet. Motion picture audiences dropped one-third early in the depression, then by 1939 boomed to a yearly box-office average of $25 per family. Like radio serials, motion pictures dispensed mostly escapist themes — because of the vigor of the Catholic-led Legion of Decency, founded in 1934, it was a less sexy escape than in the twenties. Theaters also dispensed two movies rather than one and offered give-aways of a wide variety in order to bolster the box office. As yet, the coming threat to the movies, television, was still in the engineering laboratory — a curiosity exhibited at the New York World's Fair of 1939. It was too expensive for commercial development during the depression.

Education and the Professions

The two depression factors of lack of funds and excess of leisure also operated in education. It was estimated in 1935 that one-third of the unemployed were young people. Many went to school for lack of an alternative, and high school enrollment increased by one-third between 1929 and 1935. In spite of this, economy-minded chambers of commerce and citizens' committees led a drive for cuts so deep that they carved out educational sinew along with the fat. Colleges and universities dropped in enrollment until 1935, then more than recuperated but continued to suffer budgetary crises. Vocational education was strongly emphasized on both the high school and the college level. Serious students explored social and economic questions so energetically that frightened civic and patriotic organizations warned that "pinks" were taking over the educational systems.

Alarmists feared pinks were taking over the churches also, for ministers responded as enthusiastically to the new demands for human welfare as they once had responded to the "social gospel." Of 20,000 ministers polled in 1934, nearly one-third favored socialism, and three-fifths, a "drastically reformed capitalism." The main intellectual current among ministers was toward neoorthodoxy. Reinhold Neibuhr, without disavowing political and social liberalism, found powerful psychological pressures driving man toward sin, from which man could be rescued only by faith, that is, submission to God.

Though the depression seriously cut funds for medical research, the thirties were another decade of advance in medical knowledge. Ironically, by 1935, when the American Medical Association was warning that 20 million people were suffering from malnutrition or were close to it, highly publicized discoveries in vitamin research were leading the well-fed to consume a variety of vitamin-fortified foods and to swallow vitamin pills in quantities second only to laxatives. Sulfa drugs, typhus vaccine, blood plasma, and the "artificial lung" all came into use. Life expectancy increased from fifty-six years in 1920 to sixty-four in 1940, but malnutrition, illness, and sometimes lack of good medical care wrought a heavy toll during the depression. Army medical examiners rejected almost half of the first 2 million young men the Selective Service called up in 1940–1941.

Yet doctors were ill-paid (even in 1929 half of them netted less than $3,000) and were idle much of the time. When some relief units and the Farm Security Administration offered medical aid to the destitute, the demand was overwhelming. Senator Wagner in 1938 introduced a national health bill, but it met stern opposition from the American Medical Association. Voluntary group health and hospitalization plans spread rapidly in some sixty cities and gained 3 million or more subscribers.

While scientists suffered temporary cuts in research funds, university budgets and industrial resources for research were back at a peak level by 1936; federal expenditures, by 1940. Thus the decade was one of increasing scientific investigation. The need for reorganization and reinvigoration of some of the government's scientific agencies led to the creation in 1933 of a Science Advisory Board, which tried without success to obtain a New Deal for science. In 1935 the National Resources Committee (succeeding several similar planning agencies) took over the problem and prepared a study, *Research—A National Resource* (1940). The way was being prepared for centralized scientific planning in the future.

The thirties were years of marked scientific achievement in both basic and applied research in many fields. A series of discoveries by men of many nationalities opened the way to the possibility of nuclear fission. In 1931 Harold C. Urey of Columbia discovered a heavy isotope of hydrogen—deuterium—which, combined with oxygen atoms, formed heavy water. Bombardment of deuterium atoms by various types of atom smashers brought new knowledge about the nature of the atom, knowledge that could lead to revolutionary applications. Science, a neglected stepchild of the New Deal, was to become the nation's savior in time of war.

Chapter 25. THE SECOND NEW DEAL

A Shift to the Left

Though President Roosevelt originally wished to provide for the welfare of each of the main economic and political groups in the nation, realities forced him to become the champion of the new political coalition of farmers, laborers, and the underprivileged in general. Roosevelt shifted partly because he felt that large business had defected, that it had betrayed his recovery program and was fighting politically to destroy the New Deal. Aligned against him were about 70 percent of the newspaper publishers and most of the large contributors of campaign funds.

Far more important was the threat from the left; this was mainly responsible for the gradual change in emphasis of the New Deal. In undermining this threat, Roosevelt's political pragmatism combined with his humanitarian inclinations to carry him even farther than the progressives had dared venture toward positive government action for the general welfare.

The Pressure of Politics

Through 1934 the President was still trying to hold the support of businessmen and bankers. As late as October he told the American Bankers' Association: "The time is ripe for an alliance of all forces intent upon the business of recovery. In such an alliance will be found business and banking, agriculture and industry, and labor and capital. What an all-American team that would be!" There was little chance of it. In August 1934 conservative businessmen and self-styled Jeffersonian Democrats founded the American Liberty League to fight for free enterprise, state rights, the open shop, and an end to New Deal bureaucracy.

As the congressional elections of 1934 approached, conservatives within the Liberty League and without campaigned against the New Deal on the grounds that it was destroying the Constitution and driving the country toward

bankruptcy. All they succeeded in doing was to drive the dispossessed millions closer to the New Deal. Instead of losing ground to the Republican party — which would have been normal in a midterm election — the Democrats gained an additional ten seats in the Senate and also in the House.

Throughout the nation leaders arose who promised much to those despairing people whom the New Deal had not yet rescued. An elderly physician in California, Dr. Francis E. Townsend, attracted a following of 5 million destitute old people with his plan to obtain a federal pension of $200 per month for everyone over sixty. This would have cost nearly half the national income. The Townsendites claimed, however, that since the pensions would have had to be spent within the month, "the velocity of money" would have ended the depression. The immediate realities of the movement were that its promoters raised nearly a million dollars in two years and commanded a formidable bloc of votes.

Among restless people in Northern cities, Father Charles Coughlin's politico-religious broadcasts attracted a wide following. Starting with a mixture of Papal encyclicals and Populism, he at first supported, then went far beyond, Roosevelt. Coughlin advocated expansion of silver coinage and nationalization of banks, utilities, and natural resources. Ultimately in 1938 he founded the antidemocratic, anti-Semitic Christian Front. In January 1935 he was able to demonstrate his power by inspiring an avalanche of letters and telegrams to senators protesting against the World Court. His program was vague, but the discontent he was able to tap was concrete.

From the South, Senator Huey P. Long of Louisiana succeeded in launching a far more telling assault upon the New Deal. A skillful politician, he built a powerful organization in Louisiana and a rapidly growing following that spilled out first into neighboring states, then by 1935 into the Middle West, the Pacific Coast, and indeed every part of the country. Within Louisiana, he had delighted his poverty-stricken supporters by immobilizing their traditional enemies through his strong-armed techniques. Within the state, he built bridges, roads, hospitals, and a modern educational system. It was an era of dictators in Europe, and it was easy to assail the self-styled Louisiana Kingfish with ambitions to be a Fuehrer, although his techniques were the time-honored ones of the American political boss. Ambitious to become President, he lured the masses by offering them more than Roosevelt. His "Share Our Wealth" program promised through confiscatory taxes on great fortunes to provide every family with what in those depression years seemed in itself a fortune: an income of $2,500 per year and a homestead worth $5,000. Even in Iowa, farmers guffawed when he called the Secretary of Agriculture "Lord Corn Wallace." The New Dealers' political tactician, Postmaster General James A. Farley, estimated in the spring of 1935 that Long could poll 3 or 4 million votes on a third-party ticket and possibly could throw the 1936 election to the Republicans.

The "thunder from the left" was so ominous early in 1935 that many despairing New Dealers, chafing at Roosevelt's apparent inertia, predicted defeat in 1936. Roosevelt, who never liked to explain his tactics, remarked confidentially that he had no intention of engaging in public debate with the leaders of the "lunatic fringe." Rather, he quietly went about stealing their thunder with the reform programs the New Dealers had long been planning.

The Workers' Welfare

Frances Perkins, the first woman cabinet member, had accepted the office of labor secretary only with Roosevelt's pledge that he would support a social security program. For several years, she and a group of New Dealers sought to win converts in the cabinet, in Congress, and throughout the country to their view that social insurance would not only aid the unemployed but also help prevent future depressions.

The Social Security Act of 1935 provided two types of assistance for the aged. Those who were destitute could receive federal aid up to $15 per month, depending upon the matching sums the states provided. Those who were working could receive upon retirement annuities

provided from taxes upon their earnings and their employer's payroll. The 1935 law specified payments, to begin in 1942, ranging from $10 to $85 per month, and excluded wide categories of workers from the program—but it was a beginning. The act also provided for unemployment insurance, aid for the blind and crippled, and assistance for dependent mothers and children, all such funds to be administered by the states in keeping with minimum federal standards. A Social Security Board supervised the entire system.

Social security could not immediately help those already unemployed in 1935; to aid them, Congress in April voted $5 billion to supplant direct relief with the Works Progress Administration. Work relief was more expensive but was essential to prevent the moral erosion, and if possible to save the skills, of the unemployed.

The WPA under Harry Hopkins did much to "help men keep their chins up and their hands in." It enrolled an average of 2.1 million workers between 1935 and 1941 on a wide variety of projects. Since the WPA workers were, theoretically, the least employable segment of the working force, and since almost all WPA money went for wages rather than tools and materials, its undertakings could not compare in efficiency with private construction projects. Many people tended to forget this and regard WPA as a politically inspired paradise for loafers. Nevertheless, WPA built nearly 600 airports and built or rebuilt 110,000 public buildings, more than a half-million miles of roads and streets, over 100,000 bridges, a half-million sewers, and over a million privies. In the realm of art, music, and the theater it gave opportunities to a remarkable proportion of the nation's talented people; its writers, for example, produced a useful set of state guidebooks.

The National Youth Administration, established in June 1935 as a sort of "junior WPA," aided young people between sixteen and twenty-five, seven-eighths of whom received student aid in schools and colleges.

Meanwhile, improved living quarters were being provided for working-class families. From the outset in June 1933, the Public Works Administration (PWA—not the same as WPA), through an Emergency Housing Division, began federal sponsorship of public housing. It cleared some of the nation's most notorious slum blocks, replacing them with about fifty developments containing almost 22,000 family units. The rent was an average of $26 per month, too high during these years for many previous slum dwellers to meet. Congress in 1937 finally passed Senator Wagner's bill creating the United States Housing Authority, which with $500 million (later in 1941 increased to $1.6 billion) took over and expanded the housing program to 511 projects with 161,000 units intended for the truly poor. Almost one-third of the units went to Negroes — one of the largest pieces of federal aid they had ever received.

Encouraging Unions

For those fortunate enough to be employed, Roosevelt preferred a paternalistic program of wages-and-hours guarantees and social security benefits. Union leaders wanted to use collective bargaining to gain these advantages for their workers, so they would look to the unions, not to the government.

Labor leaders had gained much of what they wanted just before the advent of the New Deal, with the passage in 1932 of the Norris-LaGuardia Act. This prohibited the courts from issuing injunctions against most ordinary collective-bargaining practices, and it made unenforceable any "yellow-dog contracts" — pledges from employees that they would not join unions. The Norris-LaGuardia Act stopped federal courts from interfering on behalf of employers in struggles with employees. It left management and the unions free to bring economic pressure upon each other as best they could in collective-bargaining procedures.

In the depression years, however, employers were usually stronger than unions. Besides, strikes could interfere with economic recovery. Hence in 1933 Section 7a of the National Industrial Recovery Act affirmed the right of labor to bargain collectively, and led to the establishment of a government agency — the National Labor Board — to settle disputes arising under Section 7a. The relatively weak board was at first favorable to employers.

While Roosevelt had always maintained cordial relations with labor leaders, he was little inclined to give them firm collective-bargaining guarantees in place of the weak Section 7a in the National Industrial Recovery Act. Congress,

under the leadership of Senator Robert F. Wagner, felt differently. In May 1935 the Senate passed Wagner's bill providing strong government protection for the unions. Roosevelt, bowing to the inevitable, signed the measure. What he had reluctantly accepted became one of the mainstays of the New Deal. The Wagner Act, passed at a time when unions were relatively weak, outlawed a number of the "unfair practices" by which management had been bludgeoning them, and created a powerful National Labor Relations Board to police the employers. Militant labor thus obtained the governmental backing essential to a drive to unionize the great mass-production industries.

AFL and CIO

Even before the adoption of the Wagner Act, union membership had risen from a depression low of less than 3 million to 4.2 million. A group of leaders of industrial unions (which offered membership to everyone within an industry) had chafed over the conservatism of the craft unions (which took in only those working at a given trade). In 1934 men like the head of the United Mine Workers, John L. Lewis, and the leaders of the two great garment unions, Sidney Hillman of the Amalgamated Clothing Workers and David Dubinsky of the International Ladies' Garment Workers, had forced President William Green of the AFL and the craft unionists to agree to charter new industrial unions in the big unorganized industries.

In 1935 organization of these industries began. It led to violent opposition not only from the corporations but also from the AFL craft unions, which feared they would be submerged by the new giant unions. Jurisdictional fights led to a schism between the AFL leadership and the industrial unionists, who formed a Committee for Industrial Organization (within the AFL) in November 1935. Industrial warfare followed, as both the AFL and the CIO mounted great rival organizational drives.

President Roosevelt and a few industrial leaders favored industrial unionism. Gerald Swope of General Electric told Roosevelt that his company could not conceivably negotiate with a large number of craft unions but might find advantages in contracting with a single industrial union. Generally, however, in the spring of 1936 much of big business had yet to see advantages in big labor. Small manufacturers were particularly hostile. They often forced young organizers to battle it out, often by physical force, with "loyal" strong-arm squads, occasionally with the police, and sometimes with rival organizers. The great difference between this and earlier periods of labor warfare was the aid the federal government provided unions through the National Labor Relations Board.

Through 1936 the United Automobile Workers gained recruits despite vigorous company opposition. There was good reason, for in 1934, at about the time the organizing drive began, nearly half the auto workers were receiving less than $1,000 per year. General Motors alone, in an effort to keep down union organization, spent almost $1 million on private detectives between 1934 and 1936. In the first two months of 1937, workers closed seventeen General Motors plants through the new device of the sit-down strike, the workers staying by their machinery inside the plants. General Motors soon recognized the UAW, and other automobile companies gradually did the same. Rubber and other industries were similarly organized. Newspapers saw in the sit-down strikes a menace to private property, and much of the public became thoroughly alarmed.

Bloody warfare in the steel industry heightened the alarm. In 1936 the CIO voted a $500,000 fund to organize the industry and began its great onslaught, winning tens of thousands of workers from company unions. United States Steel chose to capitulate rather than face a long strike just as prosperity seemed to be returning. In March 1937, to the amazement of the nation, one of the company's subsidiaries signed a contract with the Steel Workers' Organizing Committee. For the first time, "Big Steel" was unionized. But three of the "Little Steel" companies, under the leadership of Tom Girdler of Republic Steel, resisted furiously. At the Republic plant in South Chicago on Memorial Day 1937, the police killed ten strikers. Republic Steel, according to the prolabor La Follette committee, was the largest purchaser of tear gas and sickening gas in the United States; Youngstown Sheet and Tube Company owned an arsenal of over a thousand weapons. The Republic strikers lost completely, to the relief of middle-class Americans who, like the newspapers they read, blamed the strife upon the unions and the New Deal.

Yet organized labor continued to grow. By 1941 union membership totaled about 9.5 million.

More for Farmers

In January 1936 the Supreme Court held that it was unconstitutional for the AAA to regulate farm production or to impose a tax for such a purpose. Congress hastily passed a law (the Soil Conservation and Domestic Allotment Act) to meet the Court's objections and yet continue the crop-reduction effort. Under the new law, Congress appropriated money to pay farmers for conserving the soil by leaving part of their land uncultivated. The law provided that landlords must share with their tenants and sharecroppers the payments for withdrawing land from production. Nevertheless, in 1937, while the average plantation operator was grossing $8,328 of which $833 came from the soil conservation program, the average tenant family received only $385, of which $27 came from the government.

Agricultural interests pressed for a new AAA to cope with an enormous threatened surplus. The end of the drought, increased mechanization, and other improvements like the rapid spread of hybrid corn in the Middle West outmoded the crop controls of the 1936 legislation. The Agricultural Adjustment Act of 1938 – the "second AAA" – provided a number of devices to cut back production: soil conservation payments, marketing quotas, export subsidies, and crop loans. Surpluses of five nonperishable commodities upon which farmers received federal loans would be stored under government seal until needed in lean years, thus creating what Secretary Wallace termed an "ever normal granary." The surpluses so stored were to be of vital aid in feeding allies during the war years. The 1938 act also established a Surplus Marketing Administration to channel surpluses to needy persons and provide food for school lunches.

To improve the condition of the poorer farmers, those on submarginal soil, the government undertook to resettle them on better land. The Resettlement Administration (1935) and its successor, the Farm Security Administration (1937), made short-term loans for rehabilitation and long-term loans for purchasing farms but succeeded in moving only a few thousand farm families.

The more fortunate farmers were benefited by the Rural Electrification Administration, which was established in 1935 to extend power lines to farms through cooperatives. Since its activities also stimulated private power companies to extend into the country, it was effective both directly and indirectly. Power lines had reached only 4 percent of the farms in 1925; they reached 25 percent by 1940.

Less for Big Business

After the NRA had been declared unconstitutional, parts of the law were reenacted piecemeal and with alterations to form a "little NRA" that would cover industries containing a great many producers. As early as February 1935, in response to the Supreme Court invalidation of legislation to prevent the overproduction of oil, Congress passed the Connally Act prohibiting the shipment of "hot oil" (oil produced in excess of state limitations) in interstate commerce. The Guffey Act of August 1935 virtually reenacted the NRA bituminous-coal code, fixing prices, limiting production, and protecting labor. When the Supreme Court threw out the new coal-control law in 1936, Congress passed the second Guffey Act of 1937. Roosevelt feared a wages-and-hours law would be unconstitutional, but he signed the Walsh-Healey Act of August 1936, setting minimum wages and maximum hours for work done on federal contracts. To protect small retailers, the Robinson-Patman Act of 1936 prohibited wholesalers or manufacturers from giving preferential discounts or rebates to chain stores or other large buyers; the Miller-Tydings Act of 1937 fortified state "fair trade" price-fixing laws.

As yet, Roosevelt did not resort to vigorous use of the antitrust laws, but he advocated tightening the regulation of big business. In March 1935 he recommended passage of an act to prohibit after five years the pyramiding of utility holding companies, which had led to flagrant abuses in the 1920s. In the 1930s thirteen companies still controlled three-fourths of the na-

tion's electric power. They fought desperately through the summer of 1935 against what they viewed as a threatened "death sentence." One company alone spent $700,000 lobbying against the measure. In the Holding Company Act of 1935, the companies gained a partial victory; it permitted two strata of holding companies above the operating companies.

Between 1935 and 1940 Congress passed a series of other laws stiffening federal regulation. These strengthened the Federal Power Commission, brought trucks and carriers on inland waterways under the supervision of the Interstate Commerce Commission, created a new Maritime Commission to subsidize and regulate a merchant fleet, and set up a Civil Aeronautics Authority (later Board) to regulate airlines.

One of the most effective ways to regulate was to tax, and in 1935 Roosevelt proposed democratizing the federal tax structure by placing far higher levies upon big corporations and wealthy people. He pointed out that a person receiving $6,000 per year paid twice as high a tax as one receiving $4,000, yet the tax upon a $5 million income was only about five times as high as on $1 million. Conservative newspapers immediately attacked this proposal as a "soak the rich" tax scheme, but it passed Congress. It wiped away the last vestiges of Secretary Mellon's influence on tax policy, as it established the highest peacetime rates in history at the top: a maximum 75 percent income tax, 70 percent estate tax, and 15 percent corporate income tax.

Big business seemed to have grown bigger through New Deal inadvertence. The NRA relaxation of the antitrust laws had given it an opportunity to thrive at the expense of smaller business. In the two years after the end of the codes, the Attorney General initiated even fewer antitrust suits than during the NRA period.

Then, in April 1938, the President sent Congress a message vehemently denouncing the unjustifiable concentration of economic power. Less than 5 percent of all corporations in 1935 owned 87 percent of all the assets, he declared. This was leading to such a serious maldistribution of income, he pointed out, that in 1935–1936 the upper 1.5 percent of the population had a share of the national income as great as the 47 percent at the bottom—and these had less than $1,000 per year per family. The remedy, Roosevelt proposed, was to study economic concentration and enact more modern antitrust laws to cope with the newer techniques of monopoly. Undecided as to its proper course, Congress established the Temporary National Economic Committee under the chairmanship of Senator O'Mahoney. It conducted lengthy public hearings and published thirty-nine volumes of reports and forty-three scientific monographs by the end of 1941. By that time the national attention was entirely engrossed elsewhere; legislation never followed.

Meanwhile, Roosevelt launched an immediate trust-busting program through Thurman Arnold, whom he appointed head of the Antitrust Division of the Department of Justice. Arnold, who felt there was nothing wrong with existing legislation, made new and sophisticated use of the Sherman and Clayton acts as he undertook 215 major investigations and 92 test cases.

Mandate from the People

Roosevelt's vigorous reform program, enacted in its main outlines by 1936, made him a sure winner in the election of that year. Many millions felt that their personal lot had been improved by the New Deal. The violent attacks upon it from the right, and the cries of anguish over such measures as the "soak the rich" taxes, convinced them even more that Roosevelt was their friend. Despite the misgivings of many conservatives within the party, the Democratic convention in 1936 renominated him by acclamation. His control was so complete that he even obtained abrogation of the two-thirds rule through which minorities had often hamstrung conventions.

As for the Republicans, they nominated their strongest candidate. Ignoring former President Hoover and the right wing, which was crying calamity, they chose a one-time Bull Mooser who had never strayed far from the 1912 Progressive Position. This was the competent governor of Kansas, Alf M. Landon. His running mate was another Bull Mooser who had moved well to the right, the Chicago publisher Frank Knox. The Republican platform promised to do most of what the New Deal was undertaking—but more competently, constitutionally, and without running a deficit. Landon's dry voice could not match Roosevelt's radio eloquence, and Landon was further handicapped because, though he was a moderate, he had to try to hold the militant Republican right.

The election demonstrated the extent to which the New Deal depended upon a coalition of farmers, union men, and the poor. The unions were the heaviest Democratic campaign contributors, providing $1 million. Negroes switched en masse from the party of Lincoln to that of Roosevelt. The "lunatic fringe" coalition against Roosevelt stirred hardly a ripple. Huey Long had been assassinated the year before; the Union party candidate was "Liberty Bell" William Lemke—who was "cracked," some said. His ticket polled only 890,000 votes; the Socialists, 190,000; the Communists, under 80,000.

A preelection postal card poll by the *Literary Digest* had indicated that Landon would win by a big margin. How could it be so wrong? The names and addresses of those polled were taken from old telephone directories. A majority of people who could afford telephones and had not been forced to move favored Landon. In the election he received 16,680,000 popular votes, compared with 27,477,000 for Roosevelt, and got the electoral votes of only Maine and Vermont.

In the campaign Roosevelt had challenged his right-wing opponents—"economic royalists," he called them—and now he had not only received an overwhelming endorsement for himself but he carried with him many congressmen pledged to his support. Nevertheless, those economic royalists would still have the upper hand so long as the Supreme Court continued to check New Deal laws. He felt he had a mandate from the people to do something about the obstructionist Court.

Storm over the Court

Foes of the Coal Act, the Holding Company Act, the National Labor Relations Act, and the Social Security Act were openly flouting these laws, confident that the Supreme Court would disallow them as it had already done the NRA and the first AAA. The Court, through its narrow interpretation of the federal power over commerce and taxation, and its broad interpretation of freedom of contract in the Fourteenth

Amendment, seemed to have created an economic no man's land within which neither the federal nor the state governments could act.

Critics of the Court had been urging passage of some sort of constitutional amendment to provide the federal government with more extensive economic powers. Roosevelt's opinion (which subsequent Supreme Court decisions were to sustain) was that the Constitution granted adequate powers. All that was wrong was the Court's antiquated interpretation, he felt, but the four or five justices firmly opposed to the New Deal enjoyed excellent health and showed no signs of resigning. Consequently Roosevelt decided to propose adding to the Supreme Court—and to lower federal courts—new justices (presumably sharing his viewpoint) to match superannuated ones.

At this point Roosevelt's political sixth sense deserted him and, instead of presenting his proposal frankly and firmly in terms of its economic implications, he enclosed it in a larger scheme. Without informing congressional leaders in advance, in February 1937 he sent a surprise message proposing a needed general overhauling of the federal court system and the appointment of as many as six new Supreme Court justices. His nearest approach to frankness was a statement that the addition of younger blood would revitalize the courts and help them meet the needs and facts of an ever-changing world.

There was no real question about the constitutionality of Roosevelt's proposal, since Congress had from time to time changed the number of justices on the Supreme Court. Nevertheless, the plan aroused a great furor throughout the country. Many thoughtful people who had supported Roosevelt in 1936 heeded the warning of conservatives that through such constitutional shortcuts, dictators came into power. Within Congress, the controversy cut across party lines. Some Democrats fought against the "packing" of the Court, while the Republican progressive Senator Robert M. La Follette, Jr., supported the President. La Follette declared that the Court had already been "packed" for years "in the cause of Reaction and Laissez-Faire."

Some of the old-line Democratic leaders, especially from the South, had gone along with the New Deal mainly because of party loyalty and pressure from their constituents. Now that much of the electorate was turning against the

administration, these conservatives broke loose. They joined with the bulk of the Republicans to form a new conservative coalition in Congress. Roosevelt fought back by using every device of party discipline to round up votes in Congress. He might have succeeded in obtaining at least a compromise measure, had not the Supreme Court itself eliminated the necessity for one.

The justices—including Louis D. Brandeis, the oldest and most liberal—had been indignant over charges that they were too old to handle the business of the Court. Chief Justice Charles Evans Hughes even wrote a letter insisting that they were not falling behind in their work. Four of them, far to the right, were of no disposition to take a broader view of the Constitution. Three of them took a more progressive if not a New Deal view. Chief Justice Hughes on occasion voted with them, while Justice Owen J. Roberts more often voted with the conservative four.

Just before the President sent his court plan to Congress, Roberts joined with Hughes and the three more liberal justices in the case of *West Coast Hotel* v. *Parrish* to validate, by a 5 to 4 decision, a state minimum-wage law. This reversed a 5-to-4 decision of the previous year invalidating a similar law. "You may have saved the country," Hughes jubilantly told Roberts. The decision was announced on March 29, 1937. Two weeks later, the Court, again 5 to 4, upheld the Wagner Act, and in May, the Social Security Act. Since there no longer seemed to be any pressing need for judicial reform, the new conservative alliance in Congress easily dealt Roosevelt a personal defeat by voting down his court plan. At the same time, the shift of the Supreme Court's interpretation of the Constitution was a significant victory for Roosevelt and the New Deal.

Almost at once the older justices began retiring, and Roosevelt replaced them one by one with his appointees. In the next decade the Roosevelt Court rewrote large sections of constitutional law. The new justices sharply divided among themselves, but usually upon technical matters. In the main they interpreted the commerce and tax clauses so broadly and the Fourteenth Amendment so narrowly that there remained few restrictions upon economic regulation by either the federal or the state governments. For several years the judges tended to restrict governments in their interference with organized labor, but by the end of a decade, labor too was subject to firm restraints. Thus almost all constitutional impediments to government regulation of the economic system were removed.

Recovery and Recession

A sharp recession developed in the fall of 1937. It came just as many economists were fearing that an inflationary boom might get out of hand. There had been a remarkable recovery. The national income, which had dropped from $82 billion in 1929 to $40 billion in 1932, was back up to nearly $72 billion. But the depression had been so deep in 1932 that there were still 7.5 million unemployed and nearly 4.5 million families on relief.

Both Hoover and Roosevelt had been forced to incur budgetary deficits as a result of their spending programs and the depressed tax base. By 1937 the national debt had risen to $30 billion, an amount which Roosevelt found abhorrent. He actually feared another disastrous crash — one resulting from excessive government competition with private borrowers for capital. He had the Federal Reserve tighten credit and he tried to balance the budget by drastically reducing government spending. Between January and August, 1937, he cut the WPA in half, sending 1.5 million workers on unpaid "vacations." The new boom collapsed and sent the economy plummeting. The index of production dropped from 117 in August 1937 to 76 in May 1938; 4 million additional workers were thrown out of work. It seemed almost like 1932 all over again.

In October 1937 the President called Congress into special session to renew heavy public spending and to reform the "selfish interests" he incorrectly blamed for the recession. Congress passed an emergency appropriation of $5 billion; the public works and work relief programs once again poured these large sums into the economy, and by June 1938 recovery was under way at the rapid pace experienced between 1933 and 1937.

The experience of the recession of 1937–1938 and the subsequent recovery convinced Roosevelt that there was some merit in new economic theories that argued that the government could help pull the nation out of a depression by liberal expenditures and could help curb inflationary booms by means of restrictive policies. These theories, known as Keynesianism, after the British economist John Maynard Keynes, would not receive wide acceptance until much later, but never again would a national administration cut expenditures or raise taxes in the face of a recession. The public was growing accustomed to continued deficits, and it was clear to most that no disaster had befallen the nation as a result of the doubling of the federal debt during the New Deal.

Thus the New Deal entered into its final stage of reform, combining what was as new as Keynesianism with what was as old as progressivism. The trend had been toward big business, and now big government had come with the active intervention of the New Deal in so many aspects of the economy. The number of civilian government employees swelled from 588,000 in 1931 to 1,370,000 in 1941.

Since questions of constitutionality no longer seriously interfered after the changes in the Supreme Court, New Dealers fought the Fair Labor Standards Act through Congress in 1938. This established a minimum wage of 25 cents an hour (to be raised gradually to 40 cents by 1945) and a maximum work week of forty-four hours (to be lowered to forty) for most laborers, excepting agricultural, domestic, and maritime workers. It also forbade employment of children under sixteen in most areas except agriculture. Low though these standards were, they raised the pay of 300,000 workers and shortened the workweek for 1.3 million. In subsequent years the standards were raised repeatedly, and the scope of the law was broadened to include additional categories of workers.

Farewell to Reform

Roosevelt worried about the strong negative power the conservative coalition was developing in Congress. In many states, the Democratic party was under the leadership of conservatives. Postmaster General Farley, in charge of patronage, had done little to aid New Dealers who tried to challenge this leadership. In 1938 Roosevelt intervened in several primaries, mostly in the South, to try to defeat powerful conservative Democrats who headed congressional committees. Since these men had strong organizations behind them, and the New Deal candidates were relatively unknown, the conservatives won in almost every contest. The 1938 elections reflected the degree to which the prestige of Roosevelt and the New Deal were waning. The Republicans gained eighty seats in the House and seven in the Senate. Together with the conservative Democrats, the Republicans could dominate Congress.

By the end of 1938 the New Deal was close to its limits. The threat of a second world war was beginning to overshadow even the most critical domestic problems. The President could drive Congress with its Southern committee chairmen in the direction of strong defense legislation and a vigorous foreign policy only if he conciliated them by abandoning reform.

Chapter 26.   FROM ISOLATION TO INTERVENTION

American Ambivalence

Throughout the 1930s, the American people were well aware that cataclysmic events were preparing the way for the Second World War, which broke out in 1939. While the United States was seeking nationalistic but peaceable internal policies to restore prosperity, some other nations were trying to find their way out of depression by intimidating or even conquering other weaker countries. Adolf Hitler and the Nazis who won control of Germany in 1933 became an immediate and frightening menace to peace; the military leaders who determined policy in Japan continued their efforts to dominate East Asia. The American people and their government were quite ambivalent toward the acts of aggression of these nations. On the one hand, Americans wished to help the victims; on the other, they lacked the power to limit aggression by economic sanctions and did not wish the United States to become involved in armed conflict. This ambivalence continued through the thirties, as the United States more and more became involved in the struggle against the aggressors. Ultimately, through the Japanese attack on Pearl Harbor, the country was plunged into war.

Seeking Friends and Customers

In 1933, there still seemed the possibility that United States foreign policy could confine itself to economic questions growing out of the depression, and the encouragement of world disarmament. President Hoover had hoped through concessions on war debts to obtain currency stabilization and other international agreements to promote recovery. After equivocating for several months, Roosevelt decided to modify the gold standard and hence rejected stabilization until a time more favorable to the United States. In July 1933 he cabled Secretary of State Cordell Hull at the London Economic Conference a "bombshell messsage," disavowing stabilization and ending any faint possibility that the United

States would seek international routes to recovery. The debt question became a dead issue in 1934 when Roosevelt signed an act sponsored by Senator Hiram Johnson, forbidding private loans to any defaulting nations; thereupon all war-debt payments, except those of Finland, stopped altogether.

The hope of stimulating foreign trade led Roosevelt in November 1933 to recognize Soviet Russia. Since the revolution of November 1917 the Russian government had gone unrecognized while a number of irritating questions between the two nations continued to fester. Americans, hungry for what they unrealistically dreamed would be a substantial Russian trade, were eager for recognition. The Russians had even stronger motives for obtaining recognition, for they were afraid of being attacked by Japan. Maxim Litvinov, the Russian foreign minister, after discussions with Roosevelt at the White House, agreed that Russia would end its propaganda activities in the United States, guarantee religious freedom and protection in the courts to Americans resident in Russia, and negotiate a settlement of debts and claims.

By January 1934 Roosevelt was ready to listen seriously to Hull's homilies on the necessity of lowering tariff barriers in order to improve foreign trade. With Roosevelt's support, Congress in June 1934 passed Hull's cherished program, the Reciprocal Trade Agreements Act. It authorized the administration to negotiate agreements, lowering tariffs by as much as 50 percent on specified goods coming in from individual nations in return for their reducing tariffs on American goods.

The immediate effect of the reciprocal trade agreements is difficult to estimate. During the depression years they were cautiously negotiated to keep out competing products yet gain concessions for American exporters, especially of cotton and tobacco. By the end of 1938 exports of the United States to the sixteen nations with which it then had trade agreements had increased nearly 40 percent. But much of this increase would have occurred anyway, and exports were still far below 1929 levels. The long range effects were more vital. The legislation, which Congress periodically renewed, replaced the framing of new tariff legislation, and ultimately led to much lower rates.

Reciprocal trade was a key ingredient in the Good Neighbor policy toward Latin America, which the Roosevelt administration fabricated. At the Inter-American Conference at Montevideo in 1933, Hull not only offered this economic succor, he reiterated to the people of Latin America that the United States was opposed to armed intervention in Latin America. Hull even signed a convention declaring: "No state has the right to intervene in the internal or external affairs of another."

In 1933, when revolution exploded in Cuba, Summer Welles, one of the chief draftsmen of the new Latin American policy, was sent into Cuba to offer the "good offices" of the United States. Welles helped bring pacification without calling in the marines. In 1934, when a more conservative government came into power in Cuba, the United States gave up its right of intervention under the Platt Amendment. It also withdrew the last marines from Haiti and negotiated a treaty (not ratified until 1939) relaxing the restrictions upon Panama.

The new Good Neighbor policy of nonintervention received a severe testing in 1938 when Mexico expropriated all foreign oil holdings, including property valued by its American owners at $200 million. The United States conceded the right of expropriation but at first contended that the price the Mexicans wished to pay was so trivial as to be confiscation. In 1942 after years of involved controversy, a commission evaluated the property at $24 million, and the State Department then told the protesting oil companies that they must accept the settlement or receive nothing. This was a reversal of Dollar Diplomacy—a renunciation of the right to intervene for the purpose of protecting American property in Latin America. In terms of trade the new policy was of immediate benefit. As the threat of war in Europe increased, it came to mean also mutual defense, and this became paramount.

As for the Philippines, primarily the depression and secondarily isolationism brought them the long-sought but economically dubious blessing of independence. American producers of sugar, fats, and oils were determined to thrust their Filipino competitors outside the tariff wall; isolationists were eager to drop this dangerous

Far Eastern military commitment. The Tydings-McDuffie Act of 1934 thrust upon the Philippines complete independence rather than the dominion status they sought. In 1935 the Philippines entered upon a transitional commonwealth period; on July 4, 1946, they became a fully independent republic. The United States was demonstrating that it was trying to rid itself of possessions rather than seize new ones.

The New Neutrality

Meanwhile, the United States continued to assert a strong moral position to try to bring about substantial disarmament. But Hitler was bent upon rearming, not disarming, and in October 1933 withdrew from both the Geneva arms conference and the League of Nations. A new arms race was underway.

At the London Naval Conference of 1935, the Japanese withdrew after they failed to obtain equality with the Americans and British in place of the 5:5:3 ratio, and thus the way was opened for competitive naval building. The United States soon turned to building the fleet with which it was later to fight the opening battles of a Pacific war.

With the breakdown of the naval status quo and the threatened aggressions in both Asia and Europe, most Americans felt that at all costs they must stay out of impending wars. Many leaders of the peace movement—dedicated Wilsonians and advocates of the League—had become disgusted with the League's inability to stop Japanese aggression. They reasoned that internationalism had failed to maintain the peace. Others, taking an economic-determinist view of wars, concluded that Wall Streeters and munitions makers and Wilson's legalistic insistence upon outmoded neutral rights on the high seas had trapped the nation into World War I. Senate investigators, under the progressive Republican Gerald P. Nye of North Dakota, revealed exorbitant wartime profits and tax evasion and claimed that bankers had sought war to rescue their loans to the Allies.

The Nye Committee findings and similar sensational popular writings convinced a large part of the public that entrance into World War I had been a frightful mistake. The way to avoid its repetition seemed to be to legislate against the supposed causes. As Mussolini openly prepared to conquer Ethiopia in 1935, Americans feared that a general European war might develop. They felt that the way to avoid involvement was not to participate in strong deterring pressure against Italy, since Mussolini might strike back. Rather it was to isolate the nation through neutrality legislation.

President Roosevelt also favored legislation, but he and Hull desired, as Hull had proposed in 1933, a law that would enable Roosevelt to embargo war supplies to the aggressor and allow their sale to the victim. But Congress passed a neutrality act providing a mandatory embargo against both aggressor and victim and empowering the President to warn American citizens that they might travel on vessels of belligerents only at their own risk. This first Neutrality Act of 1935, a temporary measure, was renewed in 1936 and again, with even stronger provisions, in 1937.

When the attack upon Ethiopia came, in October 1935, the League branded Italy an aggressor and voted sanctions against it. England and France made gestures against Italy but showed no inclination toward determined action. Hull imposed a "moral embargo" upon oil. Mussolini easily conquered his African empire, then withdrew from the League and in October 1936 joined with Hitler to form a new Rome-Berlin axis.

The fiasco seemed to strengthen the determination of the American people to stay out of war. The new public opinion polls, based on samplings of 1,500 to 3,500 people, with a probable error of 4 to 6 percent, indicated top-heavy opinion against involvement. A typical poll in November 1935, after the attack on Ethiopia, queried: "If one foreign nation insists upon attacking another, should the United States join with other nations to compel it to stop?" The answer: yes, 28 percent; no, 67 percent; no opinion, 5 percent.

This anti-involvement sentiment continued to be the mood of the nation when a new danger arose in July 1936, as General Francisco Franco and the Falangists (modeled after the Fascists) revolted against the Republican government in Spain. Hitler and Mussolini sided with Franco; Russia, France, and to a lesser extent Great Britain favored the Loyalists. To prevent the Spanish civil war from spreading into a general European conflict, England and France agreed to send no aid to either side. Roosevelt tried to cooperate; he persuaded Congress to apply the existing Neutrality Act to civil as well as interna-

tional wars. The result was that the United States and other Western nations denied aid to Republican Spain. The Republican government came to depend increasingly upon Russia for what little aid it received. As for Franco, he received massive aid from Mussolini and Hitler, and ultimately crushed the Loyalists.

American feelings became inflamed over the invasion of Ethiopia and the Spanish civil war, but President Roosevelt voiced the majority attitude in August 1936, a month after the outbreak of the war in Spain, when he asserted: "We shun political commitments which might entangle us in foreign wars."

Japan's "New Order"

A great Japanese drive into the five northern provinces of China began in the summer of 1937. Japan avoided declaring war, and President Roosevelt did not invoke the Neutrality Act. Private American ships at their own risk could carry arms and munitions to both belligerents. The administration's purpose was to help the Chinese, who needed American supplies more than the Japanese did.

By October 1937 the administration was ready to take a firm position against Japan. The British proposed a joint arms embargo that seemed to involve no great risk. At this time and during the next four years, the consensus of the experts was that Japan was a mediocre military power. Hull persuaded Roosevelt to make a statement to counteract isolationism. The President, speaking at Chicago, went beyond his advisors and declared: "The peace-loving nations must make a concerted effort in opposition to those violations of treaties and those ignorings of humane instincts which today are creating a state of international anarchy, international instability from which there is no escape through mere isolation or neutrality." War, he asserted, was a contagion that must be quarantined by the international community.

There is evidence that Roosevelt had in mind nothing more drastic than a collective breaking off of diplomatic relations, that he did not favor economic or military sanctions. Immediate reaction was favorable, but within a few days, the "quarantine" speech had plunged the nation into a war fright. Roosevelt backtracked for several months.

Japan had no need to fear economic or military reprisals from the United States. On December 12, 1937, young Japanese aviators bombed and sank the United States gunboat *Panay* on the Yangtze River. The aviators claimed they bombed it in error, but visibility was excellent and an American flag was painted on the deck. As at the sinking of the *Maine* in 1898, a wave of excitement swept the country, but this time it was fear that the nation might become involved in war. The United States quickly accepted the profuse Japanese apologies and offers of indemnity.

At the end of 1938, as she supplanted the Open Door with the New Order, Japan was making conditions almost untenable for Americans in China. But the threat of war in Europe overshadowed the Asian impasse.

Hemispheric Solidarity

The traditional American isolationism, as exemplified by Hearst editorials and the speeches of several Senators, implied strict nonintervention in Europe but a considerably more active role in Asia—no sanctions, but an insistence upon the Open Door in China. Within the Western Hemisphere, toward both Canada and Latin America, these isolationists were ready to give the President almost a free hand. Indeed there were no more devout exponents of the Monroe Doctrine than they.

Roosevelt took full advantage of these feelings to inaugurate, within the hemisphere, policies that he could later apply across the Atlantic and the Pacific. In December 1936 he traveled all the way to Buenos Aires to put his personal prestige behind a pact to change the Monroe Doctrine into a mutual security agreement. Henceforth, if any outside power threatened the American republics, instead of the United States acting unilaterally they would all consult together for their own protection. The understanding covered disputes among the republics themselves but was specifically aimed at meeting the threat of the Axis. Roosevelt also extended hemispheric security to the north in August 1938 when he issued a declaration of solidarity with Canada.

War in Europe

By 1938 Hitler had rebuilt such a strong German army and air force that he was ready to em-

bark upon a course of intimidation and conquest. In March he proclaimed union with Austria and paraded triumphantly through Vienna. This union put western Czechoslovakia into the jaws of a German vise. Hitler began tightening it with demands on behalf of the minority of 3,500,000 Germans in Czechoslovakia. In September 1938 he brought Europe to the brink of war with his demands for the cession of the Sudeten area in which the minority lived. The Czechs, who had a strong army, were ready to fight rather than submit, but the people of other Western nations, appalled at the threat of another world conflict, were eager for a settlement on almost any terms. Roosevelt joined in the pleas to Hitler for a peaceful solution. At Munich on September 29 the French and the British signed a pact with Hitler granting his demands in Czechoslovakia. "This is the last territorial claim I have to make in Europe," he declared.

Within a few weeks, the once strong Czechoslovakia was whittled down to impotence. In March 1939 Hitler took over the remaining areas as German protectorates, thus demonstrating the worthlessness of his Munich pledge. In April he began harassing Poland. The British and French, seeing clearly that appeasement had failed, gave firm pledges to Poland and other threatened nations. They made half-hearted gestures toward Russia, which had been left out of the Munich settlement, but Stalin in August signed a nonaggression pact with Hitler. This freed Hitler to attack Poland if he could not frighten that country into submission. When Poland stood firm, Germany invaded it on September 1, 1939. True to their pledges, Great Britain and France declared war on Germany on September 3. World War II had begun.

Aiding the Allies

With the outbreak of war, Roosevelt issued a neutrality proclamation pointedly different from Wilson's 1914 plea for Americans to be impartial in thought as well as action. "This nation will remain a neutral nation," Roosevelt stated, "but I cannot ask that every American remain neutral in thought as well."

Promptly, Roosevelt called Congress into special session and, despite a heated debate, was able to muster the votes for a revision of the Neutrality Act. The 1939 measure still prohibited American ships from entering the war zones, but it allowed belligerents to purchase arms on a "cash-and-carry" basis. Had England and France been able to defeat Hitler with this limited assistance, Roosevelt probably would have been satisfied with it. Indeed, after the quick Nazi overrunning of Poland, over-optimistic American publicists, during the quiet winter of 1939–1940, asserted that the Allies were calling Hitler's bluff and, after a long and boring blockade on sea and land, would triumph. During these months of the "phony war," American indignation flared hottest over the Russian invasion of Finland. The administration applied a tight "moral embargo" on shipments of munitions to Russia but went no further.

Optimistic illusions about Hitler's weakness turned into panic in the spring of 1940 when the Nazis invaded Denmark and Norway, then swept across Holland and Belgium deep into France. On May 16, Roosevelt asked Congress for an additional billion for defense expenditures and obtained it quickly. On the premise that the United States must build great air armadas to hold off the Nazis, he set a goal of at least 50,000 airplanes a year.

On June 10, 1940, Mussolini joined the Germans by attacking France. Roosevelt that evening asserted: "The hand that held the dagger has struck it into the back of its neighbor." And, with France tottering from the German onslaught, he proclaimed that the United States would "extend to the opponents of force the material resources of this nation." He was taking the United States from a status of neutrality to one of nonbelligerency on the side of the democracies.

Twelve days later France fell, and in all western Europe only the shattered remnants of the British army that had been retrieved from Dunkirk opposed the Nazis. Already the new prime minister, Winston Churchill, was showering Roosevelt with requests for destroyers and arms of all kinds to help the British man their bastion. The odds against the British were heavy, but Roosevelt made the bold and dangerous decision to "scrape the bottom of the barrel" and make it possible for the British to buy all available matériel of war. As the Germans, preparing for an invasion, began to bomb Britain from the air, Roosevelt gave fifty over-age destroyers to the British in return for ninety-nine-year leases on eight bases from Newfoundland to British Guiana. It was, as Churchill later wrote, "a decidedly unneutral act."

Isolationists vs. Interventionists

Roosevelt threw the resources of the United States behind the British as completely as Congress would let him. He did so with the feeling that an Axis victory would mean disaster to the nation. A large part of the public seemed suddenly to agree. In March 1940 only 43 percent of those polled thought a German victory would be a threat to the United States; by July, 69 percent did. In May 1940 only 35 percent favored aid to Britain at the risk of American involvement; four months later, 60 percent did. Yet as late as November 1941 only 20 percent of those polled favored a declaration of war against Germany. Roosevelt and the American public seemed to share incompatible aims. They wished to bring about the defeat of the Axis without involving the United States in a shooting war. Some time in the next eighteen months, Roosevelt probably came to feel that American entrance was desirable; the public never did.

The whole country was pulled into a great debate on the issue of neutrality versus all-out aid to the Allies. William Allen White, the Kansas editor, headed a Committee to Defend America by Aiding the Allies, often called the White Committee. White himself (like a large percentage of Americans) favored merely aid, but a minority wanted to go further and declare war. On the anti-involvement side, a Yale student organized an America First Committee under the chairmanship of a leading Chicago businessman, General Robert E. Wood. It drew upon the oratorical talent of the aviation hero Charles Lindbergh, General Hugh Johnson, and Senators Nye and Wheeler. It won the editorial support of some large newspapers, and it appealed to a considerable segment of patriotic Americans. Inevitably it also attracted a small fringe of pro-Nazi, anti-Semitic, and American Fascist fanatics. The debate was bitter, and through the summer and fall of 1940 it was complicated by a presidential election.

Election of 1940

The Republicans met at Philadelphia in June, at the time of the collapse of France. National defense suddenly became the most important issue. Roosevelt underscored this and stole headlines from the Republican convention by appointing to his Cabinet two of the most distin-

guished Republicans. He made the elder statesman Henry L. Stimson Secretary of War, and
the 1936 vice-presidential candidate and sharp
critic of the New Deal, Frank Knox, Secretary
of the Navy.

The chagrined Republicans at Philadelphia
promptly read Stimson and Knox out of the
party but could not ignore the defense issue.
They succumbed to the grass-roots pressure,
which had been built through a careful advertising campaign, and nominated a young interna-
tionalist, Wendell Willkie. This was a startling
blow to the isolationist majority among the Republican politicians, but it provided them with a
tousle-haired, personable candidate who could
win hysterical devotion from the amateur party
workers. Both the platform and the candidate
pledged that the nation would be kept out of war
but would aid peoples fighting for liberty.

By the time the Democrats met in mid-July, it
was a foregone conclusion that they would re-
nominate Roosevelt. He was even able to force
the Democratic politicians to swallow his choice
for Vice President, Secretary of Agriculture
Henry A. Wallace, who was considered an advanced New Dealer.

Willkie embarked upon an appealing but
slightly amateurish campaign, whistle-stopping
so vigorously that he nearly lost his voice, denouncing the bad management of the New Deal
rather than its basic program.

Roosevelt, a wily old campaigner, tried to give
the appearance of not campaigning at all. Defense problems were so acute, he insisted, that
he had to spend his time touring army bases, munitions plants, and shipyards. He followed
routes that somehow took him through innumerable cities, where he cheerily greeted quantities
of voters.

Foreign policy was paramount. On this, both
Willkie and Roosevelt had much the same
views. Willkie approved of the destroyers-bases
agreement. Both made fervent antiwar statements to placate the isolationists. Willkie declared that if Roosevelt's promise to stay out of
a foreign war was no better than his pledge to
balance the budget, the boys were "already almost on the transports." This was an effective
campaign issue that cut into Roosevelt's support. In Boston, Roosevelt (making the mental
reservation that any attack upon the United
States would not be a foreign war) picked up the
challenge in words the isolationists were to

mock incessantly: "I have said this before, but I
shall say it again and again and again: Your boys
are not going to be sent into any foreign wars."

A large part of the vote of those opposing aid
to the Allies went to Willkie. Those favoring vigorous aid or even intervention (including many
who fervently opposed New Deal domestic policies) voted for Roosevelt. They preferred Roosevelt's sure leadership to Willkie's inexperi-
ence. It was a relatively close vote: 27,244,000
for Roosevelt, and 22,305,000 for Willkie; 449
electoral votes to 82. The combined third-party
vote was less than 200,000. Within a few weeks,
Wilkie was on his way to England with a letter
from Roosevelt to Churchill in his pocket.

The Lend-Lease Act

In addition to politicking, during the months
after the fall of France, Roosevelt had to build
makeshift defense machinery. With Willkie's
aid, he pushed through the Burke-Wadsworth
bill, passed in September 1940, which inaugurated the first peacetime selective service in
American history. This was the summer when
he arranged to send destroyers to England,
turned back new airplanes to the factory to be
ferried across the Atlantic, and somehow ran the
gauntlet of several anti-British, isolationist
chairmen of Senate committees.

By mid-December the British had so nearly
exhausted their financial resources that they had
practically stopped letting new contracts, yet
Churchill warned Roosevelt that their needs
would increase tenfold in the future. The Neutrality Act of 1939 and the Johnson Act of 1934
forbade American loans; a request for repeal
would have reawakened the old ill feelings about
unpaid war debts. Roosevelt, cruising in the Caribbean after the election, thought of a formula.
The United States, "to eliminate the dollar sign,"
should lend goods rather than money, while
serving as an "arsenal of democracy."

A "Lend-Lease" bill went into the congressional hopper at the right moment to bear a significant number: it became House Resolution
No. 1776. After fierce debate, the bill went
through Congress by a wide margin and in
March 1941 was signed by the President. It empowered him to spend an initial $7 billion—a
sum as large as all the controversial loans of
World War I.

THE BACKGROUND OF PEARL HARBOR

Where Historians Disagree

After the end of World War II a number of critics charged that the Roosevelt administration had deliberately brought the United States into the war by provoking the Japanese to attack Pearl Harbor. Charles A. Beard, for one, presented the case against the administration in his *President Roosevelt and the Coming of the War, 1941* (1948). According to Beard, the American government refused to compromise with Japan and allow her to buy the raw materials she needed for her military adventure in China. Hence Japan had little choice but to strike out in the southwest Pacific and take the necessary supplies by force, even at the risk of war with the United States. From decoded Japanese radio messages, Roosevelt and his advisers must have known, by late November, that Japan was about to begin hostilities. Indeed, as War Secretary Henry L. Stimson recorded in his diary, Roosevelt at a cabinet meeting "brought up the event that we were likely to be attacked" in the near future, for the Japanese were "notorious for making an attack without warning." Stimson added, significantly: "The question was how we should maneuver them into the position of firing the first shot."

In *Roosevelt from Munich to Pearl Harbor* (1950) Basil Rauch undertook to refute Beard's argument, yet Rauch conceded that the administration had had in mind a "maneuver" or sorts. "The question," he explained, "was whether the President should ask Congress for a declaration of war *prior* to a Japanese attack on the Philippines or Guam, in order to avoid giving Japan the advantage of a surprise attack, or wait until Japan attacked American territory, that is, 'maneuver' Japan into firing the first shot."

Disagreeing with both Beard and Rauch, R. N. Current contended in *Secretary Stimson: A Study in Statecraft* (1954) that Roosevelt and his advisers intended neither to provoke an attack on Pearl Harbor nor to await one on Guam or the Philippines. Stimson and the others were expecting the Japanese to move against Dutch or British but *not* American possessions. When Stimson said "we were likely to be attacked," he meant "we" in the sense of "our side," including the British and the Dutch. If he and his colleagues had really been anticipating a blow at Pearl Harbor, they obviously would not have had to worry about how to provoke the Japanese to attack there. The real question, as Stimson saw it, was how to make the Japanese *appear* to be firing on the United States—in the sense of threatening vital American interests—if and when they aggressed upon Dutch or British territory in the southwest Pacific. He assumed that such a "maneuver" as this would be necessary to persuade Congress to pass a war declaration, which he believed to be in the best interests of the United States.

The most thorough and scholarly study of the subject is *Pearl Harbor: Warning and Decision* (1962), by Roberta Wohlsetter, who on the whole is favorable to the Roosevelt policy. Today few if any historical experts hold to the Beard provocation thesis, but they continue to disagree among themselves in regard to the appropriateness of various American diplomatic and military measures preceding the attack.

Lend-Lease committed the United States formally to the policy the President had been following since the fall of France, the policy of pouring aid into Great Britain to help her withstand the German onslaught. Since Lend-Lease shipments had to cross the Atlantic to be of aid, the United States acquired a vital interest in keeping the Atlantic sea lanes open against the formidable wolf packs of German submarines, which in the spring of 1941 were destroying a half-million tons of shipping a month, twice as much as could be replaced. The President did not openly dare to convoy vessels to England as Secretary Stimson urged; isolationists in Congress were too powerful. Instead he fell back upon the device of "hemispheric defense." The American republics had proclaimed an Atlantic neutrality zone in 1939; Roosevelt in 1941 extended it far to the east, almost to Iceland, and ordered the Navy to patrol the area and give warning of aggressors. This meant radioing to the British the location of Nazi submarines. The United States occupied Greenland in April 1941 and began escorting convoys as far as Iceland in July.

Toward Belligerency

In secret, the United States had gone even further, for in the spring of 1941 American and British officers in Washington reached agreement on the strategy to be followed if the United States entered the war. President Roosevelt demonstrated publicly in August 1941 how close he had come to carrying the United States from nonbelligerency to cobelligerency with England when he met with Prime Minister Churchill off the coast of Newfoundland. Roosevelt refused to make military commitments but did sign with Churchill a press release on mutual war aims, the Atlantic Charter. In it they declared that their nations sought no additional territory, but favored self-determination and self-government for peoples who had been deprived of it, freedom of access and trade, collaboration in economic development, and mutual security from aggressors. As Churchill later pointed out, Roosevelt, representing a nation not at war, subscribed to a document that referred to "the final destruction of the Nazi tyranny" as a war aim.

In June 1941 Hitler unleashed against Russia a surprise attack so powerful that American military leaders predicted that Russia would collapse in a few weeks or months. The Russians fell back before the deep Nazi invasion but continued to fight, and in September Roosevelt, again gambling, extended Lend-Lease to them. This made it even more imperative to patrol the seas effectively.

The German answer was to strike back with submarines. In May 1941 they sank the Ameri-can ship *Robin Moor* off the coast of Brazil. In September, a submarine attacked but failed to hit the destroyer *Greer,* which was radioing the submarine's position to the British. President Roosevelt, who did not know or at least did not reveal what the *Greer* was doing, issued orders to the navy to "shoot on sight." In October another destroyer was hit, and the *Reuben James* was sunk. Congress voted legislation to arm merchantmen and allow them to sail to belligerent ports. Naval war with the Nazis was under way.

The Chief of Naval Operations, Admiral Harold R. Stark, wrote in his diary that Hitler "has every excuse in the world to declare war on us now, if he were of a mind to." But Hitler was not, and war came from the Pacific, not the Atlantic.

Pearl Harbor

The Japanese saw in the European crisis an unparalleled opportunity to extend their empire. In the summer of 1939 they forced concessions from the British which demonstrated their intentions. The United States promptly took a most serious step and gave the requisite six months' notice to terminate its 1911 commercial treaty. Beginning in January 1940 this country was free to cut off its shipments of oil, scrap iron, and other raw materials.

The United States was determined to restrain Japan, even at the risk of a war. More was at stake than tin, rubber, and other vital raw materials. In September 1940 Japan signed a defensive alliance with Germany and Italy (the Tripartite Pact); any further Japanese thrusts would damage the world status quo to which the State Department was committed. The administration policy toward Japan was inseparably interrelated with that toward Germany, and subordinate to it.

Under the Export Control Act, by the fall of 1940 the United States had placed an embargo upon aviation gasoline and almost all raw materials with military potential, including scrap iron and steel. Already war was close. The Japanese government of Prince Konoye wished to conciliate the United States if it could do so without serious concessions. Negotiations began in the spring of 1941 and dragged on into December. At first the Japanese informally suggested rather generous proposals, but by May they were making formal ones that were unacceptable: the United States should ask Chiang Kai-shek to make peace on Japan's terms, should restore normal trade with Japan, and should help Japan procure natural resources in Southeast Asia.

The German attack upon Russia relieved the Japanese of one of their greatest worries, since they thought they no longer needed to fear interference from Siberia. They decided to move into southern Indochina and Thailand. The United States had broken the Japanese code and, through intercepted messages, knew this was probably a prelude to attacks upon Singapore and the Dutch East Indies. At the end of July 1941 when the Japanese occupied southern Indochina, the United States, acting firmly with the British and the Dutch, froze Japanese assets in their respective countries, so that the Japanese could not convert these assets into cash. This put the Japanese into such a desperate plight that they would either have to abandon their aggressions or attack British or Dutch East India possessions to get needed supplies.

Roosevelt and Hull seemed to make the foolish error of thinking Japan was bluffing when she was not. Instead of granting limited concessions that would have strengthened the Japanese moderates and postponed or avoided a war the United States was in no position to fight in 1941, the American policy makers took an adamant moralistic position that played into the hands of the Japanese extremists. The Japanese made an even more grievous miscalculaton by provoking a war that few of their leaders were sure they could win.

Each nation refused to budge on the question of China. On November 20, 1941, Japan offered a modus vivendi (temporary settlement) highly favorable to herself. Hull rejected it and replied in the basic American terms, insisting that Japan get out of China. He not only knew Japan would not accept these but knew also, through intercepted Japanese messages, that she had made her last offer and that after November 29 things automatically would happen. "I have washed my hands of the Japanese situation," Hull told Stimson on November 27, "and it is now in the hands of you and Knox, the Army and Navy."

The United States knew that Japan was on the move and that war was imminent. A large Japanese convoy was moving southward through the China Sea. The administration thought an attack upon American territory unlikely. The commanders in Hawaii were routinely warned. Negligence there and in Washington, not diabolical plotting as was later charged, led to the disaster ahead. Meanwhile, on November 25, a Japanese naval task force had sailed eastward from the Kuriles.

At 7:55 on Sunday morning, December 7, 1941, the first wave of Japanese airplanes hit the United States naval base at Pearl Harbor, Hawaii; a second wave came an hour later. The attacks were successful beyond Japan's greatest expectations. Within two hours the planes destroyed or severely damaged 8 battleships, 3 light cruisers, 4 miscellaneous vessels, 188 airplanes, and important shore installations. There were 3,435 casualties. The Japanese task force withdrew without being detected, having lost 29 airplanes, 5 midget submarines, and less than 100 men. In this first strike, the United States was rendered almost impotent in the Pacific, but the bitterly wrangling nation was suddenly unified for the global war into which it had been precipitated.

"Yesterday, December 7, 1941 – a date which will live in infamy – the United States of America was suddenly and deliberately attacked by the naval and air forces of the Empire of Japan." Thus President Roosevelt addressed Congress on the Monday after the debacle at Pearl Harbor. Within four hours, the Senate unanimously, and the House 388 to 1, voted for a war resolution against Japan. Three days later Germany and Italy declared war against the United States, and on the same day, December 11, Congress reciprocated without a dissenting vote.

SELECTED READINGS

Comprehensive on American organization for World War I is F. L. Paxson, *American Democracy and the World War* (3 vols., 1936–1948). Opposition to the war and the repression of it is treated in H. C. Peterson and G. C. Fite, *Opponents of War* (1957). Good surveys of the war as a whole are H. A. De Weerd, *President Wilson Fights His War* (1968); E. M. Coffman, *The War to End All Wars* (1968); and Frank Freidel, *Over There* (1964). On the making of the peace treaty and the defeat of its ratification see T. A. Bailey, *Woodrow Wilson and the Lost Peace** (1944), and *Woodrow Wilson and the Great Betrayal** (1945); and J. A. Garraty, *Henry Cabot Lodge* (1953).

A thought-provoking short account of the 1920s is William Leuchtenburg, *The Perils of Prosperity, 1914–32** (1958); a standard survey, J. D. Hicks, *Republican Ascendancy, 1921–1933.** A brilliant critical view is A. M. Schlesinger, Jr., *The Crisis of the Old Order* (1957). On economic history, see George Soule, *Prosperity Decade* (1947); on urban development, Blake McKelvey, *The Emergence of Metropolitan America, 1915–1966* (1968). On special topics see R. K. Murray, *Red Scare** (1955); W. M. Bagby, *The Road to Normalcy** (1962), election of 1920; R. K. Murray, *The Harding Era* (1969); David Burner, *The Politics of Provincialism* (1968), Democratic party; E. D. Cronon, *Black Moses, the Story of Marcus Garvey* (1955); Burl Noggle, *Teapot Dome – Oil and Politics in the 1920's** (1962); L. E. Ellis, *Republican Foreign Policy, 1921–1933* (1968); D. R. McCoy, *Calvin Coolidge* (1967); and J. O. Tipple, comp., *Crisis of the American Dream: A History of American Social Thought, 1920–1940* (1968).

Two careful accounts of the Hoover administration are A. U. Romasco, *The Poverty of Abundance** (1965), and H. G. Warren, *Herbert Hoover and the Great Depression.* On special topics see Oscar Handlin, *Al Smith and His America** (1958); Andrew Sinclair, *Prohibition: The Era of Excess* (1966); Broadus Mitchell, *Depression Decade* (1947), the standard economic history; Milton Friedman and A. J. Schwartz, *The Great Contraction, 1929–1933** (1965); J. K. Galbraith, *The Great Crash** (1955); R. H. Ferrell, *American Diplomacy in the Great Depression* (1957); and R. N. Current, *Secretary Stimson* (1954).

The most notable single-volume survey of the New Deal is W. E. Leuchtenburg, *Franklin D. Roosevelt and the New Deal, 1932–1940** (1963). Two brilliant volumes in A. M. Schlesinger, Jr., *Age of Roosevelt,* cover domestic developments through the 1936 election: *The Coming of the New Deal** (1959) and *The Politics of Upheaval** (1960). An intellectual history is A. A. Ekirch, *Ideologies and Utopias* (1969). J. M. Burns, *Roosevelt: The Lion and the Fox** (1956) is a well-written interpretation. On special topics see Raymond Moley and E. A. Rosen, *The First New Deal* (1966); E. W. Hawley, *The New Deal and the Problem of Monopoly* (1966); J. M. Blum, *From the Morgenthau Diaries* (3 vols., 1959–1967); G. B. Tindall, *Emergence of the New South* (1968); Frank Freidel, *F. D. R. and the South** (1965); T. H. Williams, *Huey Long* (1969); F. A. Warren, *Liberals and Communism* (1966); Roy Lubove, *The Struggle for Social Security, 1900–1935* (1969); J. T. Patterson, *Congressional Conservatism and the New Deal* (1967); B. D. Karl, *Executive Reorganization and Reform in the New Deal* (1963); Bernard Sternsher, ed., *The Negro in Depression and War** (1969); Daniel Aaron, *Writers on the Left** (1961); and O. L. Graham, Jr., *The New Deal: The Critical Issues** (1971).

On foreign policy to Pearl Harbor, W. L. Langer and S. E. Gleason, *The World Crisis and American Foreign Policy* (2 vols., 1952–1953) is detailed and sympathetic; C. A. Beard, *American Foreign Policy, 1932–1940* (1946), and *President Roosevelt and the Coming of the War, 1941* (1948) are sharply critical. Cordell Hull, *Memoirs* (2 vols., 1948) extensively quotes from documents. Specialized studies include: J. W. Pratt, *Cordell Hull, 1933–1944* (2 vols., 1964); L. C. Gardner, *Economic Aspects of New Deal Diplomacy* (1964); R. P. Browder, *The Origins of Soviet-American Diplomacy* (1953); R. A. Divine, *The Reluctant Belligerent: American Entry into World War II**

(1965); A. A. Offner, *American Appeasement: United States Foreign Policy and Germany, 1933–1938* (1969); Herbert Feis, *The Road to Pearl Harbor** (1950); Selig Adler, *The Isolationist Impulse** (1957); D. W. Wyman, *Paper Walls: America and the Refugee Crisis, 1938–1941* (1968); and Roberta Wohlstetter, *Pearl Harbor: Warning and Decision* (1962).

* Titles available in paperback.

Another Foreign Crusade with Mixed Results

With the bombing of Pearl Harbor President Roosevelt turned from the New Deal to national defense and then war abroad. About a quarter of a century earlier, President Woodrow Wilson had turned from progressive reform to a foreign crusade, with disillusioning results, but Roosevelt hoped to escape the frustrations that had befallen his predecessor. In trying to avoid the "mistakes" that Wilson had made, Roosevelt pursued essentially the same objectives by almost exactly the opposite means, so that at times his policies appeared to be the very reverse of Wilson's.

Thus, during World War II, Roosevelt did not hold the United States somewhat aloof from its allies and call it merely an "associated" power, as Wilson had done during World War I. To the contrary, under Roosevelt this country took the initiative in drafting and signing a Declaration of the United Nations (January 1, 1942). The document set forth the war aims of the Atlantic Charter, committing the country's entire military and economic resources to the prosecution of the war, and pledging unlimited cooperation with the other signatories to fight on and make no separate peace. In effect, the United States was taking the lead in forming a grand alliance among the twenty-six original partners and the twenty more that signed before the war was over.

In peacemaking as in warmaking, Roosevelt followed a course quite different from Wilson's. True, the war aims he presented in the Atlantic Charter, which he cosigned with Prime Minister Winston Churchill, were vaguely reminiscent of those that Wilson had announced, unilaterally, in his Fourteen Points. But Roosevelt, with his slogan of "unconditional surrender," was determined to allow no armistice short of the enemy's utter defeat. And he was careful to keep from repeating the steps that had led the United States to a fiasco in relation to the Versailles Treaty and the League of Nations. This time there was to be no general peace conference comparable to the one at Versailles, and the new peacekeeping arrangement was to be kept quite separate from the political settlements to be made. The wartime alliance itself was to be converted into a peacekeeping body—the United Nations organization.

When, at the war's conclusion, the Senate approved American membership in the U.N. organization, many liberal Americans rejoiced that their country now was righting the wrong it presumably had done in rejecting the League. They assumed that with the United States as a member, the League would have prevented a second world war; surely the U.N. would prevent a third. The optimism soon passed. For Americans the consequences of the Second World War were to prove even more disillusioning than those of the First, as the people came to realize that the victory of the grand alliance had brought no real peace to the world.

As a result of World War II, Germany and Japan were temporarily eliminated as military powers. A "power vacuum" was left in Europe, and another in Asia. Only two really great powers remained in the world—the United States and the Soviet Union. The influence of the Russian Communists, and later that of the Chinese Communists, began to flow into the voids left by the war. The United States undertook to resist the spread of Communist power and thus came into collision with its recent allies, the Russians and the Chinese. It now sought new alliances not only with old associates like Great Britain and France but also with former foes, Germany (or a part of that country) and Japan, which it began to help revive and rebuild as strong nations. Such, in essence, was the "cold war" that commenced within two years after the end of World War II.

At first the United States appeared to hold the upper hand, for it had a monopoly of atomic weapons. But by 1949, the Russians had exploded an A-bomb of their own. The Americans got ahead again, in 1952, with the vastly more destructive hydrogen bomb, but the Russians produced an H-bomb, too, the following year. By 1957, when the Russians put the first artificial satellite into orbit, they seemed to have taken the lead in the capacity to deliver missiles with nuclear warheads. In any event, each of the great contestants now had the capability, quite literally, of destroying the other. A wholly new era had arrived, in which another world war could wipe out mankind itself. Nobody really knew whether the old rules of power politics had relevance any longer. If humanity was spared an all-out war, the reason was perhaps that the world had reached what *The New York Times* (in 1958) called a new "balance of terror."

"We face a hostile ideology—global in scope, atheistic in character, ruthless in purpose, and insidious in method. Unhappily the danger it poses promises to be of indefinite duration." So said President Eisenhower in the farewell address he directed to the American people shortly before leaving office in 1961. "A vital element in keeping the peace is our military establishment. Our arms must be mighty, ready for instant action, so that no potential aggressor may be tempted to risk his own destruction."

While warning of dangers from outside, President Eisenhower also drew attention to a possible threat arising within the nation. This was the threat of undue power accruing to the "military-industrial complex" that had developed to provide for the national defense. For the first time in their history, the American people had in their midst, on a permanent basis, the "conjunction of an immense military establishment and a large arms industry." Eisenhower did not fully describe the complex, but the military establishment consisted of the Armed Services, the Central Intelligence Agency, and other bodies provided for in the National Security Act of 1947. The arms industry included not only manufacturers of traditional armaments but also producers of a bewildering variety of new aviational, aerospace, electronic, chemical, and biological supplies. Supporting the industry and supported by it were certain labor unions and numerous scientific groups, many of these in universities that had government research contracts.

Though the peril of nuclear annihilation hung over them, the majority of the American people, in a phrase of the time, "never had it so good." They were riding a wave of prosperity much higher and longer-lasting than any previous one in the history of the country. The boom continued through the 1950s and the 1960s, with an occasional recession or minor slump but with no real depression. A generation grew up that had never experienced such a calamity and could not believe it possible.

Yet there was much to be apprehensive about, at home as well as abroad. The prosperity was largely due to the foreign dangers, for it was stimulated by government spending for defense, and there was reason to wonder how long the good times would last if by some chance there should be a sudden "outbreak of peace." And even while the prosperity lasted, a large minority of the people, perhaps as many as 30 million of them, had little or no share in it. Especially disadvantaged were the Americans of African, Mexican, and Indian descent.

Chapter 27.   THE BATTLE FOR PRODUCTION

Mobilizing for Defense

Total war made the planning of industrial production as vital as military strategy. Roosevelt, at the time of the Munich crisis in 1938, had ordered the armed forces to modernize their production plan. Just before the outbreak of war in Europe, in August 1939, he authorized the War and Navy Departments to appoint a civilian advisory committee to survey the 1939 plan. This was the War Resources Board.

At this point politics began. The unfortunate use of the word "war" rather than "defense" in the title frightened the public, especially after the invasion of Poland when even the existence of such a body seemed a move toward involvement. The firmly anti-New Deal attitude of the Board pained Roosevelt. He speedily disbanded the War Resources Board and submitted to the many pressures against substituting any new defense agencies.

With the collapse of France in the late spring of 1940, Roosevelt could delay no longer, even though he was embarking upon a presidential campaign and wished to temper isolationist hostility. Rather than ask Congress to create defense agencies, he drew upon a 1916 statute for authority and reestablished the Advisory Commission of the Council of National Defense. This time he used the word "defense" rather than "war," and carefully balanced all the major national interests.

Out of this prototype grew the many defense agencies with their shifting or nebulous lines of authority and often ill-defined powers. Out of it came many of the heads of subsequent war agencies. Out of it too came one clear fact: whatever war agencies developed, Roosevelt was of no disposition to abdicate or share his presidential powers.

In January 1941, after the Advisory Commission had almost broken down and lost its control over priorities to the military, Roosevelt established a new Office of Production Management. The new improvisations worked little better than the old, and in August 1941 Roosevelt established a new priorities board for the OPM. Finally, after American entrance into the war, Roosevelt in January 1942 organized a War Production Board under Donald Nelson. Although Nelson was personable and a good organizer, he was not strong enough to force civilian control over priorities, or a more equitable distribution of contracts among smaller manufacturers, or a well-balanced production plan. He remained head of the WPB until August 1944, but as early as October 1942 lost much of his power when President Roosevelt persuaded Justice James F. Byrnes to resign from the Supreme Court to become in effect a sort of assistant president in charge of war production. Byrnes was head at first of the Office of Economic Stabilization, then after May 1943 of the Office of War Mobilization. The OWM developed into a workable war administration.

Materials for Victory

Meanwhile, with the awarding of the first large government contracts in the summer of 1940, industry began to boom. At the time of Pearl Harbor, the United States still had little armament because so much had been shipped to Great Britain and because so many of the plants had only recently begun production. The new productive capacity was remarkably large. Despite errors and chaotic conditions, the nation was producing more combat munitions than any of the belligerent nations — indeed almost as much as Germany and Japan combined. Airplane production was up to a rate of almost 25,000 per year. The armed forces already had inducted and were training two million men. This mobilization was only a fraction of what was soon to come, for large scale construction of factories and training camps was underway. While the nation during the debate over neutrality had not built its defenses with the smoothness and speed that critics demanded, it had achieved a substantial degree of preparedness.

The Japanese attack on Pearl Harbor created almost as much chaos indirectly in American war production as it did directly in the fleet in the Pacific. The war agencies in Washington began ordering tremendous quantities — indeed far too much — of everything.

Out of the confusion a pattern gradually emerged. The basic step was to coordinate the various phases of the war production program. As late as the summer of 1942, bottlenecks were halting some assembly lines. On July 4 the vital shipbuilding program had to be cut back because of scarcities of raw materials like steel plate and glass, and of components like valves, turbines, and engines. The WPB eventually broke most of the bottlenecks through the Controlled Materials Plan, which established a balanced production of finished products and allocated precise quantities of raw materials to each manufacturer.

An indispensable adjunct of the war agencies was the Senate War Investigating Committee, headed by Harry S. Truman, previously little known. Ruling out questions of military policy, the Senators ferreted out incompetence and corruption in the war-production and military-construction programs: outrageous expense in building army camps, improper inspection of airplane engines, a quixotic scheme to build an Arctic pipeline, and the like. The Truman Committee not only uncovered and stopped hundreds of millions of dollars of waste, but by its vigor led war administrators to be more diligent in preventing further waste. In the wartime expenditure of $400 billion there was amazingly little corruption.

By the beginning of 1944 war production reached such high levels that factories had substantially turned out what seemed to be needed to win the war. The output was double that of all Axis countries combined. Cutbacks began, but they were haphazard and ill-planned, and turned out in some instances to have been premature. With the cutbacks came pressure for a resumption of the manufacture of civilian durable goods. The military leaders stanchly opposed this. However, war needs even at their peak took only about a third of American production. While manufacture of such goods as automobiles, most electrical appliances, and nondefense housing had come to a halt in 1942, production of food, clothing, and goods for repair and maintenance was continued or even slightly increased.

Transporting the Supplies

As war production grew, the problem of transporting the supplies within the country and overseas became acute. Inside the United States, the Office of Defense Transportation, established in December 1941, coordinated all forms of transport — railroads, trucking, airlines, inland waterways, and pipelines. In contrast to the system in World War I, railroads remained under private control, but functioned effectively, carrying double the traffic of 1939 with only 10 percent more locomotives and 20 percent more freight cars.

Transporting troops and supplies overseas required one of the most spectacular construction programs of all. The Germans had sunk more than 12 million tons of shipping by 1942. To replace it, the United States Maritime Commission had to abandon its program of building fast, efficient ships requiring scarce turbines, valves, and electrical equipment. As early as July 1940, Admiral Emory S. Land, head of the Commission, recommended to the President mass production of a freighter that, while slow (sailing only eleven knots), would be simple to construct and not require scarce components. By using the existing designs for an old-fashioned British tramp steamer with a reciprocating engine and steam winches, they saved six months in starting production. This "Ugly Duckling" was the Liberty ship. After a slow beginning, builders substituted welding for riveting and applied prefabrication and subassembly techniques in constructing it. In 1941 construction of Liberty ships required an average of 355 days; by the end of 1942, the time had been cut to 56 days. By 1945 the United States had over 36 million tons of ships afloat.

Scientists Against the Axis

The most revolutionary changes for the future came out of laboratories, as scientists pooled their skills in a race against those of the Axis — above all the Germans — to turn basic knowledge that was available to all into decisive weapons of war. Between the two wars, while the United States had neglected military research and development, Germany had sprinted far ahead, except in the field of radar. In the 1920s the Naval Research Laboratory in Washington had discovered the principle of radar by bouncing back a radio beam directed at a ship on the Potomac. The British had the most highly developed radar, and it was their salvation during the air blitz of 1940–1941.

Other potential weapons were in the offing which, if the Germans developed them first, could mean Nazi victory in the war. (This was one of the reasons the armed forces had decided to concentrate upon defeating Germany first.) The only way in which American scientists could catch up seemed to be through teamwork. The German threat brought creation of a government scientific agency such as the New Deal had failed to produce. A leading scientist, Vannevar Bush, persuaded President Roosevelt to create a committee for scientific research in June 1940. A year later, under the direction of Bush, it became the Office of Scientific Research and Development, which mobilized scientists with such effectiveness that in some areas they outstripped their German opponents.

The Americans and the British developed superior radar, which not only detected enemy airplanes and ships but helped direct shells against them. In these shells by 1943 one of the most effective American inventions was being used, radio-directed proximity fuses that detonated the shells as they neared their targets. American rocket research produced weapons that enormously increased the fire-power of airplanes, ships, and tanks; but the United States lagged behind the Germans, who before the end of the war were blasting London with enormous V-1 and V-2 rockets. The Germans also built the first jet airplanes and snorkel submarines, which would have been an even more serious menace if they had come into full production.

There was a danger, little publicized, that Germany might develop an atomic weapon. In the summer of 1939 a physicist, Enrico Fermi, and a mathematician, Albert Einstein, got word to President Roosevelt that German physicists had achieved atomic fission in uranium; what had long been theoretically possible had been accomplished. Next might come a bomb. The President authorized a small research project, and a race in the dark against the Nazis began.

In December 1942 physicists produced a controlled chain reaction in an atomic pile at the University of Chicago. The problem then became the enormous technical one of achieving this release of power in a bomb. Through the Manhattan District of the Army Engineer Corps, the government secretly poured nearly $2 billion into plants to produce fissionable plutonium and into another project, under the supervision of J. Robert Oppenheimer, which undertook to build a bomb. Here was an enormous and frightening gamble, against the hazards that the thing might not work and that the enemy might succeed first. Only after the war did the United States discover that the Germans were far from developing a usable atomic device. On July 16, 1945, after the end of the war in Europe, the first A-bomb was exploded, on a tower in New Mexico — producing the most blinding flash of light ever seen on earth, and then a huge billowing mushroom cloud.

Mobilization of Labor

Almost as complex as the scientific problems were those of integrating the domestic economy into the war machine: labor, agriculture, production for civilian use, and finance.

The nation, after grappling for years with the problem of millions of unemployed, found itself hard pressed for sufficient people to swell the fighting forces, man the war plants, till the fields, and keep the domestic economy functioning. There were periodic demands for national service legislation or a labor draft, but unions were so vehemently opposed that no such measure ever passed the Senate. The relatively weak War Manpower Commission tried to coerce workers into remaining at defense jobs at the risk of being drafted, but the war came to an end without any tight allocation of labor comparable to that of materials. The armed forces had first call upon men through the Selective Service, which had been in operation since the fall of 1940. Altogether draft boards registered 31 million men. Including volunteers, over 15 million men and women served in the armed forces during the war. Nevertheless the working force jumped from 46.5 million to over 53 million as the 7 million unemployed and many previously considered unemployable, the very young and the elderly, and several million women found jobs.

The number of civilian employees of the federal government trebled.

This mobilization of manpower entailed the greatest reshuffling of population within such a short time in the entire history of the nation; altogether 27.3 million people moved during the war. It meant also a heavy weight of wartime tension on American families. With the return of prosperity and the impending departure of soldiers, both marriage and birth rates rose. In 1942 and 1943 about 3 million children were born each year, compared with 2 million a year before the war. But young wives and mothers fared badly in crowded housing near defense plants or army bases, or after husbands had been shipped overseas, back home with parents. Draft boards deferred fathers as long as possible, but more than a million were ultimately inducted. More than 2.5 million wives were separated from their husbands because of the war. The divorce rate increased slowly. Because men in the armed forces could in effect not be divorced without their consent, and many estranged wives stayed married in order to continue receiving allotment checks, a heavy backlog was built for postwar divorce courts.

The great migration to war plants was stripping the agricultural South of underprivileged whites and Negroes alike, as 5 million people moved within the South, and another 1.6 million left the area completely. In the South this exodus led to the false rumor among outraged white housewives that the departing Negro domestics had formed "Eleanor Clubs," named after Mrs. Roosevelt, to "get a white woman in every kitchen by 1943." In the North, it led to explosive tension when Negroes, enjoying their new freedom, were jostled in crowded streetcars against indignant whites newly migrated from the South. A serious riot in which twenty-five Negroes and nine whites were killed shook Detroit in June 1943. New York narrowly averted a similar disaster. At the very time when the United States was fighting a war against the racist doctrines of Hitler, many whites became resentful over the rapid gains Negroes were making. In June 1941, after the head of the Pullman porters' union, A. Philip Randolph, threatened a march on Washington, President Roosevelt established the Fair Employment Practices Committee. It worked throughout the war against discrimination in employment. By 1944 2 million Negroes were at work in war indus-

tries, and many previous barriers to economic opportunities for Negroes were permanently cracked.

Not everyone shared in the new prosperity. Government economists reported in 1943 that 10 million families still received less than the $1,675 per year requisite for a minimum standard of living. Most Americans, however, were more affluent than they had been. The living standard of working people advanced rapidly; this was due less to wage increases than to payment of time-and-a-half for overtime beyond 40 hours. The average work week lengthened from 40.6 hours in 1941 to 45.2 in 1944. As living costs rose (on a 1935–1939 base of 100) from 100.4 in 1940 to 128.4 in 1945, gross weekly wages went up from $25.20 to $43.39. Working women and children also brought additional prosperity to millions of families.

Price Controls

At the beginning of the war, with a two-year supply of wheat, cotton, and corn stored in Secretary Wallace's ever-normal granary, there seemed no danger of food shortages in the United States. But within six months after Pearl Harbor, scarcities of many sorts began to develop. The United States felt the increased demand of the armed forces and its allies, and the reduction of supplies due to the loss of fibers and oils from Southeast Asia. By 1942 meat production was half again that of depression years, but American consumers with their increased buying power were eager to buy even more. Consumer income in 1943 was 65 percent above depression levels, and much of it was in the pockets of people who had not eaten adequately for years.

A Food Administrator did exist, Chester Davis, but he resigned in protest when his views (and those of the American Farm Bureau Federation) did not prevail; his successor was Marvin Jones. Neither man had the dictatorial powers to provide for agriculture the scarce supplies and manpower that the dominant farm bloc in Congress would have liked to bestow upon agricultural producers. Although farmers had to depend upon whatever the War Production Board would allocate to them, they received legislation raising the ceiling on commodity prices to 110 percent of parity. Since these increases came into conflict with the anti-inflation efforts of the administration, a dogged but indecisive struggle developed between the President and the congressional farm bloc over farm prices.

Pressures from business, farmers, and labor, combined with the scarcity of consumer goods and the burgeoning of buying power, created an almost irresistible trend toward inflation. During the defense period, the Office of Price Administration lacked real coercive power and failed to halt inflation. Between the invasion of Poland and the attack on Pearl Harbor, prices of twenty-eight basic commodities rose by nearly a fourth. Immediately thereafter, pressures became so acute that prices went up 2 percent per month. Congress hastily passed a bill authorizing only selective price-fixing and setting ceilings with a preferential trap door for agriculture.

The OPA in April 1942 issued a General Maximum Price Regulation that froze prices of consumer goods and of rents in defense areas only at their March 1942 level. The greatest weakness was the rise of farm prices toward 110 percent of parity, which drove food prices—the most conspicuous item in any index—steadily upward. This gave ammunition to labor unions' barrage against fixed wages. In October 1942 Congress, grudgingly responding to the President's demand, passed the Anti-Inflation Act. Under its authority, Roosevelt immediately froze agricultural prices, wages, salaries, and rents throughout the country.

In July 1943 Roosevelt appointed a former advertising executive with remarkable administrative talents, Chester Bowles, to head the OPA. With a small enforcement staff, Bowles braved general unpopularity to hold the increase in living costs during the next two years to 1.4 percent. Altogether, the price level went up less than 29 percent from 1939 to the end of the war, compared with 63 percent between 1914 and the armistice.

Consumers nonetheless suffered numerous irritations and discomforts. The OPA, through unpaid local volunteers manning 5,600 price and rationing boards, administered the rationing of canned goods, coffee, sugar, meat, butter and other fats, shoes, tires, gasoline, and fuel oil. The OPA could not, however, control deterioration of quality. Black-marketing and overcharging grew in proportions far beyond OPA policing capacity; in 1943 Congress slashed the funds of the enforcement division.

War Finance

One of the most important inflationary controls was the sale of war bonds and stamps to channel off some of the excess purchasing power, which for the single year 1945 mounted to nearly $60 billion. Throughout most of the war, personal incomes were at least a third greater than the available civilian goods and services. The Treasury Department, through eight war bond drives and its payroll deduction plans, but with few of the lurid or coercive touches of World War I, sold $40 billion worth of series "E" bonds to small investors, and $60 billion more to individuals and corporate entities other than banks.

Had this been the total of government loans, the effect would have been to quell inflation, but the Treasury had to borrow $87.5 billion more from commercial banks. Since in effect the Federal Reserve created new credits which the government then spent, the result was to inflate the money in circulation and increase inflationary pressures.

Taxes did much more to drain off surplus purchasing power. The government raised 41 percent of its war costs through taxation, compared with 33 percent during World War I (a measure of the greater popularity of World War II). The Revenue Act of 1942, which Roosevelt hailed as "the greatest tax bill in American history," levied a 94 percent tax on highest incomes; the President had suggested that no one should net more than $25,000 per year during the war. Also, for the first time, the income tax fell upon those in lower income brackets. To simplify payment for these new millions, Congress enacted a withholding system of payroll deductions in 1943. Corporation taxes reached a maximum of 40 percent on the largest incomes. In addition, excess profits were subject to a 90 percent tax, reclaiming for the government a large part of the return from war contracts. However, these taxes could be rebated to companies to aid them in reconversion, a provision of future significance. In effect, the government taxed away a large part of the profits of corporations, then returned it when it was needed for postwar expansion. Heavy excise taxes on transportation, communication, luxuries, and amusements completed the levies.

Between 1941 and 1945 the government raised $138 billion through taxation—nearly a $100 billion of it from income and excess profits taxes. Those in the top 5 percent of the income scale suffered a serious relative economic loss, as their share of disposable income dropped from 26 percent in 1940 to 16 percent in 1944. Few persons or corporations were able to make fortunes out of the war, and a considerable amount of economic leveling—upward more than downward—had taken place. Despite the heavy taxation, by the end of the war consumers possessed an estimated $129 billion in liquid savings.

From 1941 to 1945 the federal government spent twice as much as the total appropriations from the creation of the government to 1941, and ten times as much as the cost of World War I—a total of $321 billion. The national debt rose from $49 billion in 1941 to $259 billion in 1945, yet the black warnings of national bankruptcy that had punctuated the New Deal years all but disappeared.

Freedoms Abroad and at Home

In January 1941 Roosevelt enunciated Four Freedoms as war aims—freedom of speech and worship and freedom from want and fear. But these never caught the public imagination as Wilson's Fourteen Points had done. The public had a practical sense of the war as a necessary evil.

Conflict among government information agencies led to the establishment in June 1942 of the Office of War Information under a shrewd news commentator, Elmer Davis. Although the OWI consolidated four previous organizations, it coordinated rather than assumed the information function of domestic war agencies.

The OWI aroused the misgivings of anti-administration congressmen. They feared OWI might promote New Dealish policies and the 1944 candidacy of Roosevelt. In 1943 Congress cut funds for the Domestic Branch so drastically that it had to stop producing propaganda.

Overseas, OWI carried on a program employing 8,400 persons by V-E Day. Through "Voice of America" broadcasts begun in 1941 and propaganda of many sorts it presented American war aims and aspirations for a peaceful postwar world. As the symbol of this idealism it dramatized President Roosevelt. By the end of the war, Roosevelt was more of a hero overseas than at home, and American aims appeared more idealistic abroad than in the United States.

The war produced far less hatred and vindictiveness at home than had World War I. The energy that had gone into crude vigilantism in the earlier war went in the Second World War into serving as air raid wardens and doing similar duties for the Office of Civilian Defense. People continued to eat hamburgers and sauerkraut and listen to Wagner. They demonstrated little animus toward Americans of German background and practically none toward Italians. A few Nazi agents and American fascists were jailed, but the most ambitious effort to punish them, a sedition trial of twenty-eight, ended in a mistrial after the defendants' lawyers had engaged in long weeks of delaying tactics. A few papers like Father Coughlin's *Social Justice* were barred from the mails. But socialists went unpunished, and religious conscientious objectors who were willing to register went to Civilian Public Service camps rather than prison.

In sad contrast to this moderation, the frenzy of public fury turned on the Japanese. The fighting in the Pacific developed a fierce savagery, reflected in the public anger within the United States. On the Pacific Coast, hatred of Americans of Japanese background became extreme. Wild stories circulated about sabotage at Pearl Harbor—later proven 100 percent untrue. Under public pressure, Roosevelt in February 1942 authorized the army to remove all people of Japanese ancestry from the West Coast. Some 117,000 people, two-thirds of them United States citizens, were abruptly herded behind barbed wire, and later shipped to ten relocation centers in wild and disagreeable areas. They suffered the financial loss of at least 40 percent of their possessions and for several years were barred from lucrative employment. Yet Japanese-Americans in Hawaii were left unmolested without incident throughout the war. There were 17,600 Japanese-Americans in the armed forces. Their units, especially in Italy, established outstanding records for bravery under fire.

The Supreme Court in 1944 validated the evacuation and, in other decisions as well, upheld military control over civilians. In time of war or national emergency, United States citizens apparently could expect no court protection of their civil rights from military or executive authority.

Wartime Politics

At times the sound and fury in Washington seemed almost to drown out the clangor of war against the Axis. Despite all the platitudinous pleas to put aside politics in the interest of national unity, the struggles became if anything more virulent during the war. Conservatives saw in the war an opportunity to eradicate hated remnants of the New Deal; some liberals regarded it as an opportunity to bring Wilson's ideas to fruition, and even go beyond them to establish a global New Deal. Every one of the great pressure groups in the country fought to maintain or improve its relative position; spokesmen for large business and small, farmers and labor, jockeyed for position in Washington. The tenor of Congress continued to be conservative, and it was sensitive as always to the demands of organized constituents. Throughout the war, key committee chairmen who were leaders of the conservative coalition dominated Congress and forced their will upon President Roosevelt. Through the election of 1942, as the United States and its allies suffered unparalleled military disasters and the war administration in Washington seemed to compound confusion, the criticism rose to a crescendo. In the election, the Republicans gained forty-seven seats in the House and ten in the Senate. Within both parties the trend was toward the conservative.

President Roosevelt, to obtain crucial congressional support in prosecuting the war and planning the peace, continued to accept the sacrifice of New Deal measures. At a press conference he announced (1943) that "Dr. Win-the-War" had replaced "Dr. New Deal."

Dissatisfaction with wartime regimentation and smoldering resentments still glowing from the prewar debate over intervention seemed to give the Republicans an opportunity in 1944. They had seen auguries of a national shift toward the right in the congressional election of 1942. In their vigorous young candidate, Governor Thomas E. Dewey of New York, who ran with Governor John W. Bricker of Ohio, they seemed to have an answer to Roosevelt and the aging New Dealers.

As for President Roosevelt, it was a foregone conclusion that he would be nominated for a fourth term if he so desired. Since he was visibly aging, and thinning so that his clothes ill fit him, there was much speculation over his choice for the vice-presidential nominee. Vice President Wallace was during the war the hero of most advanced New Dealers and much of the CIO membership. But he was sneered at by party bosses and some Southern Democrats as a visionary who wished to extend the New Deal to the entire globe, to bring "a quart of milk for every Hottentot." They rallied behind James M. Byrnes of South Carolina, who had been functioning ably as unofficial assistant president — but Byrnes was unacceptable to organized labor. Out of the skirmishing among the rival factions within the Democratic party came Roosevelt's proposal of a compromise candidate acceptable to most of them, Senator Harry S. Truman of Missouri. Truman had won newspaper approval as chairman of the Senate War Investigating Committee, was a consistent New Dealer in his voting record, and was from a border state. He was popular in the Senate.

The election promised to be close — partly because the vote was likely to be small, and presumably a light vote would aid the Republicans. The possibility was like an injection of adrenalin into Roosevelt. At the end of September 1944 addressing a raucously appreciative audience of Teamsters Union members, he was at his sardonic best. He followed this triumph with a strenuous campaign in Chicago and throughout the East.

This tour de force, seemingly proving Roosevelt's capacity to serve four more years, his international leadership, and his promise to return to the New Deal after the war, were a winning combination. Organized labor, working through the CIO Political Action Committee, brought out the workers' votes. The President defeated Dewey by a margin of 432 electoral votes to 99, and a popular vote of 25,602,000 to 22,006,000. The Democrats lost one seat in the Senate, but gained twenty in the House. The Democratic victory seemed to mean a revival of the New Deal at home; and the campaign promises of both parties indicated that the United States would continue to take a lead in international affairs.

Chapter 28. VICTORY WITHOUT PEACE

The American War Machine

As Commander in Chief, President Roosevelt bore responsibility for the conduct of the war. Personally, and through assistants like Harry Hopkins and cabinet members, he coordinated the war planning of the Joint Chiefs with war production and manpower and with foreign policy. In July 1940 the War Plans Division of the Army General Staff had pointed out that civilians should decide the "what" of national policies, and the professional soldiers the "how." Roosevelt, who had always zealously guarded civilian control even in the Navy Department and the War Department, followed this course through the war. However, he depended heavily upon the advice of the Joint Chiefs of Staff and, once major policy had been decided, seldom interfered with their strategy.

The first of the great policy decisions had come in 1940 when the Americans decided that even if Japan entered the war, their primary goal would be to defeat Germany with its superior military force, war production, and weapons development. The United States confirmed this priority in the initial wartime conference with the British at the end of December 1941. This decision did not mean neglecting the war against Japan. By August 1941, when the buildup, especially of airplanes, was under way in the Philippines, and later when General MacArthur received orders to fight, the strategy was shifting to a two-front war. The war against Germany was to be offensive, while that against Japan was to be defensive. It was difficult to hold to this policy as the Japanese tide in the Pacific swelled far beyond the bounds the most pessimistic planners had anticipated.

During the first chaotic months of shocking reverses, the armed forces allotted their men and supplies piecemeal to try to meet each new Axis threat. Top strategists emphatically warned that such dissipation of effort might lead to defeat. No one was more insistent than Dwight D. Eisenhower, who had been brought to Washington after Pearl Harbor as a Far Eastern expert, and who by the spring of 1942 was head of the Operations Planning Division under General

Marshall. In emphatic memoranda he hammered away at the need to build up men and supplies in Europe for the invasion of North Africa that Roosevelt and Churchill had decided upon in their December 1941 meeting. Because of his vigor and his important role in developing an invasion plan, Eisenhower became the logical man to send to England in June 1942 as Commanding General in the European theater.

On the Defensive   1941–1942

While the United States was building and equipping its fighting forces, it had to depend upon the Russians and the British to hold back the Germans as best they could. During the discouraging first six months of American participation, the American forces had to stand perilously on the defensive in both the Atlantic and the Pacific. There even seemed danger of a breakthrough in Egypt and the Caucasus that might enable the Germans and Japanese to join forces in the Middle East or India.

Ten hours after the strike at Pearl Harbor, Japanese airplanes hit the airfields at Manila, destroying half the American bombers and two-thirds of the fighter planes. That same day the Japanese sank two British warships off Malaya, the only Allied warships in the Far East. Three days later Guam fell; then, in the weeks that followed, Wake Island and Hong Kong. The great British fortress of Singapore in Malaya surrendered in February 1942, the East Indies in March, and Burma in April. In the Philippines on May 6 the exhausted Philippine and American troops, having made brave withdrawals to the Bataan peninsula and the Island of Corregidor in Manila Bay, ran down the last American flag in the Far East.

Only one weak outpost, Port Moresby in southern New Guinea, stood as a bulwark against the invasion of Australia. It seemed likely to fall, but there containment began through the efforts on land of Australian and American troops, and on the sea, of American aircraft carriers. In the Battle of Coral Sea on May 6–7, 1942, the Americans turned back Japanese invasion forces threatening Port Moresby. Under General MacArthur, who had escaped from the Philippines, American and Australian troops began clearing the Japanese from New Guinea.

After the Battle of Coral Sea, the navy, having intercepted Japanese messages, knew the next move and rushed every available plane and vessel into the central Pacific. Near Midway Island, June 3–6, 1942, these forces inflicted heavy damage on a Japanese invasion fleet and headed off a drive to capture the island and neutralize Hawaii. The United States had achieved its goal of containment in the Pacific, and as men and supplies could be spared from the operations against the Nazis, it could assume the offensive against Japan.

In the Atlantic during the early months of 1942, the Nazis tried by means of submarines to confine the Americans to the Western Hemisphere. By mid-January, the Germans had moved so many submarines to the Atlantic coast, where at night they torpedoed tankers silhouetted against the lights of cities, that they created a critical oil shortage. Against convoys bound for Europe they made attacks with devastating success. In the first eleven months, they sank over 8 million tons of shipping – 1.2 million more than the Allies meanwhile built – and threatened to delay indefinitely the large-scale shipment of supplies and men to Europe. Gradually the United States countered by developing effective antisubmarine vessels, air patrols, detecting devices, and weapons.

The submarines made it difficult to send assistance to the British and Russians in the summer of 1942 when they needed it most. The German *Afrika Corps* raced to El Alamein, only seventy-five miles from Alexandria, Egypt, threatening the Suez Canal and the Middle East. At the same time, German armies in Russia were plunging toward the Caucasus. In May, the Russian foreign minister, Vyacheslav Molotov, visited Washington to demand an immediate second front that would divert at least forty German divisions from Russia; the alternative might be Russian collapse. Roosevelt promised to do everything possible to divert the Germans by invading France. But Churchill arrived the next month, when the Germans were threatening Egypt, and he strongly urged an invasion of North Africa instead.

The Mediterranean Offensive

The overwhelming losses in the August 1942 raid on Dieppe, France, undertaken by experienced Canadian troops, indicated the wisdom of making the first American landing on a relatively unprotected flank. Through advance negotiations with officials of the Vichy government of defeated France, the Americans hoped to make a bloodless landing in French North Africa. At the end of October 1942 the British opened a counteroffensive at El Alamein that sent the *Afrika Corps* reeling back. On November 8, Anglo-American forces landed at Oran, Algiers, and Casablanca, Morocco, with some bungling and gratifyingly few losses. They met determined Vichy French resistance only at Casablanca.

Admiral Jean Darlan, earlier one of the most notorious collaborators with the Nazis, signed an armistice with the Allies on November 12. Outraged American liberals protested against the deal with the Vichyites as opposed to cooperating with the French resistance forces under General Charles de Gaulle. Nevertheless, the Vichy gamble saved lives and speeded the liberation of North Africa.

The Germans tried to counter the invasion by attacking in Tunisia. The green American troops lost heavily, but with the aid of the British held onto their bases, gained in experience, and gradually closed a vise on the German and Italian troops. On May 12, 1943, the last Axis troops in North Africa surrendered. The Mediterranean had been reopened, and the Americans had learned lessons that would be useful in the successful invasion of France.

That invasion, despite the continued clamoring of the Russians, was not to take place immediately. The fighting in Tunisia had tied up too large a part of the Allied combat resources for too long. Nazi submarines were still taking too heavy a toll of the Allies' inadequate shipping. Some of the ships and production had to be diverted to the antisubmarine war, and others to the prosecution of the Pacific campaigns. Also, the planners in London had come to recognize that an enormous buildup was necessary for a successful cross-channel invasion. Fortunately for the Allies, the tide turned for the Russians also during the winter of 1942–1943, when they successfully held the Germans at Stalingrad in the Ukraine, eliminating an army of 250,000 men.

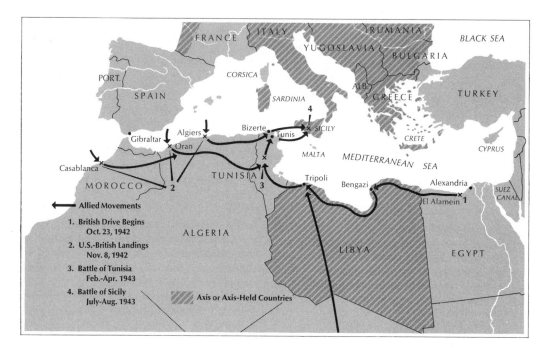

The North African and Sicilian Campaigns

As early as mid-January 1943 Roosevelt and Churchill and their staffs, while conferring at Casablanca, looked ahead to the next move. This was to be an invasion of Sicily, even though General Marshall feared it might delay the invasion of France. Churchill argued persuasively that the operation in Sicily might knock Italy out of the war and lead the Germans to tie up many divisions in defense of Italy and the Balkans.

On the night of July 9, 1943, American and British armies landed in the extreme southeast of Sicily, where defenses were comparatively light. In thirty-eight days the Allies conquered the island and looked toward the Italian mainland. Mussolini now fell from power, to be replaced by the pro-Allied Marshall Pietro Badoglio. At once Badoglio opened complicated negotiations to switch Italy to the side of the United Nations. As the negotiations went on, the Nazis moved eight strong divisions into northern Italy, concentrated other troops near Rome, and turned the country into an occupied defense bastion.

A limited but long and punishing campaign opened on the Italian peninsula on September 3, 1943. It started with the greatest optimism, for that same day the Italian government signed an armistice agreement, and the Allies quickly

seized bases and airfields in southern Italy. But the Nazi defenders fought so fiercely from hilly redoubts that by early 1944 they had stopped the slow and deliberately moving Allies at Monte Cassino. When the Allies tried to break behind the line by landing at Anzio, also south of Rome, they were almost thrown back into the sea. With relatively few divisions, the Nazis were tying down the Allies and concentrating upon Russia. Finally in May 1944 the Allies captured Cassino, pressed on from the Anzio beachhead, and on June 4 captured Rome, just before the cross-channel invasion of France began.

The Liberation of Europe

In the fall of 1943 Germany was already reeling under the incessant blows from the growing Allied air power. Great Britain had begun its mass bombing of German industrial centers in the late spring of 1942 with a thousand-plane night raid on Cologne. In August the Americans made their first experimental daytime raids on the continent. Bombing almost around the clock began on a gigantic scale in February 1944. One of the objects of these bombing raids was to draw German fighter planes into battle. By the

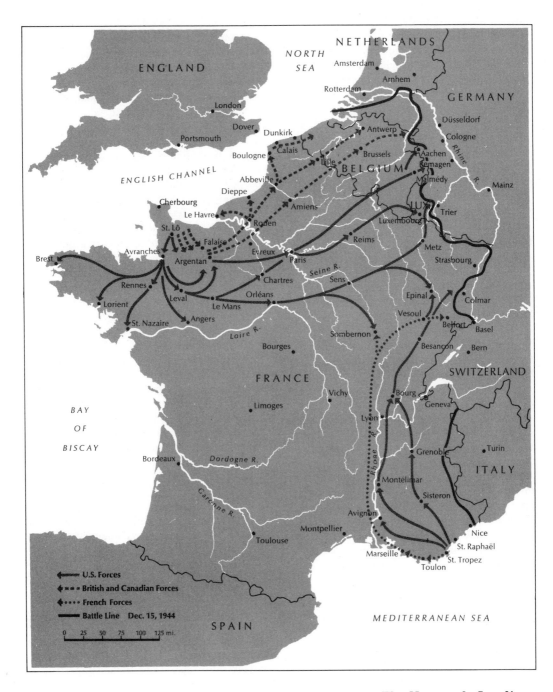

The Normandy Landings

end of the war, the Americans were flying over 7,000 bombers and 6,000 fighters in Europe, had dropped nearly a million and a half tons of bombs, and had lost nearly 10,000 bombers. British figures were similar. The bombing at-

tacks, first upon the aviation industry, then upon transportation, did much to clear the way for the invasion in the late spring. By May 1944 the *Luftwaffe* was incapable of beating off the Allied air cover for an invasion.

As D-Day (invasion day) approached, the invasion was postponed from the beginning of May until early June despite the likelihood of worsening weather, in order to obtain an additional month's production of special landing craft. A sudden storm delayed the operation for a day, but on the morning of June 6, 1944, the invasion came, not at the narrowest part of the English Channel, where the Nazis expected it, but along sixty miles of the Cotentin peninsula on the Normandy coast. While airplanes and battleships offshore incessantly bombarded the Nazi defenses, 4,000 vessels, stretching as far as the eye could see, brought in troops and supplies.

Within two weeks after the initial landings, the Allies had put ashore a million men and the equipment for them. They also had captured Cherbourg, only to find that the Germans had blocked its harbor so skillfully that it could not be used until August.

Well into July, the Allies fought mile by mile through the Normandy hedgerows. The breakthrough came on July 25, 1944, when General Omar Bradley's First Army, using its armor as cavalry had been used in earlier wars, smashed the German lines in an enormous sweep southward, then eastward. The invasion on the Mediterranean coast, beginning on August 15, quickly seized new ports (also seriously blocked) and opened new supply lines for the Allies. On August 25 Free French forces rode into Paris, jammed with cheering throngs. By mid-September, the Allied armies had driven the Germans from almost all of France and Belgium, including the port of Antwerp, and had come to a halt against a firm line of German defenses.

Cold weather, rain, and floods aided the Germans. In December they struck with desperate fury along fifty miles of front in the Ardennes Forest, driving fifty-five miles toward Antwerp before they were stopped (in the "Battle of the Bulge") at Bastogne.

While the Allies were fighting their way through France to the Westwall (German defense line) and up the Italian peninsula, the Russian armies had been sweeping westward into central Europe and the Balkans. The Russian armies advanced more rapidly than had been expected and in late January 1945 launched an offensive of over 150 divisions toward the Oder River, deep in Germany.

After liquidating the German thrust into the Ardennes, which had almost exhausted the Nazi fighting capacity, the Allied armies pushed on to the Rhine. The Americans captured Cologne on the west bank March 6, 1945, and on the next day, through remarkable luck, captured a bridge across the Rhine at Remagen. Troops poured across it. By the end of March the last great drives were under way as the British commander Montgomery with a million troops pushed across the north while Bradley's army, sweeping through central Germany, completed the encirclement and trapping of 300,000 German soldiers in the Ruhr. Russian troops were about to mount a spring offensive only thirty-five miles from Berlin.

There were fears that the Nazis were preparing for a last stand in an Alpine redoubt centering on Berchtesgaden on the Austrian border. In fact, however, the German western front had been demolished. The only real questions were where the Americans would drive next and where they would join the Russians. The Americans, capable of moving much farther eastward than had been anticipated, could have beaten the Russians to Berlin and Prague. This would have cost American lives but would have reaped political gain in Europe. General Eisenhower decided, instead, to send American troops to capture the Alpine redoubt and then halt along the Elbe River in central Germany to meet the Russians.

On May 8, 1945, the remaining German forces surrendered unconditionally. V-E (Victory in Europe) Day arrived amidst monster celebrations in western Europe and in the United States. The rejoicing was tempered only by knowledge of the continuing war against Japan.

The Pacific Offensive

The offensive strategy against the Japanese involved amphibious warfare of a type that the marine corps had been developing since the early 1920s. In the Pacific these new tactics came to be so perfected that troops were able to cross and seize vigorously defended beaches when the United States could not by-pass them and immobilize advanced Japanese strong points. The American strategy was, whenever feasible, "Hit 'em where they ain't."

The southern Solomon Islands to the east of New Guinea were being developed as a Japa-

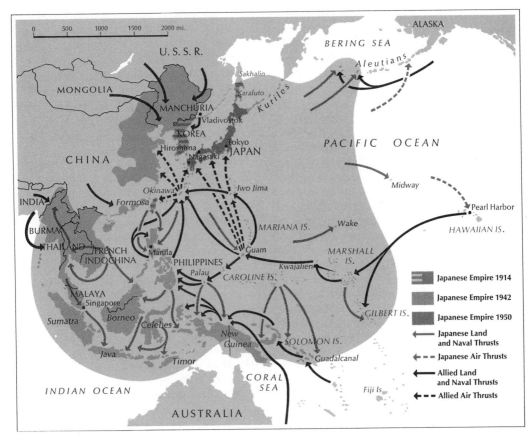

The War in the Pacific

nese base for air raids against American communications with Australia. In August 1942 the navy and marines opened an offensive against three of these islands, Gavutu, Tulagi, and Guadalcanal. Around and on Guadalcanal a struggle of unprecendented ferocity developed as the United States and Japanese navies battled for control in a series of large-scale engagements. By the time the struggle was over, the United States and its allies had lost heavily in cruisers, carriers, and destroyers, but had sunk forty-seven Japanese vessels. The Japanese navy had lost its offensive strength and thereafter concentrated upon defensive operations.

During the months when the great naval battles had been going against the United States, the Americans had gained control of the air and thus were able to sustain the marines, and subsequently the army, in their precarious jungle onslaught. By February 1943 Guadalcanal had been won. Through the year the island-hopping

continued all around the enormous Japanese-held perimeter: in the South Pacific through the northern Solomons to New Georgia and in November to Bougainville; in the Central Pacific, also in November, the marine landing on Makin and the bloody assault on Tarawa in the Gilberts; in the Northern Pacific, the inexpert reconquest of Kiska and Attu in the Aleutians.

Victories in the Marshall Islands in February 1944 cracked the Japanese outer perimeter, and before the month was out the navy had plunged far within it to wreck the bastion at Truk and raid Saipan in the Marianas. American submarines were increasingly harassing Japanese shipping, and thus hampering the economy. In 1943 they sank 284 ships; in 1944 they sank 492 — necessitating by summer a cut of nearly a quarter in skimpy Japanese food rations and creating a crucial gasoline shortage. The inner empire of Japan was coming under relentless siege.

Meanwhile, in 1942, the Japanese forced General Joseph H. Stilwell out of Burma and brought their troops as far west as the mountains bordering on India. China was so isolated that the United States could send in meager supplies only through an aerial ferry over the "hump" of the Himalayas. Through 1943, Stilwell with Chinese, Indian, and a few American troops fought back through northern Burma, constructing a road and parallel pipeline across the rugged mountains into Yunnan province, China. Meanwhile the Fourteenth Air Force (before Pearl Harbor, the "Flying Tigers") harassed the Japanese. In June 1944, from Chinese bases, B-29 bombers struck the Yawata steel mills in Japan. The Japanese retaliated in the next few months by overrunning the bases from which the bombers operated. They drove so far into the interior that they threatened the Chinese terminus of the Ledo Road, and perhaps even the center of government at Chungking.

During 1944 Japan came under heavy blockade from the sea and bombardment from the air. American submarines firing torpedoes and laying mines continued to make heavy inroads in the dwindling Japanese merchant marine.

In mid-June an enormous American armada struck the heavily fortified Mariana Islands, quickly but expensively capturing Tinian, Guam, and Saipan, 1,350 miles from Tokyo. These were among the bloodiest operations of the war. In September the Americans landed on the Western Carolines. The way was being prepared for the return to the Philippines. For weeks in advance Navy craft swept the central Pacific, and airplanes ranged over the Philippines and Formosa. Finally, on October 20 General MacArthur's troops landed on Leyte Island in the Philippines. The Japanese, threatened with being fatally cut off from their new empire in Southeast Asia, threw their remaining fleets against the invaders in three major encounters—together comprising the decisive Battle of Leyte Gulf, the largest naval engagement in history—and lost almost all their remaining sea power.

Atomic Triumph over Japan

With remarkable speed but grievous losses the American forces cut still deeper into the Japanese empire during the early months of 1945.

While fighting continued in the Philippines, the marines landed in February on the tiny volcanic island of Iwo Jima, only 750 miles from Tokyo. The Americans needed Iwo Jima to provide fighter cover for Japan-bound bombers and a landing place for crippled ones. The Japanese defended the island so grimly that the marines suffered over 20,000 casualties. It was the bloodiest battle in the history of the marine corps.

The battle for Okinawa, an island sixty-five miles long, beginning on April 1, 1945, was even bloodier. This island was 370 miles south of Japan, and its conquest clearly would be a prelude to an invasion of the main islands. On land and from the air, the Japanese fought with literally a suicidal fury. Week after week they sent Kamikaze suicide planes against the American and British ships, losing 3,500 of them but inflicting great damage. Ashore at night, Japanese troops launched equally desperate attacks on the American lines. The United States and its allies suffered nearly 50,000 casualties on land and afloat before the battle came to an end in late June 1945. The Japanese lost 110,000 killed and 7,800 prisoners.

This same sort of bitter fighting seemed to await the Americans when they invaded Japan—if indeed they should ever have to invade. There were signs that the Japanese might surrender, for they had almost no ships and few airplanes with which to fight. In July 1945 American warships stood offshore with impunity and shelled industrial targets, most of which were already in ruins from the heavy bombing attacks. Long since, moderate Japanese leaders had regarded the war as lost. Upon the invasion of Okinawa, the Emperor appointed a new premier and charged him with suing for peace. The premier could not persuade the army leaders to lay down their arms, but nevertheless he, and in early summer the Emperor himself, tried to obtain mediation through Russia.

Apparently the Russians were determined, at their own time, to enter the war. But the atomic bomb rather than Russian intervention was to be decisive in ending it. At a meeting of Allied leaders in Potsdam, Germany, in mid-July, 1945, President Truman (who had succeeded Roosevelt after his death in April) received word that the first atomic test was successful. He and Prime Minister Clement Attlee (who had succeeded Churchill) issued the Potsdam Declaration urging the Japanese to surrender or face utter devastation. The premier wished to accept the ultimatum, but the army leaders would not surrender. President Truman had set August 3 as the deadline; when it passed and the Japanese fought on, he ordered an atomic bomb to be dropped on one of four previously selected Japanese cities.

On August 6, 1945, a B-29 dropped an atomic bomb on Hiroshima, completely destroying the hitherto undamaged city, and killing 80,000 people (according to American estimates) or 200,000 (according to the Japanese). Even after the horror of Hiroshima, the Japanese army remained adamant. Russia declared war on Japan as of August 9. That same day, the air force dropped a second atomic bomb, on Nagasaki. This was the final blow. After frantic negotiations, on August 14 the Japanese government agreed to give up. On September 2, 1945, aboard the battleship *Missouri* in Tokyo Bay, the articles of surrender were signed.

World War II was at an end. All together, some 14 million men under arms had been killed, and countless millions of civilians had died. About 322,000 Americans had been killed or were missing; total United States casualties were about 1,120,000. Despite this frightful expenditure in lives and an astronomical cost in material resources, the American people faced a future made uncertain and perilous by the tensions with the Russians and the threat of future atomic wars.

The Dangerous Alliance

Only the imminent threat of Axis victory had forced an uneasy and unsatisfactory form of cooperation between Russia and its Western allies, Great Britain and the United States. As the threat began to lift in 1943, it became increasingly difficult to keep the alliance cemented together and to plan for a postwar world in which a decent peace could be maintained.

The difference between British and American strategy—the British opposing a cross-channel invasion and preferring campaigns in southern and eastern Europe—affected the two nations' dealings with the Russians. To a certain extent the United States seemed nearer to the Russian position in insisting with them upon an early invasion of France. Roosevelt personally tried

hard to establish a warm relationship with Stalin, and in his efforts he seemed at times to take a middle position between Stalin and Churchill.

At Casablanca, Morocco, in January 1943, after previous consultation with Churchill, Roosevelt announced the doctrine of unconditional surrender by the Axis. What Roosevelt seemed to desire was to avoid the sort of negotiations that had marred the 1918 armistice: causing bickerings among the Allies at the time and German misunderstandings afterwards. As the war progressed, it became clear that "unconditional surrender" left the United Nations free to state to the Axis powers the peace terms the latter might expect. Roosevelt and Churchill both emphasized that the phrase did not mean, as the Nazi propagandists charged, that extremely severe terms would be imposed. Yet, after the war, some historians charged that the "unconditional surrender" doctrine seriously discouraged the German underground, stiffened the Nazi will to fight, and thus lengthened the war.

In October 1943 Secretary Hull flew to Moscow to confer with the British and Russian foreign ministers. Hull returned elated because the Russians had agreed to create, as soon as practicable, a general international organization.

With an air of optimism Roosevelt and Churchill traveled eastward in November 1943 for a long-awaited meeting with Stalin at Teheran, Iran. On the way they stopped in Cairo to confer with Chiang Kai-shek and to prepare a statement (released after the Teheran conference) drawing a map for the postwar Far East. They proposed stripping Japan of her empire in order to restore Manchuria, the Pescadores, and Formosa to China, and to create in due course a free and independent Korea. Japan was to lose, in addition, all other territory she had acquired since 1914.

At Teheran, Roosevelt undertook to establish a friendly, intimate relationship with Stalin of the sort he enjoyed with Churchill. Stalin reaffirmed his intention to bring Russia into the Pacific war as soon as hostilities ended in Europe, and expressed his satisfaction with the Cairo communiqué on Japan. In a cordial way the three leaders discussed means, through an international organization, of keeping Germany from ever again becoming a menace. Stalin wished Russia to retain the areas she had seized in her period of collaboration with Germany, including eastern Poland as far as the so-called Curzon line proposed in 1919. Roosevelt and Churchill agreed to the Polish boundary.

Roosevelt and Churchill seem not to have recognized the nature of the peace that was being foreshadowed at Teheran. It was unrealistic to expect, as Roosevelt apparently did, that the Russians would forbear from exploiting the great European and Asian power vacuums that the defeat of Germany and Japan would create. This miscalculation led the United States into a tragic triumph—a victory without peace.

The Yalta Conference

The great conference at Yalta in the Crimea in February 1945 took place in a bleak and unpromising setting. At that time American forces were having to reduce Germany mile by mile; there seemed no reason to think Japan would be different. General MacArthur insisted on the necessity for Russian aid, taking the position that otherwise the United States would have to fight a series of difficult and expensive campaigns to overcome the Japanese in Manchuria. Consequently the Joint Chiefs did not revise their timetable calling for the defeat of Japan eighteen months after German surrender, and they continued to regard Russian aid as desirable. Roosevelt expressed to Stalin his hope that Japan could be bombed into submission without invasion—but the Americans could not count upon it.

These were the limitations upon the Americans in their bargaining at Yalta. In return for Stalin's reiterated promise to enter the Far Eastern war two or three months after German surrender, Roosevelt and Churchill promised him the Kurile Islands north of Japan and the restoration of "the former rights of Russia" lost in the Russo-Japanese War. This meant the return of southern Sakhalin Island, the return of a lease on Port Arthur as a naval base and internationalizing of the port of Dairen, Manchuria (in both instances with recognition of Russia's preeminent interests), and joint operation with China of the Chinese Eastern and South Manchurian Railroads feeding into the ports. China was to retain sovereignty over Manchuria, but Roosevelt did not clarify what "preeminent interests" meant. (For many months these clauses remained secret because Russia was still at peace with Japan.)

In its disposition of central European questions, the Yalta conference for the most part ratified previous decisions. Germany was to be divided into zones of occupation previously agreed upon. Since Berlin was to be deep in the Russian zone, the Americans and British proposed an accord providing freedom of transit into Berlin. The Russians held back, and in the general spirit of amity at Yalta, the matter was postponed. At the time, the Russian demands for heavy reparations in the form of German factories, goods, and labor seemed far more important. The British tried to scale down the Russian demand for $20 billion in such reparations, of which Russia was to obtain half. This would so strip and starve the Germans, Churchill pointed out, that the United States and Great Britain would have to feed them. Consequently he and Roosevelt agreed to the Russian figure only as a basis for discussion by a reparations commission. Already, in the light of reality, the West had left far behind the Morgenthau plan (initialed by Roosevelt and Churchill at Quebec in October 1944) for the pastoralization of Germany.

One of the touchiest questions was how to define a democratic government for Poland, a matter over which Russia and the West had negotiated for months. The Russians did not wish to allow the Polish government in exile in London or the Polish underground to assume any substantial share of power with a government the Russians established at Lublin.

At Yalta the West managed to obtain Stalin's agreement that the Lublin (Communist) government should be broadened to include democratic leaders from Poland and abroad. What the percentage should be was not specified. Subsequently the new government should hold "free and unfettered elections as soon as possible on the basis of universal suffrage and secret ballot." It would have been a satisfactory arrangement for the West if the terms had been interpreted in their Western meaning. As for the Polish boundary, it was to follow the Curzon line in the east, and the Poles were to receive territorial compensation in the north and west.

For the rest of liberated or defeated Europe, the Big Three agreed to establish interim governments "broadly representative of all democratic elements" and to provide for free elections that would create "governments responsible to the will of the people."

In the years after the war, disappointed Americans harshly criticized the Yalta agreements, especially for their violations of the Atlantic Charter. The morality of the Far Eastern arrangements is open to challenge. Their purpose was to obtain Russian aid, which top military leaders thought would shorten the war against Japan and perhaps prevent a million American casualties. The terms promised nothing to Stalin that he could not have taken anyway. The morality of the European arrangements (except perhaps for the ethnic dislocations wrought by the new Polish boundaries) was defensible if the terms received their customary Western interpretation. Roosevelt may be most severely criticized for not insisting at every point upon absolutely clear, sharply defined agreements that could receive only one interpretation in Russia—the interpretation as understood by the West. This was especially true of the question of entry into Berlin.

Roosevelt was careless in this respect because he pinned his hopes upon the good faith of the Russians and their willingness to enter into and participate actively in an international organization for the preservation of the peace.

Founding the United Nations

President Roosevelt, firmly determined to avoid Wilson's failure, included prominent Republicans in at least sketchy briefing on wartime diplomacy and let them participate more fully in postwar planning of many kinds. In this way he won their support. In March 1943 four Senators, two Republican and two Democratic, none of whom were serving on the Foreign Relations Committee, introduced a resolution calling for American leadership in establishing a United Nations organization. Public opinion polls indicated a general enthusiasm for the resolution; the Senate passed a similar declaration 85 to 5. Senator Arthur H. Vandenberg of Michigan, previously one of the most forthright isolationists, assumed Republican leadership in helping mold a "bipartisan" foreign policy. He thus gained for himself and the Republican party new power and stature.

The Big Four powers, conferring in the summer and fall of 1944 at Dumbarton Oaks, a Harvard-owned estate in Washington, drafted tentative outlines for a new international organization. These were the starting points for the drafting of a United Nations charter at a confer-

ence of fifty nations in San Francisco, opening April 25, 1945.

Basically the charter of the United Nations was a refurbishing of the old Wilsonian League covenant with the former American objections removed through giving a veto to each of the five main powers. The Americans and British, as well as the Russians, had insisted upon the veto as a seemingly necessary protection of their sovereignty. The American delegates, led by Vandenberg, succeeded in obtaining for the small nations in the General Assembly freedom to discuss and make recommendations—in effect creating "a town meeting of the world."

The Senate quickly ratified the Charter on July 28, 1945, by a vote of 80 to 2, in remarkable contrast to the slow and painful defeat it had administered to American membership in the League of Nations. But the great and growing gulf between Russia and the West destined the United Nations to be, like its predecessor, the League, a town meeting for international discussion or a sounding board for national views, rather than the forerunner of a world government.

Delayed Peacemaking

President Roosevelt lived to see neither the triumph in war nor the tragedy of peace. Already his vigor was draining away, and he could ill afford the exertions of the 1944 electoral campaign or those of the grueling trip to Yalta. Addressing Congress on his return, he was very tired and for the first time he made public reference to his paralyzed legs and his heavy steel braces as he remained seated and spoke optimistically of the Yalta agreement—which he said contained no secret provisions. Suddenly, on the afternoon of April 12, 1945, he died of a cerebral hemorrhage at his private retreat in Warm Springs, Georgia.

Roosevelt had not kept Vice President Harry S. Truman well informed, and so Truman was ill prepared for the tasks that faced him when he took over as President. But he learned fast.

During the first phase of his relations with the Russians, Truman was moderately firm but tried to give the Soviet government no cause for protest. He was chagrined when in May 1945 the Foreign Economic Administration enforced his order ending Lend-Lease so precipitately as even to call back some ships at sea. The British were the most hard hit, but Stalin complained most bitterly.

At the Potsdam conference (July 1945) Truman could secure few satisfactory agreements on questions involving occupied and liberated countries. Despite the failure at Potsdam, Truman's Secretary of State, James F. Byrnes, continued in a conciliatory fashion to seek accommodation with the Russians. The Potsdam conferees provided for a Council of Foreign Ministers to draft treaties with Italy and the former Axis satellites. During a tedious and depressing round of meetings of the Council in London, Moscow, Paris, and New York between September 1945 and December 1946, relations between the West and Russia steadily deteriorated, though five treaties were concluded. The one with Italy reflected Western demands; those with Finland, Hungary, Rumania, and Bulgaria in effect incorporated Soviet armistice terms. The United States by ratifying the three latter treaties acquiesced in the Russian domination of these nations.

The greatest obstacle to a satisfactory settlement in Europe was Germany. There a four-power Allied Control Council began sessions in Berlin marked by the same blocking and delaying tactics that made other joint conferences with the Russians so dismal. The Western nations had visualized unified controls for Germany to prevent its resurgence. But the Russians had no interest in a Germany reunified in a manner acceptable to the West; Germany was to remain split indefinitely.

In occupied Germany and Japan, meanwhile, the United States pursued firm but conflicting policies compounded of harshness and idealism. During the war the American people had come to hate the enemy leaders and were insistent that they be punished for their war crimes, especially those Nazis who were responsible for the maintenance of frightful concentration camps like Buchenwald and for the gas-chamber murder of millions of Jews. This led to the trials of thousands of Nazis and war criminals, capped by that of twenty-two key Nazi leaders before an International Military Tribunal at Nuremberg in 1945–1946. Eleven were sentenced to death.

There was an equally sweeping purge of Japan, and a trial was held for twenty-five former top Japanese military and civil officials. Seven of them, including two premiers, were executed. The dangerous precedent seemed to be established, as Churchill pointed out, that "the leaders of a nation defeated in war shall be put to death by the victors."

At first the Americans seemed bent on the pastoralization as well as reform of conquered Germany. They banned all industry directly or indirectly contributing to German war potential, including even the construction of seagoing ships, drastically cut steel and chemical production, destroyed munition plants, and allowed the dismantling of some factories for shipment to the Russians. They disbanded cartels and encouraged only agriculture and peaceful domestic industries. Along with this, they wished to foster American-style democracy in place of the repudiated Nazism.

These economic policies, coming at a time when so much of German housing and industry was rubble, and when several million exiles were making their way from the East or Czechoslovakia, reduced western Germany to a living standard not much better than that of a giant relief camp. The army undertook to feed the German people between 1945 and 1948 at a subsistence level of 950–1550 calories per day.

Even this near-starvation diet cost the British and Americans nearly half a billion dollars per year. The Russians were adding further to the economic burden by taking out of their zone (and from the western zones to the extent agreed at Potsdam) reparations totaling one and a half to three billion dollars per year. They were siphoning out of Germany more than the Americans and British could pump in.

In Japan American occupation policy suffered fewer obstacles and profited from the initial errors in Germany. During the first critical weeks General MacArthur, the Supreme Commander for the Allied Powers (SCAP), set up an overwhelmingly American occupation, based on a directive radioed him from Washington on August 29, 1945. Truman refused Stalin's demand that Russians occupy part of the northern Japanese island, Hokkaido. The irritated Russians had a voice, but no real power, on an eleven-country Far Eastern Commission in Washington and on a four-power Allied Council to advise MacArthur in Tokyo.

The American occupation authorities in Japan acted rapidly to demilitarize and democratize the country. From the outset they recognized that Japan must be left with a healthy economy, but in practice – by limiting the nation's war potential – they reduced Japan like Germany to a relief state.

Chapter 29. POSTWAR READJUSTMENTS AND THE START OF THE COLD WAR

The Postwar Military Program

The glad new day that wartime propaganda had foretold did not dawn when fighting stopped. Somehow, Americans had to readjust to the troublesome realities of postwar life. One serious political problem had to do with the adaptation of the military establishment to the new conditions — conditions that were themselves uncertain. In spite of growing menaces in Europe and Asia, the United States speedily dismantled its army, air force, and navy. At the end of the war, there was a popular demand to "bring the boys back." In April 1945 President Truman announced that nearly 7 million men had been released from the army — "the most remarkable demobilization in the history of the world, or 'disintegration,' if you want to call it that." He proposed a system of universal military training, but Congress did no more between 1946 and 1948 than to pass limited Selective Service measures. The gradual whittling of the armed forces continued, until by the spring of 1950 the army was down to 600,000 men, and the ceiling on defense expenditures, to $13 billion. Lacking land armies, the United States sought to balance the Soviet power with atomic bombs and an air force that could deliver them.

Since September 1945 the administration had been ready to negotiate an agreement with Russia that would "control and limit the use of the atomic bomb as an instrument of war" and "direct and encourage the development of atomic power for peaceful and humanitarian purposes." Great Britain and Canada joined with the United States in proposing international control of atomic energy. The United Nations Assembly responded by creating in January 1946 the United Nations Atomic Energy Commission, to which the American member, Bernard Baruch, submitted a plan in June 1946. This proposed a thoroughgoing system of control and inspection of atomic energy development through a United Nations agency. When the system became effective, the United States

would liquidate its stockpile and join in an international ban on atomic bombs.

The Russians distrusted and refused to accept the Baruch plan for international inspection and control of atomic development; instead they constantly and vociferously demanded that the United States unilaterally destroy its atom bombs. They tried to marshal world indignation against the United States while they rushed ahead with their own research on atomic weapons. American scientists and military leaders, not aware as yet of the successful Russian espionage, and underrating Russian scientific and technical proficiency, predicted that it would be many years before the Soviet Union could produce a successful bomb.

Meanwhile, Congress lengthily debated the domestic control of American atomic energy. Democrats wished to vest control in civilians; Senator Vandenberg and the Republicans urged giving it to the heads of the armed forces. A compromise was reached in the Atomic Energy Act of August 1946. This created a five-man civilian Atomic Energy Commission with complete control over research and development of fissionable materials; linked to it was a Military Liaison Committee.

Under the protection of an atomic umbrella, military leaders indulged in the luxury of a vigorous and prolonged controversy over unification of the various armed forces. This measure, proposed to bring greater efficiency and effectiveness, led instead to heightened rivalry, as the generals pushed for it, and the admirals feared for the loss of the marine corps and the relative weakening of the navy. Both sides brought the utmost pressure upon Congress. Finally in July 1947 the National Security Act provided for a Secretary of Defense to preside over separate Departments of the Army, Navy, and Air Force, with the Joint Chiefs of Staff serving as advisers to him and to the President. To coordinate diplomacy and military planning, the 1947 act also provided for a National Security Council to consist of the President, certain cabinet members, and other advisers on foreign and military policy. This Council was to be served by two other new agencies, a National Security Resources Board and a Central Intelligence Agency.

Within the reorganized Pentagon Building the old rivalries continued. Indeed, through the creation of a separate air force there now appeared to be three separate services where before there had been only two. The first Secretary of Defense, James V. Forrestal, exhausted by the struggle to make unification effective, resigned in March 1949, and committed suicide. His successor, Louis A. Johnson, became embroiled in a violent quarrel over cancellation of construction of a huge new aircraft carrier, a quarrel culminating in the resignation of the Secretary of the Navy. This crisis led to amendments to the National Security Act in August 1949, forcing greater unification of the services and formally establishing a Department of Defense.

The "Fair Deal"

On September 6, 1945, only four days after the Japanese surrender ceremonies, the President sent to Congress a twenty-one-point domestic program outlining what he later called the "Fair Deal." It called for the expansion of social security, the raising of the legal minimum wage from 40 to 65 cents an hour, a full employment bill, a permanent Fair Employment Practices Act, public housing and slum clearance, long-range planning for the protection of natural resources and building of public works (like TVA), and government promotion of scientific research. Within ten weeks, he sent additional recommendations to Congress for federal aid to education, for health insurance and prepaid medical care, and for the St. Lawrence seaway project.

Congress acted upon several of the President's recommendations. The Employment Act became law in February 1946. It established a three-man Council of Economic Advisers to aid the President and issue an annual economic report. Although the experts frequently disagreed, they became an integral part of the governmental machinery. They did much to accustom the public to the new economics that had been emerging during the New Deal and the war.

Congressional conservatives tried to steer Congress and the public away from the Fair Deal program by concentrating upon the reconversion of industry to peacetime production. Truman himself recommended, first, speedily removing all possible controls that would hamper reconversion and, second, preventing increases in prices, rents, and wages. The two aims could easily conflict.

Industry changed back to civilian production with more speed and less economic dislocation than had been expected. The gloomy forecasts of 8 million unemployed did not materialize because of the massive pent-up consumer demand for automobiles, appliances, and related products. By the end of November 1945 peacetime employment was up to the end-of-the-war total, and 93 percent of the war plants had been reconverted.

Prices and Wages

The expected glut of surplus goods did not materialize either. Instead, acute problems of scarcity arose. Shortages ranged from automobiles and appliances to men's suits, nylon stockings, and beef. Consumers commanded billions in savings and billions more in credit with which to back their demands. Added to these were the needs of the rest of the world. Against such pressures, it was impossible for the Office of Price Administration to hold prices down to the 1941–1942 level.

If prices were to be checked, wages must be also, and if wages were to be held down, so must prices be. It was a vicious circle. By January 1946 workers had gone on strike in a number of the nation's critical industries, especially steel. President Truman announced in February 1946 that labor was entitled to the 33 percent that living costs had gone up since January 1941. The Wage Stabilization Board must approve the increase; but if it cut profits below the prewar level, the companies might obtain corresponding price increases. Ultimately there was a steel settlement allowing raises of 18½ cents an hour and $5 per ton. Throughout industry, the "bulge" led to a round of similar raises in wages and prices; new strikes led to new wage increases.

Businessmen and farmers were exerting almost equal pressure upon Congress to obtain higher prices. Controls, they argued, were preventing full production, encouraging a black market, and robbing producers of a fair profit. After long debate, Congress passed a circumscribed price-control bill on June 27, 1946, just three days before the existing act was to expire. President Truman unexpectedly vetoed the bill as "a sure formula for inflation," and most price controls expired.

During the first sixteen days of July 1946, the index of prices of twenty-eight basic commodities jumped 25 percent, compared with 13 percent during the previous three years. Congress rushed through a new price-control bill only slightly stronger than the vetoed one, and on July 25 President Truman signed it. The decontrol board it created studied meat prices, decided they were unreasonable, and ordered prices rolled back to the old levels. Stockmen held back cattle until they could force abandonment of controls; angry consumers chafed in near-empty butcher shops.

For several weeks, President Truman stood firm, but as public discontent focused on the Democratic party, politicians already fearful of the worst in the congressional elections of 1946 persuaded him to relent. On October 14, 1946, he announced the immediate ending of meat controls. Meat came back, but like many other commodities, with new price tags so high that the old black-market price seemed to have become the new legal standard. Millions of consumers on small, inflexible salaries or pensions were hurt, and felt little more tender toward the Democrats. Real earning dropped 12 percent below July 1945.

"Had Enough?"

All that the Republicans needed in the fall of 1946 was the slogan, "Had Enough? Vote Republican." They captured both houses of Congress, controlling the House 246 to 188, and the Senate, 51 to 45.

President Truman, accepting the returns as a mandate to liquidate regulations, dropped almost all remaining controls on wages and prices and on the channeling of construction into low-cost homes. Congress continued rent control to March 1, 1948, but allowed rents to go up 15 percent. Retail prices moved upward 3 percent per month, canceling the gains organized labor had won in the spring of 1946. Unions fought for, and obtained, a second round of increases in 1947, and in 1948 as prices still went upward, a

third round. The spiral of inflation was creeping upward relentlessly. Workers and others in modest circumstances began to notice that it was taking place under a Republican Congress whose spokesmen had asserted that laissez faire would cure the nation's ills.

The Chairman of the House Appropriations Committee, John Taber, proclaimed that he would apply a "meat-axe to government frills." He did so. Congress refused to appropriate funds for public housing, even of a very moderate sort. It would not aid education, or extend social security; it slashed budget allowances for reclamation and power projects in the West. It passed a tax bill that, as President Truman pointed out in vetoing it, reduced the taxes of families receiving $2,400 or less by only 3 percent, but of those receiving $100,000 or more, from 48 to 65 percent.

The principal positive handiwork of the Eightieth Congress was a new basic labor law to supplant the pro-labor Wagner Act of 1935. The Taft-Hartley Labor-Management Relations Act loosened some of the previous restrictions upon employers and added several prohibitions against the unions. It also provided for "cooling-off" periods before unions could strike. President Truman stingingly vetoed it on June 20, 1947. That same day Republicans and Southern Democrats in the House overrode his veto, 331 to 83; the Senate followed three days later, 68 to 25. In practice, the Taft-Hartley Act did not cripple organized labor, partly because of the skill of labor leaders and because of President Truman's appointment to the National Labor Relations Board of members sympathetic toward labor. But the law did emphatically turn most of organized labor against the Republicans and back to the support of President Truman.

Truman Beats Dewey

Significantly, when the Republicans met at Philadelphia in June 1948 to nominate a presidential candidate, they rejected Senator Robert A. Taft, the vigorous leader of the Eightieth Congress, although he was the idol of many businessmen. Taft was hampered by his prewar isolationism and his lack of glamor as a campaigner. The Republicans again nominated Governor Thomas E. Dewey, who favored the new role of the United States in world affairs, and whose stand on domestic issues came closer to the Fair Deal than to the Republican record in Congress. His running mate was Governor Earl Warren of California, who was even more liberal. Their platform was a promise to continue all the things the Democrats had established, but do them more efficiently and cheaply.

It seemed a winning ticket and program, especially since the Democratic party suffered from two schisms. A faction to the left followed Henry A. Wallace out of the party. Wallace ran on a "Progressive" ticket to fight for thorough-going reform at home and more friendly relations with Communists overseas. Around him rallied a sprinkling of Americans who felt that the Truman domestic policies were too slow and ineffective and who feared that the foreign policies would lead to a third world war. Around him also rallied the American Communists and fellow-travelers.

At their convention in July 1948 the Democrats gloomily accepted the inevitable, the nomination of President Truman. Certain of defeat, the liberals salvaged what they could by fighting through a platform containing a strong civil-rights plank that proposed federal legislation to prevent discrimination in employment, penalize lynching, and outlaw poll taxes. This platform was expected to help Northern and city Democrats in their local and state elections.

But it drove Southern Democrats, already angered by President Truman's espousal of a strong civil-rights program, into open revolt. Waving Confederate flags, a number of them met at Birmingham, Alabama, in July 1948 to form the States Rights' Democratic Party and nominate Governor J. Strom Thurmond of South Carolina. They captured the party organization in Alabama, Louisiana, Mississippi, and South Carolina.

The revolts from both the left and the right seemed to leave President Truman in a pathetically hopeless position; all the public opinion polls showed him trailing far behind. Instead of campaigning against the cold and formal Governor Dewey, whose domestic and foreign policies were much the same as his, Truman launched his attack at the Republican Congress. Speaking extemporaneously and bluntly in a vigorous "whistle-stop" campaign, he won the strong support of organized labor, disgruntled farmers, and northern Negroes.

On election day, to the amazement of every-

one but himself, President Truman defeated Dewey, 24,106,000 to 21,969,000 in the popular vote. Thurmond's Dixiecrat ticket received 1,169,000, and Wallace 1,156,000. The Democrats also regained both houses of Congress by a margin of ninety-three seats in the House and twelve in the Senate.

Beginnings of Containment

As early as January 1946 President Truman, upset over Russian delay in withdrawing troops from Iran and Russian threats toward Turkey, wrote his Secretary of State: "Unless Russia is faced with an iron fist and strong language another war is in the making."

Truman's new policy for countering Communist aggression began to unfold in the spring of 1947. Already George F. Kennan, counselor of the American embassy in Moscow, was warning the administration that it faced "a political force committed fanatically to the belief that with the U.S. there can be no permanent *modus vivendi.*" The only answer, Kennan wrote anonymously in the July 1947 issue of *Foreign Affairs,* must be "a long-term, patient but firm and vigilant containment of Russian expansive tendencies." Russian pressure on Turkey and support of Communist guerrilla forces in Greece emphasized the immediacy of the Soviet threat. The British had been aiding the Greek government, but could no longer carry the burden. Unless Stalin were contained quickly, he might achieve the centuries-old Russian prize of the straits leading from the Black Sea into the Mediterranean. Already Russia controlled Albania on the Adriatic.

On March 12, 1947, President Truman appeared before Congress to request $400 million to bolster the armed forces of Greece and Turkey, and to enunciate the doctrine that came to bear his name: "I believe that it must be the policy of the United States to support free peoples who are resisting attempted subjugation by armed minorities or by outside pressures." Senator Vandenberg again supported him, and the Republican Congress voted the Greek-Turkish Aid Act of May 1947. The initial military aid and subsequent appropriations eased Russian pressure upon Turkey, and by the fall of 1949 brought to an end the long civil war against Communists in Greece.

ORIGINS OF THE COLD WAR

According to spokesmen for the American government, the Soviet Union was entirely to blame for the cold war. Stalin violated the Yalta agreement, imposed Russian control upon eastern Europe, and schemed to spread Communism throughout the world. The United States, reacting defensively, tried to contain Soviet expansion by means of the Truman Doctrine, the Marshall Plan, and the North Atlantic Treaty Organization. At first, American historians with few exceptions agreed substantially with the official view.

As time passed, and especially after the Vietnam War disillusioned many Americans about the containment policy, an increasing number of historians undertook to "revise" the interpretation of the cold war, as earlier historians had done with previous wars. Most of the cold war revisionists belonged to the New Left. The pioneer among them was William A. Williams, who anticipated most of the revisionist themes in his *American-Russian Relations, 1781–1947* (1952) and *The Tragedy of American Diplomacy* (1959).

According to the New Left writers, the United States was mainly if not solely responsible for the cold war. At the close of World War II, the Soviet Union was exhausted and in no position to threaten the United States. But this country, with a monopoly of nuclear weapons, was in a position to threaten the Soviet Union. In the opinion of some revisionists, Franklin D. Roosevelt would have continued the wartime Soviet-American cooperation, but Harry S. Truman abandoned the Roosevelt policy and adopted a hard line toward the Russians. In the opinion of other revisionists, the line would have been the same regardless of any change in the presidency, since American foreign policy was simply a response to the needs of American capitalism, which sought American-controlled markets throughout the world.

As early as 1948 a British physicist, P. M. S. Blackett, in *Fear, War, and the Bomb,* had written that the dropping of the atomic bombs on Hiroshima and Nagasaki was "not so much the last military act of the second World War as the first major operation of the cold diplomatic war with Russia." Taking up the idea, a New Left political economist at the University of Cambridge, England, Gar Alperovitz, suggested in his *Atomic Diplomacy* (1965) that the United States dropped the bombs on an already defeated Japan in order to impress the Russians and make them more "manageable." In *The Atomic Bomb and the End of World War II* (1966) a former official in the Roosevelt and Truman administrations, Herbert Feis, argued (as Truman himself had done) that the United States used the bombs simply to assure a quick and complete victory over Japan with a minimum loss of lives.

Reviewing the work of Williams, Alperovitz, and five other revisionist authors, Robert J. Maddox in *The New Left and the Origins of the Cold War* (1973) charged them with misusing source materials and drawing conclusions at variance with their own evidence. "There is every reason to be sharply critical of recent American foreign policy," Maddox said, "but the criticisms should rest on more substantial foundations."

In *The United States and the Origins of the Cold War, 1941–1947* (1972), John L. Gaddis maintained that a variety of preconceptions had influenced the policy makers in both Washington and Moscow. He concluded that "neither side can bear sole responsibility for the onset of the Cold War."

Military aid was not enough. The Truman Doctrine logically led to a program of economic reconstruction to bolster the stability of Europe and help eradicate the misery out of which the Communist parties in western European countries were gaining recruits. Secretary of State George C. Marshall returned in April 1947 from the Conference of Foreign Ministers in Moscow convinced that the Russians were interested only in profiting from the economic plight of Europe, not in ameliorating it. The solution, he and President Truman agreed, lay in State Department plans to aid European nations that were willing to cooperate with each other in rebuilding their economies. Speaking at the Harvard University commencement in June 1947, Secretary Marshall offered aid to all those European nations (including Russia) who would join in drafting a program for recovery.

Russia denounced the Marshall Plan as American imperialism, and intimidated the satellites and Finland and Czechoslovakia into staying away from the planning conference. Germany had no government, and Spain was not invited. Sixteen other nations of Europe joined a Committee of European Economic Cooperation, which in September 1947 presented specifications for reconstruction to create by 1951 a self-sufficient Europe. Opposition formed in Congress, but it was embarrassed from the start by possessing as unwelcome allies the American Communists, and in February 1948 it was overwhelmed by a shocked and aroused public opinion when Czech Communists seized power in Prague. In April Congress established the Economic Cooperation Administration. It cut the administration's request, but did vote an initial $4 billion.

Altogether over a three year period the United States spent $12 billion through the ECA. This helped to stimulate a remarkable recovery in Europe. By the end of 1950, industrial production was up 64 percent, economic activity was well above prewar levels, and Communist strength among voters in most areas was dwindling.

The North Atlantic Alliance

In his inaugural address, January 20, 1949, President Truman challenged the nation to aid the "more than half the people of the world" who were "living in conditions approaching misery."

Point Four of his proposals for aiding them was technical assistance and the fostering of capital investment for their development. The Point Four or Technical Cooperation program began in 1950 with an appropriation of only $35 million, but spent $400 million in the next three years.

Soviet leaders reacted vigorously against the American efforts to speed world economic recovery. They had organized their own Warsaw Alliance of nine satellite nations in September 1947 to combat "American imperialism." Through a new Cominform (Communist Information Bureau) they sought to eradicate traces of nonconformity throughout eastern Europe. Their greatest triumph was the successful coup in democratic Czechoslovakia in February 1948. Because it was as horrifying to western Europeans as it was to Americans, it helped unify the Western world against the Communist countries. Later in the year, the pressure of Stalin and the Cominform on Marshal Tito provoked him to pull Communist Yugoslavia out of their orbit, and with American aid to embark upon an independent course between Russia and the West. In western Europe, Communist parties tried to thwart the Marshall Plan, especially by calling out on strike the unions they controlled in Italy and France. Despite the strikes, progress continued.

Meanwhile, the United States moved with the British and the rather reluctant French toward the creation of a self-governing, economically strong West Germany. The culmination came on June 7, 1948, when they announced plans for a new federal West German government with sovereignty over domestic matters and full membership in the European Recovery Program. They also reformed the currency to stop the inflationary flood of marks from the Soviet zone, which was hampering recovery.

The Russians retaliated. Taking advantage of the lack of a written guarantee of land transit across the Soviet zone, they clamped a tight blockade around the western sectors of Berlin. The object was to force the Western powers to abandon either Berlin or the proposed West German republic. President Truman, unwilling to risk war by ordering in armed convoys by land, ordered the supplying of Berlin by increasing on a massive scale the airlift begun in April. Through the winter and into the spring of 1949, the airlift continued. It was a remarkable demonstration to Europeans—especially to the Germans—of what the Americans and British could achieve.

In the spring of 1949 the Russians backed down and ended the blockade. In October 1949 the German Federal Republic came into existence at Bonn in West Germany, and the Soviets established a German Democratic Republic for East Germany.

Russian intransigence led to the consolidation of the Western countries into a new grand alliance. The North Atlantic Treaty was signed April 4, 1949, by twelve nations, and subsequently also by Greece and Turkey. It declared that an armed attack against one would be considered an attack upon all, and provided for the creation of joint military forces. Under it, the signatory powers established the North Atlantic Treaty Organization to construct a defense force that, while not equal to that of the Russians, would be large enough to make an attack highly costly.

The United States began to shift from economic to military aid as the Mutual Defense Act of 1949 appropriated an initial billion dollars for armaments for the signators. The governing body of NATO, the North Atlantic Council, established military headquarters near Paris early in 1951 under the supreme command of General Dwight Eisenhower. This was SHAPE (Supreme Headquarters, Allied Powers in Europe). The number of divisions and airplanes under NATO command began gradually to grow, but while its power was still relatively feeble, its chief significance was the commitment the United States had made with the nations of western Europe to stand firm against Russian threats.

That these threats were not be be taken lightly became even more clear on September 23, 1949, when President Truman issued a press statement: "We have evidence that within recent weeks an atomic explosion occurred in the USSR." The brief postwar period of relative safety for the American people was at an end.

China Turns Red

While the United States was struggling to contain Russia in Europe between 1947 and 1949, the Chinese Communists were destroying the armies of Chiang Kai-shek.

To prevent civil war and to effect a coalition government, the Truman administration in De-

cember 1945 had sent General George C. Marshall to China. At first he obtained a cease-fire and encouraging signs of accommodation, but irreconcilable differences kept apart the two Chinese governments—the *Kuomintang* (Nationalists) and the Communists. Finally, in January 1947, Marshall returned to Washington disgusted with both governments and all factions except a handful of powerless *Kuomintang* liberals.

Full-scale war broke out. Although the Nationalist armies were larger and better equipped, they soon began to fall back before the better trained, more highly motivated Communist forces. As the inept Chiang Kai-shek government failed both on the fighting front and at home, where inflation and inefficiency were rampant, it was plunging toward defeat.

General Albert C. Wedemyer, who had been Chiang's chief of staff, recommended to Truman that the United States send 10,000 army officers together with massive material support. President Truman requested only limited aid for Chiang, and for this omission critics subsequently castigated him. But to do so might have interfered with the program of containment in Europe; it would have been unpopular and, in any event, would almost certainly have been too late. The collapse in China was rapid, and it came through lack of morale rather than shortages of arms and supplies. At the end of 1949 Chiang and the Nationalists fled to Formosa. All of China was under the new People's Republic, which ruthlessly consolidated its strength by liquidating several million dissidents, driving out American businessmen, teachers, and missionaries, and proclaiming its message to all of East Asia.

Though Great Britain and some of the western European nations recognized the new government of Red China, the United States refused to do so and blocked its entry into the United Nations.

The Japanese Ally

Beginning in 1947, the American government introduced new policies in Japan to strengthen that nation in a manner similar to the rebuilding of Germany. The American occupation in Japan brought a democratization of the government, extension of rights to women and underprivileged groups, expansion of the educational system (from a starting point as high as the goal of

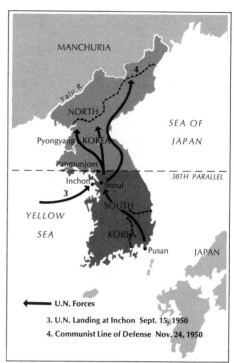

The Korean War 1950–1953

educational reform in China), land reform as drastic as that in China, a curbing of the power of the monopolistic *zaibatsu* industrial system, and an improvement in the status of labor. In Japan, more than anywhere else in Asia, the United States helped develop a dynamic alternative to Communism. In 1949, to stimulate Japanese recovery, the United States ended its reparations and stopped the dismantling of industrial combinations.

Negotiation of a Japanese peace treaty began in 1950. Aside from the fact that it stripped Japan of all her conquests, including the Ryukyu Islands directly south of Japan (most notably Okinawa), it was a generous treaty. By recognizing the right of the sovereign Japanese nation to self-defense, it opened the way to rearmament. It went into effect April 28, 1952. A security treaty, signed at the same time, permitted the United States to maintain armed forces in Japan. Two years later, a mutual-defense-assistance pact provided for Japanese rearmament with American aid, but the building of armed forces proceeded slowly. The task of defending Japan continued to rest largely with the United States.

Conflict in Korea

During the hectic days at the end of the war in the Pacific, the United States had hastily proposed that Americans accept the surrender of the Japanese in the lower half of Korea, up to the 38th parallel, and the Russians do the same in the northern half. At the moment the arrangement was useful to the United States. Afterwards, however, the Russians were willing to accept a reunited Korea only if it were Communist-dominated.

The 38th parallel became more and more an impenetrable barrier. To the north of it, the Communists developed a "peoples' government" with a strong agressive army. To the south, the United Nations held elections that led to a government under the ardently nationalistic Dr. Syngman Rhee. When the United States withdrew its forces from below the 38th parallel in June 1949, South Korea was left militarily weaker than its northern twin. In January 1950 Secretary of State Dean Acheson publicly outlined a Pacific defense perimeter that did not

5. Chinese-North Korean Attack Nov. 26, 1950
6. U.N. Line of Defense Jan. 12, 1951

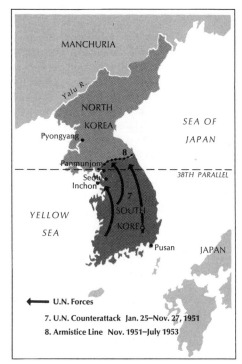

7. U.N. Counterattack Jan. 25–Nov. 27, 1951
8. Armistice Line Nov. 1951–July 1953

include Formosa or Korea. If these areas were attacked, he declared, the people invaded must rely upon themselves to resist, "and then upon the commitments of the entire civilized world under the charter of the United Nations."

The North Koreans acted swiftly, on June 24, 1950, launching a full-scale invasion that caught the South Koreans and Americans completely by surprise. Almost immediately President Truman and Congress reversed the policy of withdrawal from the Asiatic mainland. The President brought the question of the invasion before the United Nations Security Council. It could act more quickly than the Assembly, and at the moment the Russians were boycotting it, and hence had no representative present to vote a paralyzing veto. The Council on June 25 passed an American resolution demanding that the North Koreans withdraw behind the 38th parallel, and two days later called upon members of the United Nations to "furnish such assistance to the Republic of Korea as may be necessary to repel the armed attack."

President Truman on June 27 sent United States air and sea forces to the aid of the South

Koreans; on June 30 he ordered ground forces into Korea, and sent the Seventh Fleet to act as a barrier between the Chinese mainland and Formosa.

The Council of the United Nations on July 7, 1950, requested those nations providng troops to place them under a unified command headed by the United States. President Truman appointed General MacArthur commander-in-chief Some fifteen nations besides the United States and the Republic of Korea provided troops, but these never comprised more than 9 percent of the total fighting force. The United States sent about 48 percent; South Korea mustered 43 percent. What was officially a United Nations "police action" came to most Americans to seem a war on the part of the United States.

Until the United Nations could build strength in Korea, its forces withdrew toward the southern port of Pusan. Then in September 1950 General MacArthur launched an amphibious assault far behind the North Korean lines at Inchon, near Seoul. Within two weeks the North Korean armies, disrupted and demoralized, were fleeing as best they could to north of the 38th parallel.

Despite warnings from Red China that it would send troops, the United States and United Nations decided to pursue the fleeing North Koreans and, in a distinct departure from containment, to liberate North Korea. But the Joint Chiefs of Staff on September 27, 1950, ordered MacArthur under no circumstances to cross the borders of China or Russia. For several weeks the advance into northern Korea went well, then Chinese troops appeared in overwhelming numbers, forcing MacArthur's troops to retreat below the 38th parallel.

In March 1951 the Eighth Army counter-attacked, for a second and final time capturing Seoul and recrossing the 38th parallel. President Truman was ready again to seek a negotiated peace to restore the status quo.

General MacArthur, far from ready to accept the position of his commander-in-chief, repeatedly made public his eagerness to win total victory in Korea at the risk of full involvement in war with China. On March 20, 1951, he communicated his views to the Republican minority leader in the House of Representatives, Joseph W. Martin, concluding: "There is no substitute for victory."

President Truman clung to his thesis that, in the great struggle against Communism, western Europe with its concentration of heavy industry, not industrially weak Asia, was the main potential battlefield. He could not have won the support of western European partners in the United Nations for a more militant policy in Asia. He would not accept the arguments of the Asia-firsters that the United States should undertake unilateral action — "go it alone."

General MacArthur thus emerged as a major figure in American politics, trying to reverse the administration policies. Five days after Representative Martin released MacArthur's letter to the press, President Truman, on April 11, 1951, relieved General MacArthur of his commands. A groundswell of outrage swept the United States; a Gallup poll reported that 69 percent of those interviewed favored the General, only 29 percent the President. MacArthur upon his return was greeted hysterically wherever he appeared; millions watched their television sets as he addressed Congress.

Truman's policy of fighting a limited war of containment continued to baffle and exasperate a considerable part of the American people. It went too completely against the American tradi-tion of total victory. It was too hard to explain to the public or to the soldiers fighting endlessly through the rice paddies and over the hilltops of Korea.

In June 1951 the Russian delegate to the United Nations hinted that settlement was possible. Armistice negotiations began on July 10, 1951, near the 38th parallel, and continued for many weary months at Panmunjom. They came to revolve around the difficult questions of locating the cease-fire line, enforcing the armistice, and repatriating prisoners of war. By the spring of 1952 agreements had been reached upon all but the last question. Finally, in October 1952, the negotiations were recessed. By then, the nation was in the midst of a presidential campaign, and though there was no large-scale fighting in Korea, the interminable negotiations, endless skirmishing, and ever-growing casualties had worn out the patience of the American people.

To many of the American people the failures to keep China free and to achieve total victory in Korea indicated nothing less than Communist subversion within the Truman administration.

Trumanism and McCarthyism

As early as 1946 when the cold war was in its opening stages, and spy rings were being apprehended, the public became increasingly afraid that traitors within the government were betraying it to the Russians. The federal government began extensive efforts to ferret out Communists. President Truman in November 1946 established a Temporary Commission on Employee Loyalty to recommend loyalty investigation systems and safeguards of fair hearings. This led in March 1947 to the establishment of loyalty boards to undertake a sweeping investigation of all federal employees. In August 1950 the President authorized the dismissal in sensitive departments of those deemed no more than "bad security risks." By 1951 more than 3 million government employees had been cleared, over 2,000 had resigned, and 212 had been dismissed.

Against the recommendations of the Departments of Defense and Justice and of the Central Intelligence Agency, Congress passed over the President's veto the McCarran Internal Security Act of September 1950. This did not outlaw Communist organizations but required them to publish their records. It barred Communists from employment in defense plants and denied them passports.

Already in 1948 the Attorney General had obtained indictments against eleven key Communist leaders for violation of the Smith Act of 1940, which prohibited conspiring to teach the violent overthrow of the government. During their nine-month trial in 1949, the Communists engaged in elaborate harassing tactics, which further aroused the public against them. They were convicted. In June 1951, in the case of *Dennis* v. *United States,* the Supreme Court in a 6 to 2 decision rejected their appeal. Chief Justice Fred Vinson held that advocating or teaching revolution in the existing state of the world or even conspiring to do so, fell within Justice Holmes' earlier definition of what was punishable—that it constituted a "clear and present danger."

Some politicians capitalized upon the growing public hysteria over several spectacular cases. Above all there was the case of Alger Hiss, in which these politicians seemed to put on trial and condemn a whole generation of liberal intellectuals. Hiss had been a high-ranking official in the State Department. In 1948, Whittaker Chambers, a self-avowed former Communist agent, accused Hiss before the House un-American Activities Committee. When Hiss sued him for slander, Chambers produced microfilms of classified State Department documents which Hiss allegedly had given him in 1937 and 1938.

Hiss was brought to trial for perjury (the statute of limitations prevented indictment for espionage). He called upon a number of the nation's most distinguished liberals to bear witness to his character. The first trial ended with a hung jury in July 1949; the second ended with conviction in January 1950.

Among the politicians who capitalized upon the public's fears was Representative Richard M. Nixon of California. He was already on his way to the Senate and a national reputation for having kept the Hiss affair alive in its early stages. Most sensational in his rise was Senator Joseph McCarthy of Wisconsin. In February 1950 McCarthy charged that a large number of Communists and men loyal to the Communist party were still shaping foreign policy in the State Department. A subcommittee of the State Foreign Relations Committee took up his charges, but found not a single Communist or "fellow traveler."

An excited public numbering many millions eagerly swallowed McCarthy's new claims as he went on from sensation to sensation more rapidly than his detractors could refute his unsubstantiated charges. Millions wanted to believe McCarthy when he attacked as Communists the "whole group of twisted-thinking New Dealers" who had "led America near to ruin at home and abroad." McCarthy was providing a troubled nation with a scapegoat, and the Republican party with a winning issue.

A Troubled Electorate

Bipartisanship in foreign policy disappeared as the Republicans pressed their issue. They did not capture Congress in November 1950, but they gained twenty-eight seats in the House and five in the Senate. Neo-isolationists in December, heartened by the election results and no longer restrained by Senator Vandenberg, who was fatally ill, opened a "great debate" in the Senate over foreign policy. They succeeded in passing a resolution in April 1951 restraining the President from sending troops to western Europe without congressional authorization.

Meanwhile, President Truman made little headway with his Fair Deal. Congress passed the Displaced Persons Act of 1950, liberalizing the 1948 legislation which the President had denounced as discriminatory against Catholics and Jews because its quotas were unfavorable to people from southern and eastern Europe. The new law increased the number of persons to be admitted from 205,000 to 415,000—but even this latter figure was a total for a three year period, not a yearly number. Congress also implemented some of Truman's proposed reforms. The National Housing Act of 1949 provided for the construction over the succeeding six years of 810,000 housing units for lower-income families, together with a subsidy for forty years to bridge the gap between costs and the rents the tenants could afford to pay. It also provided grants for slum clearance and rural housing. Congress voted increased appropriations for power development and reclamation in the West, for TVA and for the Farmers Home Administration (which carried on the rehabilitation work of the earlier Resettlement Administration and Farm Security Administration). In contrast, the Fair Deal health-insurance program went down to crashing defeat under the vigorous opposition of the American Medical Association, which raised a $3 million fund to combat it. Federal aid for education failed because of dissension over whether aid should go to parochial schools.

Republicans undermined the Truman administration with charges of favor-peddling and corruption, which implicated men in the White House though not the President himself. The President's military aide had received as a gift a $520 deep-freeze unit; the wife of an examiner of loans for the Reconstruction Finance Corporation had acquired a $9,540 mink coat.

These became the symbols of a moral malaise in Washington. Apparently go-betweens, in return for a 5 percent fee, could obtain contracts, arrange RFC loans, and take care of tax difficulties in the Bureau of Internal Revenue. President Truman reorganized the RFC and reformed the Bureau of Internal Revenue and the Department of Justice, but much too slowly to satisfy his Republican critics.

As the election of 1952 approached, there was no indication that the majority of voters wished to reverse either Truman's foreign policy or his domestic program. They did want to "clean up the mess in Washington," and above all they wanted to see an end to the drawn-out, wearying Korean War.

Chapter 30. THE EISENHOWER YEARS

Eisenhower Elected

In Dwight D. Eisenhower, the Republican party nominated for the Presidency a successful and popular general who they felt could restore security against frightening outside threats. The conservative minority of the party had been committed to Senator Robert A. Taft. The majority sought a candidate who could pull strong support from many who had favored the Democratic foreign and domestic policies. Consequently, the Republicans looked to General Eisenhower — whom some liberal Democrats had sought to draft in 1948. Senator Richard M. Nixon of California, acceptable to conservative Republicans, was nominated for the Vice Presidency. The platform was ambiguous enough to cover disagreements between the two wings of the party.

President Truman having declined to run again, the Democrats chose Governor Adlai E. Stevenson of Illinois and, as his running mate, the liberal Senator John J. Sparkman of Alabama. The platform stated the positions of the Northern Democrats: endorsement of the Truman foreign policies, civil rights, repeal of the Taft-Hartley Act, and high price supports for farmers.

Republican campaigners played upon the triple theme of "Communism, corruption, and Korea." Speaking in Detroit on October 24, 1952, Eisenhower promised to bring the war to "an early and honorable end." To help do so, he promised he would make a personal trip to Korea. The response at the polls was overwhelming, Eisenhower polling 33,936,000 votes to 27,315,000 for Stevenson. The electoral vote was 442 to 89. But the Republicans failed to gain complete control of Congress, winning a majority of eight seats in the House and only an even split in the Senate. The Republican candidate was far more popular than his party.

John Foster Dulles

A central figure in the Eisenhower administration was John Foster Dulles, who served as secretary of state from 1953 to 1959. His sturdy moralism, his skill at bureaucratic politics, and his tireless effort made him a formidable figure. Before taking office Dulles had criticized the Democratic program of "containment" as a passive one that left the initiative to the Communists. He proposed, instead, a program of "liberation" that would lead to a "rollback" of Communist expansion. As secretary of state he continued to talk of new approaches, but Eisenhower restrained him and the Eisenhower-Dulles policy was essentially a continuation of the Truman-Acheson policy. It proved difficult even to contain Communist power, without attempting a "roll'back."

A Truce in Korea

Less than two months after President Eisenhower entered office, Stalin died, opening the possibility of an end to the Korean War and perhaps some modification of the cold war. When the new Soviet premier, Georgi Malenkov, seemed conciliatory, the President called upon the Russians to show their good faith by signing an Austrian peace treaty and supporting an armistice in Korea. The Russians did agree to an end to the occupation of Austria. On July 27, 1953, a final Korean armistice agreement was signed at Panmunjom. It provided for a cease-fire and withdrawal of both armies two kilometers back of the existing battle line, which ran from coast to coast, from just below the 38th parallel in the west to thirty miles north of it in the east.

Within three months a political conference to seek peaceful unification of Korea was to be held, but it never took place. Instead, the armistice turned into an uneasy and indefinite armed truce, marked by occasional border shootings, and unrelenting North Korean hostility.

The Korean War (officially only a "police action") had lasted more than three years and cost the United States alone 25,000 dead, 115,000 other casualties, and $22 billion. For Americans who liked to think in terms of total victory, it all seemed painfully inconclusive. The fighting had settled no problems in the Far East except to prevent the Communist conquest of South Korea.

"Massive Retaliation"

The Eisenhower administration came into office firmly committed to a Europe-first priority. Nevertheless, it maintained a tenuous compromise with the ardently nationalistic Asia-first wing of the party. The hero of the Asia-firsters was Chiang Kai-shek, and their special villain, Red China, which they insisted must be curbed or destroyed at all costs. Concurring with this group at some points were the business leaders dominant in the Eisenhower administration, who were determined that defense expenditures must fit within a balanced budget.

The solution seemed to lie in a "new look" in defense policy, equally pleasing to the secretaries of defense, the treasury, and state. This meant cutting the expensive army ground forces and basic scientific research. The United States would depend upon its thermonuclear weapons and their delivery by the air force. Popularized, this was the policy of "more bang for a buck."

A new foreign policy was necessary to make the "new look" in defense operate adequately. Secretary of the Treasury George M. Humphrey, looking at it from a standpoint of cost, asserted that the United States had "no business getting into little wars." If the nation had to intervene, he declared, "let's intervene decisively with all we have got or stay out." This was the economic basis for Secretary of State Dulles' policy of "massive retaliation." The United States would depend less on local defense, he declared in an address on January 12, 1954, and depend more on "the deterrent of massive retaliatory power . . . a great capacity to retaliate instantly, by means and at times of our own choosing."

The Indochina crisis of 1954 offered the first test of the new Eisenhower-Dulles policies. Under the leadership of Ho Chi Minh the people of Indochina, a French colony that had fallen to the Japanese in World War II, had been fighting for their independence—against the Japanese and then against the French. The end of the Korean war had enabled the Chinese Reds to provide at least indirect aid to the Indochinese nationalists, who were largely Communists, at a time when the French were tottering on the edge of military disaster. In the spring of 1954 the rebels besieged a French army of 12,000 in the frontier fortress of Dienbienphu. Already the United States was underwriting 70 percent of the French financial cost of the war, but without direct military aid, Dienbiephu and perhaps all of Indochina would be lost.

At a press conference, President Eisenhower likened the nations in Southeast Asia to a row of dominoes. The moral was implicit; the first domino must not be allowed to fall. Many of the President's advisers favored at least bombing the besieging army with carrier-based planes, but Dulles failed to gain support among allied nations. Congressional leaders had no stomach for an intervention that might involve more ground troops than the Korean War, and in which the United States might have to fight alone.

The United States did not intervene; there was no "massive retaliation." Dienbienphu fell on May 7, 1954. At a conference in Geneva, the United States, stripped of bargaining power (except for the threat of unilateral intervention) had to stand by, neither associating itself with negotiations with Red China, nor approving of the agreements in July 1954, which provided for a cease-fire and partitioning of Indochina.

After the Geneva Conference, Secretary Dulles succeeded in building a Southeast Asia Treaty Organization (SEATO) in September 1954 to serve as a counterpart of NATO and help contain Communism. SEATO was far less impressive. It did open the way for economic and military aid, but without key nations such as India, Burma, and Indonesia participating, it remained a relatively ineffective organization.

The United States continued to function in Asia as best it could on a virtually unilateral basis. Trouble with Communist China developed over some offshore islands that Chiang continued to garrison—Quemoy and the Matsu and Tachen Islands. Congress granted President Eisenhower rather indefinite emergency powers to aid Chiang. These sufficed to maintain a precarious status quo.

Our German Ally

Fortunately, the United States and its allies did not depend upon nuclear power alone. The concept of the North Atlantic Treaty Organization was embodied in its emblem of a sword and a shield. The sword stood for atomic weapons, the striking force, and the shield for conventional ground forces, to deter or withstand attack. During the Korean War the United States began to rebuild its military establishment at home and gradually to pour funds into NATO, to strengthen its defenses in terms of ground forces as well as atomic weapons.

Europeans worried over the slowness of the United States to provide arms and men, its failure (partly because of constitutional limitations) to commit itself clearly in advance to resist any armed attack on western European nations, and its desire to rearm Germany.

After receiving reassurances, France in October 1954 agreed to a treaty restoring full sovereignty to Germany (except for the stationing of allied troops in West Berlin until Germany was reunified). National armies were not to be scrambled as had been earlier planned, but the West German army was to be limited to twelve divisions, which would be supplied to NATO. Germany promised not to seek reunification or extension of her boundaries through force, and was prohibited from manufacturing atomic, biological, or chemical weapons. Germany joined NATO and thus directly became a military ally of the United States. In 1957 it contributed its first forces, five divisions totaling 120,000 men.

The Geneva Spirit

After the death of Stalin in 1953, some softening of Soviet policy led to demands from Europeans, Asians, and even Americans for a conference among the heads of state—a "summit conference"—to consider means of easing international tensions. But the greatest single motive for such a meeting was the knowledge that both the United States and Russia were manufacturing hydrogen bombs of staggering destructive power.

In August 1953, after the Russians had set off a hydrogen explosive, President Eisenhower warned that the physical security of the United States had "almost totally disappeared before the long-range bomber and the destructive power of a single bomb." The meaning of this became dramatically clear in the spring of 1954 when the United States announced that it had exploded in the Pacific a bomb powerful enough to destroy or put out of commission all of New York City.

Against this background, the American people, after an initial wariness, became enthusi-

astic about the meeting of the heads of the United States, Great Britain, France, and Russia at Geneva in July 1955. President Eisenhower, hopeful that he could wage "a war for peace," proposed at the meetings that the Russians and the United States exchange blueprints of their armed forces and permit inspection of their military installations from the air.

The affability of the Russians at Geneva immensely relieved the American people, who were hopeful for the moment that a real change of policy had come about. This "Geneva spirit," as newspapermen called it, led to a general feeling on the part of most Western nations that a nuclear war between Russia and the United States would not develop. The subsequent foreign ministers' conference, however, failed dismally to agree upon German unification, disarmament, or lowering of trade barriers. The "Geneva spirit" rapidly evaporated throughout the West.

Menace in the Middle East

Soon a new Russian drive was launched toward the Middle East, where the United States had long been deeply involved because of its conflicting interests in the people of the new state of Israel and in the oil of the Arab states.

During World War II, the British, in order not to offend the Arabs, had continued restrictions upon immigration to Palestine; both political parties in the United States favored lifting these restrictions and creating a Jewish state. After the war, the British brought the problem to the United Nations, which recommended partitioning Palestine between Jews and Arabs. The Jews successfully repelled military attacks by the Arabs and, on the day the British mandate ended, May 14, 1948, proclaimed a new government. President Truman recognized it within a few minutes, thus ending United Nations proposals to put Palestine under a temporary trusteeship. The new nation, Israel, fought off armies from surrounding Arab countries until the United Nations established an unstable truce in 1949. Although the United States tried to promote amity, relations between Israel and its neighbors continued close to the point of explosion, and other quarrels in the Middle East persisted.

Gradually the United States won over some

of the Arab nations to the Western defense system. This country leased air bases from Saudi Arabia; and through the Baghdad Pact of February 1955 Secretary Dulles managed to bring the northern bloc of Arab states, Iraq, Iran, and Pakistan, into the defense arrangement.

Dulles' diplomacy was less successful with Egypt, which for years had quarreled with the British over the Sudan and British bases along the Suez Canal. The United States tried to mediate; in 1954 the British agreed to remove their troops from the Suez area. After Gamal Abdel Nasser came to power, the State Department tried to woo him, although he proclaimed emphatic neutralist and Arab nationalist policies, and strove for leadership of the entire Arab world. Secretary Dulles tried to win him with offers of economic aid — even the sum needed to construct an enormous dam on the Nile. The Russians concluded a deal, made public in September 1955, by which they gave Nasser large quantities of armaments in exchange for cotton.

With sufficient Communist arms, Nasser might destroy Israel. He could also threaten the security system the United States was trying to build in the Middle East. Secretary Dulles met the challenge. Instead of continuing to be conciliatory toward Egypt, in July 1956, he suddenly withdrew his promise to provide funds for a dam. A week later, Nasser retaliated by seizing the Suez Canal, purportedly to obtain money for the dam. This action gave him a strangle hold on the main oil line to Europe, since two-thirds of the proven oil reserves of the world were in the Middle East, and four-fifths of the oil for western Europe was flowing from there.

During the tedious months of negotiations with Nasser which followed, Great Britain, France, and Israel all came to feel that they were not obtaining as much support as they should from the United States. Meanwhile, the armed strength of Egypt was growing rapidly. On October 29, 1956, Israeli forces struck a preventive blow at Egypt; the next day the British and French intervened to drive the Egyptian forces from the Suez Canal zone. They were militarily successful, but not before the Egyptians had thoroughly blocked the canal. The United States led the United Nations in denouncing the military intervention; the Western alliances seemed in danger of dissolving; Russia threatened to send "volunteers" to the aid of Egypt. Under these pressures, the British and French issued a cease-fire order on November 6. Another prolonged truce between Egypt and Israel began under the supervision of the United Nations.

The power vacuum in the Middle East in the weeks after the Suez cease-fire created new opportunities for the spread of Communism. Once again the American public was alarmed and incensed, since coincident with the Suez crisis came brutal Soviet suppression of an uprising in Hungary. Because of the nuclear stalemate, the United States could not intervene in Hungary. It limited itself to fostering United Nations resolutions of censure and to admitting tens of thousands of refugees.

In the Middle East more positive action afterward seemed possible. The public was receptive when the President appeared before Congress on January 5, 1957, to enunciate what came to be called the "Eisenhower Doctrine." He asked Congress to authorize military and economic aid "to secure and protect the territorial independence" of Middle Eastern nations "against overt armed aggression from any nation controlled by international communism." Congress authorized the President to use armed force as he deemed necessary, and to spend $200 million on economic aid in the area.

As an instrument of pressure upon Egypt, the Eisenhower Doctrine was of little effect. Nassar reopened the Suez Canal on his own terms, and with Soviet aid became increasingly involved in the governments of his neighbors. In April 1957 American policy seemed more successful when the United States rushed its Sixth Fleet to the eastern Mediterranean to bolster the government of Jordan. Three other states, Saudi Arabia, Iraq, and Lebanon, seemed to give at least tacit support to the Eisenhower Doctrine.

The Rocket Race

The onslaught of Communist ideology and power was especially frightening because of the failure of the United States to keep pace with the Soviet Union in the development of intercontinental ballistic missiles. In August 1957 Russia announced that she had successfully tested an intercontinental ballistic missile. In contrast, the United States had successfully tested only intermediate-range missiles that had traveled from 1,500 to 3,000 miles. The Russian claims received sobering confirmation in October when

Soviet scientists, using a rocket booster engine more powerful than any yet developed in the United States, launched the first successful satellite, the "sputnik."

Khrushchev, who in a series of bold moves had just consolidated his power in the Kremlin, now issued a series of strong statements. The intent of his "sputnik diplomacy" was clearly to shake the Western alliance and impress neutral nations. The reaction within the United States, especially when the first American attempt to launch a much smaller satellite failed, was more one of angry fear than of congratulations to the Russian scientists. Three months later the United States began launching its own, smaller satellites.

Meanwhile, extensive nuclear testing by both the United States and Russia, climaxed by the Russian explosion of several "dirty" bombs, had greatly increased the fallout of radioactive isotopes. Throughout the world there was a fear of possible harmful effects. In the spring of 1958, Khrushchev announced a unilateral abstention from nuclear tests by Russia. President Eisenhower responded that the United States and its allies would suspend tests for one year beginning October 31, 1958. The suspension would continue on a year-to-year basis, provided a proper system of control could be developed and substantial progress could be made on disarmament negotiations.

In 1959 Khrushchev made much propaganda use of the failure of the United States to catch up with Russia in astronautical feats. These feats obscured the fact that the "missile gap" between the two nations was not as great as had been feared two years earlier. The United States was successfully producing and testing its own missiles and developing plans for hiding and spreading the launching sites so that it would require ten times as many Russian missiles to destroy them. The success of the navy in constructing atomic-powered submarines that could launch missiles, and in bringing the submarines up through the ice at the North Pole, was a dramatic example of American achievement. The naval development of "Project Tepee," a radio-monitoring system that could detect missile launchings anywhere in the world, was an indication of the technical advance of American defense.

In November 1958, Khrushchev had precipitated a new crisis over Berlin, threatening to sign a separate peace treaty turning the Russian occupation functions over to East Germany. A new Secretary of State, Christian Herter, took over when Dulles, dying of cancer, resigned in April 1959. Although Herter was a strong secretary, President Eisenhower now assumed a larger measure of responsibility, and this led to new interchanges at the top with the Russians. In August 1959 Eisenhower announced that he would exchange visits with Khrushchev. On the whole Khrushchev received a cordial welcome during his tour of the United States, but discussions with Eisenhower brought no results. The President never made the return visit.

A second "summit" conference, to meet in Paris, was scheduled for May 1960. On May 1 an unarmed American "U-2" plane was downed inside the Soviet Union. The American government at first denied, then acknowledged and attempted to justify, the fact that the plane had been engaged in aerial reconnaissance of a kind the United States had been carrying on, systematically but secretly, for some time. At the Paris meeting, unsatisfied by Eisenhower's belated promise to discontinue flights over Russian territory, Khrushchev made the U-2 incident an occasion for denouncing Eisenhower and breaking up the conference.

Disgruntled Neighbors

The incessant threats against areas close to the Communist perimeter so occupied the American government and people that they paid scant attention to an area of vital worth to the United States and of growing vulnerability to Communist influence, the nations to the south. One of the minor ironies of this hectic age was the erosion of the Good Neighbor feeling between Latin American nations and the United States during the very years when this country was extending much of the Good Neighbor policy to Europe and Asia.

Above all, the problems from which Latin American peoples were suffering were economic. After the close of World War II, they could no longer sell raw materials from their farms and mines to the United States in such large quantities or at such favorable prices as before. The soaring costs of the American manufactured goods they imported further hurt them. At home they were undergoing a rapid industrial revolution, an accompanying social revolution, and an explosive population increase at the highest rate in the world, as much as 2.5 percent per year. Already their combined population had passed that of the United States. All these factors helped create acute internal problems.

Inevitably the United States would have to be involved in the solution of economic questions because the hostility of neighbors to the south would be potentially ruinous and because the two areas had become increasingly interdependent economically.

It seemed to Latin Americans that despite close economic ties, the United States was doing little to help them solve their problems — to provide adequate capital for large-scale development, to stabilize the prices of raw material at a profitable level, and to conquer inflation. They felt neglected as the American government poured billions into Europe and Asia while giving Latin America only a comparative pittance. Secretary Dulles was occupied elsewhere, and the Eisenhower administration, under the influence of conservative secretaries of the treasury, was cold to requests for government loans for economic development.

Despite riots and disorders, the Latin American discontent received little notice in the United States until May 1958, when Vice President Nixon was mobbed in Lima and Caracas. In the aftermath of the national shock, the State Department speeded changes in policy that were already slowly under way. When in June 1958 the President of Brazil called for an Operation Pan-America to speed economic development, the American government agreed to furnish nearly half the capital for a new billion-dollar Inter-American Bank to make development loans.

The administration was increasing its attention to Latin America none too soon. The full import of the Communist challenge to the south became clear in 1960. Fidel Castro, whose revolutionary accession to power had been cheered by Americans at the beginning of 1959, turned his administration increasingly to the left and indulged in shrill tirades against the United States. The Eisenhower administration, acting with restraint, was slow to retaliate economically until, in the summer of 1960, Castro systematically confiscated a billion dollars' worth of American property. At this point, the United States stopped importing Cuban sugar at a subsidized price. Castro complained to the United Nations Security Council that the United States was engaging in economic aggression.

The Soviet leader Nikita S. Khrushchev proclaimed that the Monroe Doctrine was dead and that if the United States were to intervene militarily, Soviet artillerymen could "support Cuba with rocket fire." In the fall of 1960 tension heightened as Castro tried to export his revolution to neighboring republics. President Eisenhower established a naval patrol to prevent an invasion of Guatemala or Nicaragua. At the same time, secretly, Americans were training an anti-Castro Cuban force at a camp in Guatemala. In January 1961 Castro ordered the staff of the United States embassy in Havana cut from eighty-seven to eleven. The United States then severed diplomatic relations with Cuba. Soviet influence clearly extended to within ninety miles of the United States.

Businessmen in Government

In the 1950s the majority of the voters seemed more interested in preserving their own economic gains than in remaking society. Viewing themselves as moderates, they gave wholehearted support to the moderate President, Dwight D. Eisenhower. As early as 1949 Eisenhower had indicated his own approach when, as president of Columbia University, he addressed the American Bar Association. "The path of America's future," he said then, "lies down the middle of the road between the unfettered power of concentrated wealth . . . and the unbridled power of statism or partisan interests."

Once in office, President Eisenhower established a businessmen's administration. He appointed the president of General Motors, Charles E. Wilson, to the Defense Department and other big businessmen to all the rest of the cabinet posts but one. The Secretary of Labor was the pro-Stevenson president of the plumbers' union (he was soon to resign from the cabinet). "Eight millionaires and a plumber," the *New Republic* disrespectfully remarked.

President Eisenhower's system of administering the government gave special importance to this cabinet made up preponderantly of businessmen. In the techniques that he developed, he borrowed from earlier army experience. He established his assistant, Sherman Adams, former Governor of New Hampshire, as a sort of chief of staff, and from Adams down through the cabinet he established a chain of command. Through the cabinet and numerous new committees, administrators arrived at important policy decisions, which they referred to the President. He relied heavily upon these recommendations.

"Eisenhower Prosperity"

The new administration quickly dropped almost all the price controls that had been imposed during the Korean War, and it began to restrict credit so as to prevent inflation. By the fall of 1953, however, the threat was one of deflation, and the government reversed the scarce-money policies and eased credit. By the summer of 1955 the American economy was again booming.

To avoid strikes that might unsettle economic conditions, several large industries, led by the automobile manufacturers, made new concessions to organized labor. In December 1955 the American Federation of Labor and the Congress of Industrial Organizations merged at the top into a new giant federation, the AFL-CIO. The powerful Teamsters' Brotherhood in 1957 became the focal point of a congressional investigation into labor racketeering. This led to the Labor Reform Act of 1959, which was intended to promote honest elections of union officials, safeguard union funds, ban Communist leaders, and restrict boycotting and picketing.

The great staples piled up in surplus, and from 1948 to 1956, farm prices dropped a third. The government sought to bolster the prices through $8 billion worth of purchases. The 1955 harvest was the first to be grown under a new flexible price-support system. Under the 1956 program, which was designed to cut production while creating a "soil bank" of fallow land, farmers took 12.3 million acres out of production in return for payments of over a quarter billion dollars.

The Eisenhower administration proposed federal "partnership" with local public or private enterprise in power construction. The President referred to expansion of the Tennessee Valley Authority as "creeping socialism," and the administration sought unsuccessfully to circum-

vent the TVA by contracting with the Dixon-Yates syndicate in 1954 to build a huge privately-owned steam power plant on the banks of the Mississippi. In keeping with his feeling that development of resources should be decentralized, Eisenhower signed a bill turning over to states offshore oil lands along the Gulf of Mexico and the Pacific Coast.

The President retained the basic general welfare programs that had been enacted during the previous twenty years. He took a firm stand against so-called "socialized medicine" but proposed a public health insurance program that would involve little more than limited underwriting of private insurance companies issuing health policies. Congress passed no health-insurance legislation but, in 1954, extended social security to 10 million more people, and unemployment compensation to an additional 4 million.

Decline of McCarthyism

Early in the Eisenhower administration the hunt for subversives had been intensified. Large numbers of government employees resigned or were dismissed; the administration at one point gave their total as 2,200. But most of the serious security risks had already been ousted in the Truman administration. A study of some four hundred of the Eisenhower administration cases by the Fund for the Republic of the Ford Foundation indicated that in a majority of them the charges had been insupportable, and often reinstatement ultimately followed. In July 1955 the Congress established a bipartisan Commission on Government Security to reevaluate the security program.

Senator Joseph McCarthy himself plummeted from the national limelight to relative obscurity. His downfall followed his serious blunder in obliquely attacking President Eisenhower and directly assailing Secretary of the Army Robert Stevens in January 1954. The attacks led to congressional hearings, which turned into a great national spectacle viewed by millions over television. Many people for the first time saw McCarthy in action, as for thirteen days he bullied and harried Secretary Stevens, evading issues through irrelevant countercharges and insinuations, and interrupting to object at every point. As the public watched, McCarthy seemed to change from a national hero into something of a villain, then into a low buffoon. In December 1954 the Senate voted 67 to 22 to condemn McCarthy, but his hold over the American public had already largely disintegrated.

Desegregation Begins

The Supreme Court under its new Eisenhower-appointed Chief Justice, Earl Warren, the former Governor of California, moved toward more liberal policies on both civil liberties and civil rights. In a number of cases in the 1950s the Court protected individuals who were suspected of being subversive from undue encroachment by federal or state power. These decisions attracted relatively little attention compared with the Supreme Court rulings on desegregation.

Since the late 1930s the National Association for the Advancement of Colored People had pressed a series of cases before the Supreme Court that bit by bit broke down racial segregation in public education. Their prime target was a Supreme Court decision of 1896, *Plessy* v. *Ferguson,* which had interpreted the requirement of the Fourteenth Amendment that states give "equal protection of the laws" to mean that separate but equal facilities could be furnished to Negroes. Finally, the Supreme Court reversed this doctrine in the case of *Brown* v. *Board of Education of Topeka* in May 1954. Chief Justice Earl Warren delivered the unanimous opinion of the Court: "We conclude that in the field of public education the doctrine of 'separate but equal' has no place. Separate educational facilities are inherently unequal." The Court granted that Southern states might move gradually toward desegregation.

States in the deep South and several border states resorted to every possible legal device to avoid mixed schools. Each September, mob action against integration in a few communities within the South attracted widespread attention throughout the world. By the fall of 1957, of some 3,000 biracial school districts in the South, a total of 684 had begun desegregation. Schools within these districts in large cities in the upper South or the border area, like Washington, Baltimore, Louisville, and St. Louis, opened quietly on a desegregated basis. But 2,300 districts, including all those in the deep South and Virginia, remained segregated. Some districts attempted desegregation on a very slow, "token"

basis. One of these was Little Rock, Arkansas, where intervention by the governor and threats by a mob led President Eisenhower to send federal troops to maintain order.

Pressure from growing blocs of Negro voters in the North, and from Negroes rising in economic status in the South, helped bring other changes. President Eisenhower completed the desegregation of the armed forces and tried to bring about greater integration in the government and the District of Columbia. "There must be no second-class citizens in this country," he wrote the Negro Representative Adam Clayton Powell.

Congress in August 1957, after debating sixty-three days, passed a new civil rights law — the first since Reconstruction — to give federal protection to Negroes wanting to vote. In eight Southern states with an adult Negro population of over 3.75 million, only 850,000, or 25 percent, were registered, and still fewer went to the polls. In a 1955 election in Mississippi, only about 1 percent of the adult Negroes voted. The civil-rights act empowered the federal government to remove some of the obstacles that state and local officials were placing in the way of Negro registration and voting. Federal judges were authorized to enjoin state officials from refusing to register qualified persons. The judges could fine recalcitrant officials up to $300 and could sentence them to forty-five days in jail, without a jury trial.

A Second Term for Ike

In September 1955 President Eisenhower was at the height of his popularity. Only the anti-third-term Twenty-second Amendment, ratified in 1951 as a belated slap at Roosevelt, seemed to bar him from staying in the White House as long as he chose. Apparently his health was excellent, but while vacationing in Colorado, on the morning of September 24, he suffered a heart attack. The President began to make a promising recovery, and in 1956 he and Vice President Nixon were renominated by acclamation. Stevenson triumphed again at the Democratic convention, but in the end, Eisenhower won by an even wider margin than in 1952.

It was not much of a triumph for the Republican party. The prestige of the President pulled some Republican Congressmen to narrow victories, but the Democrats continued to control both houses of Congress, as they had done since the mid-term elections of 1954.

At the close of 1957 the nation skidded into the most serious recession since the war. Although recovery began in 1958, Republicans preparing for the congressional campaign of 1958 were handicapped by the economic record. The Democrats won 13 additional seats in the Senate, giving them a 62 to 34 majority. They gained an added 47 seats in the House of Representatives, providing a majority of 282 to 153—the largest margin since Roosevelt's 1936 victory.

As prosperity returned in the spring of 1959, public opinion began to react to the incessant warnings of the President and of conservative publicists that budget balancing was the only way to avoid another ruinous round of inflation. Eisenhower succeeded in keeping down expenditures for inexpensive public housing for families displaced from slums and for other social services. He also succeeded in ending the 1960 fiscal year with a billion-dollar surplus. But by the fall of 1960, the economy had again stalled into the third recession of the Eisenhower years; tax revenue declined, and the fiscal year ended with a serious deficit.

In his final State of the Union message in January 1961, President Eisenhower granted that problems of recession and unemployment left little room for complacency. But he pointed out correctly that during his eight years in office the inflationary spiral had all but ceased and that the nation's output of goods and services had increased 25 percent; the income of the average American family increased 15 percent; and the real wages of workers increased 20 percent. "In a united determination to keep this nation strong and free and to utilize our vast resources for the advancement of all mankind," he asserted, "we have carried America to unprecedented heights."

SELECTED READINGS

A. R. Buchanan, *The United States and World War II** (2 vols., 1964) surveys military aspects of World War II. Two excellent interpretations of strategy are S. E. Morison, *Strategy and Compromise* (1958), and K. R. Greenfield, *American Strategy in World War II* (1963). A good brief account is Fletcher Pratt, *War for the World* (1950).

A monumental account of wartime diplomacy is Herbert Feis, *Churchill, Roosevelt, Stalin* (1957). Three outstanding brief interpretations are Gaddis Smith, *American Diplomacy During the Second World War, 1941–1945* (1965); J. L. Snell, *Illusion and Necessity, the Diplomacy of Global War, 1939–1945* (1963); and W. L. Neumann, *After Victory: Churchill, Roosevelt, Stalin and the Making of the Peace* (1967). An important revisionist view is Gabriel Kolko, *The Politics of War; The World and United States Foreign Policy, 1943–1945* (1968).

On production and domestic problems during World War II, see Eliot Janeway, *The Struggle for Survival* (1968 edition), which concentrates on policy and conflicts in Washington, and Bureau of the Budget, *The United States at War* (1946), which is the best survey. On special topics see J. P. Baxter III, *Scientists Against Time* (1946); R. G. Hewlett and O. E. Anderson, *A History of the United States Atomic Energy Commission* (vol. 1, 1962); and Jack Goodman, ed., *While You Were Gone: A Report on Wartime Life in the United States* (1946).

On postwar foreign policy, brief readable surveys are W. G. Carleton, *The Revolution in American Foreign Policy** (1963), and J. W. Spanier, *American Foreign Policy Since World War II** (1962). Analyses of the changes are C. E. Bohlen, *The Transformation of American Foreign Policy* (1969); R. E. Osgood, *Alliances and American Foreign Policy* (1968); and Seyom Brown, *The Faces of Power: Constancy and Change in United States Foreign Policy from Truman to Johnson* (1968). D. F. Fleming, *The Cold War and Its Origins, 1917–1960* (2 vols., 1961) places the blame upon the United States.

George Kennan, *Russia and the West under Lenin and Stalin** (1961) is an overview. Dean Acheson, *Present at the Creation; My Years in the State Department* (1969) is both witty and comprehensive. See also Norman Graebner, *Cold War Diplomacy: American Foreign Policy, 1945-1960** (1962); J. and G. Kolko, *The Limits of Power: The World and United States Foreign Policy, 1945-1954** (1972); and J. L. Gaddis, *The United States and the Origins of the Cold War, 1941-1947* (1973).

On the Truman administration: B. J. Bernstein and A. J. Matusow, *The Truman Administration: A Documentary History** (1966); E. F. Goldman, *The Crucial Decade** (1956); and A. L. Hamby, *Beyond the New Deal: Harry S. Truman and American Liberalism* (1973). Truman, *Memoirs** (2 vols., 1955) is comprehensive, and for interpretations and bibliography, see R. S. Kirkendall, ed., *The Truman Period as a Research Field* (1967).

On the Korean War, see David Rees, *Korea: The Limited War* (1964), and Carl Berger, *The Korean Knot* (1957). On the debate over foreign policy, see Norman Graebner, *The New Isolationism* (1956).

On McCarthyism, see M. P. Rogin, *The Intellectuals and McCarthy* (1967). On the type of thinking that made McCarthyism possible, see Richard Hofstadter, *The Paranoid Style in American Politics** (1965) and *Anti-Intellectualism in American Life** (1963).

On President Eisenhower and his policies, see D. D. Eisenhower, *The White House Years** (2 vols., 1963-1965); Arthur Larson, *Eisenhower: The President Nobody Knew* (1968); M. J. Pusey, *Eisenhower the President* (1956); Sherman Adams, *First Hand Report* (1961); and Richard Nixon, *Six Crises** (1962). On the Supreme Court, see C. M. Lytle, *The Warren Court and Its Critics* (1968); R. H. Sayler and others, *The Warren Court: A Critical Analysis* (1969); and Archibald Cox, *The Warren Court: Constitutional Decision as an Instrument of Reform* (1968). On the struggle for civil rights in the 1950s, see Anthony Lewis, *Portrait of a Decade, The Second American Revolution** (1964). On foreign policy, see L. L. Gerson, *John Foster Dulles* (1967); M. S. Eisenhower, *The Wine Is Bitter: The United States and Latin America* (1963); and Melvin Gurtov, *The First Vietnam Crisis: Chinese Communist Strategy and United States Involvement, 1953-1954* (1967).

* Titles available in paperback.

PART EIGHT

Man Visits Other Worlds Before He Puts His Own in Order

Foreign relations persisted as the central political preoccupations of Americans after 1960 as they continued to face a "hostile ideology" abroad. But there was a ray of hope. Russia and China were ancient enemies, with differences of interest too profound to be patched over indefinitely by the shared ideology of Communism. By 1961, signs of serious conflict appeared between the Soviet Union and the People's Republic of China. Some Americans believed that if the conflict worsened, one or both of the two Communist powers might be willing to seek or to accept improved relations with the United States. This prospect caused some to look toward an eventual "détente," relaxation of tensions in world politics. Among them was President Kennedy who, in his inaugural address advised: "Let us never negotiate out of fear. But let us never fear to negotiate." Nonetheless, during the Kennedy years, as Russia and the United States faced one another over the issues of Berlin, Cuba, and nuclear testing, the spirit of negotiation was put to severe trials. And the most dangerous crisis between the United States and the Soviet Union was yet to come. But both nations survived Vietnam without direct conflict and the achievement of some kind of détente became a real possibility during Richard Nixon's administration. Nixon failed to "bring the American people together," as he promised in his 1968 campaign; instead, he aroused increasing bitterness and division when he frustrated the hope for an early withdrawal from Vietnam. Nevertheless, he won widespread approval by finally withdrawing American troops and by redirecting basic policy in such a way as to improve the prospects for moderating the cold war and for realizing what he hailed as a "generation of peace."

Vietnam was, without question, the major tragedy of the post-1960 era. It had an enormous cost in lives and resources, set generation against generation, and drastically altered national priorities. The war also delayed détente and weakened America elsewhere in the world. The 1960s began with some promise that American society, in its exceptional prosperity, would face squarely the problems of disadvantaged peoples. President Johnson's "Great Society" program, in particular, suggested a significant revival of certain lines of progressive and New Deal reform. But President Johnson was himself to jeopardize his "Great Society" when, in 1965, he committed the country to a large-scale war in Vietnam. While starting his "war on poverty," Johnson was escalating his war in Vietnam. The enormous costs of the latter made it more and more difficult to pay for the former. And when Johnson attempted to do both, the consequence was the onset of what might prove to be the nation's most serious bout with inflation and the nation's most serious economic crisis since the Great Depression.

To many Americans, the government programs to eliminate poverty were jeopardized by the costly campaign to place an American on the moon. But to others, that campaign, climaxed by Neil Armstrong's 1969 moon landing, opened a new age of interplanetary exploration. Certainly the moon landing, the result of cooperative efforts by thousands of scientists and technicians, provided a spectacular illustration of what sociologists call "cultural lag," the failure of social and political development to keep up with technological advances. Man was visiting other worlds before he put his own in order.

Meanwhile, as the country neared the 200th anniversary of its independence, the American people were confronted with a constitutional crisis. The Constitution had provided for a balanced government, with three equal and coordinate branches, but in recent years the executive branch had greatly overbalanced the legislative. Both national security and domestic welfare demanded a strong Presidency. Constitutional and democratic government, however, required a controlled and responsible one.

Since 1960

Chapter 31. SEEKING THE "GREAT SOCIETY"

The "New Frontier"

"The world is very different now," said President John F. Kennedy in his inaugural address, January 20, 1961, "for man holds in his mortal hands the power to abolish all forms of human poverty and all forms of human life." To achieve the promise and avoid the peril was the twofold challenge of the time. This was what Kennedy called the "New Frontier" – a new challenge to the old pioneering instincts of Americans.

Kennedy had won the Democratic nomination only after a vigorous struggle in the primaries. A forty-three-year-old senator from Massachusetts and a Roman Catholic, he was thought to be handicapped by his youth and his religion. In the primaries he had to dispose of a fellow senator, Hubert Humphrey of Minnesota, who was considered more liberal than he. Then, at the convention in Los Angeles, he had to overcome the powerful opposition of Lyndon B. Johnson of Texas, the Senate majority leader. In the 1930s, Johnson had been one of the coterie of ardent New Dealers. By 1960, without entirely abandoning his earlier allegiances, he had become the most respected spokesman of the industrialized and conservative South. When Kennedy won the presidential nomination, he offered the vice-presidential nomination to Johnson, who accepted and campaigned energetically.

The Republican nomination went almost by default to Vice President Richard M. Nixon, whom President Eisenhower favored. As Vice President, Nixon had enjoyed eight years on the front pages and had even argued with Khrushchev in Moscow. Thus he was able to offer a continuation of President Eisenhower's "peace and prosperity," and – though he was only four years older than Kennedy – mature leadership.

When Kennedy challenged Nixon to a series of television debates, Nixon's advisers thought Kennedy would be no match for their man, and they agreed to four joint appearances. In the first debate, however, everything went wrong for Nixon. Not yet recovered from an illness, he appeared tired, haggard, and heavy-jowled, in con-trast to Kennedy, who seemed relaxed, self-confident, and well-informed – before an estimated 70 million television viewers. From then on, Kennedy seemed to take the lead from Nixon.

The recession of 1960–1961 also hurt the Republicans. Nevertheless, in the closing days of the campaign, a vigorous Republican campaign drive, with the aid of President Eisenhower, brought a hairline decision at the polls.

Before the election, Kennedy had hoped that on taking office he could push through Congress a legislative program as sweeping as that of Franklin D. Roosevelt during the first hundred days of the New Deal. Kennedy did not abandon his reform plans, but the closeness of the decision led him to move with caution. Unlike the Eisenhower cabinet, which had predominantly represented business, the Kennedy cabinet balanced the economic and political as well as the regional interests in the nation. The most controversial of the appointments was that of Kennedy's thirty-five-year-old brother and campaign manager, Robert F. Kennedy, as attorney general.

The Kennedy Economic Program

President Kennedy – the youngest man, except for Theodore Roosevelt, ever to occupy the White House – sent a record number of messages, twenty-five, to the first session of the Eighty-seventh Congress. Some called for long-range national undertakings: economic recovery and growth, health care for the aged, federal aid for schools, conservation and use of natural resources, highway construction, and housing and community development.

The existence of a Democratic majority in each house did not mean that Kennedy could count upon an easy enactment of his program, since many Democrats were conservative and frequently voted with the Republicans.

By dint of persuasion and compromise he managed to obtain considerable legislation. A new minimum-wage law provided considerably less coverage than the President had wished, but it did bring an additional 3,624,000 workers under the law. It raised the minimum hourly pay rate, effective in several steps over two to four years, from $1.00 to $1.25. The Housing Act of 1961 fully embodied his proposals, authorizing $4.9 billion in federal grants or loans over a four-year period for the preservation of open spaces in cities, the development of local mass transit systems, and the construction of middle-income housing. Congressional conservatives dealt the President two sharp setbacks when they defeated his bills to provide medical care for the aged and federal aid for school construction and teachers' salaries.

Kennedy obtained from Congress additional expenditures for unemployment compensation and aid to depressed areas—appropriations totaling $900 million. The only other large additions to the federal budget were $4 billion in defense spending to meet new challenges from Russia and large amounts of farm crop subsidies that had to be paid by virtue of earlier legislation. These expenditures, coupled with a vigorous expansion of the money supply by the Federal Reserve Board, brought about a substantial economic recovery by the end of 1961. But over 5 percent of the working force remained unemployed.

Unemployment declined slowly during Kennedy's administration partly because in his first two years in office he was determined to continue Eisenhower's resistence to inflation and, consequently, attempted to keep the budget in balance. He also used his powers energetically to prevent inflationary moves on the part of labor and industry. In the spring of 1962 he persuaded the United Steel Workers to accept a contract granting only small wage increases. When, almost immediately, United States Steel, followed by most other steel companies, unexpectedly announced large price increases, the President exploded with anger. During the three days that followed, he brought every variety of pressure he could muster, until the steel companies returned to their old prices. The cost to Kennedy was the hostility of much of the business community, which blamed him for a stock-market drop a few weeks later.

By January 1963 Kennedy had become convinced by his Council of Economic Advisers that he ought to shift budget policy to stimulate more rapid economic growth and to reduce persistent unemployment. Taking a middle course endorsed both by businessmen who wanted reductions in federal programs and by businessmen and liberals who adhered to Keynesian economics, Kennedy proposed to Congress a massive tax cut. The cut entailed a reduction of $13.5 billion in income taxes over a period of three years.

Kennedy and Civil Rights

Kennedy was becoming convinced that the government must do more than it had done for the Negroes—to whose votes he owed his narrow victory in the 1960 election. Nearly a decade after the Supreme Court's historic decision against segregation, the equal-rights movement was making little or no progress.

The National Association for the Advancement of Colored People (NAACP), which had led the cause, was still pressing lawsuits and seeking court orders, but more and more Negroes were growing impatient with its methods and were embittered by white obstruction of their cause. Blacks began to form more militant organizations. A desperate minority of perhaps 200,000 joined the Black Muslims and, in a spirit reminiscent of the Garvey black nationalism of the 1920s, proclaimed black supremacy and demanded a complete separation of the races. Others continued to struggle for integration but turned to direct action through new organizations such as the Congress of Racial Equality (CORE) and the Southern Christian Leadership Conference. The SCLC was led by an eloquent young Baptist minister, Dr. Martin Luther King, who gained national and international fame as an advocate of passive resistance and, for his work, was to win the Nobel Peace Prize in 1964.

In the South, beginning in 1960, youthful blacks with some white sympathizers engaged in "sit-ins" to demand the right to eat in restaurants or at lunch counters or the right to use books in the main public libraries rather than in segregated branches. Negroes and whites went on "freedom rides" to desegregate interstate buses and terminals. Thousands engaged in mass demonstrations and accepted arrest; on several occasions the jails of Southern cities were filled to overflowing. Demonstrations spread to the North in mass attacks against de facto segregation in schools and housing and against the exclusion of all but a handful of Negroes from various kinds of employment. By the summer of 1963 the movement had reached such a peak that it was being proclaimed by news magazines as the "Negro revolution." More than 200,000 demonstrators (10 to 15 percent of them white) participated in a "March on Washington," converging on the Lincoln Memorial.

In areas where federal power could be invoked, those protesting against segregation received the support of the Kennedy administration. Attorney General Robert F. Kennedy mustered federal force behind the integration of interstate transportation, and the President sent troops to the University of Mississippi to protect a Negro student, James Meredith, who had been enrolled by order of a federal court. Throughout the South campaigns were under way to enroll Negro voters under the protection of the civil rights legislation of 1957. As pressure intensified in 1963, President Kennedy threw the prestige of his administration behind the most comprehensive civil rights bill ever presented to Congress.

"Let Us Continue"

In the fall of 1963, though congressional conservatives were blocking enactment of the two major bills in the New Frontier program, the civil rights and tax-cut measures, President Kennedy felt optimistic. He was looking ahead to the election of 1964, which most observers thought would result in his reelection by a comfortable margin. He hoped that the election would bring to Washington a more liberal Congress.

To court Southern support, Kennedy visited Florida and then Texas in November 1963. As he drove through the streets of Dallas, to the cheers of an enthusiastic crowd, an assassin, shooting three times in quick succession from a sixth-floor window, killed him and seriously wounded Governor John Connally of Texas. Police arrested Lee Harvey Oswald, a self-styled Marxist who had once tried to expatriate himself in Russia, and charged him with the murder both of the President and a policeman. Two days after the shooting, while Oswald was in the Dallas city jail, he was himself murdered by a Dallas night-club operator, before an incredulous national television audience. Inevita-

bly rumors spread concerning the possibility that a ramifying plot lay behind President Kennedy's assassination. In an effort to eliminate uncertainties, a presidential commission headed by Chief Justice Warren sifted through the evidence and several months later reported to the American people that Oswald had been a lone assassin.

About two hours after the assassination, Vice President Lyndon B. Johnson was sworn in as the thirty-sixth President of the United States. When he addressed a joint session of Congress on November 27, President Johnson expressed his main theme in the words "let us continue." The most fitting memorial to Kennedy, he reminded Congress, would be the enactment of the civil rights and tax bills and, indeed, the whole agenda of the New Frontier.

The Eighty-eighth Congress responded and in its 1964 session enacted not only several vital measures of the New Frontier program but also one of President Johnson's own recommendations, an antipoverty bill designed to launch an "unconditional war on poverty." It called for the establishment of VISTA (Volunteers in Service to America), a volunteer corps of social workers, and for remedial education, vocational training, part-time employment for teen-agers and students, and federal grants to states or communities for local attacks on poverty. The initial budget was almost a billion dollars.

In his legislative programs Johnson sought to build a great national following. He courted not only people excluded from national prosperity, but also Republican businessmen. The latter were delighted with the stimulative effect of the Kennedy-Johnson tax cut that had prevented a recession and extended the economic boom. Moreover, businessmen welcomed Johnson's cutback in the anticipated federal budget for 1965. Johnson maintained ties with traditional Democratic voters by increasing expenditures on health, education, and welfare through sharp limitation of the defense budget. And he was able to remain on cordial terms with labor leaders as take-home pay rose more rapidly than prices in 1964.

Commitment to Equality

Throughout the nation the problem of civil rights was closely related to that of poverty. A large proportion of the very poor were Negroes, who were unable to obtain adequately paid, secure employment. In cities like New York, Negroes (together with Puerto Ricans) filled a large number of badly paid service positions and jobs not requiring skill. The average Harlem family received $2,000 a year less in income than its white neighbors. Of the Negroes (largely youths) 13 percent were unemployed, since the poorer jobs were the sort being most rapidly eliminated by automation. Either through discrimination or through lack of training, young people were barred from more highly skilled work. Many Northern Negroes were crowded into substandard housing, and their children were enrolled in poor schools integrated only in name.

A number of young Northerners went to Mississippi in the summer of 1964 to enroll several thousand young Negroes in "Freedom Schools" and to conduct drives registering Negroes to vote. Three of the first civil rights workers to arrive disappeared; after some weeks the FBI found their bodies buried deep beneath an earthen dam.

As the struggle intensified, President Johnson threw his weight behind the comprehensive civil rights bill that Kennedy had presented to Congress. Bipartisan leadership in the Senate finally overcame Southern opposition. In June 1964, for the first time in history, the Senate voted to end a filibuster, so that the bill could be passed. The Civil Rights Act of 1964 strengthened earlier legislation to protect the voting rights of Negroes and to expedite the desegregation of schools. It also prohibited discrimination in public accommodations and facilities and in private employment.

After the act went into effect, Negroes ate with whites for the first time in some restaurants in the deep South, stayed in the same hotels and motels, sat in "white only" sections of motion picture theaters, and swam in previously segregated swimming pools. Compliance was not universal, and several test cases challenging the constitutionality of the law were brought before federal courts.

Early in 1965 violence erupted in the South, especially in Selma, Alabama, where masses of Negroes and a few white sympathizers demonstrated against registration procedures that kept Negroes off the voting rolls. The state police brutally broke up a parade, and assassins (said to be Klansmen) murdered two white civil rights workers from the North. To protect the demonstrators, President Johnson called up the Alabama National Guard. He also urged upon Congress a bill to guarantee the right to vote in presidential, senatorial, and congressional elections. This bill provided for federal registration of voters in those states where there were literacy or other special tests for registering and where fewer than half the people of voting age actually went to the polls.

One Man, One Vote

Meanwhile, constitutional amendments and court decisions were affecting, actually or potentially, the political rights of many Americans, both Negro and white.

The Twenty-third Amendment (1961) gave the franchise in presidential elections to residents of the District of Columbia. Home rule for Washington, which had the highest percentage of Negroes of any city in the country, continued to be withheld by Congress.

The Twenty-fourth Amendment (1964) gave symbolic, if not much practical, aid to Negro voters by providing that the right to vote in any primary or other federal election should not be abridged for failure to pay a poll tax. Most states in the deep South were using other methods to try to disfranchise Negroes.

An issue involving the rights of representation of a large part of the American electorate came before the Supreme Court in 1962, in a case involving the apportionment of legislative districts in Tennessee. Although the state constitution called for reapportionment every ten years, none had taken place since 1901, with the result that rural dominance in the legislature was out of all proportion to population. Moore County, with a population of 3,454, sent one legislator; Shelby County (Memphis), with 627,019 residents, sent only three. A vote in Moore County was worth more than sixty times as much as one in Shelby County. By a 6-to-2 decision, the Supreme Court gave the federal district court a mandate to order reapportionment if it found a violation of the Constitution. Similar inequities existed in a surprising number of other states; in all but six states, fewer than 40 percent of the population could elect a majority of the legislature. As a result of the Tennessee decision, many states quickly made some reapportionment of their legislative districts, either as a result of court action or as a means of forestalling it.

An even more important Supreme Court decision (in *Reynold* v. *Sims,* 1964) held that congressional districts within a state also must be substantially equal in population. The case before the court involved the congressional district containing the city of Atlanta, Georgia, a district that had a population of 820,000 as compared with the population of 270,000 in another Georgia district.

Johnson Thrashes Goldwater

As he took up and expanded the Kennedy program, President Johnson restated the objective as the creation of the "Great Society." "For half a century we called upon unbounded invention and untiring industry to create an order of plenty for all our people," he declared in May 1964. "The challenge of the next half century is whether we have the wisdom to use that wealth to enrich and elevate our national life – and to advance the quality of American civilization."

In the presidential campaign of 1964 the moderate liberalism for which Johnson had spoken confronted extreme conservatism.

In the years following the collapse of McCarthyism, militant conservatives in the United States had organized a number of action groups. The best known was the John Birch Society, whose founder, Robert Welch, called for the impeachment of Chief Justice Earl Warren and seemed to suspect the loyalty of even President Eisenhower. Senator Barry Goldwater of Arizona, though not himself a member of the so-called "radical right" organizations, became the hero of most of these groups. At the Republican convention in San Francisco, the Goldwater forces were in complete command from the outset.

As Senator Goldwater carried the Republican party far to the right, President Johnson tried to preempt not only the center of the road but also a wide strip to both the right and the left of it. Throughout the campaign Johnson was as wary of making specific, detailed promises as Eisenhower had been in 1956 and Roosevelt in 1936; his best strategy seemed to be merely to gather the votes against Goldwater. And gather them he did. He received more votes, over 42 million, and a larger plurality than any other candidate in history.

The Johnson Program

When the Eighty-ninth Congress convened, Johnson presented to it comprehensive proposals to make a beginning toward his long-range goals. With unprecedented speed, almost all of this far-ranging program became law. The overwhelmingly Democratic majorities in Congress, which had accompanied the landslide victory over Goldwater, were Johnson's to command.

A new immigration law, in response to the demands of urban and minority groups in America, abolished the inequities of the quota system established in the 1920s. The quota for England and Ireland of 83,000 persons per year had been seldom filled; that for Greece was only 308 persons. Gradually the government eliminated these quotas and began to allot visas not on a basis of national origins but giving preference on a basis of education and skills. Soon there were complaints that only an elite of professionals could enter the United States and that other nations, especially underdeveloped ones, were suffering a "brain drain" of their doctors, engineers, and highly educated specialists. In 1966 relatives of United States citizens began to receive preference, and a quota of 17,000 was set for professionals. Immigration from northwestern Europe declined and that from southern Europe and Asia increased.

Massive sustained federal aid to education at last began. President Johnson succeeded in circumventing the impasse in Congress over the question of whether parochial schools should receive a share of federal funds. He called for grants for text and library books for students in both public and parochial schools – and significantly the grants were to be made on the basis of the needs of individual students, not schools, a formula which the Supreme Court had approved when it applied to federal funds that were to provide milk or transportation to students. The Elementary and Secondary Education Act of 1965 and subsequent legislation gave aid to schools in both urban and rural areas in proportion to the number of poverty-stricken students in them. Federal funds purchased textbooks and library materials, financed special programs for adults and for the handicapped, and strengthened state educational agencies. Total federal expenditures in education and technical training rose from less than $5 billion in 1964 to more than $12 billion in 1967.

The establishment of Medicare for the 19 million Americans over sixty-five through the Medicare-Social Security Act of 1965 altered the lives of old people and had great impact upon American medicine. The debate over Medicare, which had been bitter for twenty years, ended as the program went into effect. Large numbers of older people were now receiving care that they could not previously have obtained or that would have exhausted their savings.

Rising costs created problems for the Medicaid program, which was launched in 1968 to provide financial assistance to persons who were not old enough to qualify for Medicare but were too poor to pay their own medical bills. Under the Medicaid law each state was to set up its own plan, determining payments and standards of eligibility for them, and the federal government was to contribute from 50 to 80 percent of the expense. During the first year, however, the program cost the federal government more than ten times as much as had been expected. Congress and the state legislatures therefore changed their definition of the needy so as to make the benefits available to fewer people than had originally been covered.

Medicare and Medicaid were parts of the effort to eradicate the "pockets of poverty" within the prosperous nation. More than 9 million people classified as poor were receiving no aid from federal food programs, a Senate subcommittee learned in 1967. Figures were incomplete. There was hunger in great cities, in Appalachia, the deep South, the Southwest, and on Indian reservations. Yet over 5 million people were receiving aid through federal food programs; either they were given food or could purchase it with reduced-cost stamps. Many millions were receiving other types of relief.

The poverty program of President Johnson, continuing and expanding that of Kennedy, approached the problem in numerous ways. By 1966 the Office of Economic Opportunity, established in 1964, had put about two-fifths of its budget into a variety of Community Action Programs. Another two-fifths went into youth programs — the Job Corps, Neighborhood Youth Corps, and College Work Study. Most of the remaining funds went into the Work Experience Program. VISTA served as a kind of Peace Corps at home.

Especially among the urban Negro unemployed, the job-training programs were a disappointment. Although Negroes began to penetrate the ranks of the white-collar workers, the total numbers were small. Nominally, union restrictions against them no longer existed, yet few could gain employment as skilled, highly paid construction workers. Industries that might have hired Negroes were moving out of the cities, away from where they lived. The training programs could not easily provide the overall education and motivation that most of these unemployed Negroes lacked. Impatient urban Negroes, disappointed at the meager return that cooperation seemed to have brought them, began increasingly to turn toward other possible solutions: black power, separatism, or even violence.

Black Power

The Negro population had been increasing more rapidly than the white population since the 1920s and had been shifting from the rural South to the cities throughout the nation, especially in the North. In 1910 only about a quarter of the Negroes lived in cities, and only a tenth outside the South; by 1966 15 million Negroes, 69 percent of the Negro population, were living in metropolitan areas; 45 percent of all Negroes were living outside the South. In several of the largest cities, the proportion of Negroes at least doubled between 1950 and 1968. Negroes constituted at least 30 percent of the population of seven of these cities and 66.6 per cent of the population of Washington, D.C. A corresponding exodus of whites from the cities to the suburbs dramatically increased the areas of residential and school segregation in the "black ghettos."

While some urban Negroes were sharing in the national prosperity, their proportional gains were decidedly less than those of the whites. Indeed, the gap between their incomes and those of whites was growing wider. The number of Negroes enjoying well-paid, highly skilled employment giving them exceptional status doubled in the sixties, while the lowest-income group grew smaller. Yet 20 percent of all Negroes, the 2 million "hard-core disadvantaged" living in cities, were making no significant economic gains. They seemed trapped and were ready to blame their entrapment upon the whites.

With increasing rapidity after 1964, the

United States moved into a double crisis, compounded of rioting in the poverty-striken "black ghettos" and escalation of the American intervention in Vietnam into a major military confrontation. White students and Northern liberals shifted their efforts from the civil rights drive to concentrate on protest against the Vietnam war. Negroes increasingly sought to take their destiny into their own hands through their own organizations, independent of aid or funds from whites.

The gradual shift from white participation and leadership to Negro domination of civil rights organizations was one indication of the new mood. The Congress of Racial Equality (CORE), founded in 1941–1942, had long been the most interracial of the organizations, but by 1962 it was predominantly Negro; after 1965 CORE allowed only Negro leadership in its chapters. At their height these organizations did succeed through direct action in obtaining some votes for Negroes and political participation, even in Alabama and Mississippi. In the North they helped force open new, desirable employment opportunities for adequately educated Negroes. But they could not change the inferior conditions under which most Negroes suffered. Their failure helped stimulate feelings of separateness and militancy among Negro youth in the large cities.

Out of James Meredith's march southward from Memphis, Tennessee, to Jackson, Mississippi, in June 1966 there grew the concept of black power. Politically it meant separate action through which blocs of Negro voters would win control in Northern ghettos or the Southern black belt. Economically it meant creating Negro business to serve Negroes. CORE and SNCC (the Student Nonviolent Coordinating Committee) became associated with the concept of black power—of Negro separateness. In some respects black power seemed to critics to be retrogressive, a harking back to the proposals of Booker T. Washington; it seemed to propose a withdrawal comparable to that which white racists had been demanding. Black militants replied that Negroes by themselves must attain economic and political parity with the white population before effective integration could take place.

On August 11, 1965, a Negro crowd gathered in Watts, a Los Angeles suburb, to protest a traffic arrest; a policeman hit a bystander with his club, and several days of violence were touched off. Before the rioting was over, thirty-four people had been killed, hundreds wounded, and some $35 million in property destroyed. White Americans, hopeful that the civil rights movement was solving Negro problems, were shocked out of their optimism.

In the summer of 1966 there were forty-three outbreaks, with especially serious trouble in Chicago and Cleveland. In the summer of 1967 there were eight major riots. In the worst of these, at Detroit, forty-three persons (thirty-three Negroes and ten whites) were killed. On their television screens, the people of the nation saw alarming scenes of arson, plunder, and military action. President Johnson, calling for law and order, warned also that the only genuine long-range solution must be an attack upon the conditions that were causing despair and violence. He appointed a group of distinguished citizens to a commission to investigate the disorders and recommend preventive measures for the future.

The report of the Commission on Civil Disorders, which appeared in the spring of 1968, deflated numerous wild stories circulating during the riots: there had been few black snipers, and no organized conspiracy instigating and directing the riots. It pointed to the complexities of the problems facing the occupants of the Negro ghettos, and it recommended massive spending to erase these ghettos and the inequities their occupants suffered. "Only a commitment to national action on an unprecedented scale can shape a future compatible with the historic ideals of American society," the commission concluded. "The major need is to generate new will—the will to tax ourselves to the extent necessary to meet the vital needs of the nation." But the escalation of the war in Vietnam produced an immediate response. The enormous costs of the war and the reluctance of Congress to raise taxes, and thereby increase criticism of the war, led Congress to cut rather than to increase spending for the alleviation of urban poverty.

In April 1968 the assassination of Dr. Martin Luther King, Jr., shocked the nation but scarcely altered the mood of Congress. King, whose insistence upon Gandhi-like nonviolent techniques seemed old-fashioned to black militants, was to lead a protest march on behalf of striking garbage workers in Memphis, Tennessee. While standing on a motel balcony, he was struck by a sniper's bullet and died within a few minutes. King's death touched off the most widespread rioting the nation had yet undergone in the Negro areas of cities from coast to coast. Looting and arson were endemic; forty persons were killed. Washington was the worst hit, as fires gutted buildings within sight of the Capitol and the White House. Yet within the Negro districts, innumerable residents worked doggedly to end the disorders. Simultaneously, the nation was preoccupied with mourning the assassinated leader, as King was given a funeral bringing together an assemblage of notables and receiving television coverage exceeded only by that of President Kennedy.

Within a week Congress responded by enacting the Civil Rights Act of 1968, which had been pending for two years. It outlawed racial discrimination in the sale and rental of four-fifths of all homes and apartments. But as poor people assembled in Washington a few weeks later in the campaign that King had been planning at the time of his death, Congress was preoccupied with frugality and little disposed to provide economic aid for them.

The Spanish-Speaking Minority

As Afro-Americans enhanced their self-awareness during the 1960s, other racial minorities followed suit. Most numerous were the people of Latin American origin, most of whom had Indian ancestors, and some of whom were partly of African descent. The people of Puerto Rican background were concentrated mainly in New York, those of Cuban background mainly in Florida, and those of Mexican background mainly in California, Texas, and the Southwest.

The Mexican-Americans were the most numerous, accounting for seven of the nine million Americans of Latin American descent. They included descendants of families who had been living in Mexican territory when it was incorporated into the United States, legal immigrants and their descendants from Mexico, temporary workers ("braceros") brought in under special labor contracts, and illegal immigrants ("mojados" or "wetbacks").

The Spanish-speaking peoples had suffered from various forms of discrimination, the most visible expression of which was the "Zoot-Suit" riots in Los Angeles during June 1943. For a week mobs of white Angelenos, led by uniformed servicemen, terrorized not only the Mexican-American adolescents who sported "zoot suits," but the entire Spanish-speaking community. Beginning with that grim episode, many from the "barrios" began to join community organizations but they remained localized until the 1960s. Then for the first time large numbers of Mexican-Americans were brought together in a broad, inclusive "Chicano" (from "Mexicano") movement.

The hero of the Chicanos was César Chávez, an Arizona-born, California farm worker. The main focus of the movement was at first a farm workers' strike that Chávez called in 1965 and soon converted into a nonviolent crusade for social justice. He enlisted the cooperation of college students, church groups, and civil rights activists, including CORE and SNCC. To bring pressure on employers, who brought in strike breakers, he appealed for a nationwide boycott of California table grapes. The boycott gained the support of millions throughout the country but got no assistance from the federal government, which increased its purchases of grapes to be sent to American troops in Vietnam. Chávez won a temporary victory in 1970, when the growers of half of California's table grapes signed contracts with his union.

The Pan-Indian Movement

Joining Negroes and Chicanos in their quest for a decent share of the "Great Society" were the American Indians. They were a sizable group, numbering about 800,000 by 1970, and more than half of whom lived on or near reservations. As a group they were much worse off than other Americans, even those of African descent. Annual family income for Indians was $1,000 less than for blacks, and the unemployment rate for Indians was ten times the national rate. Suicides among Indian youth were one hundred times as frequent as among white youth.

The New Deal's Indian Reorganization Act had promised to revitalize aboriginal culture and tribal government, but Congress failed to provide sufficient funds. In 1953 Congress declared its intention to terminate federal relations with the tribes and leave them on their own. "Termination" led to further Indian impoverishment since it provided for no special assistance during the period of transition and abandoned any effort to preserve Indian culture. The Menominees of Wisconsin, for example, saw their reservation converted into Menominee County and experienced sharply declining real incomes.

During the 1960s more Indians than ever before joined a movement to bring tribes together and redress their common wrongs. In 1961 more than 400 members of 67 different tribes gathered in Chicago and drew up a Declaration of Indian Purpose, which stressed the "right to choose our own way of life" and the "responsibility of preserving our precious heritage." In 1964, while Congress was considering the Economic Opportunity Bill, hundreds of Indians and white sympathizers assembled in Washington to urge Congress to include Indians in the antipoverty program. A number of young, college-educated Indians began to speak of "red power," and some repudiated the name "Indian" —which, as they pointed out, whites had mistakenly given them—and insisted on being called "Native Americans." Congress did include Indians in the coverage of the Economic Opportunity Act, but beyond this neither the Kennedy nor the Johnson administration did anything to meet the Indians' needs and demands.

Frustrated Indians turned more and more to direct action, to confrontations with whites, to defiance of state and federal authority. In 1969 a group of Indians of various tribes, to dramatize the plight of their people, landed on Alcatraz Island, the site of an abandoned federal prison in San Francisco Bay, and claimed the place "by right of discovery." The anger and bitterness of many Indians found expression in the writings of Vine Deloria, Jr., a Sioux, who titled one of his books *Custer Died for Your Sins* (1969).

Women's Rights

American women could hardly be called a minority, since 51 percent of the population was female; yet they suffered inequities comparable to those imposed upon minority groups, and women of minority groups bore a double burden of discrimination. The 1960s became for women a period of intensified activism.

True, more and more job opportunities were opening up for women, and an increasing propor-

tion of them were working outside the home (fewer than 25 percent of women over sixteen had been counted as part of the labor force in 1940; more than 43 percent were so counted in 1970). But women were paid much less than men even for comparable work, and women had fewer chances than men to make a professional or managerial career. Moreover, they composed a smaller percentage of the college population in the 1950s than in the 1920s and were granted a smaller percentage of college degrees in 1960 than in 1930. During the 1960s they were earning only one in three of all B.A.s and M.A.s and only one in ten Ph.D.s. If anything, discrimination on the basis of sex had become more pervasive than a generation earlier.

Educated women of the middle class took the lead (as they had done in earlier feminist crusades) in the dozens of "women's liberation" movements that sprang forth in the 1960s. They were joined by women radicals who had been active in civil rights and anti-war groups but encountered discrimination even there. One of the most influential of the leaders was Betty Friedan, who in *The Feminine Mystique* (1963) denounced the American home as a "comfortable concentration camp" and called upon its inmates to free themselves. Friedan helped to found, in 1966, the most inclusive and effective of the new women's rights organizations, the National Organization for Women, or NOW. "There is no civil rights movement to speak for women as there has been for Negroes and other victims of discrimination," the organizers of NOW declared. The organization's 1967 "bill of rights" demanded an Equal Rights Amendment to the Constitution—"Equality of Rights under the law shall not be denied or abridged by the United States on account of sex"—and Congress in 1970 approved the amendment and sent it to the states for ratification. NOW also called for enforcement of the 1964 Civil Rights Act, which prohibited discrimination in employment on account of sex as well as race. Other NOW demands included the following: maternity leave for working women; public child-care centers to enable mothers to compete more freely for jobs; absolute equality of educational opportunities at all levels; and the "right of women to control their own reproductive lives" through contraception and abortion.

Chapter 32. THE "GREAT SOCIETY" ABROAD

Diversified Defense

At the time Kennedy took office, the military establishment of the United States was spending half of the federal budget and nearly a tenth of the gross national product; it was directly employing 3.5 million people. The incoming President and his new Secretary of Defense, Robert McNamara, were as determined as President Eisenhower had been in his farewell address that this vast establishment should protect but not dominate the American nation.

President Kennedy and Secretary McNamara built their plans upon the theory that the strength of thermonuclear weapons on the part of both the United States and Russia was sufficiently great to constitute a "mutual deterrent" against war. There was the assumption, however, that under the umbrella of the mutual deterrence of countering nuclear forces, the Communists would seek to gain new territories by subversion or by conventional warfare. Experts pointed to areas like South Vietnam to illustrate what they meant; nuclear deterrents were of no value there. So the President wished to develop forces expert in guerrilla and jungle warfare and equipped with special arms. A million American men were thus trained in "counterinsurgency." In addition, United States military missions aided other countries in establishing their own programs. During its first two years the administration also committed more of its defense expenditures to increasing its conventional forces. Since the inception of the Truman Doctrine (1947) and the Marshall Plan (1948), the United States had depended on economic aid as well as military power to defend many areas of the world against Communism. For both strategic and humanitarian reasons, President Eisenhower year after year requested and received huge appropriations for the mutual security program.

Most of the new, emergent nations in Asia and Africa were suffering from poverty and from a growth in population so explosive that it canceled out gains in living standards. Many of these nations were ready to accept aid from the United States, but at the same time they were also receptive both to aid and to propaganda from Communist Russia and Communist China. Even before the end of the Eisenhower administration, the United States was no longer insisting that these countries firmly align themselves on the Western side. Their right to be neutral in the cold war was conceded.

President Kennedy continued and in some ways elaborated upon the policy of financial assistance abroad. He established the Agency for International Development (AID) to coordinate various projects and to explore means of making them more effective. He sponsored the so-called Alliance for Progress, which was not really an alliance but a set of agreements between the United States and Latin American governments for cooperative undertakings in Latin America. He also brought about the establishment of the Peace Corps, which trained and sent abroad thousands of specialists, mostly young people, to work for two years in underdeveloped areas.

The returns from foreign aid were debatable. The most successful of the programs—and the least expensive—was probably the Peace Corps. Economic aid failed to work economic miracles; quite obviously economic development required far more than just the export of capital on the model of the Marshall Plan. And the amount of capital exported under programs such as the Alliance for Progress was minimal. American businessmen convinced Congress that the administration's demands for tax and land reforms, such as those included in the Alliance for Progress, were frightening investors away from the developing nations, and Latin American economic elites reinforced their advice. Consequently, foreign aid remained largely military in its substance throughout the 1960s.

Heightening Tension

The Cuban dictator Fidel Castro was drawing closer to Russia, heaping invective upon the United States, and exporting "Fidelismo" throughout Latin America. President Kennedy had declared: "Communist domination in this hemisphere can never be negotiated."

Once in office, Kennedy and his advisers faced the question of whether to go ahead with a project that the Eisenhower administration had begun. Under the direction of the Central Intelligence Agency, anti-Castro Cubans were secretly being trained and equipped in Central America for a landing in Cuba. They intended to overthrow the Castro regime with the aid of discontented groups still on the island. Kennedy decided to authorize the invasion but refused to provide United States air support. On the morning of April 17, 1961, a force of about 2,000 rebels landed at the Bay of Pigs. No accompanying revolt, such as had been expected, took place in Cuba, and the invading rebels were left to the mercy of the Cuban army and air force. Within two days the beachhead was wiped out.

In the somber aftermath of the Bay of Pigs fiasco, President Kennedy in June 1961 met Premier Khrushchev in Vienna for a frank interchange of views. It was not encouraging. Khrushchev, once he was back in Russia, set a deadline for the settlement of the Berlin issue. "A peaceful settlement in Europe must be attained this year." With or without the Western powers, he proposed to conclude a peace treaty with the East German government (the "German Democratic Republic"), which would then control access routes to West Berlin.

Suddenly, before dawn on August 13, 1961, the East German government closed the border between East and West Berlin and in the next few days began erecting elaborate concrete block and barbed wire barriers. East Germany was transformed into a vast concentration camp and West Berlin into a beleaguered island. Khrushchev had thus gained by a single act of force much that he had been seeking unsuccessfully at the conference table. The United States protested but was not ready to use armed force to destroy the new wall. Fears of thermonuclear war ran so high throughout the United States that the nation faced seriously for the first time the problem of trying to construct fallout shelters sufficient to protect the entire population. Fears were intensified during the autumn when Russia exploded approximately fifty nuclear devices, one with an estimated force of sixty-five megatons — 3,000 times more powerful than the Hiroshima bomb. The series as a whole produced double the amount of fallout of all previous atomic tests. The United States, fearing it would fall behind in the nuclear race, announced it would resume tests underground and in outer space.

Cuba: The Missile Crisis

The Berlin crisis slowly subsided during the autumn of 1961, to be succeeded a year later by a new, more frightening encounter, this time in regard to Cuba. In mid-July 1962, shiploads of Russian technicians and equipment began arriving on the island, and in August more than thirty Soviet ships unloaded two thousand technicians and instructors, together with fighter planes, surface-to-air missiles, patrol boats with missiles, and, as it turned out, equipment for offensive missiles.

The Russian move would more than redress the missile balance that had favored the United States. According to the London *Observer* (October 28, 1962): "Seen from the Pentagon, the two most alarming features of the missile buildup [in Cuba] were proximity and speed. Radar would give 15 minutes' warning of a missile attack from Russia, but only two–three minutes from Cuba. Medium-range missile bases can be constructed in hours or days. Within a month, if the U.S. sat tight, Russia could get 200–300 missiles in position — enough, at least in theory, to knock out a large part of the U.S. retaliatory forces in a surprise 'pre-emptive' attack."

How could the United States counter the Russian move? One of the two main alternatives was to strike the bases from the air; the other was to blockade Cuba. The President and his advisers decided upon a "quarantine" — a blockade. Several days of acute tension followed as the United States instituted its naval and air blockade, uncertain what would happen if a Soviet vessel among the twenty-five bound for Cuba should refuse to stop and should be sunk.

All week long the United States negotiated with Russia, and behind the stand of each side was the threat of nuclear force. Late on the evening of October 26, President Kennedy received a long, rambling letter from Khrushchev in which he compared the United States and the Soviet Union to two men tugging on a rope, pulling a knot tighter and tighter until it could be cut only by a sword. In effect, the letter said that if Kennedy would cease tugging on his end,

Khrushchev would do likewise. The letter seemed to imply that Russia would remove the missile bases provided the United States would promise not to invade Cuba. If Khrushchev would remove the missiles, Kennedy replied, the United States would end the blockade and not invade Cuba. The next day, October 27, Khrushchev accepted.

Though an armed clash had been avoided, trouble over Cuba by no means had been brought to an end. The Soviet Union did indeed remove the missiles and dismantle its bases, but Castro refused to allow on-the-spot inspection. Thousands of Soviet technicians remained, and although President Kennedy pressured Khrushchev to remove them, their return to Russia was slow. Cuban refugee groups, bewildered and angered by the no-invasion pledge, engaged in plots of their own against Castro and were resentful when the United States restrained them. In the immediate aftermath of the crisis, the national sentiment was one of profound relief, and President Kennedy's popularity rose.

Loosening of Alliances

With the onset of the cold war in 1947, world politics had become largely polarized between two power blocs: the United States and its allies, and the Soviet Union and its satellites. Though some countries, such as India, attempted to remain neutral, most of the nations of the world aligned themselves on one or the other of the two sides. By the early 1960s, however, both of the great alliances had begun to loosen somewhat. Strains were developing in the relations between the Soviet Union and Red China and in those between the United States and some of its former friends. These developments presented both new opportunities and new problems for American diplomacy.

The most notable of the American aid programs, the Marshall Plan, had helped stimulate a recovery in western Europe so remarkable that these nations in the 1960s were not only more prosperous than ever before in their history but in percentage of annual growth were in several instances outstripping the United States. Their new economic power meant that if they chose, they could either insist upon a more equal partnership or break loose to form a "third force"

between the United States and Russia, such as some French leaders had long envisaged.

At the beginning of 1963, in the aftermath of the Cuba crisis, the hopes for closer cooperation between the United States and western Europe were jolted by President Charles de Gaulle of France. Unexpectedly, de Gaulle vetoed the British application to join the European Common Market and did so because of the close British ties with the United States. At almost the same time, he proclaimed his opposition to American plans for creating a multination nuclear force within the North Atlantic Treaty Organization. De Gaulle insisted upon creating a separate small nuclear force for France, in order to gain an independent voice in European policy. Later he recognized Red China, thus asserting an independent position in Asian affairs as well.

In the summer of 1963, perhaps in part because of growing trouble with China, the Soviet Union, after years of negotiation, agreed to a treaty banning atmospheric (but not underground) tests of nuclear weapons. The treaty, the first definite step in the direction of international arms reduction since the onset of the cold war, was ratified by almost every important country except Red China (who was preparing to test its own nuclear bomb), France, and Cuba. A notable thaw in the cold war followed. President Kennedy announced that the United States would be willing to sell large quantities of surplus wheat to the Russians who were suffering from a shortage.

By 1964 many Americans were thinking hopefully of the prospect for détente with the Soviet Union. But these prospects soon declined as the United States became more and more deeply involved in an anti-Communist crusade far from home in Southeast Asia.

Involvement in Vietnam

During the presidential campaign of 1964 the Republican candidate, Senator Goldwater, urged that the United States take a much more active part in the war then going on between Communist North Vietnam and non-Communist South Vietnam. But President Johnson specifically repudiated the Goldwater policy. "There are those who say you ought to go north and drop bombs, and try to wipe out the supply lines, and they think that would escalate the war," Johnson declaimed in a campaign speech. "We don't want our American boys to do the fighting for Asian boys. We don't want to get involved in a nation (China) with 700 million people and get tied down in a land war in Asia."

In fact, Johnson himself was already preparing to enlarge the American role in Vietnam, and soon he was ordering bombs dropped on the north and was sending American boys by the hundreds of thousands to fight in that faraway land. As a consequence he lost all possibility of maintaining the "consensus" he had desired and of achieving the "Great Society" he had proclaimed. Never before had a President been elected by such a large popular majority, and never before had a President seen his popularity dwindle away so fast and so completely.

The involvement of the United States in Vietnam had developed so slowly that when it began to grow spectacularly, in 1964 and 1965, few Americans could remember how it had originated.

After the close of World War II, Vietnamese nationalists, seeking independence from France, rallied around Ho Chi Minh, a Communist who during the war had led the anti-Japanese resistance and had cooperated with the Americans. Ho issued a declaration of independence echoing the American Declaration of 1776 and began negotiations with France. When negotiations broke down, Ho and his followers resorted to arms. The American government was little concerned until the fall of Nationalist China and the outbreak of the Korean War. Then the Truman administration looked upon the French as manning a bastion to check the spread of Communism in Southeast Asia and began to send substantial aid. The Eisenhower administration increased the economic assistance and when the French forces faced disaster in 1954, considered sending large-scale military aid as well. Eisenhower held back, however, because of the opposition of Congress and because of the refusal of Great Britain to cooperate.

There followed the 1954 settlements at Geneva, establishing Laos and Cambodia, and temporarily splitting Vietnam into a Communist north and non-Communist south until free elections could be held to unify the new nation. The United States did not participate in the negotiations or sign the agreements. It promised not to use force to upset the agreements but warned that "it would view any renewal of the aggression in violation of the . . . agreements with grave concern and as seriously threatening international peace and security." Subsequently, the State Department threw its influence against free elections: they were never held.

The Eisenhower administration sought new arrangements to contain the Communists in Southeast Asia. Within two months of the Geneva agreements, Secretary Dulles succeeded in establishing the Southeast Asia Treaty Organization (SEATO), whose members agreed to consult one another regarding not only their own security but also the security of Laos, Cambodia, and South Vietnam. On October 23, 1954, President Eisenhower wrote the premier of South Vietnam, not only promising aid in return for certain reforms, but offering "to assist the Government of Viet-Nam in developing and maintaining a strong, viable state, capable of resisting attempted subversion or aggression through military means." The SEATO treaty and President Eisenhower's letter were subsequently cited as American commitments to assist South Vietnam—even though Dulles himself had told the Senate Foreign Relations Committee, when seeking its approval of SEATO, that if there should be a "revolutionary movement" in Vietnam, the SEATO members "would consult together as to what to do about it . . . but we have no undertaking to put it down; all we have is an undertaking to consult."

While the United States sought stabilization, it claimed that North Vietnam continued to seek through guerrilla activity the conquest of Laos and South Vietnam. Political turbulence and the economic dissatisfaction of many South Vietnamese made possible the successful growth of bands of Vietcong (short for Viet Communists), which by 1959 were receiving training and supplies from North Vietnam. At the end of 1960, the Vietcong established the "National Front for the Liberation of South Vietnam." Making its forays at night, murdering headmen and terrorizing villages, the Vietcong succeeded in controlling large parts of the countryside. The government of South Vietnam was confined to the cities and main lines of communication.

Gradually the United States sent increasing aid to Vietnam. Between 1954 and 1959, of $2.3 billion in aid, only two-fifths was military. American military advisers helped train the South Vietnamese army. President Kennedy, inherit-

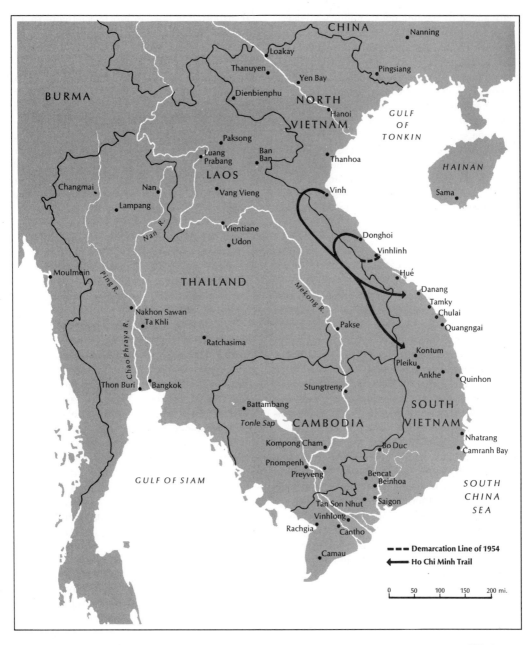

Vietnam

ing the problem, tried to build more effective resistance in Vietnam, not only through military counterinsurgency, but also through the support of the peasants. Vice President Johnson, visiting Saigon in May 1961, recommended aid but warned against direct military involvement: "American combat troop involvement is not only not required, it is not desirable. . . . Possibly Americans fail to appreciate fully the subtlety that recently colonial peoples would not look with favor upon governments which invited or accept the return this soon of Western troops."

As political and military conditions in Vietnam continued to deteriorate, President Kennedy added to the number of military advisers; by the time of his assassination in November 1963, American personnel in that country had reached a total of 15,500. Reports from American officials in Vietnam were optimistic, though internal troubles there caused newspapermen to cable home dark predictions. A new era of even greater instability had begun when the South Vietnamese army seized control of the government from the aristocratic nationalist Ngo Dinh Diem. In the summer of 1964 the political campaign in the United States overshadowed growing difficulties in Vietnam. The number of military advisers in Vietnam was up to 20,000, and on its way up to 25,000.

Escalating the War

In August 1964 there occurred an episode that was to give legal grounds for the reshaping of the war: American destroyers on patrol in international waters in the Gulf of Tonkin reported that they had been attacked by North Vietnamese torpedo boats. President Johnson concealed the fact that these destroyers were electronically gathering intelligence in support of a raid on two North Vietnamese islands by South Vietnamese. Instead he ordered a reprisal aerial attack on North Vietnam, informed the nation of his action, and then asked Congress for a supporting resolution. By a vote of 88 to 2 in the Senate and 416 to 0 in the House, Congress passed a joint resolution that authorized the President "to take all necessary measures" to protect American forces and "prevent further aggression" in Southeast Asia. Senators Wayne Morse and Ernest Gruening, the only two men in Congress to vote against the resolution, opposed it as being a "predated declaration of war power." Subsequently the resolution did serve as legal authorization for the escalation of the conflict.

By the beginning of 1965 the Vietcong, aided not only by supplies but also by military units coming from North Vietnam along the jungle "Ho Chi Minh trail" through Laos, were in ascendency. The American "advisers" had gradually become combatants and were already suffering serious casualties. At this point the United States began a rapid build-up of troops in Vietnam and the launching of regular bombing attacks upon supply depots, army camps, and

transportation lines in North Vietnam. In 1965 United States armed forces in Vietnam grew from 23,000 to over 180,000; in 1966, the number was doubled; by the end of 1967, it was approaching an authorized half-million. Air sorties were intensified until the tonnage of bombs being dropped exceeded that dropped in Europe during World War II. Casualties mounted. By every statistic, the Vietnam War was becoming one of the most serious in United States history.

According to Johnson, the purpose of this enormous effort was to stop aggression and preserve the freedom of the South Vietnamese people. "We want nothing for ourselves," he declared in 1965, "—only that the people of South Vietnam be allowed to guide their own country in their own way." Yet the Johnson administration supported the military dictatorship of General Nguyen Van Thieu, who in 1965 seized control of the South Vietnamese government.

While the United States increased its economic and military aid to the Thieu regime, the Soviet Union and the People's Republic of China provided larger and larger shipments of arms and other supplies to the Ho Chi Minh government of North Vietnam, and the North Vietnamese stepped up their military action and their assistance to the Vietcong. American intervention seemed to unite the rival Communist superpowers, who had a mutual interest in preventing a Communist defeat in Vietnam. There appeared to be a danger that if the United States should press its intervention to the point of victory for Thieu, the Chinese might intervene with their own troops as they had done in Korea.

On occasions, the United States limited or halted its bombings and other offensive actions in efforts to persuade the North Vietnamese to begin negotiations. Each time North Vietnam refused, for the most part adhering to the position that the United States must unconditionally and permanently end all bombing. At times a further stipulation was attached to this condition: all American forces were to leave Vietnam.

President Johnson and his advisers refused to end the bombing unconditionally and permanently. They pointed out that during each bombing halt at the time of a holiday truce the North Vietnamese rushed men and supplies southward or prepared for new attacks. American military leaders, following a policy of seeking out and destroying enemy forces, were confident at the beginning of 1968 that with enough men and supplies they could eventually triumph.

Deescalation Begins

In the United States, where television brought pictures of the cruelty and destruction of the war into every living room, the war became more and more unpopular. Liberals and university students participated vigorously in demonstrations, "teach-ins," and "sit-ins." Some young men burned their draft cards. Senator J. William Fulbright of Arkansas and a group of his colleagues became bitter critics of President Johnson and Secretary of State Dean Rusk. Public opinion polls indicated that a majority of Americans still supported the Vietnam War, but it had become the transcendent issue in the nation.

The drain of enthusiasm for the Vietnam War accelerated rapidly in the early months of 1968. During a truce in the fighting to observe Tet — the Chinese New Year — the Vietcong suddenly struck in almost every city of South Vietnam. They were dislodged only after days of bitter fighting, great devastation, and heavy casualties. The single blow destroyed the homes of a half-million South Vietnamese. The Tet offensive intensified pressure against the war among a growing segment of the American voters.

In the fall of 1967 Senator Eugene McCarthy of Minnesota, an opponent of the war, began what seemed to be a futile protest campaign for the Presidency. He had behind him only a handful of liberals and a growing group of enthusiastic students. In the first of the primary campaigns in New Hampshire, some of the young men cut their long hair and shaved their beards before ringing doorbells for McCarthy. In the voting, McCarthy was startlingly strong against Johnson, winning almost all the delegates to the convention. The next day, Senator Robert Kennedy of New York, also a critic of the Vietnam War, announced his candidacy. There were indications that the challenge to President Johnson would be so strong that he might not be able to win renomination.

For months President Johnson had been considering a change in his course of action. On the evening of March 31, 1968, in a telecast to the nation, he suddenly announced that he was ordering a halt in the attacks upon the populous areas of North Vietnam and was inviting the North Vietnamese to join him in a "series of mutual moves toward peace": "Tonight in the hope that this action will lead to early talks, I am taking the first step to deescalate the conflict. We are reducing — substantially reducing — the present level of hostilities. And we are doing so unilaterally, and at once." At the close of his talk he made an announcement that removed any possibility that the deescalation could be looked upon as a political gesture: "I shall not seek and I will not accept the nomination of my party for another term."

The North Vietnamese government accepted President Johnson's invitation, and in May 1968 negotiations began in Paris.

Election of 1968

During 1967 and 1968, the issues of the Vietnam War and urban violence became the focus of the preconvention presidential campaigns.

Significantly, the successful Republican contender, Richard Nixon, took no clear-cut stand on Vietnam. According to public opinion polls, Nixon was running so far ahead in the first of the primary campaigns in New Hampshire that his principal opponent, Governor George Romney of Michigan, withdrew before the balloting. Nixon easily fended off last-minute threats from Governor Ronald Reagan of California on the right, and Governor Nelson Rockefeller of New York to the left, to win nomination on the first ballot. He chose Spiro Agnew, governor of Maryland, as his running mate.

The Vietnam debate, by contrast, wracked the Democratic party. After Johnson announced his decision not to run for another term, only Eugene McCarthy and Robert Kennedy (holding much the same views on Vietnam and domestic problems) were left to battle each other in the Democratic primaries. In late April, too late to become embroiled in the primaries, Vice President Hubert H. Humphrey entered the campaign. So many Democratic leaders in states without primaries backed Humphrey that he became an immediate favorite to win the nomination. Public attention focused on the primary contests. Kennedy won Indiana, lost Oregon to McCarthy, and then in the last primary in California, won again. At a Los Angeles hotel, on June 5, just after he had exhorted his cheering followers to seek victory with him at the Democratic convention, he was shot and killed by an assassin. National mourning for Kennedy brought a temporary cessation in the campaigning.

At the Democratic convention in Chicago, McCarthy (and some Kennedy followers backing Senator George McGovern of South Dakota) were unable to prevent the nomination of Humphrey on the first ballot. The critics of Humphrey, who was heir to administration policies, were bitter. Adding to their bitterness were the rough tactics of the Chicago police who shoved and harassed delegates and spectators to the convention, and before television cameras, clubbed and manhandled demonstrators in the streets of Chicago. An investigating committee subsequently referred to the violent police reactions to the taunts and attacks by the demonstrators as a "police riot." During the campaign, Humphrey (who had been distinguished for his liberalism throughout his political career) received little support from those who had followed McCarthy and Kennedy.

The candidate who evoked the most enthusiastic responses and violent heckling wherever he spoke throughout the country was former Governor George Wallace of Alabama, running with General Curtis LeMay on the American Independent party ticket. "We are not talking about race," Wallace declared again and again, as he whipped up enthusiasm among audiences largely made up of white workers. General LeMay, who had been Chief of Staff of the Air Force, favored a hard line toward Vietnam. Public opinion polls showed Wallace at one point to be the favorite of a fifth of the voters; he hoped to throw the election into the House of Representatives. By election day his support had dropped substantially.

Neither of the major candidates evoked much enthusiasm. Nixon, campaigning methodically, seemed far ahead from the outset. On the two main issues—law and order at home and the Vietnam war—Nixon favored conciliation from a position of strength. He declared in his acceptance address that he would heed "the voice of the great majority of Americans, the forgotten Americans, the non-shouters, the non-demonstrators, that are not racists or sick, that are not guilty of the crime that plagues the land." Regarding the Vietnam war, he pointed out that he had been a critic of the administration, while Humphrey had been its defender; beyond that comment he made little commitment.

In contrast to Nixon's campaign, Humphrey's seemed deficient in both planning and finance. On Vietnam, he and his opponent differed little, but on the problem of poverty he pledged federal aid for a massive "Marshall Plan for the cities" in contrast to Nixon's insistence that private capital must help the poor to help themselves. During the last weeks of the campaign, Humphrey's standing in the public opinion polls increased markedly, and the statements of both candidates became sharper. Yet, as the front runner, Nixon refused to debate Humphrey on television. Both candidates were occupying middle positions, with Nixon to the right and Humphrey to the left of center.

By the fairly narrow margin of some 500,000 votes, out of more than 73 million cast, Nixon defeated Humphrey. The electoral vote was far more decisive, 302 for Nixon to 191 for Humphrey and 45 for Wallace. In his victory statement, Nixon returned to a theme he had frequently touched upon during the campaign and asserted that "the great objective of this Administration at the outset" would be "to bring the American people together."

Chapter 33. THE NIXON YEARS

The Nixon-Kissinger Approach

Even more than Presidents Kennedy and Johnson, President Nixon preoccupied himself with foreign affairs. On the basis of his earlier experience as Vice President, Nixon considered himself something of an expert in diplomacy. During his first term as President, he depended on Secretary of State William P. Rogers, a New York corporation lawyer, to administer the State Department. But he relied mainly on his special assistant for national security affairs, Henry A. Kissinger, a Harvard professor of international politics. For four years, Kissinger's White House office overshadowed the Department of State. Then, after the inauguration of Nixon for a second term, the President put Kissinger at the head of the department.

Before his appointment as Nixon's security adviser, Kissinger in books and articles had criticized the assumptions on which American policy was based. To him, as well as to some other observers, it seemed that the developments of the 1960s had made obsolete the containment policy of the 1950s. The signs of growing antagonism between Communist China and Communist Russia belied the concept of a single, combined program of Communist aggression. No longer were there only two power centers, the United States and the Soviet Union; there were now at least three, with China, and potentially others if western Europe and Japan were included. For this new "multipolar" world, Kissinger proposed a flexible, many-sided balance-of-power system to take the place of the rigid, two-sided system that had prevailed since the start of the cold war.

When Nixon decided to open relations with the Chinese People's Republic and to improve relations with the Soviet Union, his decision was in keeping with the new diplomacy that he and Kissinger had proposed. Meanwhile Nixon continued the war in Vietnam, though Kissinger believed that American involvement had been based on "an outmoded foreign policy concept." Nixon undertook to "Vietnamize" the war—

that is, to shift the burden of actual combat from Americans to the South Vietnamese, in accordance with the Nixon Doctrine—but the process was painfully slow.

Vietnamization 1969-1972

Regarding Vietnam, Nixon said in May 1969 that he hoped to achieve "a peace we can live with and a peace to be proud of." He did not specify the kind of peace he had in mind, but presumably it would be one that kept the Thieu regime in power in Saigon. Whatever the details, his kind of peace, like Lyndon B. Johnson's, remained unacceptable to the Ho Chi Minh government of Hanoi. In Paris the talks went on among the representatives of the United States, South Vietnam, North Vietnam, and the National Liberation Front; but rumors of progress toward a settlement proved disappointing again and again.

As the months passed and no end to the fighting appeared in sight, "Johnson's war" began to be looked upon as "Nixon's war," and by the summer's end an opinion poll showed a clear majority of the American people believed the involvement in Vietnam was a mistake. Nixon turned opinion in favor of his Vietnam policy, however, by a televised speech on November 3, 1969. He said the "silent majority" agreed with him that a "precipitate withdrawal" would be "disastrous for the future of peace" in the world. Vice President Agnew afterward denounced the peace demonstrators as an "effete corps of impudent snobs" and reprimanded newspaper and television commentators for daring to question the Nixon policy.

Making a concession to the war's critics, Nixon had announced earlier the beginning of partial troop withdrawals, the first of which would reduce by 60,000 the United States force of about 540,000 men in Vietnam. These withdrawals, he explained, were steps toward the "Vietnamization" of the war. That is, the South Vietnamese themselves would be trained and equipped to take over the defense of their country as the American fighting men were gradually pulled out.

Nixon also sought to lessen opposition by reforming the draft, which because of its uncertainties and inequities added to the difficulty of justifying the sacrifice of American lives in a small and distant country. To its critics, the draft seemed all the worse because of the high-handed way in which it was administered. Its director persisted in advising local draft boards to punish antiwar demonstrators by conscripting them, even after a federal court had held this to be illegal. Nixon recommended that the conscription law be changed so as to provide for a "draft lottery" that would take only nineteen-year-olds and would take them at random. Such a lottery went into effect in 1970. Going still further, Nixon urged the formation of an all-volunteer army, with improved pay and other incentives for enlistment. By 1973, Americans were no longer being drafted.

The Vietnamization plan was going so well, Nixon announced in April 1970, that he would bring home 150,000 additional men within a year or so. Suddenly, before the end of April, he broke the startling news that he had ordered American troops to cross into neutral Cambodia and, with their South Vietnamese allies, to seize military bases that the enemy had been using for operations in South Vietnam. He explained that "increased military aggression" by the Communists in Cambodia had begun to jeopardize the continuing success of the Vietnamization program.

Up to this point, Nixon said, it had been American policy "to scrupulously respect the neutrality" of Cambodia. What he did not tell the people was that the United States was already deliberately and systematically violating Cambodian neutrality. For more than a year he had personally authorized the secret bombing of suspected North Vietnamese bases on the Cambodian side of the border. For several years American ground forces had been carrying on clandestine operations in Cambodia and in Laos as well. If these facts had been made public at the time, the popular protest in the United States might have gone to even greater extremes than it actually went.

At the news of the Cambodian incursion, the languishing peace movement came to life. On campuses all over this country, during May,

youthful protesters demanded that the universities close down in a "strike" against the government's war policy. A radical minority resorted to violence, smashing windows and fire-bombing buildings. Policemen and national guardsmen arrived to face rock-throwing mobs, which they tried to disperse with tear gas and, in a few instances, with gunfire. Four students (all white) were shot and killed at Kent State University in Ohio, and two (both black) at Jackson State University in Mississippi. A few months later a physicist died when antiwar protesters set off an explosion that wrecked several buildings at the University of Wisconsin in Madison.

After ending the invasion of Cambodia in June 1970, Nixon launched an invasion of Laos, in February 1971. This time he sent no American ground troops (Congress in the Defense Appropriations Act of 1970 had prohibited their use in Laos) but gave American air support to the invading South Vietnamese army. "The South Vietnamese by themselves can hack it," he declared. This was a test of his Vietnamization program, and it proved a failure. Within a few weeks the badly mauled army scrambled back to the relative safety of South Vietnam.

American critics of "Nixon's war," like those of "Johnson's war," were appalled by the horrible sufferings it brought upon civilians, both South Vietnamese and North Vietnamese. Millions of them were deprived of life, health, shelter, or livelihood as a result of American action —napalm bombing, population transfer, village destruction, crop burning, and forest defoliation. Hundreds were shot or bayoneted by American soldiers, as in the "My Lai massacre" (March 16, 1968), for which Lieutenant William L. Calley, Jr., was convicted of premeditated murder in 1971.

Continuing troop withdrawals, Nixon announced in January 1972 that the total of American troops in Vietnam would shortly be reduced to 69,000, the lowest figure in nearly seven years. As troops were withdrawn, American casualties in the war decreased, and so did the outcry at home. Yet, while taking out ground forces, Nixon was sending in more and more air and naval forces. Eventually he authorized the dropping of a greater tonnage of bombs than Johnson had, and these bombs killed far more civilians than the 102 that Calley was charged with murdering at My Lai. Nixon ordered his greatest escalation of the war against the Vietnamese Communists after he had dramatically displayed his friendship with the Chinese and Russian Communists.

Rapprochement with China

Until 1949 the United States had sought to maintain the Open Door policy in China. Then, after the Communists under Mao Tse-tung and Chou En-lai got control of the Chinese mainland, the doors were closed on both sides. The Peking government taught hatred of Americans and excluded them from the country. The Washington government prohibited trade between the United States and the Chinese mainland, refused to recognize the Mao regime, and opposed its being represented in the United Nations. Washington continued to treat Chiang Kai-shek, after his flight to the island of Taiwan, as an ally and as the rightful head of all China.

From 1949 to 1971, no American in national politics had opposed the recognition of the Peking government more resolutely than had Richard M. Nixon. Eventually, making a complete turnabout, he reopened relations in a spectacular display of presidential diplomacy.

Recognition was long past due. China was the largest nation in the world, with about a quarter of all the world's people. It was one of the nuclear powers, having set off its first atomic bomb in 1964 and its first hydrogen bomb in 1967. By making friends with the Peking leaders, Nixon could hope to get their cooperation in ending the Vietnam War. He could also hope to use China as a counterbalance to the Soviet Union and thus as a means of inducing in the Russians a conciliatory mood and hastening a détente. The Chinese leaders, for their part, were eager to have the United States as a potentiality in their own balance-of-power arrangement against the Soviet Union. They feared that the Russians might attack China in an attempt to destroy the Chinese nuclear installations.

Early in 1971 Nixon hinted at a change in American policy when, in a public statement, he used the legitimate name "People's Republic of China" for what he and other American officials always had called simply "Red China" or "Communist China." That spring the Peking government invited a team of American table-tennis players to visit China, and the Nixon administration gave them permission to go. Such "Ping-Pong diplomacy" led to speculation about higher-level contacts between the two countries but hardly prepared the American people for the startling announcement Nixon made in July. He said he himself had received an invitation to visit the People's Republic (an invitation that Kissinger had arranged on a secret trip to Peking) and would make the visit within the next several months.

To succeed in his new China policy, Nixon would have to approve the admission of the People's Republic to the United Nations. In the past the American delegates to the U.N. had repeatedly managed to prevent the seating of a Peking delegate. Now the United States representative proposed giving a seat on the Security Council to the People's Republic while keeping a place for Nationalist China, that is, Taiwan. The Chinese Communists insisted, however, that the Chinese Nationalists must go. In October 1971 the United Nations admitted the People's Republic and expelled Nationalist China.

Nixon's China visit, when it finally came in February 1972, proved to be a theatrical success. For a whole week American television followed the President and his entourage. Never before had a summit meeting been so elaborately staged or so extensively viewed. One effect was to reduce, if not to reverse, the anti-Chinese feelings that had been instilled in the American people for a generation.

The summit meeting was also something of a diplomatic success. In Peking the leaders of the two countries agreed to scientific, cultural, journalistic, and other exchanges and to the development of trade. They did not agree to the immediate establishment of formal relations, with an exchange of ambassadors. The Communists, looking on Taiwan as part of their country, refused to accept an embassy from the United States so long as Taiwan had one. The United States must first break off diplomatic relations with Nationalist China. If the summit conferees arrived at any understanding in regard to the Vietnam War, they made no public announcement of the fact.

On subsequent journeys to Peking, Kissinger worked out details of trade arrangements and other matters and managed, as he put it, to "accelerate the normalization of relations." A year after the Nixon visit, the two countries agreed to set up "liaison offices" in each other's capitals. Except in name, these offices practically amounted to embassies. The United States was expected soon to remove some of the 9,000 American troops on Taiwan. By 1973, it appeared that relations with China were getting back to normal, after nearly a quarter century of nonrecognition and estrangement.

Détente with Russia

Nixon had been the first American President to make a trip, while in office, to China; he was the second to travel to Russia. His Russian visit, in May 1972, was even more important than the one in Peking. From both the Russian and the American points of view, the time was ripe for a move toward a new understanding. The Soviet government, under the leadership of Communist party chief Leonid Brezhnev, looked to the United States for possible future support against China, for aid in overcoming Russia's technological lag, and for wheat and other foodstuffs to make up for her serious crop shortages. Having achieved something like nuclear parity with the United States, the Russians also were interested in the economies of slowing down the arms race. Nixon and his advisers shared the desire for a limitation of nuclear armaments, wished to promote American trade, and hoped for Soviet cooperation in ending the war in Vietnam and preventing war in other parts of the world, especially in the Middle East.

By 1972 the United States still led the Soviet Union in the number of long-range planes kept in readiness for delivering nuclear bombs. Moreover, this country had almost twice as many submarines equipped with nuclear missiles. But the Soviet Union had moved ahead in regard to land-based intercontinental ballistic missiles, or ICBMs, which could carry nuclear explosives all the way from the one country to the other.

The two superpowers were engaged in a "doomsday game" of competition in the development of more and more deadly weapons and delivery systems. Each of the two was testing a multiple independently targeted reentry vehicle, or MIRV, a device that could be sent into orbit and then directed back into the earth's atmosphere above the enemy's territory, where it would drop separate nuclear warheads on widely scattered targets. Each nation was also planning an antiballistic-missile system, or ABM, which was intended to protect population centers or ICBM emplacements against missile attack. In the ABM system, nuclear "antimissile missiles" would be launched to intercept and explode approaching enemy missiles before these could reach their targets. The Nixon administration's ABM project aroused considerable opposition in the United States. Critics said the ABM would have little effect on ICBMs and still less on MIRVs but would endanger civilians in its vicinity and would intensify the arms race.

The two superpowers took a step toward lessening the competition between them when, in 1969, American and Russian diplomats met in Helsinki to begin discussion of a strategic arms limitation treaty, or SALT. After continuing their talks in Vienna for two and a half years, the negotiators arrived at a temporary agreement. This first-phase treaty, or SALT I, would limit each country to only two ABMs and the existing number of ICBMs. The compromise would leave the United States superior in numbers of warheads and the Soviet Union, with its warheads of greater size, superior in total megatonnage. The limitations were to last for five years. Applying only to quantity and not to quality, they would do nothing to prevent a continuing and even heightening contest for arms improvements in the meantime.

At their Moscow meeting in 1972, Nixon and Brezhnev signed SALT I and several other agreements. One of these promised a vast expansion of trade through American tariff reductions and credit extensions. A gigantic "wheat deal" led immediately to the sale of about a fourth of the total American wheat supply at a bargain price, one well below the market price, and the American government was to make up the difference by means of subsidies to the American wheat sellers. The prospect of a reduction in arms spending, however, did not last long. After Nixon's return from Moscow, the administration asked Congress to approve the largest military budget ever except during a declared war.

In June 1973 Nixon welcomed Brezhnev to Washington. A series of new agreements were confirmed and those of the previous year were extended. The two countries pledged to abstain from nuclear war, to speed up the conclusion of SALT II for a permanent "freeze" on offensive nuclear arms, and to cooperate in various economic, scientific, and cultural fields. Toasting his Russian guest at a dinner, Nixon said: "The question is: Shall the world's two strongest nations constantly confront one another in areas which might lead to war, or shall we work together for peace?" The question remained to be answered, despite all the talk of détente.

Exit from Indochina

Nixon's China and Russia diplomacy gave him added strength in his conduct of the Vietnam War. Neither China nor Russia stopped sending military supplies to North Vietnam, but both powers indicated that there were limits to their aid. Apparently each was somewhat reluctant to risk damaging its new relationship with the United States.

Between Nixon's China visit and his Russia visit, the fighting in Vietnam actually intensified, going in some respects to greater lengths than ever before. In March 1972 the North Vietnamese launched their heaviest attack since the Tet offensive of 1968. Well equipped with tanks and artillery, they crossed into South Vietnam and proceeded to overrun much of its territory. In April Nixon responded by sending B-52 bombers to strike near Hanoi and Haiphong, thus reversing Johnson's 1968 decision to deescalate the air war in the north. On May 8 — just before his scheduled trip to Peking — Nixon ordered the mining of Haiphong harbor and six other North Vietnamese ports, so as to prevent the delivery of war supplies by ship from China or the Soviet Union. Johnson had refrained from this extreme measure for fear it would provoke retaliation from one or both of those two countries. Now they confined themselves to comparatively mild protests.

In Paris, Kissinger and North Vietnamese Foreign Secretary Le Duc Tho were meeting separately and secretly, and were nearing a cease-fire agreement. "Peace is at hand," Kissinger finally announced on October 26, just before the 1972 presidential election. The North Vietnamese government was ready and eager to accept the terms that Kissinger and Tho had arrived at, but President Thieu of South Vietnam raised objections, and Nixon refused to give his approval. On December 16, after Kissinger and Tho had broken off negotiations, Kissinger declared that the agreement was 99 percent complete, but he did not explain what the missing 1 percent consisted of.

The next day, December 17, without any announcement from the White House, American planes began to bomb North Vietnamese cities in the heaviest and most destructive raids of the entire war. The targets were docks, airfields, railyards, power plants, antiaircraft defenses, and the like, but these were located in or near residential areas, and homes, shops, schools, and even hospitals were hit. The destruction was achieved at considerable cost to the Americans. In the previous seven years of the Vietnam War, only one B-52 bomber had been lost in combat. Now, in two weeks of round-the-clock raiding, fifteen of the high-flying giant planes fell when struck by Russian-made surface-to-air missiles. On December 30 Nixon called off the bombing and announced that the North Vietnamese had consented to resume the secret peace talks.

On January 27, 1973, representatives of the four parties (the United States and South Vietnam, North Vietnam and the "Provisional Revolutionary Government" of South Vietnam, that is, the Vietcong) signed an "agreement on ending the war and restoring peace in Vietnam." The main provisions of this agreement were the same as those of the October 1972 agreement, which Nixon had refused to approve. There was to be an immediate cease-fire, and within sixty days prisoners of war were to be returned and foreign military forces in South Vietnam were to be withdrawn. Contradictorily, both the South Vietnamese right of self-determination and the unity of all Vietnam, North and South, were recognized. Laos and Cambodia were to be evacuated, and their independence and neutrality were to be respected. An international commission was to supervise the cease-fire.

Nixon proclaimed that at last he had won a "peace with honor." In fact, he had gained two things in the peace arrangement. One was the return of several hundred American prisoners of war (whose numbers, incidentally, he had recently increased through the Christmas-season bombing and the exposure of downed B-52 crews to capture). The other gain for Nixon was to keep Thieu in power in South Vietnam for the time being. But Nixon had also yielded a lot in the truce terms. These included several references to the 1954 Geneva settlement, which the United States had never signed. They reconfirmed the Geneva principle of the ultimate reunification of Vietnam. That was what the North Vietnamese and the Vietcong had been fighting for, and at the time of the cease-fire they were in a strong position for achieving it, since they now occupied a large part of South Vietnam's territory.

Such were the inconclusive results of more than a decade of direct American military involvement in Vietnam, and they had been accomplished at a staggering cost. In money, this exceeded $100 billion for the United States alone. In lives, it was approximately 1.2 million Vietnamese and 55,000 Americans. Some 300,000 Americans were wounded, half of them seriously, and many of these were permanently maimed. A total of about 3 million Americans served in the war, most of them unwillingly. Perhaps as many as 70,000 evaded service by dodging the draft or deserting after enlistment. Thousands of deserters and draft dodgers remained in hiding at home or in refuge abroad, particularly in Canada and Sweden, as Nixon with the backing of a public majority vowed to grant no amnesty. The psychological cost to Americans, both veterans and nonveterans, was incalculable. Never since the Civil War had the people been so badly divided. Understandably, the announcement of peace, after the longest war in American history, provoked no such demonstrations of popular rejoicing as had followed World War I and World War II.

There was no peace in Vietnam. The international commission, set up to supervise the cease-fire, was powerless to keep the Communists and the non-Communists apart. During the first year after the cease-fire the Vietnamese (both sides together) suffered more battle deaths than the Americans had suffered during the ten years before it. In Laos the fighting ended about a month after the cease-fire, when the Communists were left in control of more than half the country. In Cambodia the war continued, and Nixon refused to stop the bombing of Cambodia until Congress compelled him to do so.

Congress had been growing more and more critical of the President's assertion of warmaking powers without any congressional declaration of war, and both the Senate and the House had begun to consider proposals for holding him to constitutional limits. In 1969 the Senate advised the President that in the future he should get the approval of Congress before committing the United States to the use of armed forces abroad. In 1971 Congress repealed the 1964 Gulf of Tonkin resolution, which Johnson and

Nixon had treated as the equivalent of a war declaration. Congress could have stopped the war by cutting off appropriations for it, but this would have been unpopular, since it would have looked like American soldiers were being abandoned in the field. Nixon maintained that as commander in chief, he had the power to use the armed forces as he saw fit in order to protect the troops while he was withdrawing them under his Vietnamization plan.

After the signing of the cease-fire and the withdrawal of the troops, Nixon no longer had that justification for waging war as he saw fit. When he persisted in bombing Cambodia, despite congressional protests, Congress set August 15, 1973, as a deadline for the cessation of all American military activity in Indochina, including the air warfare in Cambodia. Nixon discontinued the bombing only at the last minute.

Several months later Congress passed, over Nixon's veto, a measure intended to prevent a President from involving the country in future wars without congressional approval. Under this war-powers resolution of 1973, the President could order no troops into action without reporting to Congress, and he would have to halt the action immediately if Congress objected, or in ninety days if Congress failed to give its positive permission. The new law was a response to a growth in presidential power that Congresses as well as Presidents had been fostering for many years. Whether the measure was wise for the nuclear age, and whether it would work in any case, only time could tell.

Old Friendships Under Strain

While relations with China and Russia were improving, relations with Japan, West Germany, Great Britain, and other allies were getting worse.

The American conduct of the Vietnam War antagonized many Europeans. Some felt the United States was neglecting western Europe while preoccupying itself with Southeast Asia. Some were outraged by the warfare upon Vietnamese civilians, and especially by the 1972 Christmas-season bombing of North Vietnamese cities.

The switch in American policy toward China and Russia disturbed the leaders of Japan and the western European countries. In response, Kissinger declared 1973 to be "the year of Europe" and proposed a "new Atlantic Charter" that would include Japan. Nixon was expected to offset his summit diplomacy with China and Russia by going to Japan and Europe to conclude new understandings with them. But his trips were repeatedly postponed. Moreover, in response to popular demand, some of the Democrats in Congress were proposing to compel a reduction in the number of American troops abroad in NATO. And the Nixon administration insisted that the allies, now that they were financially strong, ought to make larger contributions than they had been making to the common defense.

Toward the European Economic Community (the Common Market), the American government's attitude had become ambivalent by 1973. On the one hand, the United States still officially favored the strengthening of the EEC and approved its enlargement when Great Britain was finally admitted, along with Ireland and Denmark. On the other hand, the United States seemed to fear the economic competition of the EEC and complained that it was discriminating against American exports.

Already there was a crisis in trade and monetary relations between the United States and both Japan and Europe. For years, the American government and American citizens had been spending larger and larger quantities of dollars abroad, for tourist travel, foreign goods, capital investments, and economic and military aid. The expenditures on the Vietnam War, after its escalation in 1964, added greatly to the dollar outflow. All together, Americans increasingly spent far more in foreign countries than foreigners spent in the United States. Europeans doubted the ability of America to adhere to the gold standard and the dollar tended to lose value in relation to foreign currencies.

By 1971 the Nixon administration felt compelled to take drastic steps. It put a temporary 10 percent surcharge on imports. Then it stopped giving up gold in return for the dollars that foreign governments held. This meant that the exchange rates were no longer controlled, and the dollar price of other currencies, especially the mark and the yen, began to rise. Finally Nixon did what no President since Franklin D. Roosevelt had done—he officially devalued the dollar. He raised the official price

of gold from $35 to $38 an ounce. In 1973 he further devalued the dollar, raising the gold price to $42.

Devaluation was intended to overcome the balance-of-payments deficit by causing Americans to buy less of foreign goods and services, and foreigners to buy more of American goods and services. But the deficit kept growing, and the dollar kept falling. To cut down imports, the Nixon administration threatened to raise tariffs and to impose other trade controls; the Japanese and the Europeans protested. By this time, exports had begun to increase, with large shipments abroad of American wheat and other crops. Now, to cut down on exports and prevent shortages at home, the administration put limits on the foreign sale of farm commodities and steel scrap, thus provoking new protests, especially on the part of Japan.

The international trade and monetary system of the preceding quarter century appeared to have broken down, and economic conflicts between the United States and its allies were putting a serious strain on the alliances.

Trouble in Nonpower Regions

The Nixon-Kissinger theory of five power centers left a subordinate place for the nonpower regions of the world, the distinctly weaker countries of Latin America, Asia, and Africa. Yet clashes arising in these areas could jeopardize relations among the powerful, as the Vietnam War at times had seemed likely to do.

During Nixon's presidency, the relations of the United States with many of the Latin American countries deteriorated. New military governments in Peru and Bolivia seized the property of American corporations. The constitutionally elected government of the radical Salvador Allende did the same in Chile. In retaliation, Nixon undertook to block financial aid, from either American or international sources, to Chile and other countries that failed to compensate American property owners satisfactorily. It was revealed that officials of the International Telephone and Telegraph Company, an American-based multinational corporation having extensive holdings in Chile, had consulted with officials of the Central Intelligence Agency about possible methods of preventing Allende's election to the Chilean presidency. This revelation lent some credence to the charge, in 1973, after Allende's overthrow and death in a military coup, that the American government had connived with his opponents.

The Middle East, the scene of continual fighting between Arabs and Israelis, presented a particularly acute dilemma for the Nixon administration, as it had done for previous administrations. Israel had many sympathizers, both Jewish and non-Jewish, within the United States. They could exert considerable pressure in American politics. The Arab countries could count upon no such American constituency, but they possessed two-thirds of the world's known oil reserves, and they occupied areas that were of strategic importance to the United States in its global conflict with the Soviet Union.

Violence in the Middle East had been renewed in 1967, after a United Nations peacekeeping force had been withdrawn at the demand of Egypt. Expecting an attack from Egypt, which was well equipped with Russian arms, Israel struck and in the Six-Day War defeated Egypt, Jordan, and Syria and occupied parts of their territory. A 1967 U.N. resolution called upon Israel to withdraw her armed forces from the occupied territories, but recognized the right of every nation in the area to "live in peace within secure and recognized boundaries." Israel refused to budge without guarantees of her security. After the 1967 war Israel rearmed with American aid, and Egypt and Syria with Russian aid. Intermittent shelling and raiding went on across the borders between Israel and her neighbors.

The Nixon administration, at first, attempted an "even-handed" policy in the Middle East. Nixon hoped for a compromise and the Russians cooperated to the extent of agreeing to U.N. mediation, which resulted in a brief truce, in 1970. Then Palestinian Arabs, living as refugees in Jordan, revolted against Jordan's King Hussein, who was trying to stay on good terms with Israel and the United States. While Hussein was putting down the rebellion, Nixon made a display of naval strength in the Mediterranean Sea, presumably as a warning to Russia against allowing Egypt to intervene in Jordan. Thereafter the Soviet Union rapidly increased its naval force in the Mediterranean, and Russian ships soon outnumbered American vessels there.

After 1972 the détente between the United States and the Soviet Union could have been expected to defuse the explosive Middle Eastern situation. In October 1973, however, war again erupted, when on the Jewish holy day of Yom Kippur the Egyptians and the Syrians suddenly attacked. Both they and the Israelis quickly lost huge quantities of tanks, aircraft, and other equipment, and both the Russians and the Americans resorted to airlifts to make up for the losses. Only after the Israelis had got the upper hand did the Russians show any interest in ending the war. Then Kissinger and Brezhnev worked out, and the U.N. Security Council adopted, resolutions calling for an immediate cease-fire and for the beginning of peace negotiations on the basis of the 1967 resolution—which would presumably require Israel to give up most if not all of her 1967 conquests in return for some guarantee of her continued existence.

As the shooting died down, the American-Russian détente seemed belatedly to be having an effect in the Middle East. All at once Nixon made the startling announcement that he was putting American forces throughout the world on a stand-by alert. He was doing so, administration spokesmen said, because the Russians were increasing their already large naval force in the Mediterranean and were preparing to fly troops to the Middle East to enforce the cease-fire. The Russians sent no troops, and a new U.N. peacekeeping force began to arrive. Relaxing the alert, Nixon declared that the United States had just passed through its most dangerous war crisis since the Cuban missile crisis of 1962. "Without détente," he said, "we might have had a major confrontation in the Mid-east."

While Egypt and Israel disputed over the details of the cease-fire and threatened to resume hostilities, the Arab countries announced plans to reduce oil production and to cut off petroleum sales to the United States. The Arabs intended, by withholding oil from Israel's friends, to pressure them into supporting a Middle Eastern settlement that would force Israel to leave the Arab territories she had conquered in 1967. Japan and western Europe, which had been getting respectively 82 percent and 72 percent of their petroleum from Arab sources, were much more vulnerable than the United States, which had depended on those sources for only 11 percent of its supply. Understandably, Japan and the leading powers of western Europe were careful not to offend the Arabs. The United States seemed likely to become careful, too, as the American people increasingly felt the pinch of the oil embargo during the winter of 1973–1974.

Meanwhile the "Yom Kippur war" intensified the strains within the North Atlantic Treaty Alliance. None of the principal NATO allies had backed the United States in its support of Israel. During the airlift several of them had forbidden American transport planes to refuel in their territories or even to fly over them. After the war the Nixon administration made its anger known to the allies. They, in turn, complained that the American government had disregarded their desperate need for Arab oil and had failed to consult them about its intentions, particularly about its intention to order a world-wide military alert. The alliance now appeared to be more badly shaken than at any time since 1956, when France and Great Britain had joined Israel in invading Egypt, and the United States had sided with the Soviet Union in bringing about U.N. action against the invaders.

The Imperial Presidency

President Nixon, though full of ideas about foreign affairs, took office in 1969 without having given much thought to a domestic program. He favored what he called "reform," which seemed to mean a reversal of the policies his immediate predecessors had sponsored under the slogans of "the New Frontier" and "the Great Society." He looked for a slogan of his own and came up with "the New Federalism." This implied that he would, in his words, "reverse the flow of power and resources from the states and communities to Washington and start power and resources flowing back . . . to the people all over America."

In fact, while reversing certain policies, Nixon did not stop the trend toward the centralization of power. Rather, he encouraged a development that had been accelerating since the presidency of Franklin D. Roosevelt. With respect to domestic as well as foreign affairs, Nixon undertook to concentrate more and more authority in the White House.

"I've always thought this country could run itself domestically without a President," Nixon had said in 1967. "All you need is a competent Cabinet to run the country at home." Actually,

the cabinet had been losing influence on policy making ever since World War II, and it continued to do so under Nixon. His own cabinet was distinguished by little competence and still less continuity. He appointed few outstanding public figures to it, and during his first five years he made more changes in its membership than any other President had made during any length of time. For the most part, the members merely administered their own departments, seldom if ever consulting with one another as a group or even individually with the President. An exception was John Mitchell, Nixon's former law partner, his 1968 campaign manager, and from 1969 to 1972 his attorney general and chief adviser on politics. Mitchell had direct access to the White House.

Few other department heads, government officials of lesser rank, or congressmen or senators could approach the President directly. Almost all of them had to deal with him through his top White House aide, the "keeper of the gates," H. R. Haldeman, or through the chief of his domestic policy staff, John Ehrlichman. These two, old friends and veteran Nixon campaigners, now subject only to the President himself, ran the executive office with respect to domestic affairs from 1969 to 1973. The executive office was a large and rapidly swelling bureaucracy, whose numbers during that four-year period grew from 2,000 to more than 4,200.

By 1969 the domestic programs of the federal government and the agencies to administer them had become so numerous that they were difficult if not impossible for the President to control. Nixon proposed a new plan for bringing together the widely scattered threads of administration. The central proposal, approved by Congress, was to create the Office of Management and Budget, which would oversee the financing and directing of all administrative agencies. Nixon also proposed to reorganize and reduce the number of executive departments. When Congress failed to approve, the President in 1973 went ahead on his own. By executive order he raised three of the department heads to the level of "presidential councillors" and directed that the others report to one of the three, who in turn would report to a presidential aide (Erhlichman). With the three councillors constituting a "super cabinet," the authority and prestige of the traditional cabinet would be still further reduced.

Nixon also claimed unprecedented authority for the presidential office in relation to the legislative branch, especially after his reelection in 1972. Asserting "executive privilege" seemingly without limit, he took the position that congressional committees could not question administrative officials without the President's consent. Implying that the President, not Congress, should have the power of the purse, he ordered administrative agencies not to spend appropriated money after Congress had overridden his vetoes of appropriation bills.

By the beginning of his second term, Nixon faced a congressional revolt. His critics in Congress—including some members of the Republican minority as well as the Democratic majority—talked of a constitutional crisis. For many years Congress had been allowing Presidents more and more discretion, particularly in foreign affairs. Now Nixon, while stretching to the utmost his powers as commander in chief in Southeast Asia, was thought to be doing the same with his powers as chief executive at home. Unless Congress acted soon to regain its lost authority, some of the critics believed, the checks and balances of the Constitution would become meaningless in actual practice.

Law and Order

From the beginning of his first term, President Nixon hoped to alter the direction of the Supreme Court. As Chief Justice Warren approached retirement, President Johnson had tried to replace him with Abe Fortas, whom Johnson earlier had appointed as an associate justice. Fortas, a liberal, could have been expected to keep the Court on essentially the same track it had been following under Warren. The Republicans in the Senate blocked the Fortas appointment and thus gave Nixon an opportunity to choose his own chief justice. Nixon— who insisted that it was "the job of the courts to interpret the law, not make the law"—chose a conservative strict constructionist who agreed with him. This was Warren Burger, who had served on the United States Court of Appeals for the District of Columbia and who had spoken out against what he considered the Supreme Court's protection of the rights of criminals.

Nixon soon had a chance to put another man of his choice on the Supreme Court, but this time he ran into difficulty and embarrassment. The opening occurred when Justice Fortas resigned after the revelation that he had received a salary payment from a foundation whose donor was under indictment for fraud. To take Fortas' place, Nixon named a federal circuit court judge from South Carolina, C. F. Haynsworth, whose past decisions showed that he lagged considerably behind the Warren Court in his devotion to civil rights. Spokesmen for black organizations and for labor unions were joined in opposition to Haynsworth's nomination by others, including prominent Republicans, when it was revealed that Haynsworth had sat on cases involving corporations in which he himself had a financial interest. Eventually the Senate rejected the Haynsworth nomination, and Nixon then named G. Harrold Carswell, a Florida judge who lacked Haynsworth's legal eminence and who was shown to have made racist statements in the past. When the Senate turned down Carswell also, Nixon angrily charged the Senate majority with bias against the South. The Senate finally accepted the appointment of Harry A. Blackmun, who, like Chief Justice Burger, came from Minnesota and had a reputation as a conservative jurist.

Before Nixon had been in office three years, two more Supreme Court vacancies arose, and again he ran into trouble in trying to fill them. The American Bar Association refused to endorse his first two choices, one of whom was a woman. Nixon then nominated, and the Senate approved, Lewis F. Powell, Jr., a Virginian and a former head of the American Bar Association, and William H. Rehnquist, assistant attorney general in the Nixon administration and a Goldwater Republican from Arizona. "I shall continue to appoint judges," Nixon later said, "who share my philosophy that we must strengthen the peace forces against the criminal forces in America."

By 1969, a decade and a half after the Court's historic decision outlawing segregation, only about 20 percent of the black children in the South were attending mixed schools. And, in September 1969, the Nixon administration suddenly ceased to insist on immediate steps toward integration, and granted Mississippi an additional delay in eliminating its dual school system. Several weeks later the Court overruled the administration and demanded that Mississippi integrate its schools "at once." But Nixon pre-

THE NIXON YEARS 377

vented the HEW Department from cutting off funds from noncomplying districts and continued to delay the carrying out of its desegregation plans.

In many areas the achievement of racial balance in schools would require the transporting of children from one neighborhood to another. When federal courts began to order such busing, Nixon spoke out with the many who denounced it as unthinkable if not unconstitutional. Nevertheless, the Supreme Court unanimously upheld it in a 1971 case involving Charlotte, North Carolina. The next year Nixon tried, unsuccessfully, to induce Congress to pass an antibusing law. Meanwhile, opponents of busing in northern cities violently resisted court-ordered busing; those in Denver, Colorado, and Pontiac, Michigan, resorted to the fire-bombing of school buses. There was also resistance in the South, but on the whole desegregation proceeded faster there than in the North. Before the end of Nixon's first term — thanks to the federal courts rather than the President — the proportion of Southern blacks in all-black schools had declined from about 80 to less than 20 percent.

Comparatively few blacks, North or South, approved of Nixon's policies on schools or other matters, but the urban black communities had apparently come to the conclusion that rioting did them more harm than good. The antiwar groups also calmed down after their campus eruptions at the time of the Cambodian invasion in 1970. It was as if events had numbed the erstwhile protesters for peace. But Indians resumed their demonstrations, sometimes with violence.

In 1969, the hopes of Indians had been raised when Nixon appointed a Mohawk-Sioux as Commissioner of Indian Affairs, and again in 1970 when Nixon promised Indians "self-determination without termination," that is, an increase in control over their own affairs and at the same time an increase in federal aid. The promises were not fulfilled, however, and among Indians anger and frustration took the place of hope. In November 1972 nearly a thousand protesters forcibly took over the Bureau of Indian Affairs building in Washington and, after six days, left it with damage to files and furniture that government officials estimated at $500,000 to $2 million. Later that winter members of the militant American Indian Movement occupied the hamlet of Wounded Knee on the Pine Ridge res-

ervation in South Dakota, fortified the place (the site of a one-sided, bloody engagement between the United States cavalry and a group of Sioux in 1890), and held it for more than two months.

The General Welfare

In dealing with the problem of poverty, Nixon appeared to follow a zigzag course. In 1969, Nixon proposed a new Family Assistance Plan, which his special adviser on urban and poverty problems, Daniel P. Moynihan, had devised. Under the Moynihan plan, every unemployed family of four would receive at least $1,600 a year. The working poor would get this minimum and would be allowed to keep part of their pay until their earned income reached $4,000, when the benefits would be discontinued.

The Moynihan plan had much to recommend it, but it provoked a bitter controversy. Black militants, welfare recipients, and social workers opposed it as inadequate. Congress neither adopted it nor agreed on a substitute, and Nixon himself soon lost interest in the plan. He turned to recommending, instead, that welfare expenditures be cut and that payments to "ineligibles" be stopped.

Already Nixon had begun to undo the Johnson poverty program by closing more than half of the Job Corps training centers. He also reduced spending on other social-welfare agencies, including the National Institutes of Health. In his budget for 1973–1974 he proposed to abolish more than a hundred federal grant programs that were giving aid to the unemployed, the mentally ill, veterans, college students, small businessmen, and other groups. He also proposed to discontinue spending for urban renewal, to end assistance for hospital construction, and to reduce expenditures on lunches for schoolchildren. In 1973 he proceeded, without congressional approval, to break up the Office of Economic Opportunity, which had been the main agency of Johnson's "war on poverty."

To replace many of the federal grants for specific purposes, Nixon had been urging that the federal government transfer funds to the states and cities, which would then be responsible for their own social programs. Such "revenue sharing" he viewed as the finest example of the New Federalism in practice. Congress approved, and revenue sharing began in 1973, when the federal government turned about $5 billion over to state and local governments. Big-city mayors soon lost their enthusiasm for revenue sharing, since it promised them less money for dealing with urban problems than the specific grants, now being reduced or eliminated, had provided.

Many Americans had hoped that, once the United States was finally out of the Vietnam War, the government could cut its military spending and could afford to increase its domestic expenditures. Yet in his first postwar budget, the one for 1973–1974, Nixon not only demanded a reduction in domestic expenditures but also asked for an increase in military spending, from $74.8 billion to $79 billion. The extra money was to go largely for the development of new weapons and for pay raises to attract recruits to the all-volunteer armed forces.

The Nixon Economy

When Nixon talked of reducing expenditures on social programs, he justified it as a necessary means of controlling inflation. He had inherited the inflation problem from his predecessor, Johnson, who had built up a tremendous inflationary pressure by increasing expenditures for both the Great Society and the Vietnam War without raising taxes. Nixon faced a dilemma, since rising prices could mean booming business, while deflationary policies might bring on widespread unemployment. In handling the problem he proved to be neither consistent nor successful.

At the outset, in 1969, Nixon announced a deflationary "game plan." He was going to maintain a balanced budget by spending less and taxing more, yet he signed a tax bill that enlarged exemptions and thus reduced revenue. He was also going to tighten bank credit and raise interest rates through the operations of the Federal Reserve System, and he succeeded in doing so. As a consequence a recession ensued. But anticipations of continued inflation were so strong and widespread that prices continued to rise. The country began to suffer from "stagflation," stagnation and inflation together.

The Economic Stabilization Act of 1970 authorized the President to impose direct controls on prices and also wages if and when he saw fit to do so. Nixon said: "I will not take this nation down the road of wage and price controls, how-

ever politically expedient that may seem." One year later he put into effect a two-phase control system. In Phase I, to last for ninety days, nearly all wages and prices were frozen at their existing levels. In Phase II, to last indefinitely, most wage and price increases were kept within strict limits. Inflation now slowed down temporarily, but the business recession continued, and the unemployment rate rose to more than 6 percent of the labor force for 1971, as compared with less than 4 percent for 1969.

If these economic conditions had persisted, they might have threatened the reelection of Nixon in 1972, just as they had contributed to the failure of Nixon's 1960 campaign. So, in 1971, he suddenly reversed his original game plan of tight credit and a balanced budget. He got from Congress a bill further reducing taxes. The Federal Reserve Board lowered interest rates and encouraged borrowing from banks. Government agencies began to spend at a rate of $1 billion a month more than had previously been planned. The Department of Agriculture increased its crop subsidies to farmers (for taking land out of production) from $3.1 billion to $4.1 billion a year. Altogether, the government paid out so much more than it took in that the deficit for 1972 was by far the largest for any year since World War II. By Election Day, incomes were up and unemployment was down. Politically, the combination of easy credit and deficit spending proved a great success.

The economic consequences, however, were disastrous. Foods and other raw materials were already becoming more scarce throughout the world. Nixon's wheat deal with the Soviet Union made the food shortage worse than it would otherwise have been in the United States. Meanwhile, food production in the United States was declining as a result of Nixon's election-year farm policy. By pushing exports and restricting output, the administration was decreasing the available supply of foodstuffs within the country. By loosening credit and pouring out money, it was increasing the effective demand. Thus it was creating an explosive inflationary force. At this critical moment, early in 1973, Nixon chose to discontinue the strict wage-price controls of Phase II, which he replaced with the flexible, largely voluntary guidelines of what came to be called Phase III.

There followed the most rapid and extreme rise in the cost of living since the end of World

War II. Prices of meat and grain products soared the highest. Responding to consumer protests, the administration finally put a ceiling on the retail prices of meat and other foods but not on the prices of livestock or grain. This haphazard attempt at price fixing only worsened the food shortage. Squeezed between rising costs and fixed prices, some poultrymen killed baby chicks, and some packers and bakers went out of business.

After his reelection in 1972, Nixon ended the government's spending spree and renewed his demands for economizing on social programs. He opposed a tax increase and argued that if an increase should become necessary, Congress would be to blame because of its extravagance. To forestall a recession, he sought to moderate the business boom that had been under way in 1972 and that was to last through most of 1973. But, by mid-1974 budget policy and Federal Reserve policy had become so restrictive that the feared recession became a reality.

Prosperity became even more difficult to preserve when, in the fall of 1973, the Arab nations cut back their oil production and put an embargo on petroleum shipments to the United States. There had already been, in this country, scattered shortages of fuel oil during the winter of 1972–1973 and gasoline during the summer of 1973. For the winter of 1973–1974, a much greater and more general shortage was anticipated, but experts differed as to how great it would actually prove to be. Natural gas and electric power were also in short supply. To meet the "energy crisis," the federal and state governments took a variety of steps. These included an appeal to homeowners to lower their thermostats, allotments of fuel to airlines and a consequent elimination of many flights, allocation of fuel oil and gasoline to dealers, a reduction of highway speed limits to fifty-five miles an hour, a ban on Sunday sales of gasoline, and a contingency plan for gasoline rationing. Prices of gasoline and fuel oil started to take a steep rise. The shortage threatened to curtail production as well as transportation, since many industries depended directly or indirectly on petroleum for power, and others (such as those making or using plastics or synthetic fibers) depended on it also for raw material. By March 1974, the outlook was dim, with long lines of cars waiting for gas at filling stations in many parts of the country. The next month the pros-

pect brightened temporarily when the Arab oil ban was lifted. But the shortage had both enhanced the forces of recession and contributed to increased inflation.

A Triumphant Reelection

According to a 1970 book, the "real majority" in the United States was "unyoung, unblack, and unpoor." The mature, white, well-off citizens were most concerned about such things as campus protests, school integration, street crimes, and welfare costs. If these worried people could be induced to vote for Nixon, his reelection would be assured. This prospect formed the basis for the campaign strategy that Nixon's attorney general and political adviser, John Mitchell, adopted for 1972. In particular, Mitchell planned to attract to Nixon the voters who in 1968 had favored the American party candidate, George Wallace of Alabama. In addition to these Southern whites, the Republicans hoped to win over many Northern workers, especially the Catholics of immigrant background. Thus the Nixon forces might break up the already shaky Democratic coalition — which Franklin D. Roosevelt had put together in the 1930s — and replace it with a permanent Republican majority.

To Republican strategists it was hardly encouraging when, in 1970, Congress passed a bill to lower the voting age to eighteen. Nixon signed the bill, despite the widespread assumption that most of the young would vote Democratic. The Supreme Court ruled the new law constitutional for federal but not for state or local elections. The Twenty-sixth Amendment, ratified in time for the elections of 1972, made eighteen the minimum age for voters in state and local as well as federal contests.

Nixon's chances for reelection improved when, in May 1972, in a Maryland shopping center, a would-be assassin shot George Wallace, leaving him partially paralyzed and incapable of continuing his presidential campaign. Nixon's chances improved still further when, in July, the Democratic nominating convention met in Miami.

On the first ballot the convention chose George M. McGovern, an opponent of the Vietnam War and an advocate of a $1,000 tax credit for every citizen. While still a relatively unknown senator from South Dakota, McGovern had begun openly to seek the presidency far in advance, in January 1971. In the primaries he outdid the early favorite, Senator Edmund Muskie of Maine, and the previous candidate, Senator Hubert Humphrey of Minnesota. At the convention, McGovern benefited from reforms he himself had helped to bring about. The "McGovern rules" were intended to make the convention broadly representative of the party by requiring certain proportions of women, blacks, and youths among the delegates. But the rules antagonized old-line politicians and had a very divisive effect on the party, especially when the convention unseated a powerful boss, Mayor Richard J. Daley of Chicago.

The very qualities that had brought McGovern the nomination—the qualities that appealed to liberals within the Democratic party—made him a weak candidate in the election. From the make-up of the convention, many voters got the impression that he was the candidate of hippies, aggressive women, and militant blacks.

While McGovern campaigned strenuously with limited financial resources, which came mainly from small contributors, Nixon had an easy "non-campaign." He had the advantage of more money, most of it from large corporations, than any other presidential candidate had ever had at his disposal. Seldom appearing, Nixon was an "invisible candidate." His choice for a second time as Vice President, Spiro Agnew, together with other government officials, carried the campaign burden for Nixon, never mentioning him by name but always referring to him as "the President." By virtue of his China and Russia visits and the Vietnam negotiations he appeared to be a bringer of peace. Since business was finally booming, he could be credited with prosperity. As a foe of busing for racial balance in schools, he had the gratitude of race-conscious whites. Through his "law and order" statements and his court appointments, he had made himself the apparent champion of peace at home as well as abroad.

Nixon won by one of the most decisive margins in history. He received the largest share of the popular vote (60.8 percent) of any candidate except Johnson (61.1 percent) in 1964. He received the largest proportion of the electoral vote (521 of 538) since Roosevelt (523 of 531) in 1936. McGovern carried only Massachusetts and the District of Columbia. But the presidential victory, overwhelming though it was, probably meant less an endorsement of Nixon than a rejection of his opponent.

Watergate

As he began his second term, in January 1973, President Nixon stood at the height of his power and popularity. Soon his popularity, as measured by opinion polls, began to drop. It fell faster than that of any other President since such polls were first taken, in Franklin D. Roosevelt's time. Within a year, public confidence in Nixon was so low that serious doubts arose as to whether he should, or could, continue to lead the people. The reason for the sudden collapse of his prestige could be summed up in a word that became familiar to all newspaper readers and television viewers—"Watergate." That word designated a bewildering assortment of political scandals, easily the worst in American history.

The Watergate was a deluxe hotel-apartment-office complex in Washington. In it were located the headquarters of the Democratic National Committee. There, at about two o'clock on the morning of June 17, 1972, police arrested five men who had broken into the headquarters to "bug" them and to copy documents. Later two others were arrested, one of them the general counsel for Nixon's personal campaign organization, the Committee for the Re-election of the President (CREEP). Two months after the burglary, however, Nixon stated that "no one in the White House staff, no one in this Administration presently employed, was involved in this very bizarre incident." He added: "This kind of activity, as I have often indicated, has no place whatsoever in our political process."

When, after the election, the captured burglars went on trial, all but one of them pleaded guilty, and that one refused to talk. The Justice Department prosecutors failed to implicate anyone higher up than those arrested, but Federal District Judge John J. Sirica suspected that the whole truth had not been told. While sentencing the defendants to long terms in prison, Sirica intimated that if they would cooperate in getting at the truth, he would reduce the sentences. One of the defendants, James W. McCord, Jr., a former CIA agent and a "security coordinator" for CREEP, now agreed to testify before a federal

THE NIXON YEARS 381

grand jury and a Senate investigating committee, which was headed by Senator Sam J. Ervin of North Carolina. McCord led a long parade of witnesses who appeared, voluntarily or under subpoena, before the grand jury and the Ervin committee. The committee hearings, televised, gave the public an opportunity to draw its own conclusions about the character and conduct of the men around the President. The testimony was so conflicting and confusing, however, that only with difficulty could the threads of the developing story be untangled.

Certain undisputed facts stood out. Nixon had been much concerned about the leaking of government secrets, especially the leaking of a Defense Department study of the Vietnam War, which *The New York Times* and other journals published as "The Pentagon Papers" in 1971. So, to plug the leaks, he set up and put Ehrlichman in charge of a special group of White House employees, who called themselves "the plumbers," and who tapped the telephones of newsmen and members of Kissinger's staff. Nixon ordered the plumbers to investigate the background of Daniel Ellsberg, the man responsible for leaking the Pentagon Papers. Using White House funds, two of the plumbers led a team of burglars who broke into the Los Angeles office of Ellsberg's psychiatrist to search for Ellsberg's psychiatric files. Nixon was eager to prosecute and convict Ellsberg. While Ellsberg was on trial before a federal court, Nixon told Ehrlichman to approach the trial judge and find out if he would be interested in a promotion to the post of FBI director. The judge dismissed the case.

Four of the burglars of the psychiatrist's office, including the two leaders, took part, with CREEP financing, in the Watergate break-in. After the arrests, CREEP members and other government officials hastily destroyed a tremendous quantity of their records. Nixon told Haldeman and Ehrlichman to meet with top CIA officials, and the CIA director concluded that the White House was trying to "use" the agency as a means of slowing down an FBI probe and covering up CREEP activities. A White House attorney suggested to one of the Watergate defendants that he, the defendant, would get a presidential pardon after a short time in prison if he would keep silent about his superiors' involvement in the affair. Nixon's personal attorney and other White House staffers covertly passed more than $400,000, mostly from Nixon

campaign contributions, to the defendants, their families, and their lawyers.

Besides the Watergate burglary, CREEP agents had perpetrated a variety of "dirty tricks" before and during the campaign, the worst of them having been intended to destroy the reputation of Nixon's strongest potential rival, Senator Muskie, and thereby prevent his getting the Democratic nomination. "I have often thought we had too much money," one of Nixon's campaign workers said afterward. Part of the money came from corporations that were making unlawful contributions, part of it from persons or groups who were receiving specific government favors. Most visibly, the Justice Department compromised an antitrust suit against the International Telephone and Telegraph Company after the ITT had agreed to contribute.

A President Resigns

Many of Nixon's friends, advisers, and aides were indicted on, and some of them were convicted of, charges growing out of illegal campaign activities. The question became more and more insistent: Was Nixon himself guilty? Did he authorize any of the illegal activities or any of the attempts to cover them up? Did he have any knowledge of the misdeeds or the cover-up and fail to act on his knowledge, fail to stop what was going on and see that those responsible were punished? (Misprision of felony is itself a crime.) In a succession of statements Nixon altered and added to his original story, but he continued to maintain that he was innocent of any wrongdoing. "I am not a crook," he declared at one news conference. There was a possible way of testing, at certain points, his veracity as against that of his accusers. At his direction—as one of the very few who knew about it revealed in the midst of the Senate hearings—hidden tape recorders had been recording White House conversations. But Nixon refused to give up the relevant tapes until after Judge Sirica had ruled that he must, and then Nixon's spokesmen let it be known that two of the most important tapes were nonexistent and a third had a peculiar gap in it. A team of experts concluded that part of this tape had been deliberately erased.

To a growing number of Americans it seemed that, at the very least, Nixon had shown remarkably poor judgment in choosing some of his subordinates. It turned out that he had certainly been no judge of character when he twice endorsed Spiro Agnew for the vice presidency. Late in 1973 Agnew, the stern advocate of law and order, resigned as Vice President and pleaded nolo contendere (no contest) to a charge of income-tax evasion, the federal prosecutors agreeing in return to refrain from pressing charges of soliciting and accepting bribes. To replace Agnew, Nixon named the House Republican leader, Gerald Ford of Michigan. After a thorough investigation, Congress gave Ford its approval. He appeared to be, if not an imaginative or inspiring statesman, at least an honest politician.

With Ford as the prospective successor, old demands for the resignation or impeachment of Nixon were renewed. As 1974 began, Nixon still refused to resign. The Judiciary Committee of the House was busily gathering evidence for the decision whether or not to impeach. After requesting a number of the presidential tapes, the committee served the President with a subpoena when he refused to give them up. Finally, at the end of April, he responded, not by delivering the tapes, but by sending in and at the same time publishing 1200 pages of selected and edited transcripts. He and other Republican spokesmen claimed that these told the whole story of his relation to the Watergate scandal and completely exonerated him. Others, especially Democrats, drew a quite different conclusion. By a partisan vote, the committee ruled that Nixon had not made an adequate response to the subpoena.

By the summer of 1974, nine men — in adddition to the "Watergate seven," the burglars and their accomplices — had confessed to or been convicted of Watergate-related offenses. These nine were former members of CREEP or of the White House staff, the highest ranking of them being Erlichman. Several others, including Haldeman and Mitchell, had been indicted and were awaiting trial. Nixon himself had been named as an "unindicted co-conspirator" by a federal grand jury.

For use as evidence in these cases the special prosecutor for the Justice Department, Leon Jaworski, asked for tape recordings of sixty-four White House conversations. Nixon refused to give them up, claiming that "executive privilege" justified him in thus protecting the confidentiality of his office. In the case of *United States* v. *Richard M. Nixon* the Supreme Court decided unanimously against the President in July 1974.

A few days later, after several months of thorough inquiry, the House Judiciary Committee voted to recommend three articles of impeachment. These charged that Nixon had (1) obstructed justice by helping to cover up the Watergate crimes, (2) misused federal agencies so as to violate the rights of citizens, and (3) interfered with congressional powers by refusing to turn over tapes and other materials that the committee had subpoenaed.

Though Nixon continued to assert his innocence, more and more signs of his complicity were coming to light. Newly released tapes proved what he had always denied — that he had been aware of and indeed had directed the Watergate cover-up from the beginning. With impeachment and conviction finally looming as unavoidable, he did what no President had ever done before. He resigned. Immediately, on August 9, 1974, Gerald Ford was sworn in as Nixon's successor. For the first time, there was a President who had not reached the office by going through a national election.

The Ford Administration

Gerald Ford's Presidency was certain to be far more modest in every way than that of his predecessor. The constitutional crisis that had vaulted Ford into the Oval Office meant that any new President would have to be cautious in advancing his prerogatives. The fact that Ford had not obtained a popular mandate would limit the length of the "honeymoon" with Congress that a new President traditionally enjoyed and would restrict his ability to appeal directly to the public for support. Also, Ford was thoroughly a man of the Congress. He had been first elected to the House of Representatives in 1948, was reelected a dozen times after that, and served for nearly ten years, until he became Vice President, as House minority leader. With that history, and his consequent respect for Congressional expertise, it was unlikely that Ford would continue Nixon's initiatives in centralized executive planning. And Ford appeared to have far less taste for the trappings and show of Presidential power than had Richard Nixon. Ford reduced the population of ornamental eagles that Nixon had perched in the Oval Office and removed the 307 battle streamers, commemorating engagements from Ticonderoga to Vietnam, that his predecessor had displayed behind the Presidential chair.

Without an electoral endorsement, Ford had to pay close attention to enhancing his power. To end speculation that he intended to be only a care-taker President and simply serve out the rest of his term, he announced that he would be a candidate for reelection in 1976. He made significant, popular gestures to the liberal wing of the Republican Party and to sympathetic Democrats. He named Nelson Rockefeller, ex-governor of New York, as Vice President. By that same act he may well have eliminated from the ring his most powerful contender for the 1976 Republican nomination. And he retained Henry Kissinger as Secretary of State. However, partly to contain Kissinger's influence within the administration he retained Nixon's last Secretary of Defense, James Schlesinger, a powerful figure known to be at odds with Kissinger over some strategic questions.

All of those actions boded well for Ford's political future, but he offset their effect by his handling of the lingering Watergate affair. In September he extended a full pardon to Richard Nixon, explaining that Nixon's health was in jeopardy and that he had suffered enough. Nixon accepted the pardon, thereby admitting some element of guilt, and was, for a time, gravely ill from complications of phlebitis. But much of the American public was dissatisfied with the outcome, particularly when Ford followed the pardon with an amnesty plan for Vietnam draft-evaders and deserters that was quite narrow in scope. Ford's ratings in public opinion polls nose-dived as a consequence, falling to a 50 percent approval rate by late September 1974 from a favorable rating of 71 percent a week after he took office—the sharpest two-month decline in 35 years. And the memory of Watergate refused to dissipate. In January 1975 John Ehrlichman, H. R. Haldeman, and John Mitchell were convicted of conspiracy, obstruction of justice, and giving false testimony. In February they were sentenced to a minimum of 30 months in prison, and their subsequent appeals promised to keep the cases in the public eye for some time to come.

Yet another Watergate-related scandal began to emerge in January 1975 when a *N.Y. Times* reporter broke the story that the CIA, beginning in the 1950s, had engaged in extensive domestic surveillance. Such activity, while legally sanctioned in limited form by the National Security Council for the purposes of counterintelligence, had reached such proportions by the 1960s that it appeared that the CIA had violated its Congressional mandate. The participation of ex-CIA agents in Nixon administration "capers" and the implication of the CIA in their "cover-up" appeared to some to be part of a larger pattern of secret government at home. The CIA's director of counterintelligence for twenty years resigned in the wake of the exposé, and Ford, bowing to public opinion, appointed a blue-ribbon panel to investigate the CIA's domestic activity. But again Ford's popularity declined when he appointed to the panel several individuals, including its chairman, Nelson Rockefeller, who in the past had in some way been involved with or shown vigorous support for the CIA.

The Ford-Kissinger foreign policy progressed uncertainly in its European and Middle Eastern dimensions and the administration could do little more than watch the final victory of Communist forces in Vietman and Cambodia. But a Ford trip to Vladivostok appeared to advance détente and Ford escaped the testing of a major foreign crisis. However, Ford was unable to avoid the trials of a major domestic calamity—the transformation of the mild recession into the worst economic reversal since the Great Depression. The reversal was not the new President's responsibility. In a sense, the severity of the recession resulted from the protracted inflation that had occurred over the preceding decade. If the Johnson administration and Congress had been willing to check the expansion before it had soared out of control, if the Nixon administration had allowed the recession of 1969–1970 to continue until inflation had subsided, or if the Nixon administration had embarked upon serious wage and price controls, the recession facing Gerald Ford would not have been as grave. Inflationary pressures had become so intense that even by mid-1975, when unemployment reached nearly 10 percent, prices continued to rise, although finally at a reduced pace.

In his policies of coping with the combination of inflation and recession, Ford avoided extremes of action and switched positions rather dramatically. Beginning with a posture of stringent opposition to inflation, Ford turned, by January 1975, to a warrior against unemployment and had endorsed the biggest deficit — more than $50 billion — in peacetime history for fiscal year 1976. He proposed a program of stimulation of employment through a $15 billion tax cut. Wanting even more stimulation, Congress passed and the President approved a tax cut of more than $22 billion — the biggest ever in the nation's history. That action, taken in early April, contributed to the economic recovery which had begun by the summer of 1975 and continued, although more slowly, through 1976. However, the program of economic stimulation, which Congress expanded to include a deficit of nearly $60 billion, contributed to inflationary pressures. Price increases in 1975 and 1976, although less severe than those before the 1974–1975 recession, pinched most family budgets. One result was a sharp increase in the number of wives and teen-agers who sought employment to supplement eroding family incomes. The surge of new entrants into the labor force, coupled with the incompleteness of recovery from the recession, kept the rate of unemployment at nearly 8 percent even by the end of 1976.

Election of 1976

When Ford first took office, he seemed to reassure the American people with his refreshing candor, simplicity, physical vigor, and Midwestern origins (Grand Rapids, Michigan). However, his pardon of Richard Nixon and the persistence of the frustrating conjunction of inflation and high unemployment left Ford highly vulnerable as a candidate for reelection.

Recognizing Ford's vulnerability, more than a dozen Democratic leaders entered the campaign for their party's nomination. The competition in the primaries was intense, but a former Governor of Georgia, James ("Jimmy") E. Carter, Jr., demonstrated the ability to attract support from a wide range of Democratic voters and emerged as the only contender to win pluralities with some consistency. By convention time almost all the other leading candidates had dropped out of the race, leaving the way clear for a smooth, party-uniting Carter nomination. Carter took liberal Senator Walter F. Mondale of Minnesota as his running mate.

Compounding the problems that a united

Democratic party created for Ford, Ronald Reagan, the former Governor of California, challenged Ford for the Republican nomination. As the leading spokesman for conservative Republicans, he proved to be a formidable candidate; but Ford, with greater leverage over the party machinery and drawing on the united support of liberal Republicans, won the nomination. With a small margin of victory he was forced to take a conservative, Senator Robert J. Dole of Kansas, as his running mate, and the Republican party emerged from its August convention badly divided. Ford began his contest with Carter trailing the Democrat by more than thirty points in both the Harris and the Gallup polls.

Before the primaries Jimmy Carter had been virtually unknown outside the South. A graduate of the U.S. Naval Academy, a former career naval-officer (on nuclear submarines), a moderately wealthy, small-town (Plains, Georgia) peanut farmer, Carter's political experience had been limited to service in the Georgia legislature and a single term as Governor of Georgia. Carter campaigned as an outsider from the Washington establishment; he made much of his small-town origins; he described himself as a "populist"; he made no effort to conceal his religious faith as a "second-born" Christian; and he ran on a platform stressing the need for greater economic stimulation and vigorous central planning to set national priorities. Ford waged his campaign largely from the White House. He put strong emphasis on his successes in foreign policy. Television advertisements stressed his sincerity, decency, and warm family life and accused Carter of extreme liberalism, inconsistency on the issues, excessive ambition, and poor judgment.

Neither candidate managed to capture the imagination of the American electorate, although by election day Ford had pulled even with Carter in the public opinion polls. The very closeness of the contest seemed to stimulate voter turnout, and Carter defeated the incumbent. Carter's electoral vote margin was small, but his popular vote margin was substantially greater than Kennedy's in 1960 or Nixon's in 1968. That popular endorsement and the election of a strongly Democratic Congress created the promise of significant policy departures during Carter's Presidency.

Chapter 34. TOWARD THE TWENTY-FIRST CENTURY

The Promise of Technology

Generation after generation, Americans had been preoccupied with material progress. Those of the late twentieth century saw technological achievements even more startling than those of earlier times. A future of increasing abundance seemed to be promised by the continuing development of technical innovations summed up in the term "automation."

Essential to automation as it developed after World War II were electronic controls and the development of computer systems. The first electronic computer went into operation in 1946. Its name was descriptive: ENIAC, which stood for Electronic Numerical Integrator and Calculator. At first computers were large, cumbersome, and expensive, but the discovery that complicated electronic circuits, which had been assembled by hand, could be printed on cardboard or plastic and that compact durable transistors (invented in 1948) could replace fragile vacuum tubes made possible the rapid and spectacular advance in computer technology. By the end of the sixties, computers were a hundred times faster, ten times smaller in their electronic components, and provided information in a thousandth of the time of earlier ones.

Computers, capable of answering in a few minutes problems that would require a thousand man-hours of calculation, were bringing a revolution in information processing. Jerome B. Wiesner, who had been President Kennedy's science adviser, described the change this way: "The computer, with its promise of a millionfold increase in man's capacity to handle information, will undoubtedly have the most far-reaching consequences of any contemporary technical development. The potential for good in the computer, and the danger inherent in its misuse, exceed our ability to imagine."

Computers could give answers to innumerable informational problems previously so complex as to be unmanageable. They were helping industry control inventories to eliminate the periodic scarcity or glut that had contributed to irregularities in the business cycle. They could fly jet planes, guide rockets to the moon, or control almost any sort of machinery. They could, critics feared, through data storage on every individual, destroy privacy; through the tasks they could guide, they might create serious unemployment.

The high rates of unemployment during the 1950s engendered fears that automation threatened chronic unemployment. Some suggested that American society would have to develop means, such as a guaranteed annual wage, for separating income from increasingly scarce productive-work. However, during the 1960s, these fears diminished when unemployment rates declined significantly even before the Vietnam mobilization. Automation, and all innovation that enhanced productivity, became generally regarded as contributing to increased employment. Meanwhile, the problem of the "hardcore" unemployed became more widely interpreted as the result of discrimination and inadequate education, rather than automation.

As production grew, the United States began to change from a "have" to a "have-not" nation in natural resources, but innovations postponed the danger of disastrous shortages. Between 1900 and 1950, the production of bituminous coal rose two and a half times, of copper three times, of iron ore three and a half times, and of crude oil thirty times. Although Gifford Pinchot, writing in the Progressive era, had feared that bituminous coal would soon be exhausted, exhaustion was still far off. In fact, the Department of the Interior was still researching new uses—such as liquefication and gasification—for bituminous coal. In 1877 Secretary of the Interior Carl Schurz warned of a "timber famine" only twenty years away, but according to a 1962 estimate, forests at that time were growing at a rate that exceeded by 60 percent the amount of timber cut. Synthetic substances, plastics, and metals had cut the demand for forest products. As the rich iron deposits began to dwindle, steel companies developed processes to make use of lower-grade ore. Once the huge investment had been made in plants that produced high-grade pellets from taconite ores, the steel companies reaped the advantage of higher productivity from furnaces into which they fed the pellets. New ore deposits were opened in Labrador. The United States became the largest importer of copper, lead, and zinc, leading to a flow of dollars overseas.

Scientific Research

Applications of scientific knowledge, both civilian and military, were being developed at such a rapid pace that they created a sharp pressure for additional basic research. In 1957 a Department of Defense research officer declared: "We have been chewing up the findings of basic research since World War II at a speed faster than they are being produced in the laboratories and ivory towers."

The chief agency for promotion of basic scientific research was the National Science Foundation. In 1945 Dr. Vannevar Bush, who had been wartime director of the Office of Scientific Research and Development, proposed the establishment of a peacetime government agency to promote basic research. The United States could no longer depend upon Europe, Bush warned. In 1950 Congress established the National Science Foundation, but limited its annual appropriations to $15 million per year and appropriated less than that until the 1956 fiscal year. In the 1959 budget, after the sputnik crisis, President Eisenhower asked for $140 million for the National Science Foundation. Thereafter its budget, and its impact upon scientific research, increased significantly.

Overall federal expenditures on research and development—no more than a tenth of it for basic research—rose so spectacularly that by the end of the sixties they totaled more than the entire federal budget before Pearl Harbor. These sums were so large that many universities were dependent upon them for a considerable portion of their budgets. Concentration of expenditures in a few universities (68 percent of federal research funds were going to twenty-five institutions) had important side effects.

Scientific and engineering work at Harvard and the Massachusetts Institute of Technology had helped attract science-based industry, espe-

cially in electronics, to Highway 128 ringing Boston; the University of California and Stanford had brought similar industry to the San Francisco Bay region. Understandably, there developed considerable pressure to allocate more scientific grants to the Middle West and other areas in the United States. The House Appropriations Committee forbade the granting of more than 10 percent of the National Science Foundation fellowships to the residents of any one state.

The most comprehensive and spectacular of basic research enterprises, in which the United States cooperated with sixty-two other countries including Russia, was the International Geophysical Year, from July 1, 1957, to the end of 1958. It involved exploring the globe from pole to pole and from ionosphere to core, and included the launching of satellites and the establishment of an American base at the South Pole. The research in Antarctica developed into a long-range scientific program, centering in a permanent base at McMurdo Sound, which supplied a number of outlying stations. By international treaty, national territorial holdings and armaments were barred from the continent; the United States, the Soviet Union, and a number of other nations carried on scientific work and shared information without friction.

In medical research, the most visible advance was the development of an effective polio vaccine by Dr. Jonas Salk of the University of Pittsburgh. The vaccine was first used on a large scale in 1955, and within two years the polio rate in the United States dropped 80 percent. Many spectacular innovations were made possible by electronic or atomic advances. The transplant of kidneys and even of a human heart were aided by chemical treatment and radiation to prevent rejection of the new organ. A number of mechanical and electronic inventions—among them artificial kidneys and miniature electronic generators to keep a heart beating at the right pace—helped to save lives. The laser beam, a ray of concentrated light, became a tool of eye surgery to repair damage to the retina.

But the most dramatic breakthrough came not in medical technology but in the fundamental understanding of the chemistry of life. In 1953 James D. Watson of Harvard University and Francis H. C. Crick of Cambridge University worked out the chemical structure of DNA, the material in the genes that carries the hereditary information. The genes control the biochemical activities of the cell, and following the discovery of their structure came research that revealed the mechanisms by which the genes control cell activity. This biological revolution, gathering force during the 1960s, produced an explosion of knowledge of basic cell biochemistry, which promised to unravel the mysteries of a number of hitherto intractable diseases. It also brought from the realm of science fiction the possibility of man's controlling human heredity.

The Space Race Begins

At the same time that mankind was dramatically advancing knowledge of its own inner space, it was venturing into outer space. However, that enterprise began not out of interest in pure science but because of the cold war.

The American government had shown little interest in space exploration until October 1957, when the Soviet Union put its first satellite, Sputnik I, into orbit. Already the United States was carrying on a program of rocket research under the direction of Wernher von Braun, a German-born expert whose team had designed and built for the Hitler regime the V-2 rockets that devastated London during the final stages of World War II. As the Russians advanced into Germany in 1945, they captured a few of the top men and hundreds of the technicians engaged in the V-2 project. Braun and others turned themselves over to the United States Army. In the early postwar years, however, the Americans were slower than the Russians in using German expertise to produce ballistic missiles, and still slower in using it to develop space rockets.

"Our satellite program has never been conducted as a race with other nations," President Eisenhower declared as he congratulated the Soviet Union on the launching of Sputnik I. But most Americans, including prominent public figures, assumed that a race was indeed on, and the United States appeared to be lagging far behind. Sputnik II carried a dog into space in November 1957 while Braun and his coworkers were still trying to launch a tiny, three-pound sphere, which they did not succeed in orbiting until January 1958. In October of that year, twelve months after the appearance of Sputnik I, the American government set up the National Aeronautics and Space Administration (NASA) to coordinate the nation's space efforts, but gave it only a small budget.

By 1961, when Kennedy took over the presidency from Eisenhower, the United States appeared to be making some gains. This country was ahead of the Soviet Union in the number of satellites put into orbit — thirty-three to nine. The total weight of the nine Soviet satellites, however, was more than twice as great as that of all thirty-three American ones, and the Russians were rumored to be testing a five-ton spaceship that could take a man into orbit. To the Russians, Kennedy said in his inaugural: "Let us explore the stars together." But the Russians showed little interest in that. In April 1961 they sent the world's first cosmonaut, Yuri Gagarin, once around the earth. After reentering the atmosphere and parachuting to safety, Gagarin issued the boastful challenge: "Now let the other countries try to catch us."

Eight days after Gagarin's flight (and just one day after the Bay of Pigs fiasco in Cuba) President Kennedy directed a memorandum to Vice President Johnson, whom he had named as chairman of an advisory Space Council. "Do we have a chance of beating the Soviets," Kennedy asked, "by putting a laboratory in space, or by a trip around the moon, or by a rocket to land on the moon, or by a rocket to go to the moon and back with a man?" The best the United States could do for the time being was to propel Alan Shepard into a suborbital flight that went some 100 miles up to the edge of space and some 300 miles out into the Atlantic Ocean. Three weeks later, May 25, 1961, Kennedy appealed to Congress: "I believe this nation should commit itself to achieving the goal, before the decade is out, of landing a man on the moon and returning him safely to earth." Congress soon responded by making the first of the necessary appropriations.

The moon program, Project Apollo, was expected to cost $20 billion, ten times as much as the development of the atom bomb (but less than the Vietnam War was to cost for a single year). Advocates of the program maintained that it would be well worth the price on account of its scientific and economic benefits as well as its enhancement of national prestige. One space official declared: "Each improvement in our ability to fly unmanned and manned spacecraft results in a corresponding improvement in our ability to solve nature's mysteries."

To the Moon and Beyond

Until 1965 the United States continued to trail the Soviet Union in the launching of manned spacecraft, though not in the firing of unmanned satellites. A Russian cosmonaut circled the globe seventeen times (August 1961) before the first American, John Glenn, was put into space (February 1962), to return to earth after making only three orbits. Another and yet another American went around in one-man Mercury capsules similar to Glenn's, but the Russians kept the lead in flight endurance and took the lead in orbiting two vehicles close together, in launching two-man and then three-man craft, and in releasing a man from one of the ships to float in nothingness. But the United States was putting up, all together, more than twice as many satellites as the Soviet Union. Some of these were intended for scientific purposes — to study solar radiation, the earth's magnetic field, and weather phenomena. Others, such as Telstar, facilitated around-the-world communication by telephone and television. Still others, such as the "eye in the sky" satellites Samos and Midas, gave the military new means of observation or espionage. Meanwhile, from 1963 to 1965, the Americans discontinued manned flights and concentrated on the design and construction of improved space vehicles.

By 1965 the Americans were ready to achieve some firsts of their own with men in space. The new two-man Gemini, unlike the latest Soviet spaceships, was maneuverable; it was equipped with small rockets that could change its course in mid-orbit, as its pilots demonstrated on their first flight. On a second flight an astronaut stepped into space and, with a small oxygen-spitting gun, pulled the vehicle about on a tether. The third of the Geminis, orbiting for nearly 191 hours, broke the endurance record that the Russians had set. On a later launching, in 1966, a Gemini succeeded in overtaking an orbiting craft and joining up or "docking" with it — a manuever essential for a moon trip. The United States now appeared to hold the lead in manned as well as unmanned flights.

The next stage involved the Apollo, a three-man spacecraft which, with over 2 million parts, was far more complicated than the Gemini or the Mercury. The project was set back and the nation was stunned when early in 1967, a fire killed the three astronauts while they were re-hearsing for the first Apollo take-off. While the craft was being redesigned and retested, a succession of Surveyors, unmanned, were being rocketed to the moon and were sending back tens of thousands of pictures of the lunar surface. One of the Surveyors landed on the moon and then took off from it, as a manned vehicle was scheduled to do eventually. In late 1968, after Apollo 7 had carried three men around the earth, Apollo 8 carried three others around the moon, the first men to leave the earth's gravitational field. During the next few months, Apollo 9 tested a lunar module (the landing craft that was to leave and rejoin the mother ship) in an earth orbit, and Apollo 10 tested one in a moon orbit.

At last, in July 1969, Apollo 11 was blasted off on its epochal flight to land men on the moon. Ahead of them streaked a Russian spacecraft, Luna 15, heading for lunar orbit, but Luna carried no crew. Its launching seemed to show dramatically that in space enterprises the Soviet Union was still competing rather than cooperating — and now competing at a decided disadvantage. Not that sovereignty over the moon was at stake: by a treaty signed in 1966 the two superpowers had agreed that the moon should be a no man's land open to exploration and use by all nations. At issue were national prestige and (to the extent that the space programs yielded new techniques of warfare) military advantage.

The flight of Apollo 11 was a beginning, not an ending. During the next three years the United States launched a series of six additional Apollos, five of which succeeded in putting men on the moon, and all of which returned safely to the earth. Meanwhile both the United States and the Soviet Union sent space probes to Mars and Venus, and in 1973 the United States sent others to Jupiter and Mercury. Discontinuing lunar explorations for the time being, the Americans now concentrated their man-in-space efforts on experimental earth orbits. In 1973 they launched a two-story laboratory, Skylab, and three three-man crews in succession visited it to survey the earth's resources, test man's ability to live in space for long periods, and carry on other observations and experiments. At last, by an agreement of 1972, the Americans and the Russians were beginning to cooperate. They undertook a joint earth-orbiting mission in 1975.

"There is no question but that we will go to Mars and colonize the moon, probably sooner than we now think," a NASA official said in 1972. "I think it will also become a reality that we'll pick up communications from other intelligence in the universe."

The Crowding Country

In 1967 the demographic clock of the Census Bureau indicated that the population of the United States had passed the 200-million mark. In 1970 the census takers counted a total of 203,184,772. That was almost twice as large as it had been in 1920 and about 24 million larger than in 1960.

The rapid population growth after World War II belied the predictions of demographic experts who, on the basis of birth rates that had fallen for more than a century, had expected a leveling-off. The baby boom of the 1950s caused pessimists to go to the opposite extreme. At the postwar rate of growth, some predicted, the population within 800 years would be so large that each American would have only one square foot of land to stand on. During the 1960s, however, the birth rate dropped even lower than it had been during the depression. By 1972 it was down to 2.11 per woman. This was a "zero population growth" rate, one that could mean eventually (after two more generations of childbearing women) just enough births to offset the number of deaths. Meanwhile the birth rate might rise again, and so population predicting remained as uncertain as ever.

Immigration accounted for less than a half million, or about 20 percent, of the population increase during the decade 1960–1970. The immigration act of 1965 eliminated the national-origins quota system, which had allowed only a certain percentage of each nationality to enter the country. The new law provided that, from 1969 on, there would be a ceiling of 120,000 on immigration from the Western Hemisphere and 170,000 from the rest of the world. The law allowed parents, spouses, and children of United States citizens to enter the country without regard to the overall limitations. Thereafter the largest numbers of immigrants no longer came from Canada and the United Kingdom but from Italy and the Philippines.

Mobility continued to characterize Americans, as it had always done. In 1970 more than one-fourth of the natives of the United States were living in a state other than the one they were born in (in 1850 the proportion had been about the same). During the 1960s, as during previous decades, the greatest interstate movement was to the Far West, especially to California, already the most populous state by 1960 and the home of nearly 20 million people in 1970. A reversal seemed under way in 1970 when, for the first time in a hundred years, as many people moved out of California as moved into it. From 1920 to 1960 so many blacks had left the South that the region lost more than it gained by migration, but during the 1960s it gained 1.8 million whites from the North while losing 1.4 million blacks to the North. As a whole, the black population grew 33 percent faster than the white during the decade and constituted about 11 percent of the nation's total population in 1970.

The flight from the farm continued at an accelerating speed. In 1920 the people had been distributed about evenly between city and country. By 1970 the rural population had increased slightly, but the urban population had nearly tripled. The number of farms (and farmers) actually declined after 1935, from a peak of 6.8 million in that year to less than 3 million in 1970, and the figure was expected to be below 2 million by 1980. In 1970, some 63 million people were classified as rural (most of them nonfarm), about 62 million as strictly urban (living in cities proper), and 75 million as suburban.

Rise of the Megalopolis

During the decades after World War II, metropolitan areas expanded until they met and merged with one another. From north of Boston to south of Washington a single urban region—a megalopolis—was coming into being. Other supercities were taking form along the Great Lakes from Milwaukee to Buffalo and on the Pacific coast from San Diego to Los Angeles.

The proper governing of these areas was a problem. It was complicated by the escape of affluent whites from city jurisdictions and tax collectors to the suburbs, and by the concentration of poor blacks in the inner cities. While the city governments needed more and more financial resources, the tax basis was growing very slowly or actually shrinking.

Because individual metropolitan problems

transcended city and sometimes state lines, special governmental authorities to deal with matters like harbor development or transit had come into existence. Together with traditional governments they led to a multiplicity of governmental agencies. Within the 212 standard metropolitan areas in the 1960s there were some 18,000 units of government, ranging from counties to school boards. There was little cooperation among them: most of these governments were ready to give little or no aid to the ailing cities. Many state, county, and suburban officials resisted the establishment of the federal Department of Housing and Urban Development, in 1965.

The problems with which metropolis and the merging megalopolis had to grapple were those long faced by city dwellers: improvement of housing, transportation, living conditions, educational and cultural opportunities, and above all the economic base for both the family and community; conversely, the elimination of pollution, blight, crime, and violence. The size of the new metropolitan areas made these problems far larger and sometimes more complex than in earlier generations.

Federal aid in one form or another had helped make possible the vast growth of suburbia since 1945 — and then the white exodus from cities into suburbs. By 1963, 5 million families owned houses built with FHA aid; millions more lived in houses financed through the GI Bill of Rights. Federal guarantees had helped 27 million home owners borrow money for repairs. The government encouraged the deposit of money in savings and loan associations, which issued millions of mortgages, by insuring the deposits and by limiting the ability of commercial banks to compete with the associations for deposits.

Simultaneously with the growth of suburbs, attempts were made to rejuvenate decaying central cities through federal aid. Urban renewal projects were to transform slums into business and cultural areas and above all into attractive apartment complexes. The new buildings were expected to bring a fivefold increase in taxes, thus helping to solve urban financial problems.

A small beginning during the New Deal had involved federal clearing of slums and construction of public housing. From 1937 on, the federal government helped cities in the undertaking. The 1949 legislation provided for a bold departure. The federal government would help cities finance the purchase of slum land, which would then be sold to private entrepreneurs at reduced costs. Federal loans or mortgage insurance gave these builders a further profit incentive. Thus private enterprise would be persuaded to rebuild the cities.

For five years the program made little progress and thereafter seemed most effective in producing profits for the entrepreneurs. There were numerous complaints that it was the land where the poorest people (often Negroes) lived that was being taken over, and that these people seldom received adequate housing elsewhere at rents they could afford. Sometimes land was cleared and left idle for years while builders were sought. Sometimes the new construction was a complex of luxury apartments, as in the West End of Boston.

Beautification, cleanliness, and safety were also problems requiring community and even national action. Cities in an affluent society produced ever-increasing quantities of waste. Keeping streets and vacant lots clean was relatively simple compared with disposing of the innumerable tons of sewage, garbage, and trash. In 1920 the average person threw away less than 3 pounds of refuse per day; by the mid-sixties he was discarding 4.5 pounds. Household and industrial waste had turned many of the nation's rivers into huge sewers. Smoke and fumes from industries, automobiles, incinerators, and burning dumps created acute smog hazards in widespread areas.

The Transportation Headache

Increasingly, after World War II, older modes of conveyance deteriorated. Streetcars, which had taken over America in the early years of the twentieth century, almost completely disappeared, to be supplanted by buses or additional subways. Transit lines, unable to meet rising costs with revenues that failed to keep pace, faced bankruptcy. Municipally owned systems ran heavier and heavier deficits. Between 1955 and 1965 the number of riders on public transit lines declined 25 percent. Railroads, to cut losses, tried to drop commuter services. The number of passengers commuting by train declined 45 percent between 1929 and 1963 and continued to decline thereafter. City dwellers and suburbanites depended more and more upon automobiles, but automobiles required six to forty-five times more space on highways per passenger than did buses, and multiple-unit rail cars were even more efficient.

While public transportation languished, the federal government helped subsidize the building of 6,000 miles of expressways. This forced the leveling of countless blocks of urban buildings (including a disproportionate amount of poor peoples' housing), and other buildings were leveled to provide parking lots. As a consequence, still more automobiles poured into the cities, compounding traffic problems and, during public transportation strikes, creating chaos. An opposite approach at both the local and federal level was to try to improve public transit or even to develop new systems as, most spectacularly, in the San Francisco Bay region. In 1966 Congress created a new Department of Transportation.

National transportation problems were interrelated, as railroad passenger service rapidly declined, and trucks became an increasingly important factor in carrying freight. The large-scale program of turnpike building that marked the first decade after World War II came to an end as thousands of miles of toll-free superhighways were built, beginning with the Interstate Highway Act of 1956, which set standards for the roads (no grade crossings, for example) and provided federal funds for 90 percent of the cost. For public transportation, Americans had to depend either upon buses or airlines.

By the mid-fifties, airlines, which had been luxury transportation before World War II, were carrying over 30 million passengers per year. By the mid-sixties, the figure had nearly quadrupled and was expected to double again within a decade. Especially along the northeast coast, the air lanes were so crowded that at the height of the evening rush, about 100 planes would be landing or about to land at the three major New York area airports, while another 250 private planes were also taking off or landing at these and smaller fields. Despite an occasional collision, and numerous near collisions, the airlines were able to boast a remarkable safety record. But the congestion of people at the major airports worsened with the appearance, in 1970, of the "jumbo jet" carrying more than twice as many passengers as any previous airliner.

For the future, when airlines might not be able to meet the passenger demands along the north-east corridor between Washington and Boston, the federal government was fostering high-speed train service, which it hoped ultimately would carry passengers at 160 miles an hour. The Metroliner, with a speed of 120 miles an hour, was operating between New York and Washington by 1969. There might be a future along a few congested routes for rail passenger service of this sort. In the early 1970s a government-owned corporation, Amtrak, was running passenger trains on a number of railroad lines and was attracting more and more riders, despite the handicap of poor roadbeds and rolling stock. The principal railroad companies of the Northeast were bankrupt or facing bankruptcy, however, and only massive federal aid could keep them in business.

The Costs of Abundance

For the American people as a whole, the quarter century following World War II was a time of unprecedented enjoyment of material things. But abundance had its costs in the pollution of the environment and the depletion of natural resources. By the 1970s some believed that the age of plenty was about over and a new age of scarcity was at hand.

In the 1960s most Americans were still enjoying a living standard far higher than any they had previously known. Though the population had been growing, the output of goods and services had been growing much faster. Even allowing for the rise in prices and in taxes, the average person was better off than ever before. True, income continued to be very unevenly distributed, the top 5 percent of the people receiving 20 percent of the income, yet workers were getting more pay for less work than in the past. With a forty-hour instead of a forty-four-hour week, and with paid vacations, the average industrial employee enjoyed much more free time than his father or grandfather had in 1900. Workers could afford to spend a smaller proportion of their wages for food, clothing, and shelter and a larger proportion for automobiles, appliances, medical care, recreation, and other luxuries. Even among families classified as living in "poverty" (having an income of less than $4,000 a year), 60 percent owned automobiles in 1960. In 1964, 93 percent of the homes, including those of the poor as well as the rich, contained television sets.

The goods that came forth in such abundance were produced by industries the ownership and control of which were more and more highly concentrated. In 1960 the eighty-seven largest corporations held 26 percent of the total of corporate assets, and in 1970 they held 46 percent. During the 1960s companies merged at a faster rate than ever, usually to form conglomerates. Many of these became "multi-national" firms by acquiring subsidiaries in foreign countries. Corporations, "agribusinesses," took over a larger and larger share of agriculture in the United States, and the average size of farms increased as the number of farms declined.

While consumers enjoyed the bounty that industry provided, a growing number of them complained that too many of the products were useless, dangerous, falsely advertised, overpriced, defective, or lacking in durability. The complaints resulted in an accelerating movement for consumer protection. As early as the 1920s the Consumers Union had begun to test products and issue reports on them. In 1966 Ralph Nader emerged as a leading advocate of the new consumerism when he published a book, *Unsafe at Any Speed,* exposing the built-in hazards of many American cars. Nader started a number of consumer organizations to bring public pressure on both business and government.

Public services were less plentiful and of lower quality than commercial services and commodities. As population grew, the construction and maintenance of schools, hospitals, streets, sewers, public housing, and other community facilities fell behind the mounting needs. The times were characterized by private wealth and public poverty. That was the theme of John K. Galbraith's widely quoted book *The Affluent Society* (1958). "The line which divides our area of wealth from our area of poverty," Galbraith wrote, "is roughly that which divides privately produced and marketed goods and services from publicly rendered services." The contrast was symbolized by the picture he described of a prosperous middle-class family drivng in an air-conditioned car, over poorly paved and trash-littered streets and billboard-cluttered highways, to lunch on "exquisitely packaged food from a portable ice box" at a picinic spot beside a polluted stream.

There seemed to be, in some material re-

spects, a lowering of the quality of American life, and for much of this the population growth itself was responsible. The results of growth, as the sociologist Dennis H. Wrong pointed out, included "traffic jams, spreading urban and suburban blight, the overcrowding and destruction of beaches, parks, and other outdoor recreational facilities, water shortages, air pollution," and "deterioration in professional and social services resulting from shortages of trained personnel."

The worsening pollution of the environment resulted not only from population growth but, much more, from the great increase in factory output and from the development of new industrial processes and products. The production of synthetic fibers, for example, used more energy and hence directly or indirectly yielded more pollutants than the production of cotton or wool. Synthetic detergents, plastic materials, and aluminum cans were not biodegradable as were the objects for which they were substituted.

One of the worst offenders, with regard to air pollution, was the automobile. Motor vehicle registrations, which had amounted to only 8,000 in 1900, rose from 31 million in 1945 to 109 million in 1970. Thus the number of vehicles grew by more than 300 percent while the number of people was growing by about 50 percent. Many of the newer cars and trucks had more powerful, higher-compression engines than earlier models and gave poorer mileage while using high-test gasoline that contained a lead compound, an additional pollutant.

The befouling of air and water posed an immediate threat to human well-being and an ultimate threat to human existence. Environmentalists raised a demand for government action, and Congress responded with the Clean Air Acts of 1963, 1965, and 1970. These encouraged states and municipalities to set up their own programs for controlling pollution from stationary sources and required car manufacturers to see that vehicle emissions were drastically cut by 1975. Pittsburgh had long since set an example for other municipalities by starting, in 1941, a smoke-abatement program which, by the 1950s, had changed the city from one of the smoggiest and grimiest to one of the cleanest. Most communities, however, were slow to act, though some of them experimented with methods of transforming waste into salable products—converting fly ash from incinerators into an ingredient for concrete, manufacturing fertilizer from garbage and sewage, and retrieving metal from dumps. Industrialists generally resisted the application of antipollution measures to their own industries, since such measures tended to raise production costs and to place their products at a competitive disadvantage.

The war effort of 1941–1945 had used up tremendous quantities of raw materials, and the ensuing production boom used up still larger quantities, especially of fossil fuel. After the war, Americans turned more and more away from coal to oil and natural gas for generating electrical energy as well as for heating houses and other buildings. Manufacturers of plastics, synthetic fibers, and petrochemicals demanded increasing quantities of petroleum as a raw material. Drivers of cars, trucks, and buses added greatly to the demand, and the air force added further with its fueling of bombers in Vietnam.

Signs of an approaching "energy crisis" appeared in the United States as early as the mid-1960s, with the sudden failures of the electrical supply and the temporary blackouts of New York City and other areas in the Northeast. The events of 1973–1974 — the restrictions on oil exports by the Arabs and the fantastic price increases by the Arabs and other foreign producers — only made acute a condition that was already on the way to becoming chronic. For the indefinite future, Americans faced recurring energy shortages and price increases. They could take little comfort in the probability that they would not be quite so bad off as the Europeans or the Japanese.

The United States still possessed considerable oil resources, already discovered or yet to be discovered, in addition to vast shale deposits that eventually could be made to yield petroleum. The country had enough coal in the ground to last for centuries. It also had the capacity to build additional atomic-power plants. But the exploitation of petroleum, coal, or atomic fission endangered the environment in one way or another — through possible spills from drilling, damage to surroundings from oil transportation (as in the case of the Alaska pipeline to bring oil south from new Alaskan fields), destruction of mountains to get at shale, scarring of land by strip mining, pollution of air by the burning of low-grade coal, leakage of radioactive wastes from an atomic reactor, or some even more deadly accident with an atomic power plant.

In time the harnessing of the sun's rays might provide clean energy, but other resources would remain scarce in comparison with the abundant supplies of the past. Seemingly, as they advanced toward the twenty-first century, Americans would have to face the necessity of stabilizing their population and using energy and raw materials more efficiently.

Education

The prosperity of the postwar era both depended upon and supported the rapid growth of education systems. After World War II, critics of public education charged that the schools were neglecting things of the mind in favor of athletics, band contests, vocational training, and "life adjustment." When the Soviet Union launched the first artificial satellite, sputnik, in 1957, many Americans assumed that the Russians had proved the superiority of their education in science and technology. A demand arose for fewer "frills" and more intellectual rigor, and school officials, teachers, and pupils responded. So did Congress. In 1958 it passed the National Defense Education Act, which provided for the spending of nearly a billion dollars over a four-year period to encourage the study of science, mathematics, and foreign languages.

Nevertheless, the schools continued to be criticized for their performance. At the end of the 1960s it appeared that 10 to 15 of every 100 pupils entering the fourth grade could not read (in ghetto schools, 35 to 50 of every 100). About 25 million adults in the nation as a whole were functionally illiterate, unable to comprehend a newspaper or magazine article or to fill out an application form. Most of these people were school dropouts.

With the gaining momentum of the civil rights movement, the emphasis of school reformers had shifted from academic excellence to equality of educational opportunity. This presumably would help the poor to rise out of poverty. But Christopher Jencks and seven associates at Harvard University's Center for Educational Policy Research questioned the assumption in a 1972 report. "If we want economic equality in our society," Jencks wrote, "we will have to get it by changing our economic institutions, not by changing the schools."

In fact, educational equality was yet to be tried. Annual expenditures per pupil ranged from a few hundred dollars in some schools to several thousand in others, even within the same state. Schools depended mainly on local property taxes, and resources therefore varied tremendously as between the poorest and the wealthiest districts. In the early 1970s, after the supreme court of California had declared the reliance on local school taxes unconstitutional in that state, suits were brought against similar financing arrangements in more than thirty other states.

The swelling enrollments of the 1950s and 1960s necessitated costly programs of school construction. At first the voters responded willingly by approving the issue of construction bonds, but eventually they grew more and more reluctant. In 1960 they approved nearly 90 percent of the bond issues put to referendums; in 1970, less than 47 percent. Undoubtedly the people were reacting against rising taxes, but they also seemed to be expressing a decline of confidence in the public schools.

During World War II, colleges and universities suffered from a loss of male students to the draft. The federal government helped many institutions by contracting with them to educate and train various kinds of specialists for the armed forces. After the war the government contributed to a sudden bulge in enrollments by paying the college expenses of veterans under the "GI Bill of Rights." During the 1950s and 1960s, attendance continued to swell, and at a faster rate than the college-age population, for a larger and larger proportion of young people were going on to secondary and higher education. And, at the same time, demand for professional workers grew rapidly. Consequently, graduate and professional schools were especially thriving, as the demand for university teachers and other professional workers grew. The federal government heavily subsidized many programs that were directly or indirectly related to the national defense. State universities multiplied as teachers' colleges were converted into general colleges and these were raised, at least in name, to university status. Large campuses grew larger still—there were thirty-nine

with more than 20,000 students in 1969 as compared with only two in 1941.

By the early 1970s the quarter-century-long academic boom appeared to be at an end. Federal support had been curtailed. Enrollments were leveling off and, in many institutions, even falling, while unemployment rose among holders of the Ph.D. and other advanced degrees. Private institutions, having had to raise tuition charges repeatedly to meet rising costs, had lagged far behind in the recruitment of students. Now many of the smaller and financially weaker private colleges faced the threat of extinction.

The first postwar generation of college students—especially the veterans, or GIs—seemed to be mainly interested in getting a degree to get ahead. A survey of members of the class of '49 concluded that they were "curiously old before their time" and were concentrating on the pursuit of economic security. Students of the 1950s also appeared to be looking ahead to jobs, especially corporation jobs. The prevailing campus spirit was quiet and conformist.

Then in 1964 the campus of the University of California at Berkeley erupted, and during the next several years other large universities from coast to coast experienced a succession of student riots, with the rioters taking over and sometimes fire-bombing university buildings and vandalizing business properties in the neighborhood. The rioters were giving expression to a variety of complaints—the impersonality of the gigantic and complex "multiversity," the irrelevance of its curriculum to their personal needs, and the complicity of the universities in the Vietnam War (through war-related research and through the training of military officers in the ROTC).

Colleges and universities responded to demands for "relevance" and personal involvement by relaxing requirements, adding courses in "black studies," "environmental studies," and other contemporary concerns, and giving students some voice in administration. Some institutions, such as the City University of New York, adopted a policy of "open admissions," eliminating most entrance requirements. By the 1970s these new programs appeared to have wrought little basic change in the substance of higher education. And the economic contraction of the mid-1970s, with its high unemployment rate for young people and its tightening of university budgets, encouraged resumed enthusiasm on the part of both students and administrators for traditional programs with clear vocational objectives.

The "Counter Culture"

During the 1960s the growing university population of upper-middle-class white youth formed the core of participants in what became known as the "counter culture." These young people, joined by some of their elders, rejected prevailing cultural norms. There was a political dimension to this challenge: a criticism of racial and sexual discrimination, of restrictions on sexual behavior, of the war in Vietnam, and of national growth policies that threatened the physical environment. But what was unique and distinctive was a fervent assault on reason, systematic knowledge, the work ethic, and the related presumption that wealth and power ought to be distributed according to productivity. In its most extreme forms, this enthusiasm included experimentation with drugs, mysticism, witchcraft, astrology, evangelical religion, and "acid rock." The movement found articulate descriptions in Theodore Roszak's *The Making of a Counter Culture* (1969) and Charles Reich's *The Greening of America* (1970). Roszak wrote: "Nothing less is required than the subversion of the scientific world view with its entrenched commitment to an egocentric and cerebral mode of consciousness. In its place, there must be a new culture in which the non-intellective capacities of personality — those capacities that take fire from visionary splendor and the experiences of human communion — become the arbiters of the true, the good and the beautiful."

By the 1970s the most exaggerated forms of the counter-culture movement were on the wane. They appeared to have been the special product of an unusually large population of young people (a result of the baby boom of the 1940s); the high prosperity of the 1960s, which released young people from pressing material concerns; the inhumanity of the Vietnam War and the threat of the draft; and the unusual pressures created by parents who had reacted to the crises of depression and world war by turning inward to emphasize family "togetherness." During the 1970s the end of the Vietnam War, the return of economic depression, the declines in fertility rate, family size, and the relative number of young people, and the growing tolerance of the adult population stemmed the cultural excesses of the 1960s.

The "Permissive" Society

Much of the nation believed that the cultural revolution of the 1960s was simply a youthful phenomenon, but in fact adults participated as well — not only in the antiwar, environmental, and feminist crusades, but in the recasting of sexual norms. This was nothing new. Significant deviation from Victorian sexual ideals had begun after World War I, and it was possible, in any case, that Victorian norms had never accurately reflected actual behavior.

Perhaps in reaction to the unusually intense enthusiasm for traditional family life that had followed World War II (and had produced high fertility rates), the rate of divorce increased dramatically during the 1960s. In 1960, there was one annulment or divorce for every four marriages; by 1970, one for every three. Contributing to that increase was the growing independence and the enhanced self-image of women, more and more of whom were working outside the home.

There was talk of a "sexual revolution" in the 1960s as sex relations outside of marriage appeared to become much more widespread than ever before. Presumably oral contraceptives (the "pill") and the erosion of the "double standard" for sexual behavior encouraged extramarital intercourse. But studies by Dr. Alfred C. Kinsey and his Institute for Sex Research at Indiana University, cast doubt on the idea of a revolution. Kinsey's *Sexual Behavior in the Human Male* (1948) showed that among the preceding generation of Americans sex activity had been much more varied than laws or morals would have led anyone to believe. "People talk more freely about sex nowadays, and young people are far more tolerant and permissive regarding sex," Kinsey's successor observed in the 1960s. Yet, though premarital intercourse had increased, it had not risen suddenly or dramatically; "it has been on the rise ever since the turn of the century."

For some women, sexual freedom meant freedom from unwanted children, not only through contraception but, when necessary, through abortion. Advocates of abortion-on-demand asserted the right of a woman to control her own body. Opponents insisted on the right of the unborn to the enjoyment of life. A few states liberalized their laws to permit abortion under a wide range of conditions, but most of the states retained laws that made it difficult if not impossible —except for illegal and often dangerous practitioners. In 1973 the Supreme Court struck down those state laws that prohibited abortion during the first three months of pregnancy.

Freedom of sexual expression in words and pictures raised another constitutional issue, that of freedom of speech and the press. In 1957 the Supreme Court narrowed the legal definition of obscenity to include only those works that were morally offensive by prevailing national standards and were "utterly without redeeming social value." This decision put the burden of proof on local authorities in obscenity cases. It opened the way for an unprecedented flood of pornography. President Johnson appointed a Commission on Obscenity and Pornography to study the effects. The commission finally reported, in 1970, that "exposure to explicit sexual materials" apparently had little or nothing to do with causing emotional disorders, delinquency, or crime. The commission recommended the repeal of all laws forbidding the dissemination of such materials to consenting adults. Instead of acting on that recommendation, President Nixon denounced the report as "morally bankrupt," and the Senate condemned it by a vote of 60 to 5. The Supreme Court, instead of further relaxing its stand, soon practically reversed itself. In 1973 it held that works were obscene if they lacked "serious literary, artistic, political, or scientific value" and if they were offensive by the standards of the local community. The burden of proof was now on the defendant, and local authorities here and there began successfully to prosecute.

The Arts and Literature

Despite the flowering of rock-and-roll, the blossoming of mass pornography, and the antiformalism of the counter culture, the American public continued to have a keen taste for tradi-

tional artistic modes during the 1960s. Indeed, never had so many Americans shown so much interest in literature, art, and music as they did during the age of affluence that followed World War II. To some extent the federal and state governments encouraged cultural activity, the federal government establishing (1966) the Federal Arts and Humanities Endowments and a Federal Council on the Arts, and each of the states setting up its own arts council or commission. Some of the councils made financial grants, and private foundations provided more substantial sums. Most of the activity, however, was financed by individual spending.

The catering to cultural interests became a big business in itself. By the end of the 1960s, total expenditures were approaching $7 billion a year. (They had been $3 billion in 1960.) People were spending twice as much on the arts as on recreation in general and six times as much as on sports.

Despite continuing predictions of its imminent demise, the novel continued to be the most popular medium of literary expression and a continuing source of artistic excitement. The most prestigious figures in American writing during the quarter century after World War II were those who had made their reputations in earlier decades. Through the fifties, Ernest Hemingway and William Faulkner remained two of the patriarchs of literature for the Western world as well as for the United States. These men of great reputation were joined by a large new generation of vigorous writers. Among the novelists, their work ranged from the realism of John O'Hara and James Gould Cozzens, portrayers of the upper middle class, through a variety of newer styles and themes. The work of Robert Penn Warren, who won the Pulitzer Prize in both poetry and fiction, transcended Southern regionalism, but his most widely read novel, *All the King's Men* (1946), was a study of a political leader resembling Huey Long of Louisiana. In 1948 Norman Mailer produced the most acclaimed of the novels that came out of World War II, *The Naked and the Dead,* but in his subsequent work was more successful as a writer of nonfiction. J. D. Salinger through his account of the inward torture of an adolescent boy, *Catcher in the Rye* (1951), and subsequent stories about the precocious members of the Glass family (*Franny and Zooey,* 1962) became the spokesman for the generation of the 1950s.

Through the writings of several of the novelists ran a theme of alienation from, or at least serious questioning of, their culture. Saul Bellow began his work in this vein with *Dangling Man* (1944) and continued it in a number of successful novels, including *The Adventures of Augie March* (1953) and *Herzog* (1964). Nelson Algren wrote with blunt clarity about the flotsam of society, the men and women who had never had a chance, in his stories and novels, most notably, *The Man with the Golden Arm* (1949). Several Negro writers fell within this pattern. The most famous was James Baldwin, perhaps at his best in works of nonfiction like *The Fire Next Time* (1963); the most bitter, the poet and playwright, LeRoi Jones, especially effective in his one-act plays; and the most distinguished, Ralph Ellison, for a single novel, *Invisible Man* (1952). When the New York *Herald Tribune Book Week* in 1965 queried some 200 critics, authors, and editors, their consensus was that the work of fiction of the previous two decades most memorable and most likely to endure was *Invisible Man*. It is the sweeping, at times fantastic, drama of a young Negro's quest for identity.

Among the novelists who emerged in the 1960s, perhaps the most notable were John Barth, Joseph Heller, Kurt Vonnegut, Jr., and Thomas Pynchon. Each dealt in his own way with what seemed to all of them like the cosmic absurdity of contemporary life. They were less interested in developing character or plot than in creating effects of intellectual ambiguity and emotional contradiction. In his mock-picaresque novel *The Sot-Weed Factor* (1961) Barth gave the impression that people could find no meaning in life except for the realization that they were merely acting their parts in a farce that had been written for them. In *Catch-22* (1964) Heller ridiculed the insanity and regimentation of war and, by implication, the insanity and regimentation of business society. In *Slaughterhouse-Five* (1969), his sixth novel, Vonnegut used his experience in World War II as a springboard for science fiction in which horror was mixed with humor. In his third novel, *Gravity's Rainbow* (1973), Pynchon made his central figure a German V-2 rocket of World War II. Baffling, jarring, full of complex symbolism, Pynchon's book gave an apocalyptic vision of man's place in the universe. Some reviewers hailed it as the greatest American novel since *Moby Dick*.

The Role of Television

Television changed the leisure habits of the American people, made them better informed on the news and issues of the day, and even modified the patterns of American politics. In 1947 fewer than 10,000 people owned television sets with which they could view programs a few hours a day from a handful of stations. A decade later over 40 million sets in homes, hotels, and bars were tuned in to 467 stations. Motion-picture attendance dropped from a wartime high of 90 million a week to about 40 million. Not until the sixties did Hollywood begin to recuperate, by producing pictures that were better than before, or at least bolder. Professional sports, especially football and basketball, flourished as television brought them to millions of spectators at a time.

Television even more than radio meant mass communication to a nationwide audience. One musical show, telecast on 245 stations one night in March 1957 reached an estimated audience of 100 million — enough people to fill a Broadway theater every night for 165 years. Beginning with the 1952 campaign, television remade presidential elections as candidates began to make extensive and expensive use of the new medium. Radio was far from superseded, especially in the transistorized portable form that took over not only the United States but the entire world during these years.

Advertisers paid for the vast outpouring from commercial television and radio stations. They spent enormous sums to compete for the attention of the average television viewer who, surveys indicated, sat in front of his set as much as six hours a day. The manufacturers of one headache remedy, for example, spent nearly $750,000 in one month in 1958; their two nearest competitors spent a combined total of nearly $1 million that same month. In consequence, programs were patterned to draw the largest number of viewers, and when surveys indicated that the sets were tuned in elsewhere, the programs were ruthlessly pruned. Television lost one of its biggest sources of income when the federal government banned cigarette commercials after January 1, 1971.

One critic, Richard Schickel, commented that, to literate people, television was "an unparalleled purveyor of trash." Nevertheless, "we sit there, eyes glued to the set, watching this explication of the obvious in hateful fascination." A Canadian scholar, Marshall McLuhan, won a large following by extolling in confusing but thought-provoking prose the new era of mass media. He wrote, in *The Medium Is the Message* (1967): "The contained, the distinct, the separate — our western legacy — are being replaced by the flowing, the unified, the fused." The electronic medium of communication made its impressions all at once, he said, in contrast to the print medium, which made its impressions one after another. One reason for the generation gap and the youth revolt, he suggested, was the influence of the new medium on the young, who for the first time had been exposed to it in their formative years.

Foundations and the federal government tried to further the positive role of television. The Carnegie and Ford foundations proposed that educational stations be encouraged to take advantage of television's educational and cultural potentialities. The Public Broadcasting Act of 1967 authorized, though it provided no financing for, a noncommercial television network. Soon university-affiliated and other stations from coast to coast were providing high-quality theater, musical performances, and lecture courses with the cooperation of the Public Broadcasting System.

Commercial stations received and transmitted a large share of their programs from one or another of three great networks, the American Broadcasting Company, the National Broadcasting Company, and the Columbia Broadcasting System. These sources provided not only entertainment but also news and opinion for their affiliated stations. Bringing world events, or chosen segments of them, visibly into the home, the network programs had a much greater emotional impact (as in reporting the Vietnam War) than did newspaper accounts. A comparatively small number of prestigious commentators, outstanding among them Walter Cronkite of CBS, dominated the presentation of TV news. Hence questions arose regarding the breadth and balance of the coverage.

Vice President Agnew and other spokesmen for the Nixon administration, as well as Nixon himself, objected strongly to what they considered hostile treatment by the news media, especially television. Agnew demanded that commentators be "made more responsible to the views of the nation." The director of the White House Office of Telecommunications Policy attacked TV newsmen as "so-called professionals who confuse sensation with sense and who dispense elitist gossip in the guise of news analysis." He proposed a law that would put the responsibility on local stations for assuring "fairness," and the administration threatened to revoke the licenses of stations that failed to meet its standards.

An independent study (1973) by the Twentieth Century Fund concluded, however, that "presidential television" gave the President a great advantage over his critics. "Presidential television means the ability to appear simultaneously on all national radio and television networks at prime, large-audience evening hours, virtually whenever and however he wishes." Nixon exploited this advantage even more than his predecessors, taking as much TV time during his first eighteen months in office as Eisenhower, Kennedy, and Johnson together had taken during theirs. Congress, the courts, the opposition party could not keep up with the President in his ability to command free time on the air. Television appeared to be one of the factors that had increased the power of the executive as against that of the other branches of government. But at the same time, television exposure no doubt accelerated the demise of the Nixon administration as the relentless flow of Watergate developments on the nightly news contributed powerfully to the building of hostile public opinion. As a result some pundits speculated that the nation had entered an era of short-term Presidents since television coverage meant that they could not obscure their errors as effectively as their predecessors had. At the very least, the medium of television meant that Americans had come to participate in the communal life of a giant nation with unprecedented intimacy and intensity. That participation would no doubt keep the pace of cultural change close to the frenetic level reached during the 1960s.

On the Kennedy and Johnson administrations, see A. M. Schlesinger, Jr., *A Thousand Days: John F. Kennedy in the White House** (1965), a superb memoir and first-rate history. See also T. C. Sorensen, *Kennedy** (1965); Tom Wicker, *JFK and LBJ: The Influence of Personality upon Politics* (1968); A. D. Donald, ed., *John F. Kennedy and the New Frontier** (1966); J. F. Heath, *John F. Kennedy and the Business Community* (1969); T. H. White, *The Making of the President, 1960** (1961); Rowland Evans and Robert Novak, *Lyndon B. Johnson: The Exercise of Power** (1966); and E. F. Goldman, *The Tragedy of Lyndon Johnson** (1969).

On prosperity and poverty: H. G. Vatter, *The U.S. Economy in the 1950's** (1963); Walter Heller, *New Dimensions of Political Economy* (1966); Michael Harrington, *The Other America: Poverty in the United States* (1962); H. P. Miller, *Rich Man, Poor Man** (1964); Oscar Lewis, *La Vida: A Puerto Rican Family in the Culture of Poverty—San Juan and New York** (1966); H. M. Caudill, *Night Comes to the Cumberlands* (1963), on poverty in the Appalachians; J. D. Donovan, *The Politics of Poverty* (1967); Sar Levitan, *The Great Society's Poor Law: A New Approach to Poverty* (1969).

On civil rights and blacks: M. L. King, Jr., *Stride Toward Freedom** (1958) and *Why We Can't Wait** (1964); James Baldwin, *The Fire Next Time* (1963); *The Autobiography of Malcolm X** (1966); James Farmer, *Freedom—When?* (1966); Stokely Carmichael and C. V. Hamilton, *Black Power: The Politics of Liberation in America** (1967); Anthony Lewis, *Portrait of a Decade: The Second American Revolution* (1964); Louis Harlan, *Separate and Unequal** (1961), on segregated schools; A. P. Blaustein and C. C. Ferguson, *Desegregation and the Law** (1962); J. W. Silver, *Mississippi: The Closed Society** (1964); A. I. Waskow, *From Race Riot to Sit-In: 1919 and the 1960's* (1966); James Peck, *Freedom Ride* (1962); D. R. Matthews and J. W. Prothro, *Negroes and the New Southern Politics** (1966); N. V. Bartley, *The Rise of Massive Resistance: Race and Politics in the South During the 1950's* (1969); Lee Rainwater and W. L. Yancey, *The Moynihan Report and the Politics of Controversy** (1967); *Report of the National Advisory Committee on Civil Disorders** (1968); and A. Meier and E. Rudwick, *CORE: A Study in the Civil Rights Movement, 1942–1968* (1973).

On Indians and Chicanos: Stan Steiner, *The New Indians** (1968); Vine Deloria, Jr., *Custer Died for Your Sins* (1969); H. W. Hertzberg, *The Search for an American Indian Identity: Modern Pan-Indian Movements* (1971); W. E. Washburn, *Red Man's Land/White Man's Law: A Study of the Past and Present Status of the American Indian* (1971); A. M. Josephy, ed., *Red Power** (1971); S. A. Levitan and B. Hetrick, *Big Brother's Indian Programs* (1972); Wayne Moquin, ed., *A Documentary History of the Mexican-Americans* (1971); Stan Steiner, *La Raza** (1970); and M. S. Meier and F. Rivera, *The Chicanos: A History of Mexican Americans* (1972).

On woman's place: W. H. Chafe, *The American Woman: Her Changing Social, Economic, and Political Roles, 1920–1970* (1972); Judith Hole and Ellen Levine, eds., *Rebirth of Feminism* (1972); and Elizabeth Janeway, *Man's World, Woman's Place: A Study in Social Mythology* (1971).

On the Nixon administration: T. H. White, *The Making of the President, 1968** (1969); J. McGinniss, *The Selling of the President, 1968* (1970); Garry Wills, *Nixon Agonistes** (1970); R. M. Scammon and B. J. Wattenberg, *The Real Majority* (1970); and Carl Bernstein and Bob Woodward, *All the President's Men** (1974).

On the Vietnam War and its background: David Halberstam, *The Making of a Quagmire* (1956); A. M. Schlesinger, Jr., *The Bitter Heritage: Vietnam and American Democracy, 1941–1966* (1967); Neil Sheehan and others, *The Pentagon Papers** (1971); David Halberstam, *The Best and the Brightest** (1972).

On American society and culture in the 1960s, see: B. J. Wattenberg and R. M. Scammon, *This U.S.A., An Unexpected Family Portrait . . . Drawn from the Census* (1965); National Commission on Technology, Automation and Economic Progress, *Technology and the American Economy* (1966); W. W. Heller, *New Dimensions of Political Economy* (1966); J. K. Galbraith, *The New Industrial State* (1967); Herbert Stein, *The Fiscal Revolution in America* (1969); D. K. Price, *The Scientific Estate* (1965); J. N. Wilford, *We Reach the Moon* (1969); Charles Abrams, *The City Is the Frontier** (1965); President's Commission on Law Enforcement and Administration of Justice, *The Challenge of Crime in a Free Society* (1967); Frank Graham, *Disaster by Default: Politics and Water Pollution* (1966); Ronald Berman, *America in the Sixties: An Intellectual History* (1968); Richard Kostelanetz, ed., *The New American Arts** (1965); Barbara Rose, *American Art Since 1900** (1967); R. Kostelanetz, ed., *On Contemporary American Literature** (1969); E. H. Erikson, *Identity: Youth and Crisis* (1968); M. E. Marty *et al., What Do We Believe? The Stance of Religion in America* (1968); and W. L. O'Neill, *Coming Apart: An Informal History of America in the 1960s* (1971).

* Titles available in paperback.

Appendices

The Declaration of Independence

In Congress, July 4, 1776,

THE UNANIMOUS DECLARATION OF THE THIRTEEN UNITED STATES OF AMERICA

When, in the course of human events, it becomes necessary for one people to dissolve the political bands which have connected them with another, and to assume, among the powers of the earth, the separate and equal station to which the laws of nature and of nature's God entitle them, a decent respect to the opinions of mankind requires that they should declare the causes which impel them to the separation.

We hold these truths to be self-evident, that all men are created equal; that they are endowed by their Creator with certain unalienable rights; that among these, are life, liberty, and the pursuit of happiness. That, to secure these rights, governments are instituted among men, deriving their just powers from the consent of the governed; that, whenever any form of government becomes destructive of these ends, it is the right of the people to alter or to abolish it, and to institute a new government, laying its foundation on such principles, and organizing its powers in such form, as to them shall seem most likely to effect their safety and happiness. Prudence, indeed, will dictate that governments long established, should not be changed for light and transient causes; and, accordingly, all experience hath shown, that mankind are more disposed to suffer, while evils are sufferable, than to right themselves by abolishing the forms to which they are accustomed. But, when a long train of abuses and usurpations, pursuing invariably the same object, evinces a design to reduce them under absolute despotism, it is their right, it is their duty, to throw off such government and to provide new guards for their future security. Such has been the patient sufferance of these colonies, and such is now the necessity which constrains them to alter their former systems of government. The history of the present King of Great Britain is a history of repeated injuries and usurpations, all having, in direct object, the establishment of an absolute tyranny over these States. To prove this, let facts be submitted to a candid world: —

He has refused his assent to laws the most wholesome and necessary for the public good.

He has forbidden his governors to pass laws of immediate and pressing importance, unless suspended in their operation till his assent should be obtained; and, when so suspended, he has utterly neglected to attend to them.

He has refused to pass other laws for the accommodation of large districts of people, unless those people would relinquish the right of representation in the legislature; a right inestimable to them, and formidable to tyrants only.

He has called together legislative bodies at places unusual, uncomfortable, and distant from the depository of their public records, for the sole purpose of fatiguing them into compliance with his measures.

He has dissolved representative houses repeatedly for opposing, with manly firmness, his invasions on the rights of the people.

He has refused, for a long time after such dissolutions, to cause others to be elected; whereby the legislative powers, incapable of annihilation, have returned to the people at large for their exercise; the state remaining, in the meantime, exposed to all the danger of invasion from without, and convulsions within.

He has endeavored to prevent the population of these States; for that purpose, obstructing the laws for naturalization of foreigners, refusing to pass others to encourage their migration hither, and raising the conditions of new appropriations of lands.

He has obstructed the administration of justice, by refusing his assent to laws for establishing judiciary powers.

He has made judges dependent on his will alone, for the tenure of their offices, and the amount and payment of their salaries.

He has erected a multitude of new offices, and sent hither swarms of officers to harass our people, and eat out their substance.

He has kept among us, in time of peace, standing armies, without the consent of our legislatures.

He has affected to render the military independent of, and superior to, the civil power.

He has combined, with others, to subject us to a jurisdiction foreign to our Constitution, and unacknowledged by our laws; giving his assent to their acts of pretended legislation:

For quartering large bodies of armed troops among us:

For protecting them by a mock trial, from punishment, for any murders which they should commit on the inhabitants of these States:

For cutting off our trade with all parts of the world:

For imposing taxes on us without our consent:

For depriving us, in many cases, of the benefit of trial by jury:

For transporting us beyond seas to be tried for pretended offences:

For abolishing the free system of English laws in a neighboring province, establishing therein an arbitrary government, and enlarging its boundaries, so as to render it at once an example and fit instrument for introducing the same absolute rule into these colonies:

For taking away our charters, abolishing our most valuable laws, and altering, fundamentally, the powers of our governments:

For suspending our own legislatures, and declaring themselves invested with power to legislate for us in all cases whatsoever.

He has abdicated government here, by declaring us out of his protection, and waging war against us.

He has plundered our seas, ravaged our coasts, burnt our towns, and destroyed the lives of our people.

He is, at this time, transporting large armies of foreign mercenaries to complete the works of death, desolation, and tyranny, already begun, with circumstances of cruelty and perfidy scarcely paralleled in the most barbarous ages, and totally unworthy the head of a civilized nation.

He has constrained our fellow citizens, taken captive on the high seas, to bear arms against their country, to become the executioners of their friends, and brethren, or to fall themselves by their hands.

He has excited domestic insurrections amongst us, and has endeavored to bring on the inhabitants of our frontiers, the merciless Indian savages, whose known rule of warfare is an undistinguished destruction of all ages, sexes, and conditions.

In every stage of these oppressions, we have petitioned for redress, in the most humble terms; our repeated petitions have been answered only by repeated injury. A prince, whose character is thus marked by every act which may define a tyrant, is unfit to be the ruler of a free people.

Nor have we been wanting in attention to our British brethren. We have warned them, from time to time, of attempts made by their legislature to extend an unwarrantable jurisdiction over us. We have reminded them of the circumstances of our emigration and settlement here. We have appealed to their native justice and magnanimity, and we have conjured them, by the ties of our common kindred, to disavow these usurpations, which would inevitably interrupt our connections and correspondence. They, too, have been deaf to the voice of justice and consanguinity. We must, therefore, acquiesce in the necessity which denounces our separation, and hold them as we hold the rest of mankind, enemies in war, in peace, friends.

We, therefore, the representatives of the United States of America, in general Congress assembled, appealing to the Supreme Judge of the world for the rectitude of our intentions, do, in the name, and by the authority of the good people of these colonies, solemnly publish and declare, that these united colonies are, and of right ought to be, free and independent states: that they are absolved from all allegiance to the British Crown, and that all political connection between them and the state of Great Britain is, and ought to be, totally dissolved; and that, as free and independent states, they have full power to levy war, conclude peace, contract alliances, establish commerce, and to do all other acts and things which independent states may of right do. And, for the support of this declaration, with a firm reliance on the protection of Divine Providence, we mutually pledge to each other our lives, our fortunes, and our sacred honor.

The foregoing Declaration was, by order of Congress, engrossed, and signed by the following members:

JOHN HANCOCK

New Hampshire

Josiah Bartlett
William Whipple
Matthew Thornton

Massachusetts Bay

Samuel Adams
John Adams
Robert Treat Paine
Elbridge Gerry

Rhode Island

Stephen Hopkins
William Ellery

Connecticut

Roger Sherman
Samuel Huntington
William Williams
Oliver Wolcott

New York

William Floyd
Philip Livingston
Francis Lewis
Lewis Morris

New Jersey

Richard Stockton
John Witherspoon
Francis Hopkinson
John Hart
Abraham Clark

Pennsylvania

Robert Morris
Benjamin Rush
Benjamin Franklin
John Morton
George Clymer
James Smith
George Taylor
James Wilson
George Ross

Delaware

Caesar Rodney
George Read
Thomas M'Kean

Maryland

Samuel Chase
William Paca
Thomas Stone
Charles Carroll,
  of Carrollton

Virginia

George Wythe
Richard Henry Lee
Thomas Jefferson
Benjamin Harrison
Thomas Nelson, Jr.
Francis Lightfoot Lee
Carter Braxton

North Carolina

William Hooper
Joseph Hewes
John Penn

South Carolina

Edward Rutledge
Thomas Heyward, Jr.
Thomas Lynch, Jr.
Arthur Middleton

Georgia

Button Gwinnett
Lyman Hall
George Walton

Resolved, That copies of the Declaration be sent to the several assemblies, conventions, and committees, or councils of safety, and to the several commanding officers of the continental troops; that it be proclaimed in each of the United States, at the head of the army.

The Constitution of the United States of America[1]

WE the People of the United States, in Order to form a more perfect Union, establish Justice, insure domestic Tranquility, provide for the common defence, promote the general Welfare, and secure the Blessings of Liberty to ourselves and our Posterity, do ordain and establish this CONSTITUTION for the United States of America.

Article I

SECTION 1.

All legislative Powers herein granted shall be vested in a Congress of the United States, which shall consist of a Senate and House of Representatives.

SECTION 2.

The House of Representatives shall be composed of Members chosen every second Year by the People of the several States, and the Electors in each State shall have the Qualifications requisite for Electors of the most numerous Branch of the State Legislature.

No Person shall be a Representative who shall not have attained to the Age of twenty-five Years, and been seven Years a Citizen of the United States, and who shall not, when elected, be an Inhabitant of that State in which he shall be chosen.

[Representatives and direct Taxes[2] shall be apportioned among the several States which may be included within this Union, according to their respective Numbers, which shall be determined by adding to the whole Number of free Persons, including those bound to Service for a Term of Years, and excluding Indians not taxed, three fifths of all other Persons.][3] The actual Enumeration shall be made within three Years after the first Meeting of the Congress of the United States, and within every subsequent Term of ten Years, in such Manner as they shall by Law direct. The Number of Representatives shall not exceed one for every thirty Thousand, but each State shall have at Least one Representative; and until such enumeration shall be made, the State of New Hampshire shall be entitled to chuse three, Massachusetts eight, Rhode-Island and Providence Plantations one, Connecticut five, New York six, New Jersey four, Pennsylvania eight, Delaware one, Maryland six, Virginia ten, North Carolina five, South Carolina five, and Georgia three.

When vacancies happen in the Representation from any State, the Executive Authority thereof shall issue Writs of Election to fill such Vacancies.

The House of Representatives shall chuse their Speaker and other Officers; and shall have the sole Power of Impeachment.

SECTION 3.

The Senate of the United States shall be composed of two Senators from each State, chosen by the Legislature thereof, for six Years; and each Senator shall have one Vote.

Immediately after they shall be assembled in Consequence of the first Election, they shall be divided as equally as may be into three Classes. The Seats of the Senators of the first Class shall be vacated at the Expiration of the second Year, of the second Class at the Expiration of the fourth Year, and of the third Class at the Expiration of the sixth Year, so that one-third may be chosen every second Year; and if Vacancies happen by Resignation, or otherwise, during the Recess of the Legislature of any State, the Executive thereof may make temporary Appointments until the next Meeting of the Legislature, which shall then fill such Vacancies.

No Person shall be a Senator who shall not have attained to the Age of thirty Years, and been nine Years a Citizen of the United States, and who shall not, when elected, be an Inhabitant of that State for which he shall be chosen.

[1]This version, which follows the original Constitution in capitalization and spelling, was published by the United States Department of the Interior, Office of Education, in 1935.
[2]Altered by the Sixteenth Amendment.
[3]Negated by the Fourteenth Amendment.

The Vice President of the United States shall be President of the Senate, but shall have no vote, unless they be equally divided.

The Senate shall chuse their other Officers, and also a President pro tempore, in the absence of the Vice President, or when he shall exercise the Office of President of the United States.

The Senate shall have the sole Power to try all Impeachments. When sitting for that purpose, they shall be on Oath or Affirmation. When the President of the United States is tried, the Chief Justice shall preside: And no person shall be convicted without the Concurrence of two thirds of the Members present.

Judgment in Cases of Impeachment shall not extend further than to removal from Office, and disqualification to hold and enjoy any Office of honor, Trust, or Profit under the United States: but the Party convicted shall nevertheless be liable and subject to Indictment, Trial, Judgment, and Punishment, according to Law.

SECTION 4.

The Times, Places and Manner of holding Elections for Senators and Representatives, shall be prescribed in each State by the Legislature thereof; but the Congress may at any time by Law make or alter such Regulations, except as to the Places of Chusing Senators.

The Congress shall assemble at least once in every Year, and such Meeting shall be on the first Monday in December, unless they shall by Law appoint a different Day.

SECTION 5.

Each House shall be the Judge of the Elections, Returns and Qualifications of its own Members, and a Majority of each shall constitute a Quorum to do Business; but a smaller number may adjourn from day to day, and may be authorized to compel the Attendance of absent Members, in such Manner, and under such Penalties, as each House may provide.

Each House may determine the Rules of its Proceedings, punish its Members for disorderly Behaviour, and, with the Concurrence of two thirds, expel a Member.

Each House shall keep a Journal of its Proceedings, and from time to time publish the same, excepting such Parts as may in their Judgment require Secrecy; and the Yeas and Nays of the Members of either House on any question shall, at the Desire of one fifth of those Present, be entered on the Journal.

Neither House, during the Session of Congress, shall, without the Consent of the other, adjourn for more than three days, nor to any other Place than that in which the two Houses shall be sitting.

SECTION 6.

The Senators and Representatives shall receive a Compensation for their Services, to be ascertained by Law, and paid out of the Treasury of the United States. They shall in all Cases, except Treason, Felony, and Breach of the Peace, be privileged from Arrest during their Attendance at the Session of their respective Houses, and in going to and returning from the same; and for any Speech or Debate in either House, they shall not be questioned in any other Place.

No Senator or Representative shall, during the Time for which he was elected, be appointed to any civil Office under the Authority of the United States, which shall have been created, or the Emoluments whereof shall have been increased, during such time; and no Person holding any Office under the United States shall be a Member of either House during his continuance in Office.

SECTION 7.

All Bills for raising Revenue shall originate in the House of Representatives; but the Senate may propose or concur with Amendments as on other bills.

Every Bill which shall have passed the House of Representatives and the Senate, shall, before it become a Law, be presented to the President of the United States; If he approve he shall sign it, but if not he shall return it, with his Objections, to that House in which it shall have originated, who shall enter the Objections at large on their Journal, and proceed to reconsider it. If after such Reconsideration two thirds of that House shall agree to pass the bill, it shall be sent, together with the objections, to the other House, by which it shall likewise be reconsidered, and if approved by two thirds of that House, it shall become a Law. But in all such Cases the Votes of both Houses shall be determined by Yeas and Nays, and the Names of the Persons voting for and against the Bill shall be entered on the Journal of each House respectively. If any Bill shall not be returned by the President within ten Days (Sundays excepted) after it shall have been presented to him, the Same shall be a Law, in like Manner as if he had signed it, unless the Congress by their Adjournment prevent its Return, in which Case it shall not be a Law.

Every Order, Resolution, or Vote to which the Concurrence of the Senate and House of Representatives may be necessary (except on a question of Adjournment) shall be presented to the President of the United States; and before the Same shall take Effect, shall be approved by him, or being disapproved by him, shall be repassed by two thirds of the Senate and House of Representatives, according to the Rules and Limitations prescribed in the Case of a Bill.

SECTION 8.

The Congress shall have Power To lay and collect Taxes, Duties, Imposts and Excises, to pay the Debts and provide for the common Defence and general Welfare of the United States; but all Duties, Imposts and Excises shall be uniform throughout the United States;

To borrow money on the credit of the United States;

To regulate Commerce with foreign Nations, and among the several States, and with the Indian Tribes;

To establish an uniform Rule of Naturalization, and uniform Laws on the subject of Bankruptcies throughout the United States;

To coin Money, regulate the Value thereof, and of foreign Coin, and fix the Standard of Weights and Measures;

To provide for the Punishment of counterfeiting the Securities and current Coin of the United States;

To establish Post Offices and post Roads;

To promote the Progress of Science and useful Arts, by securing for limited Times to Authors and Inventors the exclusive Right to their respective Writings and Discoveries;

To constitute Tribunals inferior to the Supreme Court;

To define and punish Piracies and Felonies committed on the high Seas, and Offenses against the Law of Nations;

To declare War, grant Letters of Marque and Reprisal, and make Rules concerning Captures on Land and Water;

To raise and support Armies, but no Appropriation of Money to that Use shall be for a longer Term than two Years;

To provide and maintain a Navy;

To make Rules for the Government and Regulation of the land and naval forces;

To provide for calling forth the Militia to execute the Laws of the Union, suppress Insurrections and repel Invasions;

To provide for organizing, arming, and disciplining the Militia, and for governing such Part of them as may be employed in the Service of the United States, reserving to the States respectively, the Appointment of the Officers, and the Authority of training the Militia according to the discipline prescribed by Congress;

To exercise exclusive Legislation in all Cases whatsoever, over such District (not exceeding ten Miles square) as may, by Cession of particular States, and the acceptance of Congress, become the Seat of the Government of the United States, and to exercise like Authority over all Places purchased by the Consent of the Legislature of the State in which the Same shall be, for the Erection of Forts, Magazines, Arsenals, Dock-yards, and other needful Buildings; – And

To make all Laws which shall be necessary and proper for carrying into Execution the foregoing Powers, and all other Powers vested by this Constitution in the Government of the United States, or in any Department or Officer thereof.

SECTION 9.

The Migration or Importation of such Persons as any of the States now existing shall think proper to admit, shall not be prohibited by the Congress prior to the Year one thousand eight hundred and eight, but a tax or duty may be imposed on such Importation, not exceeding ten dollars for each Person.

The privilege of the Writ of Habeas Corpus shall not be suspended, unless when in Cases of Rebellion or Invasion the public Safety may require it.

No bill of Attainder or ex post facto Law shall be passed.

No capitation, or other direct, Tax shall be laid unless in Proportion to the Census or Enumeration herein before directed to be taken.

No Tax or Duty shall be laid on Articles exported from any State.

No Preference shall be given by any Regulation of Commerce or Revenue to the Ports of one State over those of another: nor shall Vessels bound to, or from, one State, be obliged to enter, clear, or pay Duties in another.

No Money shall be drawn from the Treasury, but in Consequence of Appropriations made by Law; and a regular Statement and Account of the Receipts and Expenditures of all public Money shall be published from time to time.

No Title of Nobility shall be granted by the United States: And no Person holding any Office of Profit or Trust under them, shall, without the Consent of the Congress, accept of any present, Emolument, Office, or Title, of any kind whatever, from any King, Prince, or foreign State.

SECTION 10.

No State shall enter into any Treaty, Alliance, or Confederation; grant Letters of Marque and Reprisal; coin Money; emit Bills of Credit; make any Thing but gold and silver Coin a Tender in Payment of Debts; pass any Bill of Attainder, ex post facto Law, or Law impairing the Obligation of Contracts, or grant any Title of Nobility.

No State shall, without the Consent of the Congress, lay any Imposts or Duties on Imports or Exports, except what may be absolutely necessary for executing its inspection Laws: and the net Produce of all Duties and Imposts, laid by any State on Imports or Exports, shall be for the Use of the Treasury of the United States; and all such Laws shall be subject to the Revision and Control of the Congress.

No state shall, without the Consent of Congress, lay any duty of Tonnage, keep Troops, or Ships of War in time of Peace, enter into any Agreement or Compact with another State, or with a foreign Power, or engage in War, unless actually invaded, or in such imminent Danger as will not admit of delay.

Article II

SECTION 1.

The executive Power shall be vested in a President of the United States of America. He shall hold his Office during the Term of four years, and, together with the Vice President, chosen for the same Term, be elected, as follows:

Each State shall appoint, in such Manner as the Legislature thereof may direct, a Number of Electors, equal to the whole Number of Senators and Representatives to which the State may be entitled in the Congress: but no Senator or Representative, or Person holding an Office of Trust or Profit under the United States, shall be appointed an Elector.

[The Electors shall meet in their respective States, and vote by Ballot for two persons, of whom one at least shall not be an Inhabitant of the same State with themselves. And they shall make a List of all the Persons voted for, and of the Number of Votes for each; which List they shall sign and certify, and transmit sealed to the Seat of the Government of the United States, directed to the President of the Senate. The President of the Senate shall, in the Presence of the Senate and House of Representatives, open all the Certificates, and the Votes shall then be counted. The Person having the greatest Number of Votes shall be the President, if such Number be a Majority of the whole Number of Electors appointed; and if there be more than one who have such Majority, and have an equal Number of Votes, then the House of Representatives shall immediately chuse by Ballot one of them for President; and if no Person have a Majority, then from the five highest on the List the said House shall in the Manner chuse the President. But in chusing the President, the Votes shall be taken by States, the Representation from each State having one Vote; a quorum for this Purpose shall consist of a Member or Members from two-thirds of the States, and a Majority of all the States shall be necessary to a Choice. In every Case, after the Choice of the President, the Person having the greatest Number of Votes of the Electors shall be the Vice President. But if there should remain two or more who have equal votes, the Senate shall chuse from them by Ballot the Vice President.][4]

The Congress may determine the Time of chusing the Electors, and the Day on which they shall give their Votes; which Day shall be the same throughout the United States.

No person except a natural-born Citizen, or a Citizen of the United States, at the time of the Adoption of this Constitution, shall be eligible to the Office of President; neither shall any Person be eligible to that Office who shall not have attained to the Age of thirty-five years, and been fourteen Years a Resident within the United States.

[1]Revised by the Twelfth Amendment.

In Case of the Removal of the President from Office, or of his Death, Resignation, or Inability to discharge the Powers and Duties of the said Office, the same shall devolve on the Vice President, and the Congress may by Law provide for the Case of Removal, Death, Resignation, or Inability, both of the President and Vice President, declaring what Officer shall then act as President, and such Officer shall act accordingly, until the disability be removed, or a President shall be elected.

The President shall, at stated Times, receive for his Services a Compensation, which shall neither be increased nor diminished during the Period for which he shall have been elected, and he shall not receive within that Period any other Emolument from the United States, or any of them.

Before he enter on the execution of his Office, he shall take the following Oath or Affirmation: – "I do solemnly swear (or affirm) that I will faithfully execute the Office of President of the United States, and will, to the best of my Ability, preserve, protect, and defend the Constitution of the United States."

SECTION 2.

The President shall be Commander in Chief of the Army and Navy of the United States, and of the Militia of the several States, when called into the actual Service of the United States; he may require the Opinion, in writing, of the principal Officer in each of the executive Departments, upon any subject relating to the Duties of their respective Offices, and he shall have Power to Grant Reprieves and Pardons for Offenses against the United States, except in Cases of Impeachment.

He shall have Power, by and with the Advice and Consent of the Senate, to make Treaties, provided two-thirds of the Senators present concur; and he shall nominate, and by and with the Advice and Consent of the Senate, shall appoint Ambassadors, other public Ministers and Consuls, Judges of the supreme Court, and all other Officers of the United States, whose Appointments are not herein otherwise provided for, and which shall be established by Law: but the Congress may by Law vest the Appointment of such inferior Officers, as they think proper, in the President alone, in the Courts of Law, or in the Heads of Departments.

The President shall have Power to fill up all Vacancies that may happen during the Re-

cess of the Senate, by granting Commissions which shall expire at the End of their next Session.

SECTION 3.

He shall from time to time give to the Congress Information of the State of the Union, and recommend to their Consideration such Measures as he shall judge necessary and expedient; he may, on extraordinary occasions, convene both Houses, or either of them, and in Case of Disagreement between them, with respect to the Time of Adjournment, he may adjourn them to such Time as he shall think proper; he shall receive Ambassadors and other public Ministers; he shall take care that the Laws be faithfully executed, and shall Commission all the Officers of the United States.

SECTION 4.

The President, Vice President and all civil Officers of the United States, shall be removed from Office on Impeachment for, and Conviction of, Treason, Bribery, or other high Crimes and Misdemeanors.

Article III

SECTION 1.

The judicial Power of the United States, shall be vested in one supreme Court, and in such inferior Courts as the Congress may from time to time ordain and establish. The Judges, both of the supreme and inferior Courts, shall hold their Offices during good Behaviour, and shall, at stated Times, receive for their Services, a Compensation, which shall not be diminished during their Continuance in Office.

SECTION 2.

The judicial Power shall extend to all Cases, in Law and Equity, arising under this Constitution, the Laws of the United States, and Treaties made, or which shall be made, under their Authority; – to all Cases affecting ambassadors, other public ministers and consuls; – to all cases of admiralty and maritime Jurisdiction; – to Controversies to which the United States shall be a Party; – to Controversies between two or more States; – between a State and Citizens of another State;[5] – between Citizens of

---

[5]Qualified by the Eleventh Amendment.

different States, — between Citizens of the same State claiming Lands under Grants of different States, and between a State, or the Citizens thereof, and foreign States, Citizens or Subjects.

In all Cases affecting Ambassadors, other public Ministers and Consuls, and those in which a State shall be Party, the supreme Court shall have original Jurisdiction. In all the other Cases before mentioned, the supreme Court shall have appellate Jurisdiction, both as to Law and Fact, with such Exceptions, and under such Regulations as the Congress shall make.

The trial of all Crimes, except in Cases of Impeachment, shall be by Jury; and such Trial shall be held in the State where the said Crimes shall have been committed; but when not committed within any State, the Trial shall be at such Place or Places as the Congress may by Law have directed.

SECTION 3.

Treason against the United States, shall consist only in levying War against them, or in adhering to their Enemies, giving them Aid and Comfort. No Person shall be convicted of Treason unless on the Testimony of two Witnesses to the same overt Act, or on Confession in open Court.

The Congress shall have power to declare the Punishment of Treason, but no Attainder of Treason shall work Corruption of Blood, or Forfeiture except during the Life of the Person attainted.

Article IV

SECTION 1.

Full Faith and Credit shall be given in each State to the public Acts, Records, and judicial Proceedings of every other State. And the Congress may by general Laws prescribe the Manner in which such Acts, Records and Proceedings shall be proved, and the Effect thereof.

SECTION 2.

The Citizens of each State shall be entitled to all Privileges and Immunities of Citizens in the several States.

A Person charged in any State with Treason, Felony, or other Crime, who shall flee from Justice, and be found in another State, shall on demand of the executive Authority of the State from which he fled, be delivered up, to be removed to the State having Jurisdiction of the crime.

No Person held to Service or Labour in one State, under the Laws thereof, escaping into another, shall, in Consequence of any Law or Regulation therein, be discharged from such Service or Labour, but shall be delivered up on Claim of the Party to whom such Service or Labour may be due.

SECTION 3.

New States may be admitted by the Congress into this Union; but no new State shall be formed or erected within the Jurisdiction of any other State; nor any State be formed by the Junction of two or more States, or parts of States, without the Consent of the Legislatures of the States concerned as well as of the Congress.

The Congress shall have Power to dispose of and make all needful Rules and Regulations respecting the Territory or other Property belonging to the United States; and nothing in this Constitution shall be so construed as to Prejudice any Claims of the United States, or of any particular State.

SECTION 4.

The United States shall guarantee to every State in this Union a Republican Form of Government, and shall protect each of them against Invasion; and on Application of the Legislature, or of the Executive (when the Legislature cannot be convened) against domestic Violence.

Article V

The Congress, whenever two-thirds of both Houses shall deem it necessary, shall propose Amendments to this Constitution, or, on the Application of the Legislatures of two-thirds of the several States, shall call a Convention for proposing Amendments, which, in either Case, shall be valid to all Intents and Purposes, as part of this Constitution, when ratified by the Legislatures of three-fourths of the several States, or by Conventions in three-fourths thereof, as the one or the other Mode of Ratification may be proposed by the Congress; Provided that no Amendment which may be made prior to the Year One thousand eight hundred and eight shall in any Manner affect the first and fourth Clauses in the Ninth Section of the first Article; and that no State, without its Consent, shall be deprived of its equal Suffrage in the Senate.

Article VI

All Debts contracted and Engagements entered into, before the Adoption of this Constitution, shall be as valid against the United States under this Constitution, as under the Confederation.

This Constitution, and the Laws of the United States which shall be made in Pursuance thereof; and all Treaties made, or which shall be made, under the Authority of the United States, shall be the supreme Law of the Land; and the Judges in every State shall be bound thereby, any Thing in the Constitution or Laws of any State to the Contrary notwithstanding.

The Senators and Representatives before mentioned, and the Members of the several State Legislatures, and all executive and judicial Officers, both of the United States and of the several States, shall be bound by Oath or Affirmation to support this Constitution; but no religious Test shall ever be required as a qualification to any Office or public Trust under the United States.

Article VII

The Ratification of the Conventions of nine States shall be sufficient for the Establishment of this Constitution between the States so ratifying the same.

Done in Convention by the Unanimous Consent of the States present the Seventeenth Day of September in the Year of our Lord one thousand seven hundred and Eighty seven, and of the Independence of the United States of America the Twelfth. In Witness whereof We have hereunto subscribed our Names.[6]

George Washington

President and deputy from Virginia

New Hampshire

John Langdon
Nicholas Gilman

Massachusetts

Nathaniel Gorham
Rufus King

Connecticut

William Samuel Johnson
Roger Sherman

New York

Alexander Hamilton

New Jersey

William Livingston
David Brearley
William Paterson
Jonathan Dayton

Pennsylvania

Benjamin Franklin
Thomas Mifflin
Robert Morris
George Clymer
Thomas FitzSimons
Jared Ingersoll
James Wilson
Gouverneur Morris

Delaware

George Read
Gunning Bedford, Jr.
John Dickinson
Richard Bassett
Jacob Broom

Maryland

James McHenry
Daniel of
    St. Thomas Jenifer
Daniel Carroll

Virginia

John Blair
James Madison, Jr.

North Carolina

William Blount
Richard Dobbs Spaight
Hugh Williamson

South Carolina

John Rutledge
Charles Cotesworth Pinckney
Charles Pinckney
Pierce Butler

Georgia

William Few
Abraham Baldwin

[6]These are the full names of the signers, which in some cases are not the signatures on the document.

Articles in Addition to, and Amendment of, the Constitution of the United States of America, Proposed by Congress, and Ratified by the Legislatures of the Several States, Pursuant to the Fifth Article of the Original Constitution[7]

[Article I]

Congress shall make no law respecting an establishment of religion, or prohibiting the free exercise thereof; or abridging the freedom of speech, or of the press; or the right of the people peaceably to assemble, and to petition the Government for a redress of grievances.

[Article II]

A well regulated Militia, being necessary to the security of a free State, the right of the people to keep and bear Arms shall not be infringed.

[Article III]

No Soldier shall, in time of peace, be quartered in any house, without the consent of the Owner, nor in time of war, but in a manner to be prescribed by law.

[Article IV]

The right of the people to be secure in their persons, houses, papers, and effects, against unreasonable searches and seizures, shall not be violated, and no Warrants shall issue, but upon probable cause, supported by Oath or affirmation, and particularly describing the place to be searched, and the persons or things to be seized.

[Article V]

No person shall be held to answer for a capital or otherwise infamous crime, unless on a presentment or indictment of a Grand Jury, except in cases arising in the land or naval forces, or in

[7]This heading appears only in the joint resolution submitting the first ten amendments.

the Militia, when in actual service in time of War or public danger; nor shall any person be subject for the same offence to be twice put in jeopardy of life or limb; nor shall be compelled in any criminal case to be a witness against himself, nor be deprived of life, liberty, or property, without due process of law; nor shall private property be taken for public use, without just compensation.

[Article VI]

In all criminal prosecutions, the accused shall enjoy the right to a speedy and public trial, by an impartial jury of the State and district wherein the crime shall have been committed, which district shall have been previously ascertained by law, and to be informed of the nature and cause of the accusation; to be confronted with the witnesses against him; to have compulsory process for obtaining witnesses in his favour, and to have the Assistance of Counsel for his defence.

[Article VII]

In suits at common law, where the value in controversy shall exceed twenty dollars, the right of trial by jury shall be preserved, and no fact tried by a jury, shall be otherwise reexamined in any Court of the United States, than according to the rules of the common law.

[Article VIII]

Excessive bail shall not be required, nor excessive fines imposed, nor cruel and unusual punishments inflicted.

[Article IX]

The enumeration in the Constitution, of certain rights, shall not be construed to deny or disparage others retained by the people.

[Article X]

The powers not delegated to the United States by the Constitution, nor prohibited by it to the

States, are reserved to the States respectively, or to the people.

[Amendments I – X, in force 1791.]

[Article XI][8]

The Judicial power of the United States shall not be construed to extend to any suit in law or equity, commenced or prosecuted against one of the United States by Citizens of another State, or by Citizens or Subjects of any Foreign State.

[Article XII][9]

The Electors shall meet in their respective States and vote by ballot for President and Vice-President, one of whom, at least, shall not be an inhabitant of the same State with themselves; they shall name in their ballots the person voted for as President, and in distinct ballots the person voted for as Vice-President, and they shall make distinct lists of all persons voted for as President, and of all persons voted for as Vice-President, and of the number of votes for each, which lists they shall sign and certify, and transmit sealed to the seat of the government of the United States, directed to the President of the Senate; – The President of the Senate shall, in the presence of the Senate and House of Representatives, open all the certificates and the votes shall then be counted; – The person having the greatest number of votes for President, shall be the President, if such number be a majority of the whole number of Electors appointed; and if no person have such majority, then from the persons having the highest numbers not exceeding three on the list of those voted for as President, the House of Representatives shall choose immediately, by ballot, the President. But in choosing the President, the votes shall be taken by states, the representation from each state having one vote; a quorum for this purpose shall consist of a member or members from two-thirds of the states, and a majority of all the

states shall be necessary to a choice. And if the House of Representatives shall not choose a President whenever the right of choice shall devolve upon them, before the fourth day of March next following, then the Vice-President shall act as President, as in the case of the death or other constitutional disability of the President. – The person having the greatest number of votes as Vice-President, shall be the Vice-President, if such number be a majority of the whole number of Electors appointed, and if no person have a majority, then from the two highest numbers on the list, the Senate shall choose the Vice-President: a quorum for the purpose shall consist of two-thirds of the whole number of Senators, and a majority of the whole number shall be necessary to a choice. But no person constitutionally ineligible to the office of President shall be eligible to that of Vice-President of the United States.

[Article XIII][10]

SECTION 1.

Neither slavery nor involuntary servitude, except as a punishment for crime whereof the party shall have been duly convicted, shall exist within the United States, or any place subject to their jurisdiction.

SECTION 2.

Congress shall have power to enforce this article by appropriate legislation.

[Article XIV][11]

SECTION 1.

All persons born or naturalized in the United States, and subject to the jurisdiction thereof, are citizens of the United States and of the State wherein they reside. No State shall abridge the privileges or immunities of citizens of the United States; nor shall any State deprive any person of life, liberty, or property, without due process of law; nor deny to any person within its jurisdiction the equal protection of the laws.

---

[8]Adopted in 1798.
[9]Adopted in 1804.

[10]Adopted in 1865.
[11]Adopted in 1868.

SECTION 2.

Representatives shall be apportioned among the several States according to their respective numbers, counting the whole number of persons in each State, excluding Indians not taxed. But when the right to vote at any election for the choice of electors for President and Vice-President of the United States, Representatives in Congress, the Executive and Judicial officers of a State, or the members of the Legislature thereof, is denied to any of the male inhabitants of such State, being twenty-one years of age, and citizens of the United States, or in any way abridged, except for participation in rebellion, or other crime, the basis of representation therein shall be reduced in the proportion which the number of such male citizens shall bear to the whole number of male citizens twenty-one years of age in such State.

SECTION 3.

No person shall be a Senator or Representative in Congress, or elector of President and Vice-President, or hold any office, civil or military, under the United States, or under any State, who, having previously taken an oath, as a member of Congress, or as an officer of the United States, or as a member of any State legislature, or as an executive or judicial officer of any State, to support the Constitution of the United States, shall have engaged in insurrection or rebellion against the same, or given aid or comfort to the enemies thereof. But Congress may by a vote of two-thirds of each House, remove such disability.

SECTION 4.

The validity of the public debt of the United States, authorized by law, including debts incurred for payment of pensions and bounties for services in suppressing insurrection or rebellion, shall not be questioned. But neither the United States nor any State shall assume or pay any debts or obligation incurred in aid of insurrection or rebellion against the United States, or any claim for the loss or emancipation of any slave; but all such debts, obligations, and claims shall be held illegal and void.

SECTION 5.

The Congress shall have the power to enforce, by appropriate legislation, the provisions of this article.

[Article XV][12]

SECTION 1.

The right of citizens of the United States to vote shall not be denied or abridged by the United States or by any State on account of race, color, or previous condition of servitude —

SECTION 2.

The Congress shall have power to enforce this article by appropriate legislation.

[Article XVI][13]

The Congress shall have power to lay and collect taxes on incomes, from whatever source derived, without apportionment among the several States, and without regard to any census or enumeration.

[Article XVII][14]

The Senate of the United States shall be composed of two Senators from each State, elected by the people thereof, for six years; and each Senator shall have one vote. The electors in each State shall have the qualifications requisite for electors of the most numerous branch of the State legislatures.

When vacancies happen in the representation of any State in the Senate, the executive authority of such State shall issue writs of election to fill such vacancies: *Provided,* That the legislature of any State may empower the executive thereof to make temporary appointments until the people fill the vacancies by election as the legislature may direct.

This amendment shall not be so construed as to affect the election or term of any Senator chosen before it becomes valid as part of the Constitution.

[Article XVIII][15]

SECTION 1.

After one year from the ratification of this article the manufacture, sale, or transportation of

[12]Adopted in 1870.
[13]Adopted in 1913.
[14]Adopted in 1913.
[15]Adopted in 1918.

intoxicating liquors within, the importation thereof into, or the exportation thereof from the United States and all territory subject to the jurisdiction thereof for beverage purposes is hereby prohibited.

SECTION 2.
The Congress and the several States shall have concurrent power to enforce this article by appropriate legislation.

SECTION 3.
This article shall be inoperative unless it shall have been ratified as an amendment to the Constitution by the legislatures of the several States, as provided in the Constitution, within seven years from the date of the submission hereof to the States by the Congress.

[Article XIX][16]

The right of citizens of the United States to vote shall not be denied or abridged by the United States or by any State on account of sex.

Congress shall have power to enforce this article by appropriate legislation.

[Article XX][17]

SECTION 1.
The terms of the President and Vice-President shall end at noon on the 20th day of January, and the terms of Senators and Representatives at noon on the 3d day of January, of the years in which such terms would have ended if this article had not been ratified; and the terms of their successors shall then begin.

SECTION 2.
The Congress shall assemble at least once in every year, and such meeting shall begin at noon on the 3d day of January, unless they shall by law appoint a different day.

SECTION 3.
If, at the time fixed for the beginning of the term of the President, the President elect shall have died, the Vice-President elect shall become President. If a President shall not have been chosen before the time fixed for the be-

ginning of his term, or if the President elect shall have failed to qualify, then the Vice-President elect shall act as President until a President shall have qualified; and the Congress may by law provide for the case wherein neither a President elect nor a Vice-President elect shall have qualified, declaring who shall then act as President, or the manner in which one who is to act shall be selected, and such person shall act accordingly until a President or Vice-President shall have qualified.

SECTION 4.
The Congress may by law provide for the case of the death of any of the persons from whom the House of Representatives may choose a President whenever the right of choice shall have devolved upon them, and for the case of the death of any of the persons from whom the Senate may choose a Vice-President whenever the right of choice shall have devolved upon them.

SECTION 5.
Sections 1 and 2 shall take effect on the 15th day of October following the ratification of this article.

SECTION 6.
This article shall be inoperative unless it shall have been ratified as an amendment to the Constitution by the legislatures of three-fourths of the several States within seven years from the date of its submission.

[Article XXI][18]

SECTION 1.
The eighteenth article of amendment to the Constitution of the United States is hereby repealed.

SECTION 2.
The transportation or importation into any State, Territory, or possession of the United States for delivery or use therein of intoxicating liquors, in violation of the laws thereof, is hereby prohibited.

SECTION 3.
This article shall be inoperative unless it shall have been ratified as an amendment to the

[16]Adopted in 1920.
[17]Adopted in 1933.

[18]Adopted in 1933.

Constitution by conventions in the several States, as provided in the Constitution, within seven years from the date of the submission hereof to the States by the Congress.

[Article XXII][19]

No person shall be elected to the office of the President more than twice, and no person who has held the office of President, or acted as President, for more than two years of a term to which some other person was elected President shall be elected to the office of the President more than once.

But this Article shall not apply to any person holding the office of President when this Article was proposed by the Congress, and shall not prevent any person who may be holding the office of President, or acting as President, during the term within which this Article becomes operative from holding the office of President or acting as President during the remainder of such term.

This article shall be inoperative unless it shall have been ratified as an amendment to the Constitution by the legislatures of three-fourths of the several states within seven years from the date of its submission to the states by the Congress.

[Article XXIII][20]

SECTION 1.
The District constituting the seat of Government of the United States shall appoint in such manner as the Congress may direct:

A number of electors of President and Vice-President equal to the whole number of Senators and Representatives in Congress to which the District would be entitled if it were a State, but in no event more than the least populous State; they shall be in addition to those appointed by the States, but they shall be considered, for the purposes of the election of President and Vice-President, to be electors appointed by a State; and they shall meet in the District and perform such duties as provided by the twelfth article of amendment.

SECTION 2.
The Congress shall have power to enforce this article by appropriate legislation.

[Article XXIV][21]

SECTION 1.
The right of citizens of the United States to vote in any primary or other election for President or Vice President, for electors for President or Vice President, or for Senator or Representative in Congress, shall not be denied or abridged by the United States or any state by reason of failure to pay any poll tax or other tax.

SECTION 2.
The Congress shall have the power to enforce this article by appropriate legislation.

[Article XXV][22]

SECTION 1.
In case of the removal of the President from office or of his death or resignation, the Vice President shall become President.

SECTION 2.
Whenever there is a vacancy in the office of the Vice President, the President shall nominate a Vice President who shall take office upon confirmation by a majority vote of both Houses of Congress.

SECTION 3.
Whenever the President transmits to the President Pro Tempore of the Senate and the Speaker of the House of Representatives his written declaration that he is unable to discharge the powers and duties of his office, and until he transmits to them a written declaration to the contrary, such powers and duties shall be discharged by the Vice President as Acting President.

SECTION 4.
Whenever the Vice President and a majority of either the principal officers of the executive departments or of such other body as Congress may by law provide, transmit to the President Pro Tempore of the Senate and the Speaker of

[19]Adopted in 1951.
[20]Adopted in 1961.

[21]Adopted in 1964.
[22]Adopted in 1967.

the House of Representatives their written declaration that the President is unable to discharge the powers and duties of his office, the Vice President shall immediately assume the powers and duties of the office as Acting President.

Thereafter, when the President transmits to the President Pro Tempore of the Senate and the Speaker of the House of Representatives his written declaration that no inability exists, he shall resume the powers and duties of his office unless the Vice President and a majority of either the principal officers of the executive departments or of such other body as Congress may by law provide, transmit within four days to the President Pro Tempore of the Senate and the Speaker of the House of Representatives their written declaration that the President is unable to discharge the powers and duties of his office. Thereupon Congress shall decide the issue, assembling within forty-eight hours for that purpose if not in session. If the Congress, within twenty-one days after receipt of the latter written declaration, or, if Congress is not in session, within twenty-one days after Congress is required to assemble, determines by two-thirds vote of both Houses that the President is unable to discharge the powers and duties of his office, the Vice President shall continue to discharge the same as Acting President; otherwise, the President shall resume the powers and duties of his office.

[**Article XXVI**][23]

SECTION 1.

The right of citizens of the United States, who are eighteen years of age or older, to vote shall not be denied or abridged by the United States or by any State on account of age.

SECTION 2.

The Congress shall have power to enforce this article by appropriate legislation.

[23]Adopted in 1971.

Admission of States to the Union*

1	Delaware	*Dec. 7, 1787*	26	Michigan	*Jan. 26, 1837*
2	Pennsylvania	*Dec. 12, 1787*	27	Florida	*Mar. 3, 1845*
3	New Jersey	*Dec. 18, 1787*	28	Texas	*Dec. 29, 1845*
4	Georgia	*Jan. 2, 1788*	29	Iowa	*Dec. 28, 1846*
5	Connecticut	*Jan. 9, 1788*	30	Wisconsin	*May 29, 1848*
6	Massachusetts	*Feb. 6, 1788*	31	California	*Sept. 9, 1850*
7	Maryland	*Apr. 28, 1788*	32	Minnesota	*May 11, 1858*
8	South Carolina	*May 23, 1788*	33	Oregon	*Feb. 14, 1859*
9	New Hampshire	*June 21, 1788*	34	Kansas	*Jan. 29, 1861*
10	Virginia	*June 25, 1788*	35	West Virginia	*June 19, 1863*
11	New York	*July 26, 1788*	36	Nevada	*Oct. 31, 1864*
12	North Carolina	*Nov. 21, 1789*	37	Nebraska	*Mar. 1, 1867*
13	Rhode Island	*May 29, 1790*	38	Colorado	*Aug. 1, 1876*
14	Vermont	*Mar. 4, 1791*	39	North Dakota	*Nov. 2, 1889*
15	Kentucky	*June 1, 1792*	40	South Dakota	*Nov. 2, 1889*
16	Tennessee	*June 1, 1796*	41	Montana	*Nov. 8, 1889*
17	Ohio	*Mar. 1, 1803*	42	Washington	*Nov. 11, 1889*
18	Louisiana	*Apr. 30, 1812*	43	Idaho	*July 3, 1890*
19	Indiana	*Dec. 11, 1816*	44	Wyoming	*July 10, 1890*
20	Mississippi	*Dec. 10, 1817*	45	Utah	*Jan. 4, 1896*
21	Illinois	*Dec. 3, 1818*	46	Oklahoma	*Nov. 16, 1907*
22	Alabama	*Dec. 14, 1819*	47	New Mexico	*Jan. 6, 1912*
23	Maine	*Mar. 15, 1820*	48	Arizona	*Feb. 14, 1912*
24	Missouri	*Aug. 10, 1821*	49	Alaska	*Jan. 3, 1959*
25	Arkansas	*June 15, 1836*	50	Hawaii	*Aug. 21, 1959*

*In the case of the first thirteen states, the date given is that of ratification of the Constitution.

Year	Candidates	Parties	Popular Vote	Electoral Vote
1789	**GEORGE WASHINGTON** (Va.)*			69
	John Adams			34
	Others			35
1792	**GEORGE WASHINGTON** (Va.)			132
	John Adams			77
	George Clinton			50
	Others			5
1796	**JOHN ADAMS** (Mass.)	Federalist		71
	Thomas Jefferson	Democratic-Republican		68
	Thomas Pinckney	Federalist		59
	Aaron Burr	Dem.-Rep.		30
	Others			48
1800	**THOMAS JEFFERSON** (Va.)	Dem.-Rep.		73
	Aaron Burr	Dem.-Rep.		73
	John Adams	Federalist		65
	C. C. Pinckney	Federalist		64
	John Jay	Federalist		1
1804	**THOMAS JEFFERSON** (Va.)	Dem.-Rep.		162
	C. C. Pinckney	Federalist		14
1808	**JAMES MADISON** (Va.)	Dem.-Rep.		122
	C. C. Pinckney	Federalist		47
	George Clinton	Dem.-Rep.		6
1812	**JAMES MADISON** (Va.)	Dem.-Rep.		128
	De Witt Clinton	Federalist		89
1816	**JAMES MONROE** (Va.)	Dem.-Rep.		183
	Rufus King	Federalist		34
1820	**JAMES MONROE** (Va.)	Dem.-Rep.		231
	John Quincy Adams	Dem.-Rep.		1
1824	**JOHN Q. ADAMS** (Mass.)	Dem.-Rep.	108,740	84
	Andrew Jackson	Dem.-Rep.	153,544	99
	William H. Crawford	Dem.-Rep.	46,618	41
	Henry Clay	Dem.-Rep.	47,136	37
1828	**ANDREW JACKSON** (Tenn.)	Democrat	647,286	178
	John Quincy Adams	National Republican	508,064	83

*State of residence at time of election.

Year	Candidates	Parties	Popular Vote	Electoral Vote
1832	**ANDREW JACKSON** (Tenn.)	Democrat	687,502	219
	Henry Clay	National Republican	530,189	49
	John Floyd	Independent		11
	William Wirt	Anti-Mason	33,108	7
1836	**MARTIN VAN BUREN** (N.Y.)	Democrat	765,483	170
	W. H. Harrison	Whig		73
	Hugh L. White	Whig	739,795	26
	Daniel Webster	Whig		14
	W. P. Mangum	Independent		11
1840	**WILLIAM H. HARRISON** (Ohio)	Whig	1,274,624	234
	Martin Van Buren	Democrat	1,127,781	60
	J. G. Birney	Liberty	7,069	—
1844	**JAMES K. POLK** (Tenn.)	Democrat	1,338,464	170
	Henry Clay	Whig	1,300,097	105
	J. G. Birney	Liberty	62,300	—
1848	**ZACHARY TAYLOR** (La.)	Whig	1,360,967	163
	Lewis Cass	Democrat	1,222,342	127
	Martin Van Buren	Free-Soil	291,263	—
1852	**FRANKLIN PIERCE** (N.H.)	Democrat	1,601,117	254
	Winfield Scott	Whig	1,385,453	42
	John P. Hale	Free-Soil	155,825	—
1856	**JAMES BUCHANAN** (Pa.)	Democrat	1,832,955	174
	John C. Frémont	Republican	1,339,932	114
	Millard Fillmore	American	871,731	8
1860	**ABRAHAM LINCOLN** (Ill.)	Republican	1,865,593	180
	Stephen A. Douglas	Democrat	1,382,713	12
	John C. Breckinridge	Democrat	848,356	72
	John Bell	Union	592,906	39
1864	**ABRAHAM LINCOLN** (Ill.)	Republican	2,213,655	212
	George B. McClellan	Democrat	1,805,237	21
1868	**ULYSSES S. GRANT** (Ill.)	Republican	3,012,833	214
	Horatio Seymour	Democrat	2,703,249	80
1872	**ULYSSES S. GRANT** (Ill.)	Republican	3,597,132	286
	Horace Greeley	Democrat; Liberal Republican	2,834,125	66
1876	**RUTHERFORD B. HAYES** (Ohio)	Republican	4,036,298	185
	Samuel J. Tilden	Democrat	4,300,590	184
1880	**JAMES A. GARFIELD** (Ohio)	Republican	4,454,416	214
	Winfield S. Hancock	Democrat	4,444,952	155

Year	Candidates	Parties	Popular Vote	Electoral Vote
1884	**GROVER CLEVELAND** (N.Y.)	Democrat	4,874,986	219
	James G. Blaine	Republican	4,851,981	182
1888	**BENJAMIN HARRISON** (Ind.)	Republican	5,439,853	233
	Grover Cleveland	Democrat	5,540,309	168
1892	**GROVER CLEVELAND** (N.Y.)	Democrat	5,556,918	277
	Benjamin Harrison	Republican	5,176,108	145
	James B. Weaver	People's	1,041,028	22
1896	**WILLIAM McKINLEY** (Ohio)	Republican	7,104,779	271
	William J. Bryan	Democrat-People's	6,502,925	176
1900	**WILLIAM McKINLEY** (Ohio)	Republican	7,207,923	292
	William J. Bryan	Dem.-Populist	6,358,133	155
1904	**THEODORE ROOSEVELT** (N.Y.)	Republican	7,623,486	336
	Alton B. Parker	Democrat	5,077,911	140
	Eugene V. Debs	Socialist	402,283	—
1908	**WILLIAM H. TAFT** (Ohio)	Republican	7,678,908	321
	William J. Bryan	Democrat	6,409,104	162
	Eugene V. Debs	Socialist	420,793	—
1912	**WOODROW WILSON** (N.J.)	Democrat	6,293,454	435
	Theodore Roosevelt	Progressive	4,119,538	88
	William H. Taft	Republican	3,484,980	8
	Eugene V. Debs	Socialist	900,672	—
1916	**WOODROW WILSON** (N.J.)	Democrat	9,129,606	277
	Charles E. Hughes	Republican	8,538,221	254
	A. L. Benson	Socialist	585,113	—
1920	**WARREN G. HARDING** (Ohio)	Republican	16,152,200	404
	James M. Cox	Democrat	9,147,353	127
	Eugene V. Debs	Socialist	919,799	—
1924	**CALVIN COOLIDGE** (Mass.)	Republican	15,725,016	382
	John W. Davis	Democrat	8,386,503	136
	Robert M. LaFollette	Progressive	4,822,856	13
1928	**HERBERT HOOVER** (Calif.)	Republican	21,391,381	444
	Alfred E. Smith	Democrat	15,016,443	87
	Norman Thomas	Socialist	267,835	—
1932	**FRANKLIN D. ROOSEVELT** (N.Y.)	Democrat	22,821,857	472
	Herbert Hoover	Republican	15,761,841	59
	Norman Thomas	Socialist	881,951	—
1936	**FRANKLIN D. ROOSEVELT** (N.Y.)	Democrat	27,751,597	523
	Alfred M. Landon	Republican	16,679,583	8
	William Lemke	Union and others	882,479	—
1940	**FRANKLIN D. ROOSEVELT** (N.Y.)	Democrat	27,244,160	449
	Wendell L. Willkie	Republican	22,305,198	82

Year	Candidates	Parties	Popular Vote	Electoral Vote
1944	**FRANKLIN D. ROOSEVELT (N.Y.)**	Democrat	25,602,504	432
	Thomas E. Dewey	Republican	22,006,285	99
1948	**HARRY S. TRUMAN (Mo.)**	Democrat	24,105,695	304
	Thomas E. Dewey	Republican	21,969,170	189
	J. Strom Thurmond	State-Rights Democrat	1,169,021	38
	Henry A. Wallace	Progressive	1,156,103	—
1952	**DWIGHT D. EISENHOWER (N.Y.)**	Republican	33,936,252	442
	Adlai E. Stevenson	Democrat	27,314,992	89
1956	**DWIGHT D. EISENHOWER (N.Y.)**	Republican	35,575,420	457
	Adlai E. Stevenson	Democrat	26,033,066	73
	Other	—	—	1
1960	**JOHN F. KENNEDY (Mass.)**	Democrat	34,227,096	303
	Richard M. Nixon	Republican	34,108,546	219
	Other	—	—	15
1964	**LYNDON B. JOHNSON (Tex.)**	Democrat	43,126,506	486
	Barry M. Goldwater	Republican	27,176,799	52
1968	**RICHARD M. NIXON (N.Y.)**	Republican	31,770,237	301
	Hubert H. Humphrey	Democrat	31,270,533	191
	George Wallace	American Indep.	9,906,141	46
1972	**RICHARD M. NIXON (N.Y.)**	Republican	47,169,911	520
	George S. McGovern	Democrat	29,170,383	17
	Other	—	—	1
1976	***JAMES E. CARTER, JR. (Ga.)**	Democrat	40,287,283	297
	Gerald R. Ford	Republican	38,557,855	241

*Based on returns from 99 percent of the precincts.

Presidents and Vice Presidents

President	Vice President
1. George Washington, Federalist 1789	John Adams, Federalist 1789
2. John Adams, Federalist 1797	Thomas Jefferson, Dem.-Rep. 1797
3. Thomas Jefferson, Dem.-Rep. 1801	Aaron Burr, Dem.-Rep. 1801 George Clinton, Dem.-Rep. 1805
4. James Madison, Dem.-Rep. 1809	George Clinton, Dem.-Rep. 1809 Elbridge Gerry, Dem.-Rep. 1813
5. James Monroe, Dem.-Rep. 1817	D. D. Tompkins, Dem.-Rep. 1817
6. John Quincy Adams, Dem.-Rep. 1825	John C. Calhoun, Dem.-Rep. 1825
7. Andrew Jackson, Democratic 1829	John C. Calhoun, Democratic 1829 Martin Van Buren, Democratic 1833
8. Martin Van Buren, Democratic 1837	Richard M. Johnson, Democratic 1837
9. William H. Harrison, Whig 1841	John Tyler, Whig 1841
10. John Tyler, Whig and Democratic 1841	

11. James K. Polk, Democratic 1845	George M. Dallas, Democratic 1845
12. Zachary Taylor, Whig 1849	Millard Fillmore, Whig 1849
13. Millard Fillmore, Whig 1850	
14. Franklin Pierce, Democratic 1853	William R. D. King, Democratic 1853
15. James Buchanan, Democratic 1857	John C. Breckinridge, Democratic 1857
16. Abraham Lincoln, Republican 1861	Hannibal Hamlin, Republican 1861 Andrew Johnson, Unionist 1865
17. Andrew Johnson, Unionist 1865	
18. Ulysses S. Grant, Republican 1869	Schuyler Colfax, Republican 1869 Henry Wilson, Republican 1873
19. Rutherford B. Hayes, Republican 1877	William A. Wheeler, Republican 1877
20. James A. Garfield, Republican 1881	Chester A. Arthur, Republican 1881
21. Chester A. Arthur, Republican 1881	
22. Grover Cleveland, Democratic 1885	T. A. Hendricks, Democratic 1885
23. Benjamin Harrison, Republican 1889	Levi P. Morton, Republican 1889
24. Grover Cleveland, Democratic 1893	Adlai E. Stevenson, Democratic 1893
25. William McKinley, Republican 1897	Garret A. Hobart, Republican 1897 Theodore Roosevelt, Republican 1901

President	Vice President
26. Theodore Roosevelt, Republican 1901	Chas. W. Fairbanks, Republican 1905
27. William H. Taft, Republican 1909	James S. Sherman, Republican 1909
28. Woodrow Wilson, Democratic 1913	Thomas R. Marshall, Democratic 1913
29. Warren G. Harding, Republican 1921	Calvin Coolidge, Republican 1921
30. Calvin Coolidge, Republican 1923	Charles G. Dawes, Republican 1925
31. Herbert Hoover, Republican 1929	Charles Curtis, Republican 1929
32. Franklin D. Roosevelt, Democratic 1933	John Nance Garner, Democratic 1933 Henry A. Wallace, Democratic 1941 Harry S. Truman, Democratic 1945
33. Harry S. Truman, Democratic 1945	Alben W. Barkley, Democratic 1949
34. Dwight D. Eisenhower, Republican 1953	Richard M. Nixon, Republican 1953
35. John F. Kennedy, Democratic 1961	Lyndon B. Johnson, Democratic 1961
36. Lyndon B. Johnson, Democratic 1963	Hubert H. Humphrey, Democratic 1965
37. Richard M. Nixon, Republican 1969	Spiro T. Agnew, Republican 1969 Gerald R. Ford, Republican 1973
38. Gerald R. Ford, Republican 1974	Nelson A. Rockefeller, Republican 1974
39. James E. Carter, Jr., Democrat 1977	Walter F. Mondale, Democrat 1977

Population of the United States

Division and State	1790	1800	1810	1820	1830	1840	1850	1860	1870
United States	3,929,214	5,308,483	7,239,881	9,638,453	12,866,020	17,069,453	23,191,876	31,443,321	39,818,449
GEOGRAPHIC DIVISIONS									
New England	1,009,408	1,233,011	1,471,973	1,660,071	1,954,717	2,234,822	2,728,116	3,135,283	3,487,924
Middle Atlantic	952,632	1,402,565	2,014,702	2,699,845	3,587,664	4,526,260	5,898,735	7,458,985	8,810,806
South Atlantic	1,851,806	2,286,494	2,674,891	3,061,063	3,645,752	3,925,299	4,679,090	5,364,703	5,853,610
East South Central	109,368	335,407	708,590	1,190,489	1,815,969	2,575,445	3,363,271	4,020,991	4,404,445
West South Central			77,618	167,680	246,127	449,985	940,251	1,747,667	2,029,965
East North Central		51,006	272,324	792,719	1,470,018	2,924,728	4,523,260	6,926,884	9,124,517
West North Central			19,783	66,586	140,455	426,814	880,335	2,169,832	3,856,594
Mountain							72,927	174,923	315,385
Pacific							105,871	444,053	675,125
NEW ENGLAND									
Maine	96,540	151,719	228,705	298,335	399,455	501,793	583,169	628,279	626,915
New Hampshire	141,885	183,858	214,460	244,161	269,328	284,574	317,976	326,073	318,300
Vermont	85,425	154,465	217,895	235,981	280,652	291,948	314,120	315,098	330,551
Massachusetts	378,787	422,845	472,040	523,287	610,408	737,699	994,514	1,231,066	1,457,351
Rhode Island	68,825	69,122	76,931	83,059	97,199	108,830	147,545	174,620	217,353
Connecticut	237,946	251,002	261,942	275,248	297,675	309,978	370,792	460,147	537,454
MIDDLE ATLANTIC									
New York	340,120	589,051	959,049	1,372,812	1,918,608	2,428,921	3,097,394	3,880,735	4,382,759
New Jersey	184,139	211,149	245,562	277,575	320,823	373,306	489,555	672,035	906,096
Pennsylvania	434,373	602,365	810,091	1,049,458	1,348,233	1,724,033	2,311,786	2,906,215	3,521,951
SOUTH ATLANTIC									
Delaware	59,096	64,273	72,674	72,749	76,748	78,085	91,532	112,216	125,015
Maryland	319,728	341,548	380,546	407,350	447,040	470,019	583,034	687,049	780,894
Dist. of Columbia		14,093	24,023	33,039	39,834	43,712	51,687	75,080	131,700
Virginia	747,610	880,200	974,600	1,065,366	1,211,405	1,239,797	1,421,661	1,596,318	1,225,163
West Virginia									442,014
North Carolina	393,751	478,103	555,500	638,829	737,987	753,419	869,039	992,622	1,071,361
South Carolina	249,073	345,591	415,115	502,741	581,185	594,398	668,507	703,708	705,606
Georgia	82,548	162,686	252,433	340,989	516,823	691,392	906,185	1,057,286	1,184,109
Florida					34,730	54,477	87,445	140,424	187,748
EAST SOUTH CENTRAL									
Kentucky	73,677	220,955	406,511	564,317	687,917	779,828	982,405	1,155,684	1,321,011
Tennessee	35,691	105,602	261,727	422,823	681,904	829,210	1,002,717	1,109,801	1,258,520
Alabama				127,901	309,527	590,756	771,623	964,201	996,992
Mississippi		8,850	40,352	75,448	136,621	375,651	606,526	791,305	827,922
WEST SOUTH CENTRAL									
Arkansas			1,062	14,273	30,388	97,574	209,897	435,450	484,471
Louisiana			76,556	153,407	215,739	352,411	517,762	708,002	726,915
Texas							212,592	604,215	818,579

EAST NORTH CENTRAL								
Ohio	45,365	230,760	581,434	937,903	1,519,467	1,980,329	2,339,511	2,665,260
Indiana	5,641	24,520	147,178	343,031	685,866	988,416	1,350,428	1,680,637
Illinois		12,282	55,211	157,445	476,183	851,470	1,711,951	2,539,981
Michigan		4,762	8,896	31,639	212,267	397,654	749,113	1,184,059
Wisconsin					30,945	305,391	775,881	1,054,670
WEST NORTH CENTRAL								
Minnesota						6,077	172,023	439,706
Iowa					43,112	192,214	674,913	1,194,020
Missouri		19,783	66,586	140,455	383,702	682,044	1,182,012	1,721,295
North Dakota								2,405
South Dakota								11,776
Nebraska							28,841	122,993
Kansas							107,206	364,399
MOUNTAIN								
Montana								20,595
Idaho								14,999
Wyoming								9,118
Colorado							34,277	39,864
New Mexico						61,547	93,516	91,874
Arizona								9,658
Utah						11,380	40,273	86,786
Nevada							6,857	42,491
PACIFIC								
Washington							11,594	23,955
Oregon						13,294	52,465	90,923
California						92,597	379,994	560,247

Division and State	1880	1890	1900	1910	1920	1930	1940	1950	1960	1970
UNITED STATES	50,155,783	62,947,714	75,994,575	91,972,266	105,710,620	122,775,046	131,669,275	150,697,361	179,323,175	203,211,926
GEOGRAPHIC DIVISIONS										
New England	4,010,529	4,700,749	5,592,017	6,552,681	7,400,909	8,166,341	8,437,290	9,314,453	10,509,367	11,841,663
Middle Atlantic	10,496,878	12,706,220	15,454,678	19,315,892	22,261,144	26,260,750	27,539,487	30,163,533	34,168,452	37,199,040
South Atlantic	7,597,197	8,857,922	10,443,480	12,194,895	13,990,272	15,793,589	17,823,151	21,182,335	25,971,732	30,671,337
East South Central	5,585,151	6,429,154	7,547,757	8,409,901	8,893,307	9,887,214	10,778,225	11,477,181	12,050,126	12,803,470
West South Central	3,334,220	4,740,983	6,532,290	8,784,534	10,242,224	12,176,830	13,064,525	14,537,572	16,951,255	19,320,560
East North Central	11,206,668	13,478,305	15,985,581	18,250,621	21,475,543	25,297,185	26,626,342	30,399,368	36,225,024	40,252,476
West North Central	6,157,443	8,932,112	10,347,423	11,637,921	12,544,249	13,296,915	13,516,990	14,061,394	15,394,115	16,319,187
Mountain	653,119	1,213,935	1,674,657	2,633,517	3,336,101	3,701,789	4,150,003	5,074,998	6,855,060	8,281,562
Pacific	1,114,578	1,888,334	2,416,692	4,192,304	5,566,871	8,194,433	9,733,262	14,486,527	20,339,105	25,453,688
Noncontiguous									858,939	1,068,943
NEW ENGLAND										
Maine	648,936	661,086	694,466	742,371	768,014	797,423	847,226	913,774	969,265	992,048
New Hampshire	346,991	376,530	411,588	430,572	443,083	465,293	491,524	533,242	606,921	731,681
Vermont	332,286	332,422	343,641	355,956	352,428	359,611	359,231	377,747	389,881	444,330
Massachusetts	1,783,085	2,238,947	2,805,346	3,366,416	3,852,356	4,249,614	4,316,721	4,690,514	5,148,578	5,689,110
Rhode Island	276,531	345,506	428,556	542,610	604,397	687,497	713,346	791,896	859,488	946,725
Connecticut	622,700	746,258	908,420	1,114,756	1,380,631	1,606,903	1,709,242	2,007,280	2,535,234	3,031,709
MIDDLE ATLANTIC										
New York	5,082,871	6,003,174	7,268,894	9,113,614	10,385,227	12,588,066	13,479,142	14,830,192	16,782,304	18,236,967
New Jersey	1,131,116	1,444,933	1,883,669	2,537,167	3,155,900	4,041,334	4,160,165	4,835,329	6,066,782	7,168,164
Pennsylvania	4,282,891	5,258,113	6,302,115	7,665,111	8,720,017	9,631,350	9,900,180	10,498,012	11,319,366	11,793,909
SOUTH ATLANTIC										
Delaware	146,608	168,493	184,735	202,322	223,003	238,380	266,505	318,085	446,292	548,104
Maryland	934,943	1,042,390	1,188,044	1,295,346	1,449,661	1,631,526	1,821,244	2,343,001	3,100,689	3,922,399
Dist. of Columbia	177,624	230,392	278,718	331,069	437,571	486,869	663,091	802,178	763,956	756,510
Virginia	1,512,565	1,655,980	1,854,184	2,061,612	2,309,187	2,421,851	2,677,773	3,318,680	3,966,949	4,648,494
West Virginia	618,457	762,794	958,800	1,221,119	1,463,701	1,729,205	1,901,974	2,005,552	1,860,421	1,744,237
North Carolina	1,399,750	1,617,949	1,893,810	2,206,287	2,559,123	3,170,276	3,571,623	4,061,929	4,556,155	5,082,059
South Carolina	995,577	1,151,149	1,340,316	1,515,400	1,683,724	1,738,765	1,899,804	2,117,027	2,382,594	2,590,516
Georgia	1,542,180	1,837,353	2,216,331	2,609,121	2,895,832	2,908,506	3,123,723	3,444,578	3,943,116	4,589,575
Florida	269,493	391,422	528,542	752,619	968,470	1,468,211	1,897,414	2,771,305	4,951,560	6,789,443
EAST SOUTH CENTRAL										
Kentucky	1,648,690	1,858,635	2,147,174	2,289,905	2,416,630	2,614,589	2,845,627	2,944,806	3,038,156	3,218,706
Tennessee	1,542,359	1,767,518	2,020,616	2,184,789	2,337,885	2,616,556	2,915,841	3,291,718	3,567,089	3,923,687
Alabama	1,262,505	1,513,401	1,828,697	2,138,093	2,348,174	2,646,248	2,832,961	3,061,743	3,266,740	3,444,165
Mississippi	1,131,597	1,289,600	1,551,270	1,797,114	1,790,618	2,009,821	2,183,796	2,178,914	2,178,141	2,216,912
WEST SOUTH CENTRAL										
Arkansas	802,525	1,128,211	1,311,564	1,574,449	1,752,204	1,854,482	1,949,387	1,909,511	1,786,272	1,923,285
Louisiana	939,946	1,118,588	1,381,625	1,656,388	1,798,509	2,101,593	2,363,880	2,683,516	3,257,022	3,641,306
Oklahoma		258,657	790,391	1,657,155	2,028,283	2,396,040	2,336,434	2,233,351	2,328,284	2,559,229
Texas	1,591,749	2,235,527	3,048,710	3,896,542	4,663,228	5,824,715	6,414,824	7,711,194	9,579,677	11,196,730
EAST NORTH CENTRAL										
Ohio	3,198,062	3,672,329	4,157,545	4,767,121	5,759,394	6,646,697	6,907,612	7,946,627	9,706,397	10,652,017
Indiana	1,978,301	2,192,404	2,516,462	2,700,876	2,930,390	3,238,503	3,427,796	3,934,224	4,662,498	5,193,669
Illinois	3,077,871	3,826,352	4,821,550	5,638,591	6,485,280	7,630,654	7,897,241	8,712,176	10,081,158	11,113,976
Michigan	1,636,937	2,093,890	2,420,982	2,810,173	3,668,412	4,842,325	5,256,106	6,371,766	7,823,194	8,875,083
Wisconsin	1,315,497	1,693,330	2,069,042	2,333,860	2,632,067	2,939,006	3,137,587	3,434,576	3,951,777	4,417,731

WEST NORTH CENTRAL										
Minnesota	780,773	1,310,283	1,751,394	2,075,708	2,387,125	2,563,953	2,792,300	2,982,483	3,413,864	3,804,971
Iowa	1,624,615	1,912,297	2,231,853	2,224,771	2,404,021	2,470,939	2,538,268	2,621,073	2,757,537	2,824,376
Missouri	2,168,380	2,679,185	3,106,665	3,293,335	3,404,055	3,629,367	3,784,664	3,954,653	4,319,813	4,676,501
North Dakota	36,909	190,983	319,146	577,056	646,872	680,845	641,935	619,636	632,446	617,761
South Dakota	98,268	348,600	401,570	583,888	636,547	692,849	642,961	652,740	680,514	665,507
Nebraska	452,402	1,062,656	1,066,300	1,192,214	1,296,372	1,377,963	1,315,834	1,325,510	1,411,330	1,483,493
Kansas	996,096	1,428,108	1,470,495	1,690,949	1,769,257	1,880,999	1,801,028	1,905,299	2,178,611	2,246,578
MOUNTAIN										
Montana	39,159	142,924	243,329	376,053	548,889	537,606	559,456	591,024	674,767	694,409
Idaho	32,610	88,548	161,772	325,594	431,866	445,032	524,873	588,637	667,191	712,567
Wyoming	20,789	62,555	92,531	145,965	194,402	225,565	250,742	290,529	330,066	332,416
Colorado	194,327	413,249	539,700	799,024	939,629	1,035,791	1,123,296	1,325,089	1,753,947	2,207,259
New Mexico	119,565	160,282	195,310	327,301	360,350	423,317	531,818	681,187	951,023	1,016,000
Arizona	40,440	88,243	122,931	204,354	334,162	435,573	499,261	749,587	1,302,161	1,770,900
Utah	143,963	210,779	276,749	373,351	449,396	507,847	550,310	688,862	890,627	1,059,273
Nevada	62,266	47,355	42,335	81,875	77,407	91,058	110,247	160,083	285,278	488,738
PACIFIC										
Washington	75,116	357,232	518,103	1,141,990	1,356,621	1,563,396	1,736,191	2,378,963	2,853,214	3,409,169
Oregon	174,768	317,704	413,536	672,765	783,389	953,786	1,089,684	1,521,341	1,768,687	2,091,385
California	864,694	1,213,398	1,485,053	2,377,549	3,426,861	5,677,251	6,907,387	10,586,223	15,717,204	19,953,134
NONCONTIGUOUS										
Alaska									226,167	300,382
Hawaii									632,772	786,561

About the Authors

RICHARD N. CURRENT is University Distinguished Professor of History at the University of North Carolina at Greensboro. He is co-author of the Bancroft Prize-winning *Lincoln the President*. His books include: *Three Carpetbag Governors; The Lincoln Nobody Knows; Daniel Webster and the Rise of National Conservatism;* and *Secretary Stimson*. Professor Current has lectured on U.S. history in Europe, Asia, South America, Australia, and Antarctica. He has been a Fulbright Lecturer at the University of Munich and the University of Chile at Santiago, and has served as Harmsworth Professor of American History at Oxford. He is President of the Southern Historical Association.

T. HARRY WILLIAMS is Boyd Professor of History at Louisiana State University. He was awarded both the 1969 Pulitzer Prize and National Book Award for his biography of *Huey Long*. His books include: *Lincoln and His Generals; Lincoln and the Radicals; P. G. T. Beauregard; Americans at War; Romance and Realism in Southern Politics; Hayes of the Twenty-Third; McClellan, Sherman, and Grant; The Union Sundered;* and *The Union Restored*. Professor Williams has been a Harmsworth Professor of American History at Oxford and President of both the Southern Historical Association and the Organization of American Historians.

FRANK FREIDEL is Charles Warren Professor of History at Harvard University. He is writing a six-volume biography of Franklin D. Roosevelt, four volumes of which have been published. Among his other books are: *Our Country's Presidents; F.D.R. and the South;* and *America in the Twentieth Century*. He is co-editor of the 1974 edition of the *Harvard Guide to American History,* and Vice President of the Organization of American Historians. He is also a former president of the New England Historical Society.

W. ELLIOT BROWNLEE is an Associate Professor of History at the University of California, Santa Barbara. He received his Ph.D. from the University of Wisconsin. His area of specialization is U.S. economic history. He received a Haynes Foundation Fellowship in 1969. His published works include *Progressivism and Economic Growth: The Wisconsin Income Tax, 1911–1929; Women in the American Economy: A Documentary History, 1675 to 1929;* and *Dynamics of Ascent: A History of the American Economy*. In addition he has contributed to professional journals that include *Explorations in Economic History, Economic History Review,* and *Wisconsin Magazine of History*.

A NOTE ON THE TYPE

The text of this book was set in Linofilm Times Roman, adapted from the Linotype face designed by Stanley Morison for The Times (London), and introduced by that newspaper in 1932.

Among typographers and designers of the twentieth century, Stanley Morison has been a strong forming influence, as typographical advisor to the English Monotype Corporation, as a director of two distinguished English publishing houses, and as a writer of sensibility, erudition, and keen practical sense.